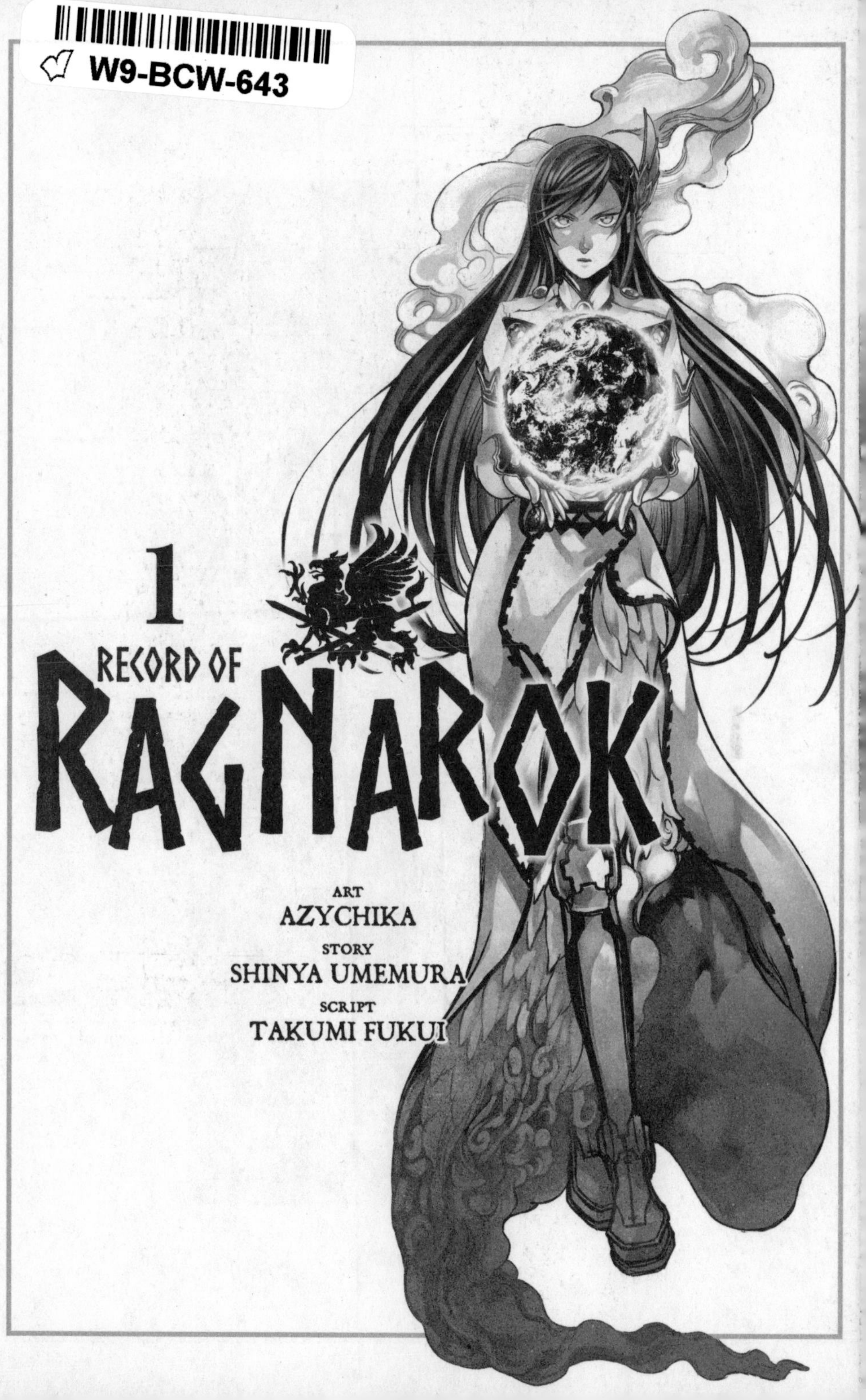

1

RECORD OF RAGNAROK

ART
AZYCHIKA

STORY
SHINYA UMEMURA

SCRIPT
TAKUMI FUKUI

RECORD OF RAGNAROK

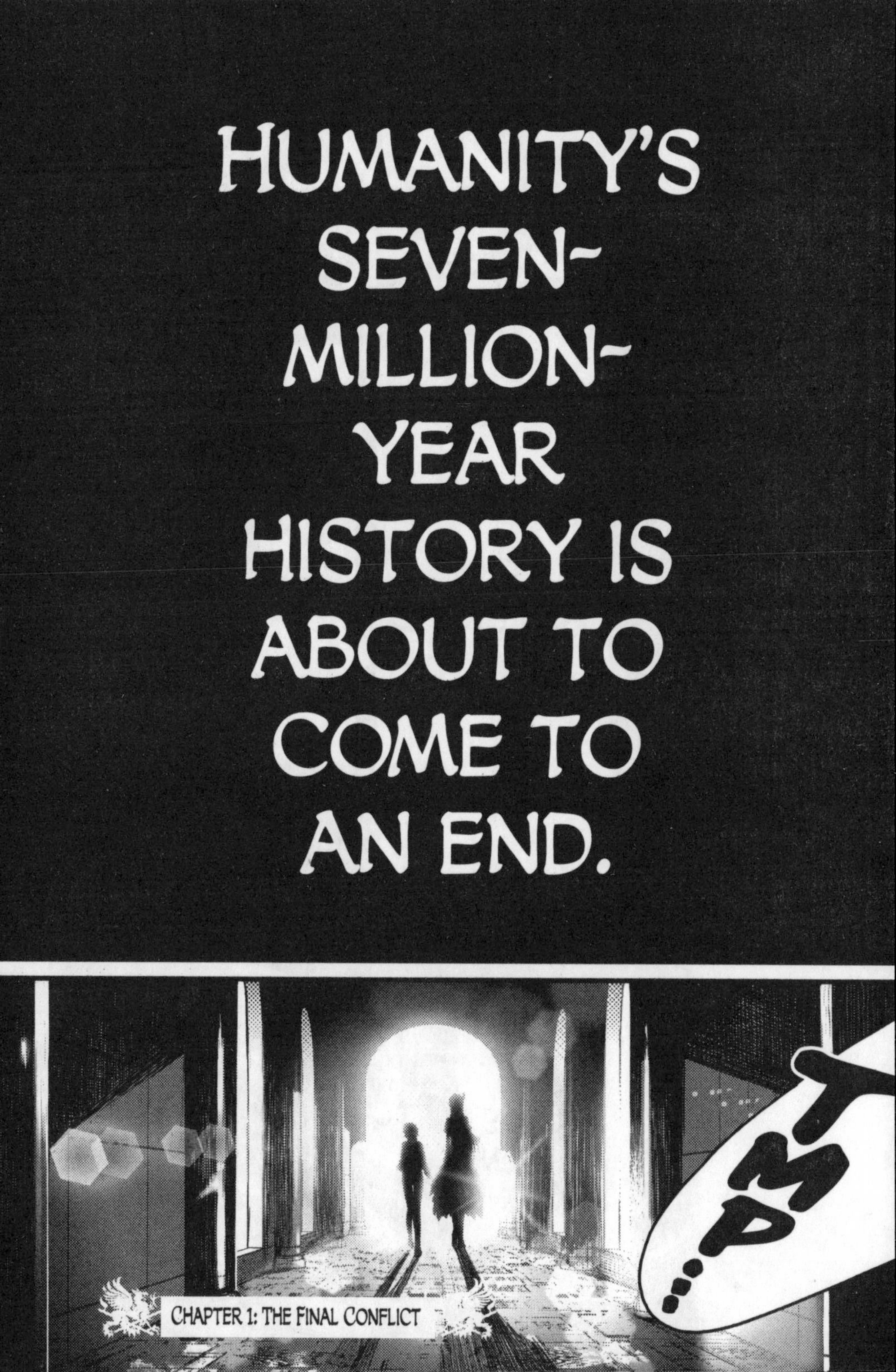
HUMANITY'S SEVEN-MILLION-YEAR HISTORY IS ABOUT TO COME TO AN END.
TMP...
CHAPTER 1: THE FINAL CONFLICT

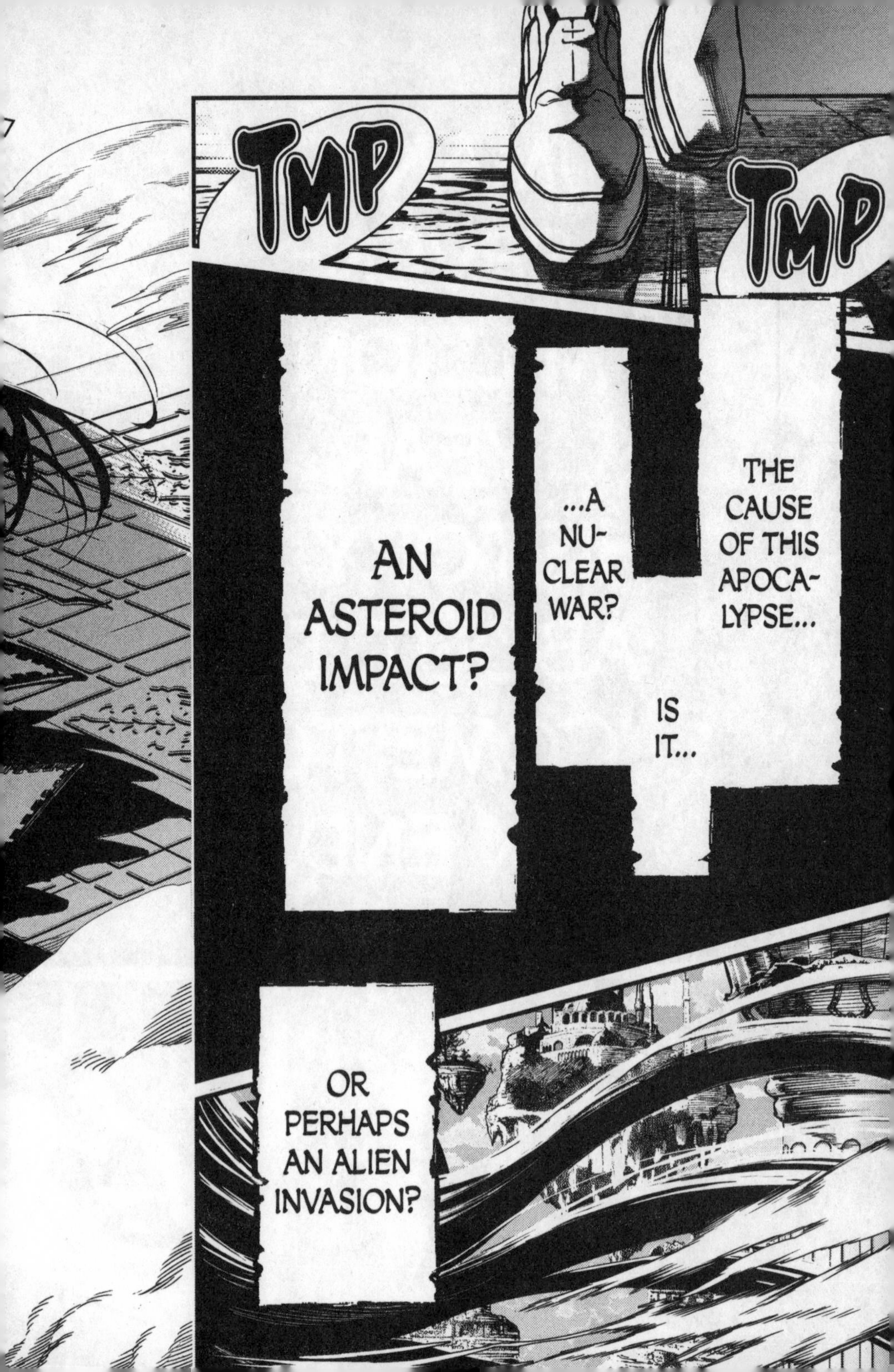
TMP
TMP
THE CAUSE OF THIS APOCA-LYPSE...
IS IT...
...A NU-CLEAR WAR?
AN ASTEROID IMPACT?
OR PERHAPS AN ALIEN INVASION?

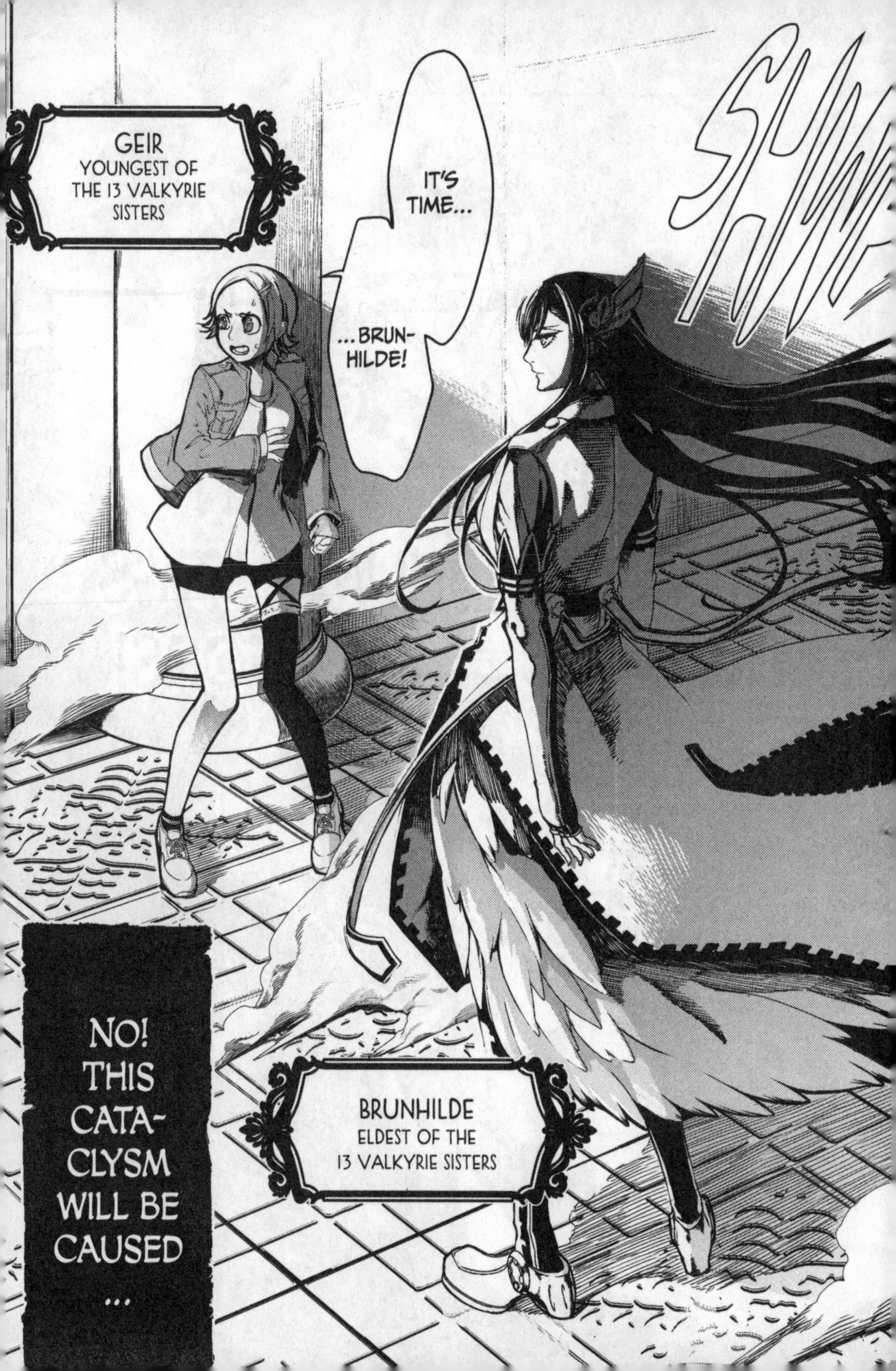
IT'S TIME... ...BRUNHILDE!
GEIR
YOUNGEST OF THE 13 VALKYRIE SISTERS
BRUNHILDE
ELDEST OF THE 13 VALKYRIE SISTERS
NO! THIS CATACLYSM WILL BE CAUSED ...

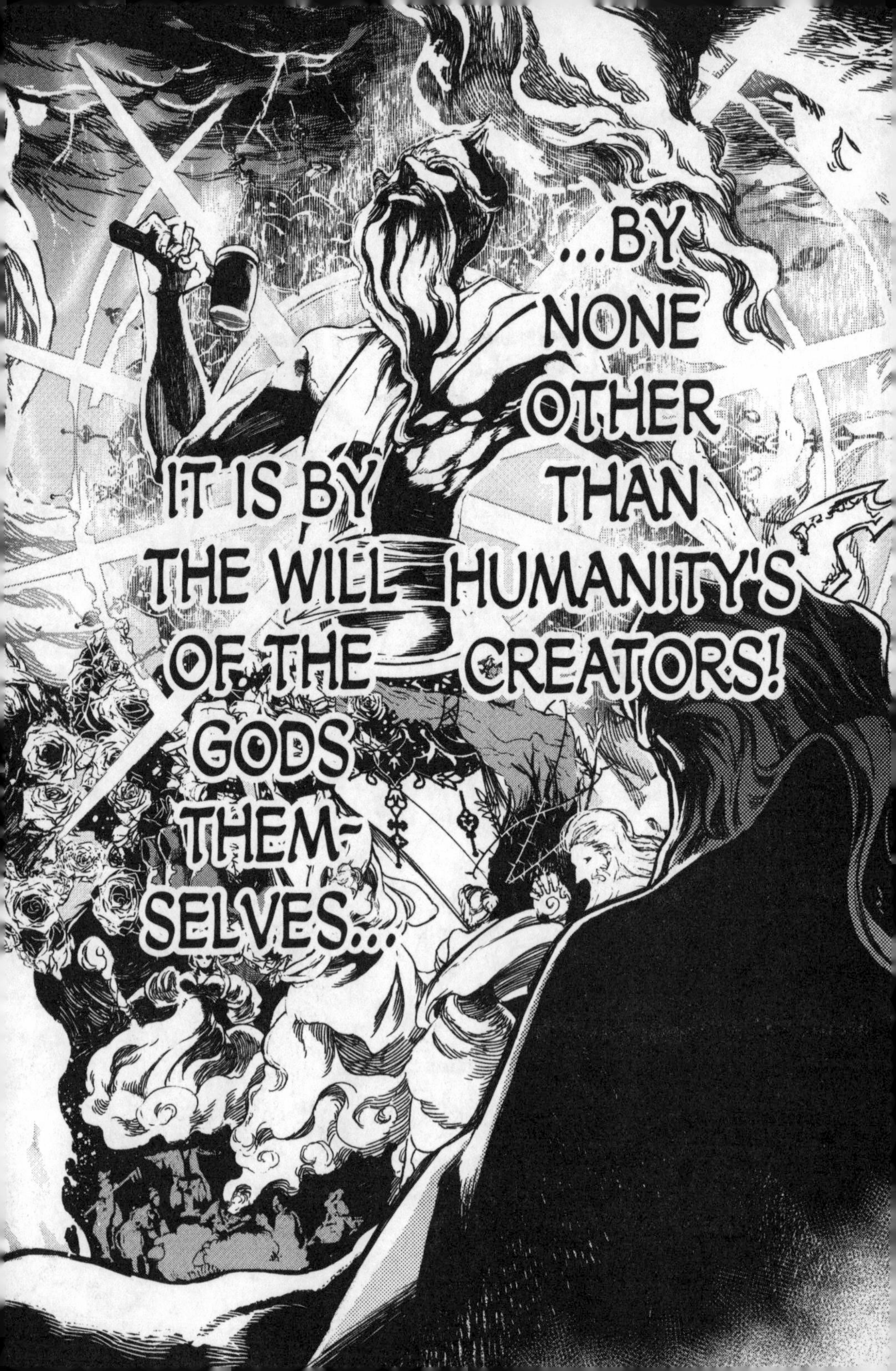
IT IS BY THE WILL OF THE GODS THEM-SELVES...
...BY NONE OTHER THAN HUMANITY'S CREATORS!

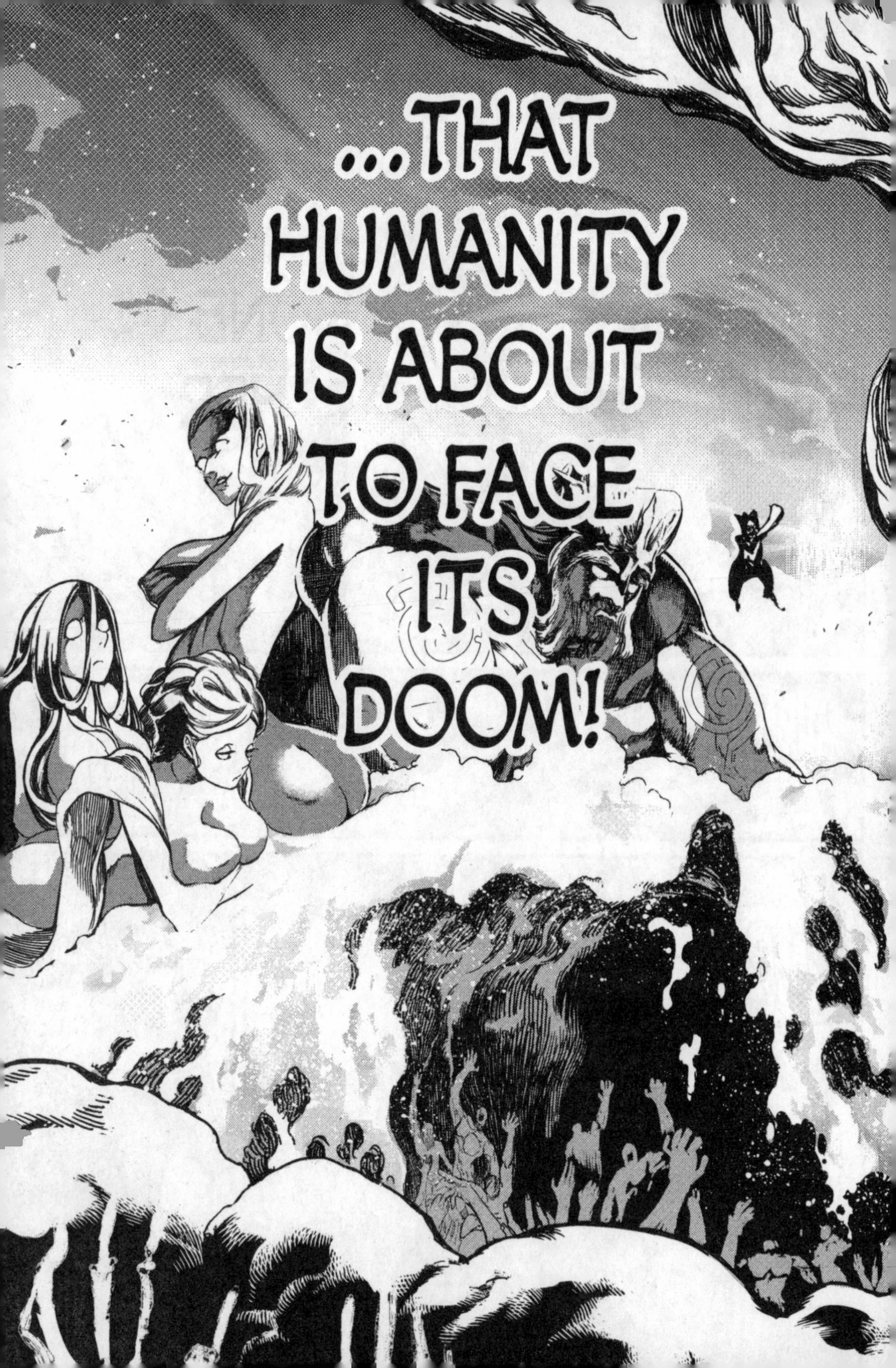
...THAT HUMANITY IS ABOUT TO FACE ITS DOOM!

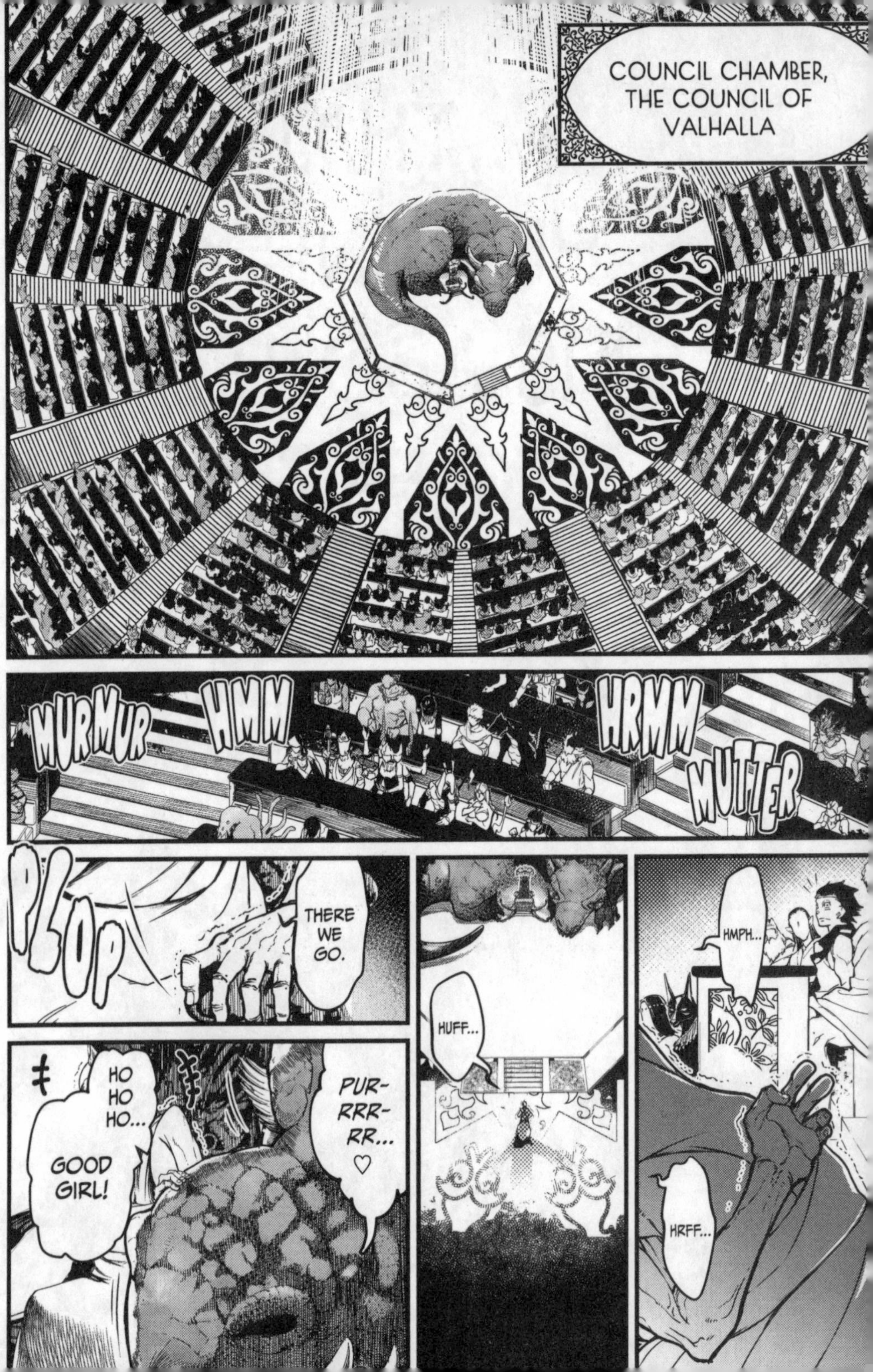
COUNCIL CHAMBER, THE COUNCIL OF VALHALLA
MUTTER
HRMM
HMM
MURMUR
HMPH...
HRFF...
HUFF...
THERE WE GO.
PLOP
PUR-RRR-RR... ♡
HO HO HO...
GOOD GIRL!

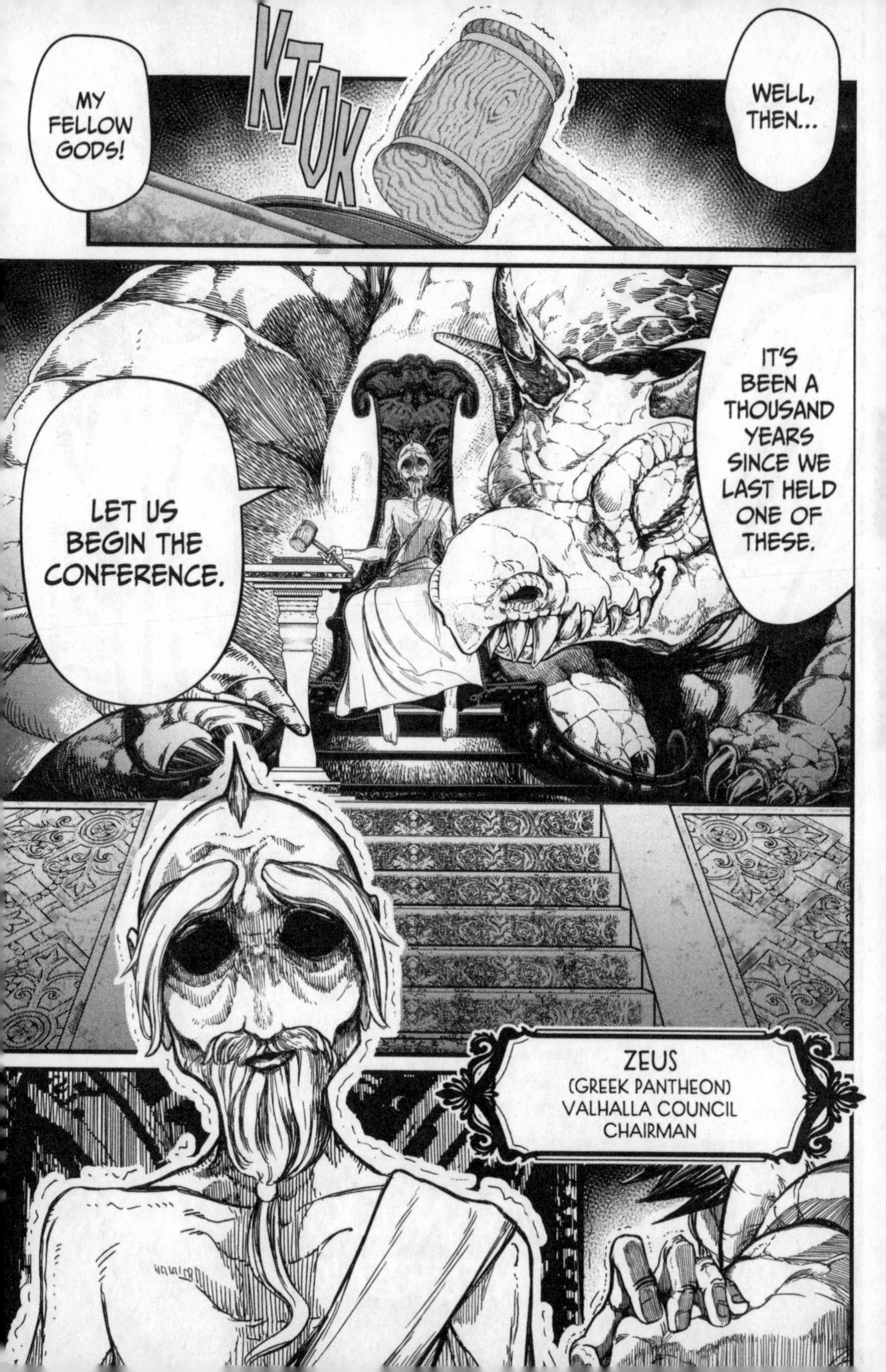
WELL, THEN...
KTOK
MY FELLOW GODS!
IT'S BEEN A THOUSAND YEARS SINCE WE LAST HELD ONE OF THESE.
LET US BEGIN THE CONFERENCE.
ZEUS
(GREEK PANTHEON)
VALHALLA COUNCIL
CHAIRMAN

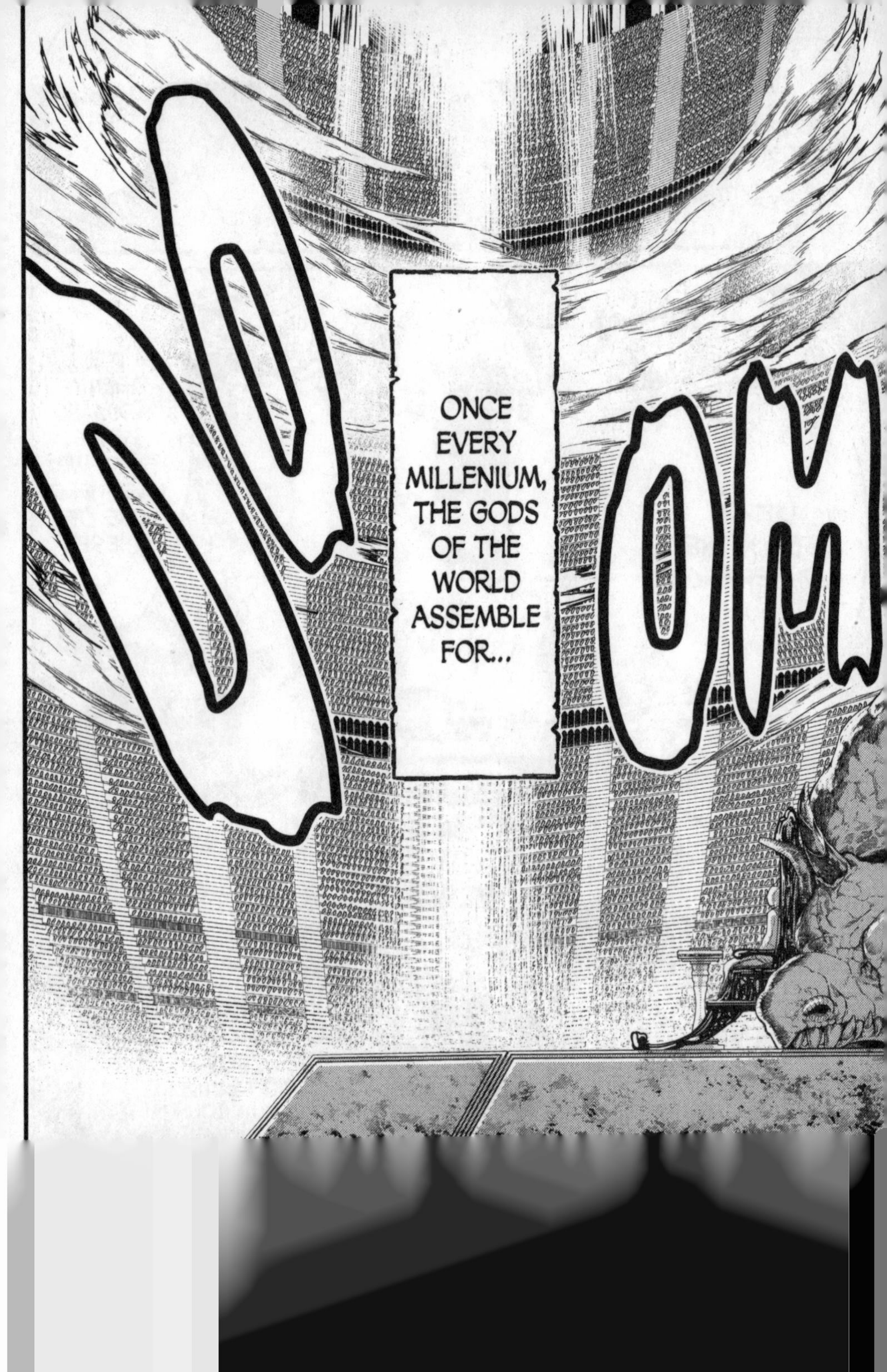
ONCE EVERY MILLENIUM, THE GODS OF THE WORLD ASSEMBLE FOR...

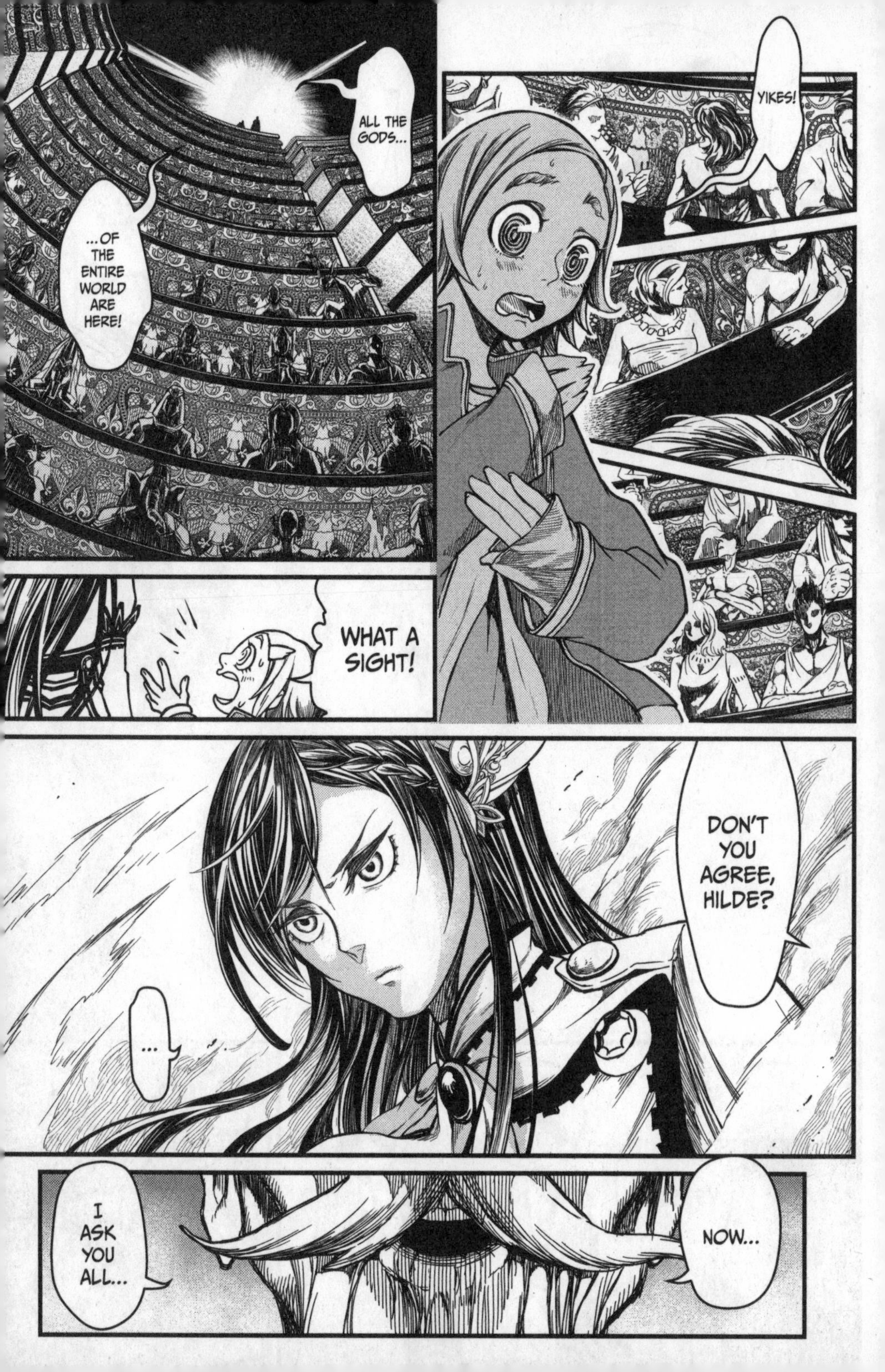
YIKES!
ALL THE GODS...
...OF THE ENTIRE WORLD ARE HERE!
WHAT A SIGHT!
DON'T YOU AGREE, HILDE?
...
NOW...
I ASK YOU ALL...

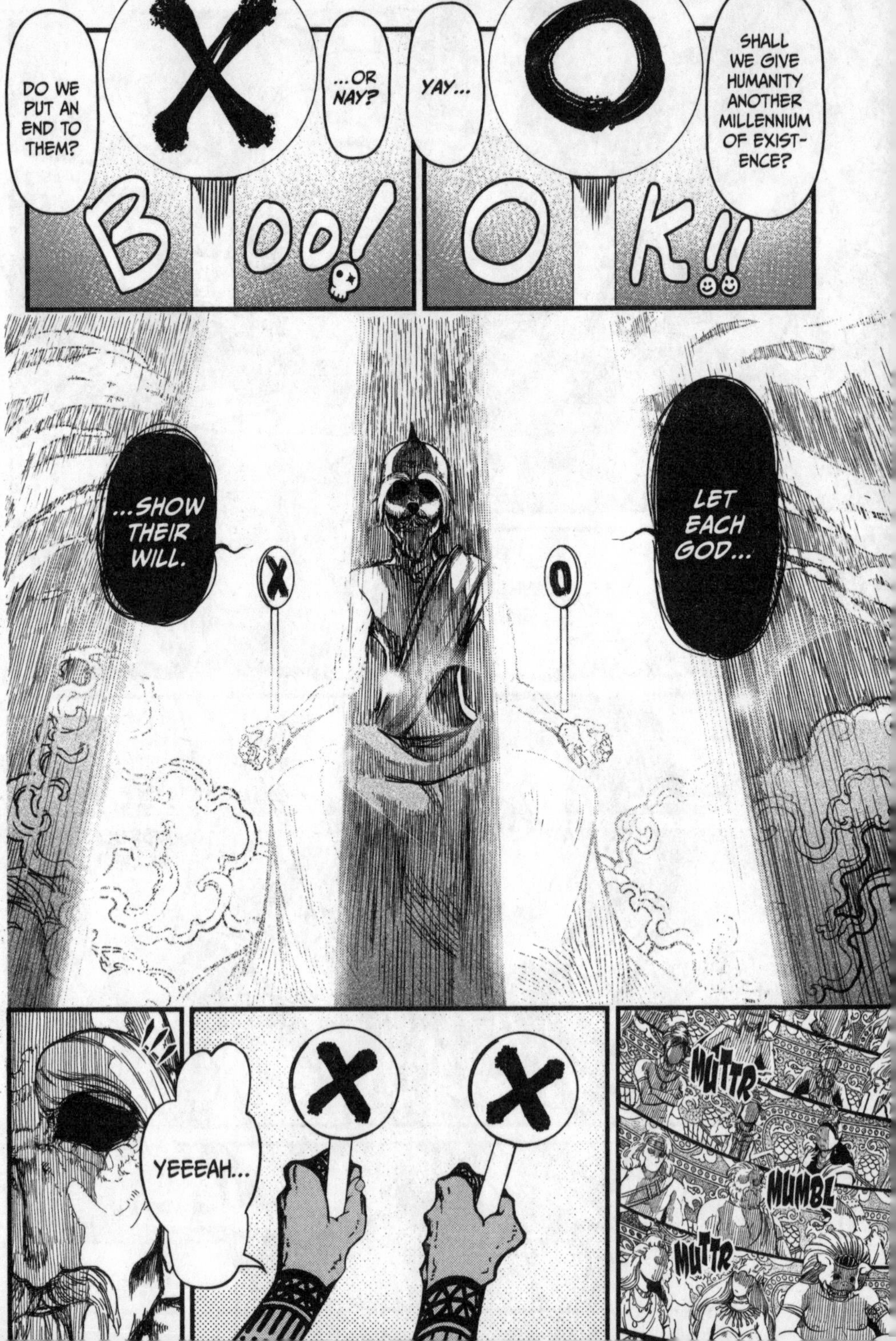
SHALL WE GIVE HUMANITY ANOTHER MILLENNIUM OF EXIST-ENCE?
YAY...
OK!!
...OR NAY?
DO WE PUT AN END TO THEM?
BOO!
LET EACH GOD...
...SHOW THEIR WILL.
MUTTR
MUMBL
MUTTR
YEEEAH...

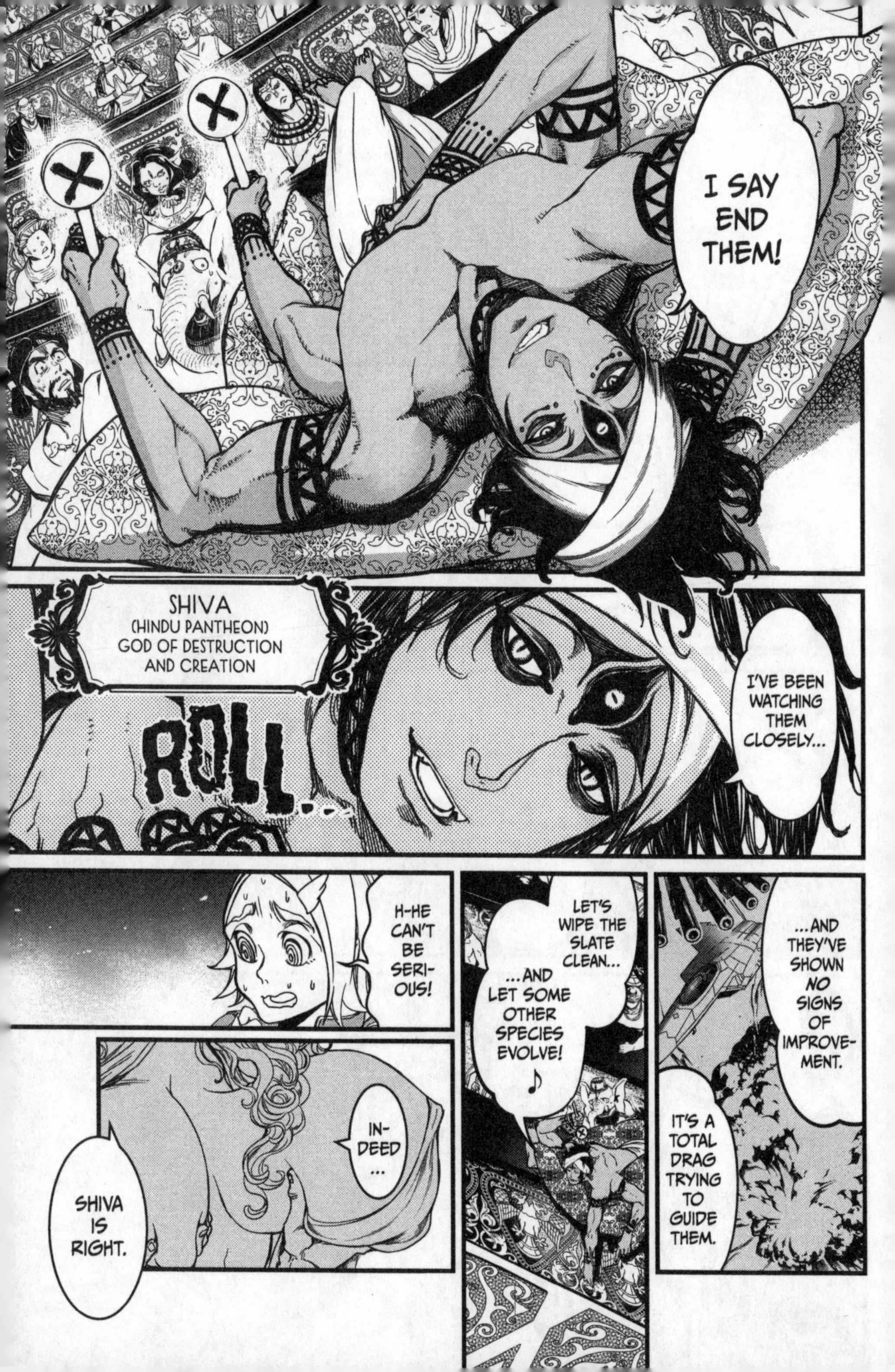
I SAY END THEM!
I'VE BEEN WATCHING THEM CLOSELY...
SHIVA (HINDU PANTHEON) GOD OF DESTRUCTION AND CREATION
ROLL...
...AND THEY'VE SHOWN NO SIGNS OF IMPROVEMENT.
IT'S A TOTAL DRAG TRYING TO GUIDE THEM.
LET'S WIPE THE SLATE CLEAN...
...AND LET SOME OTHER SPECIES EVOLVE! ♪
H-HE CAN'T BE SERI-OUS!
IN-DEED...
SHIVA IS RIGHT.

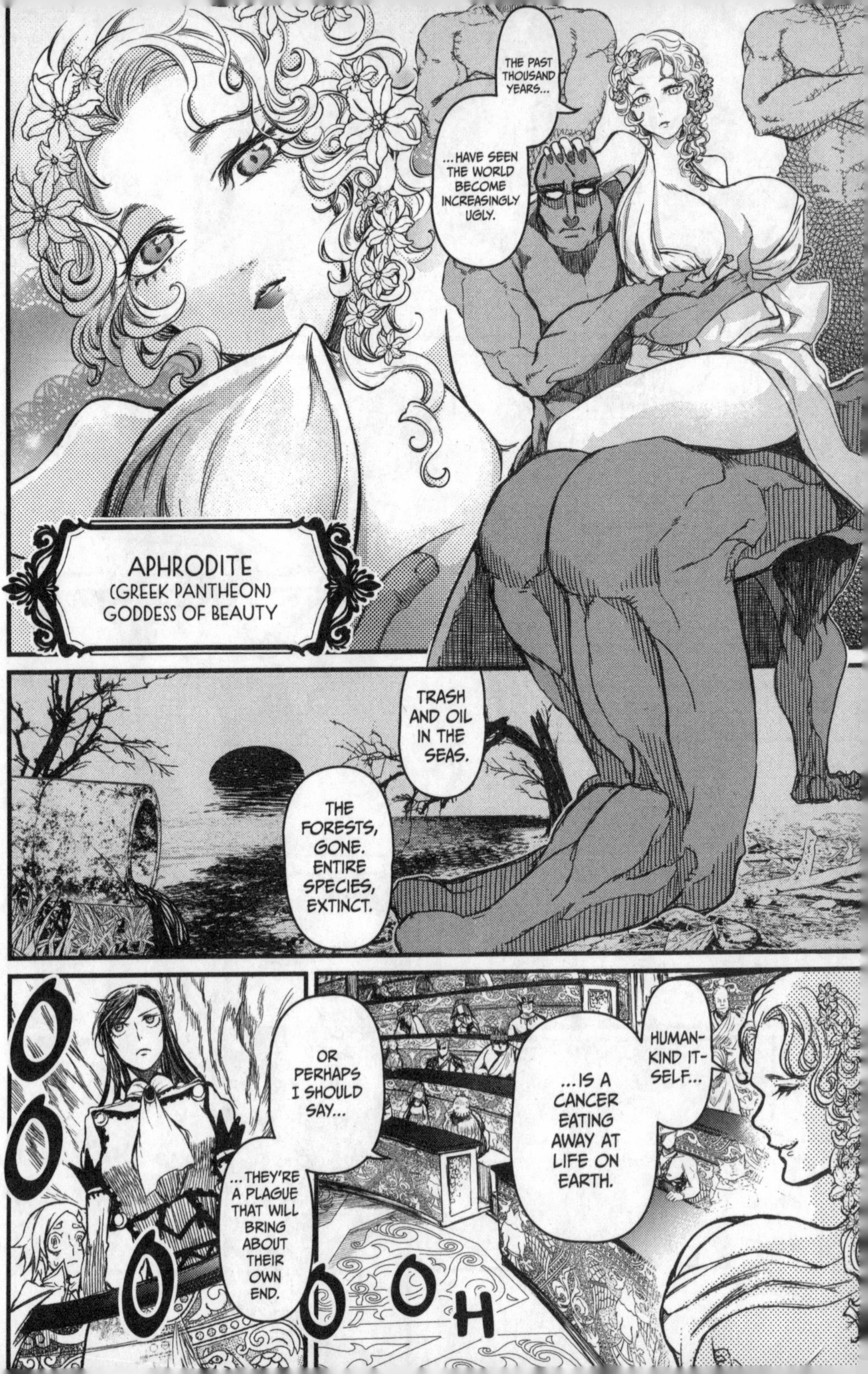
THE PAST THOUSAND YEARS...
...HAVE SEEN THE WORLD BECOME INCREASINGLY UGLY.
APHRODITE (GREEK PANTHEON) GODDESS OF BEAUTY
TRASH AND OIL IN THE SEAS.
THE FORESTS, GONE. ENTIRE SPECIES, EXTINCT.
HUMAN-KIND IT-SELF...
...IS A CANCER EATING AWAY AT LIFE ON EARTH.
OR PERHAPS I SHOULD SAY...
...THEY'RE A PLAGUE THAT WILL BRING ABOUT THEIR OWN END.
OOOOOOOH

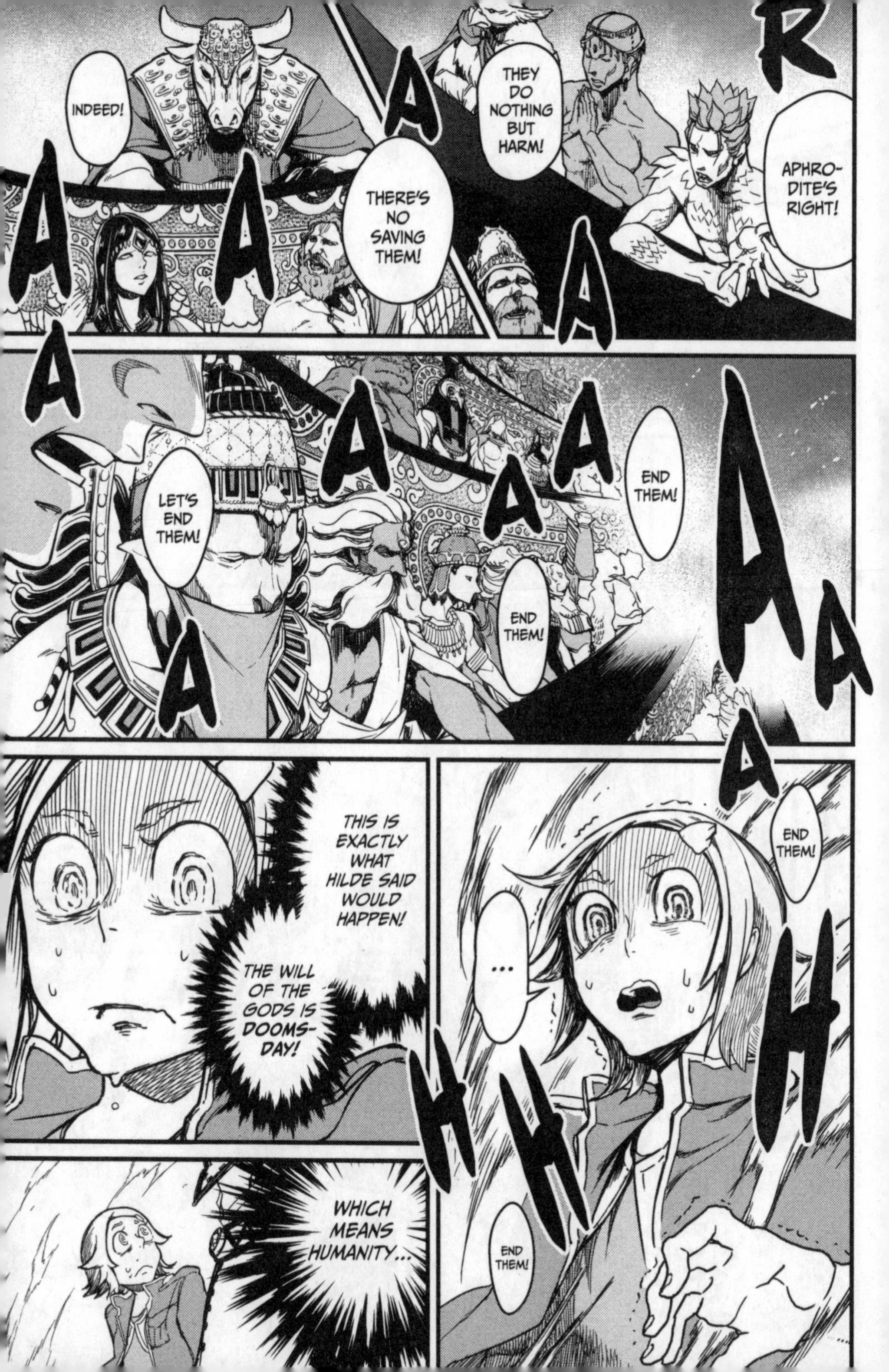
RAAAAAAAAAAAAAHHHH
APHRO-DITE'S RIGHT!
THEY DO NOTHING BUT HARM!
THERE'S NO SAVING THEM!
INDEED!
END THEM!
END THEM!
LET'S END THEM!
END THEM!
...
THIS IS EXACTLY WHAT HILDE SAID WOULD HAPPEN!
THE WILL OF THE GODS IS DOOMS-DAY!
END THEM!
WHICH MEANS HUMANITY...

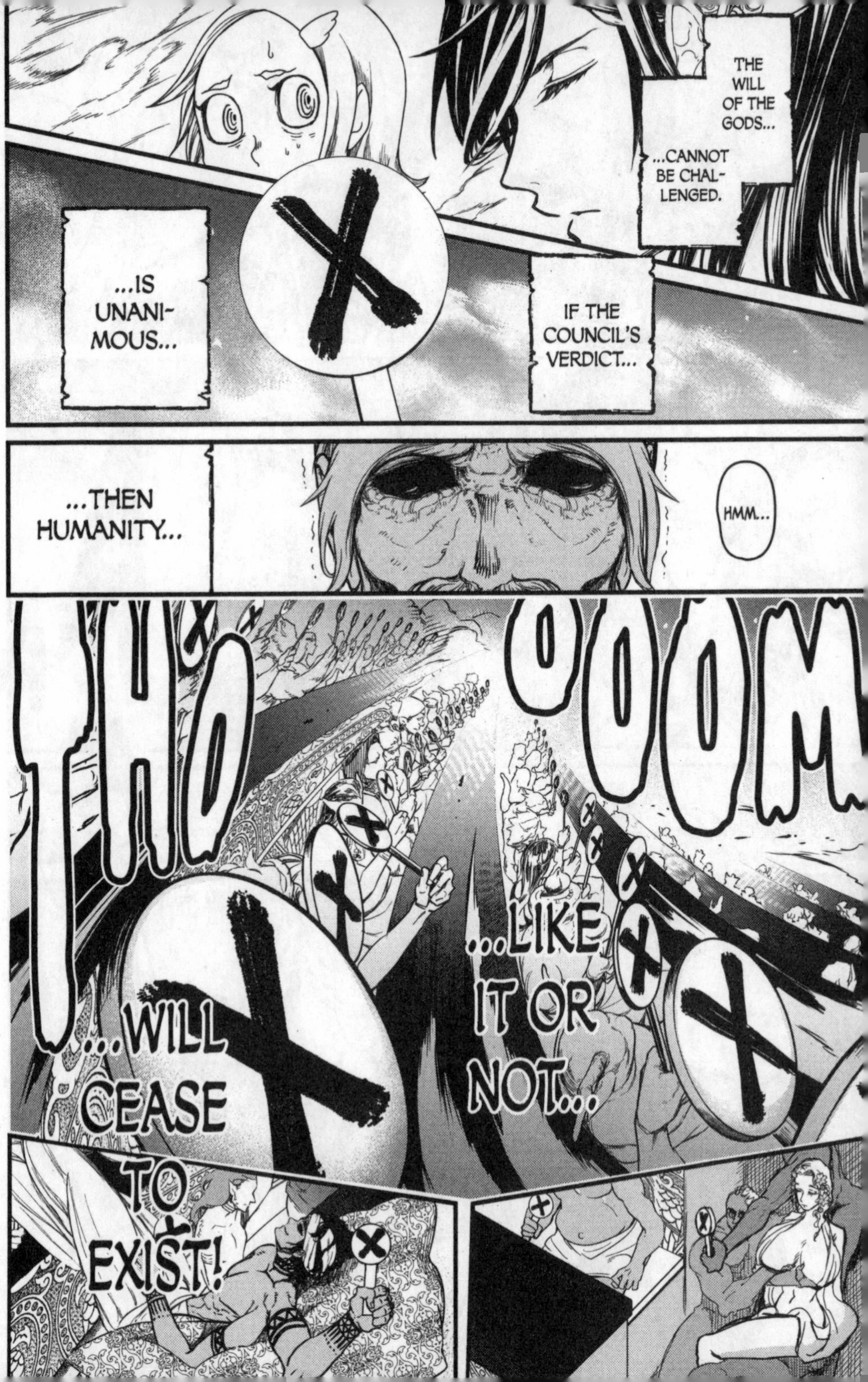

THE WILL OF THE GODS...
...CANNOT BE CHAL-LENGED.
IF THE COUNCIL'S VERDICT...
...IS UNANI-MOUS...
HMM...
...THEN HUMANITY...
THOOOM
...LIKE IT OR NOT...
...WILL CEASE TO EXIST!

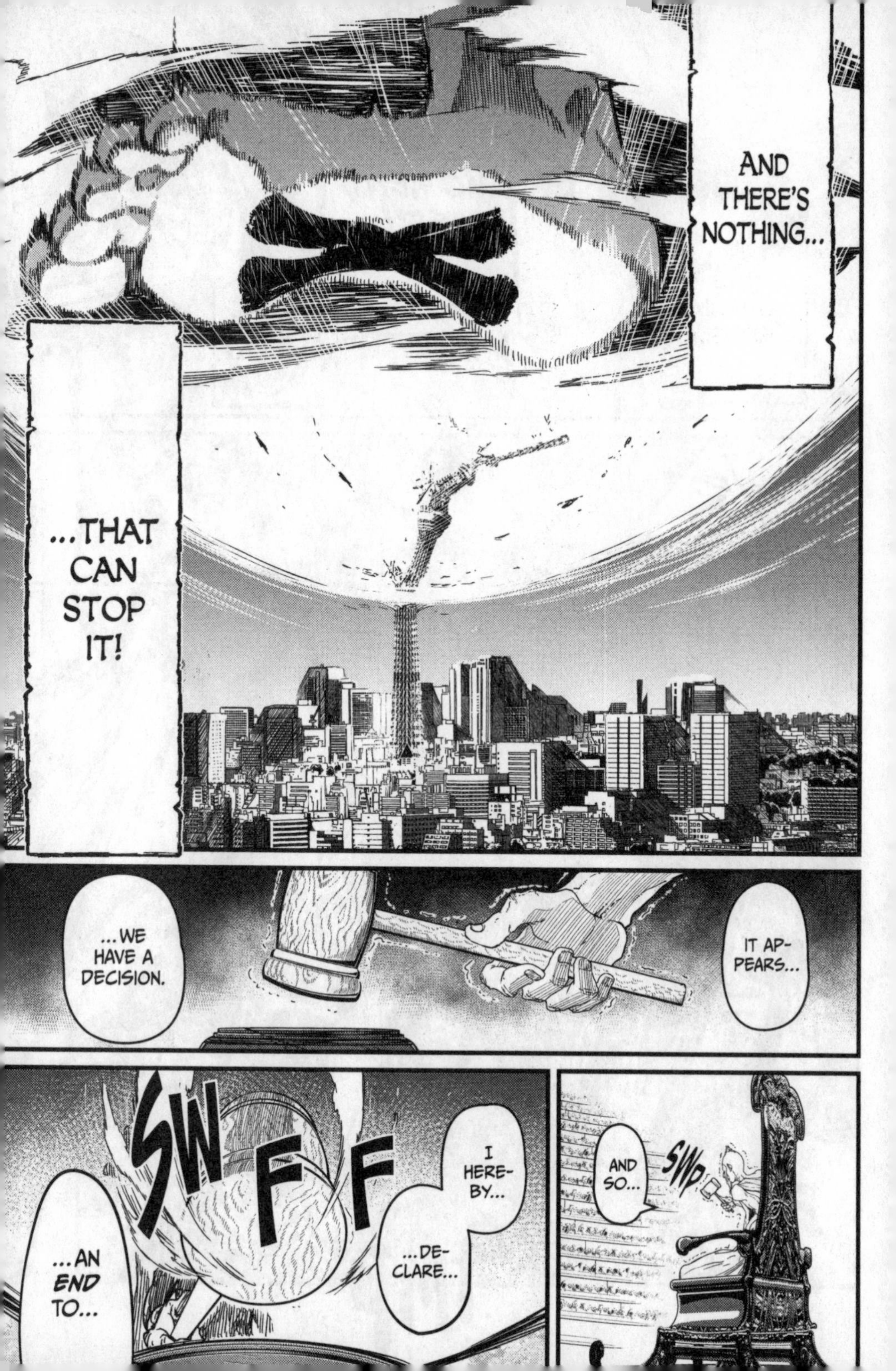
AND THERE'S NOTHING...
...THAT CAN STOP IT!
IT AP-PEARS...
...WE HAVE A DECISION.
AND SO...
SWP
I HERE-BY...
...DE-CLARE...
SWFF
...AN END TO...

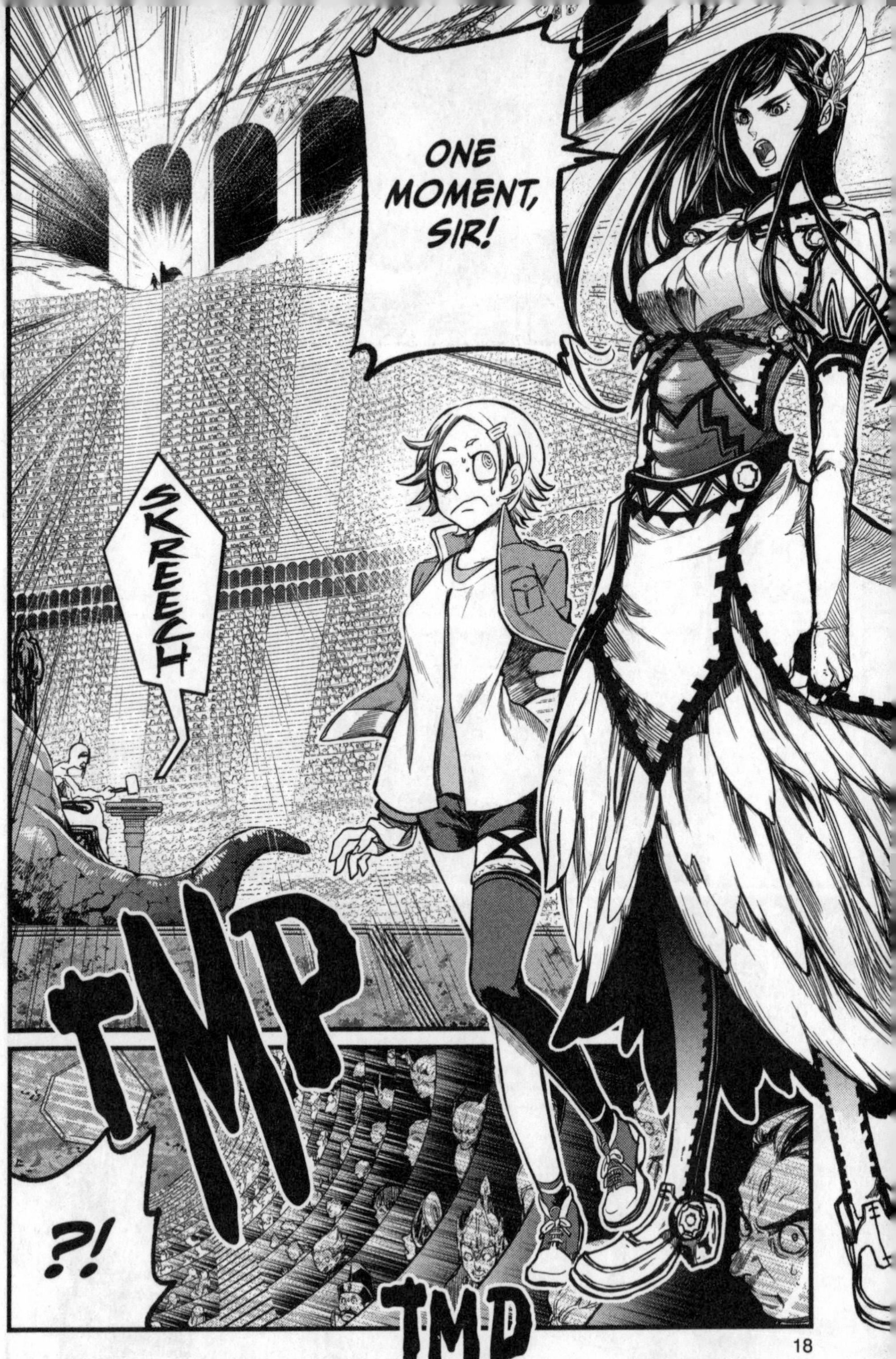
ONE MOMENT, SIR!
SKREECH
TMP
?!
TMP

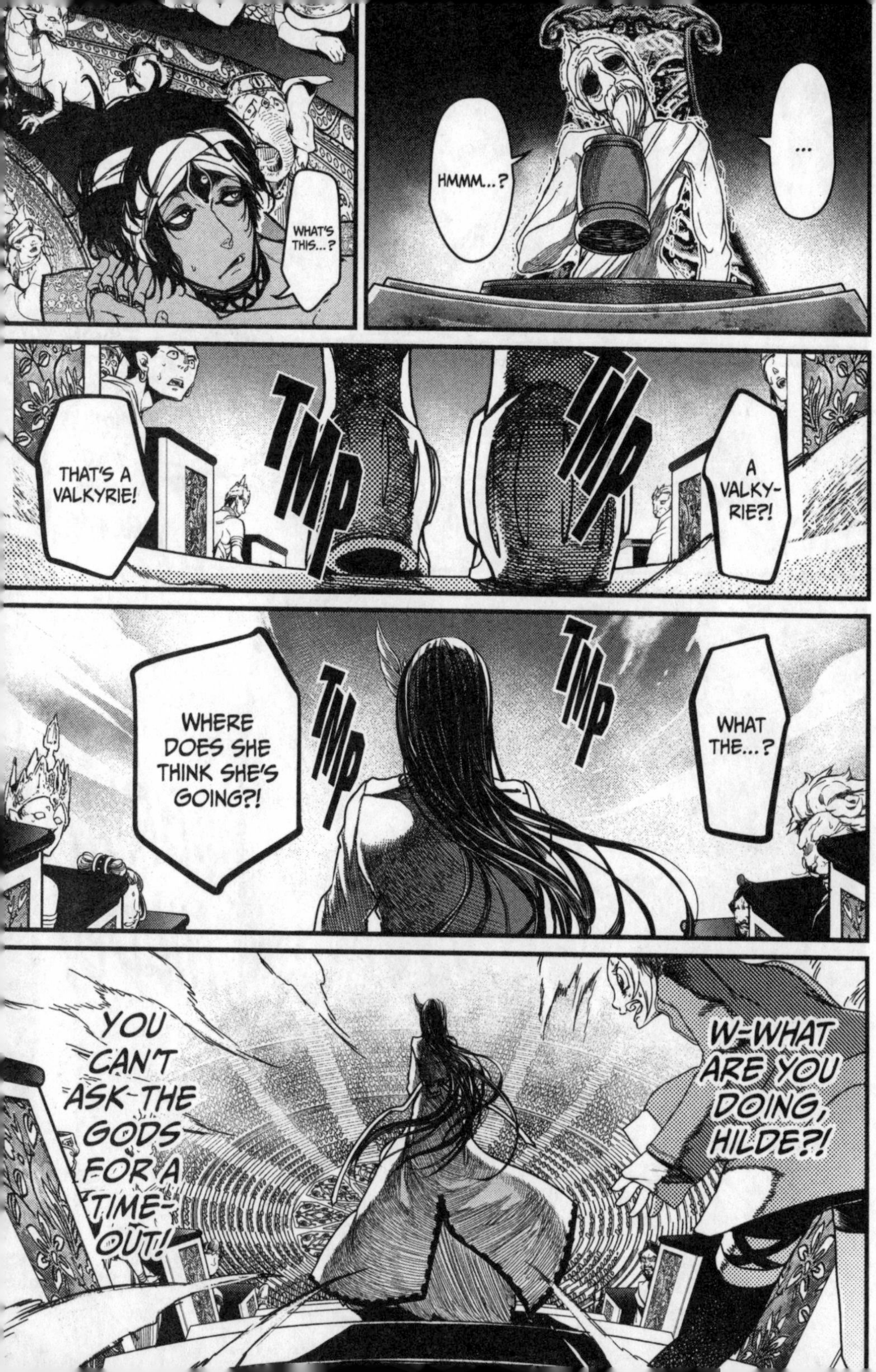
...
HMMM...?
WHAT'S THIS...?
A VALKY-RIE?!
TMP
TMP
THAT'S A VALKYRIE!
WHAT THE...?
TMP
TMP
WHERE DOES SHE THINK SHE'S GOING?!
W-WHAT ARE YOU DOING, HILDE?!
YOU CAN'T ASK THE GODS FOR A TIME-OUT!

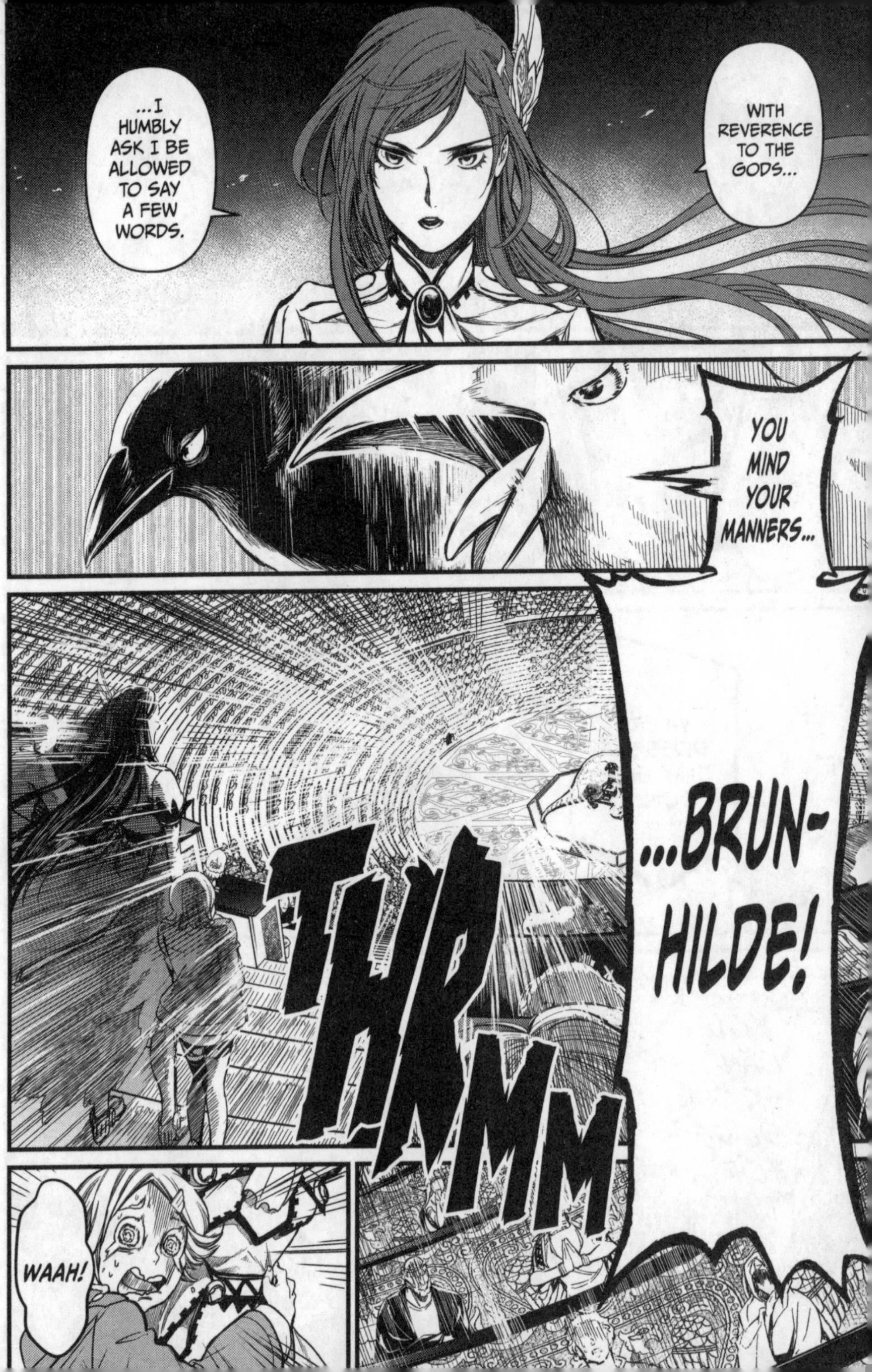
WITH REVERENCE TO THE GODS...
...I HUMBLY ASK I BE ALLOWED TO SAY A FEW WORDS.
YOU MIND YOUR MANNERS...
...BRUN-HILDE!
THMM
WAAH!

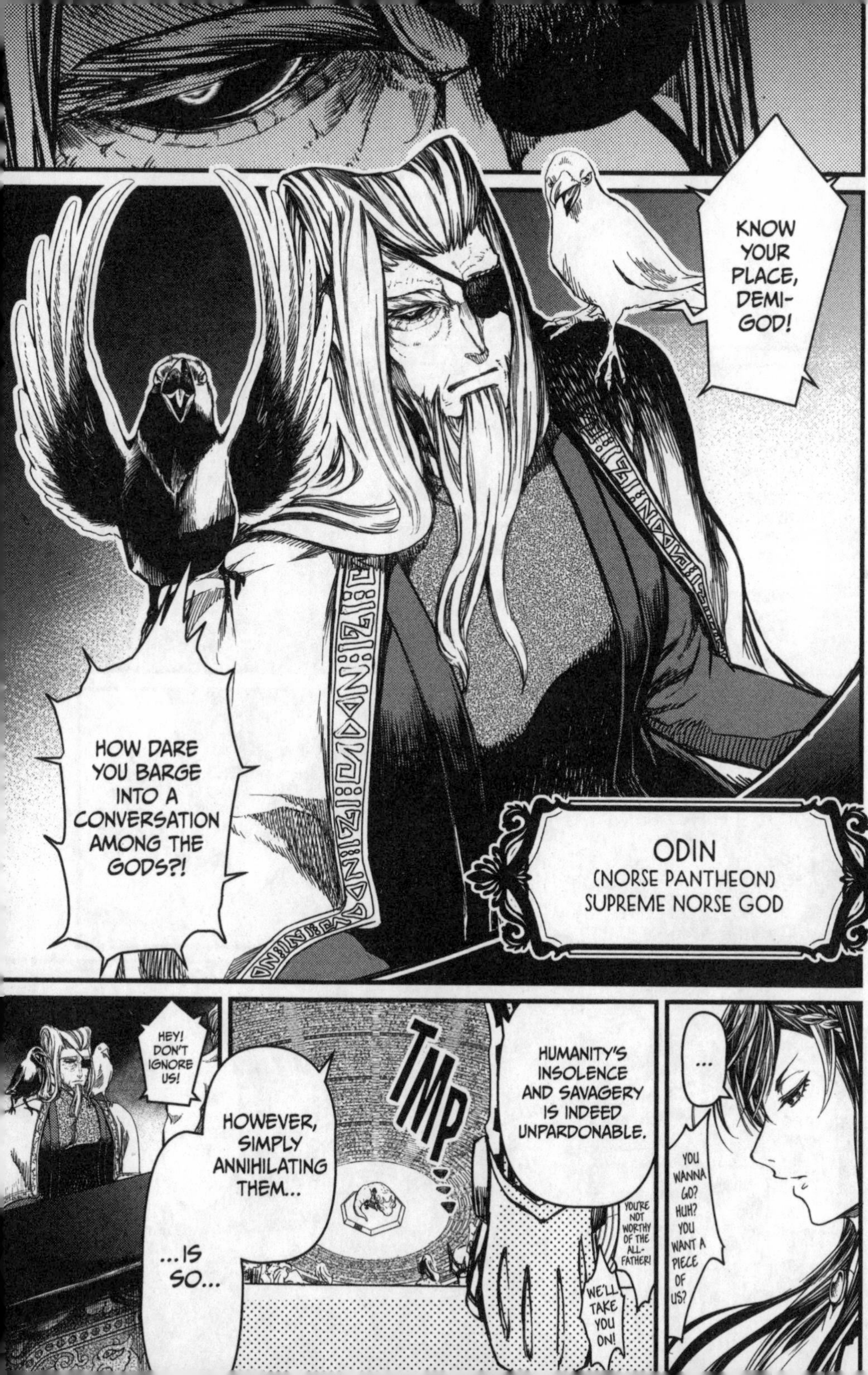
KNOW YOUR PLACE, DEMI-GOD!
HOW DARE YOU BARGE INTO A CONVERSATION AMONG THE GODS?!
ODIN
(NORSE PANTHEON)
SUPREME NORSE GOD
...
YOU WANNA GO? HUH? YOU WANT A PIECE OF US?
HUMANITY'S INSOLENCE AND SAVAGERY IS INDEED UNPARDONABLE.
YOU'RE NOT WORTHY OF THE ALL-FATHER!
WE'LL TAKE YOU ON!
TMP
HOWEVER, SIMPLY ANNIHILATING THEM...
...IS SO...
HEY! DON'T IGNORE US!

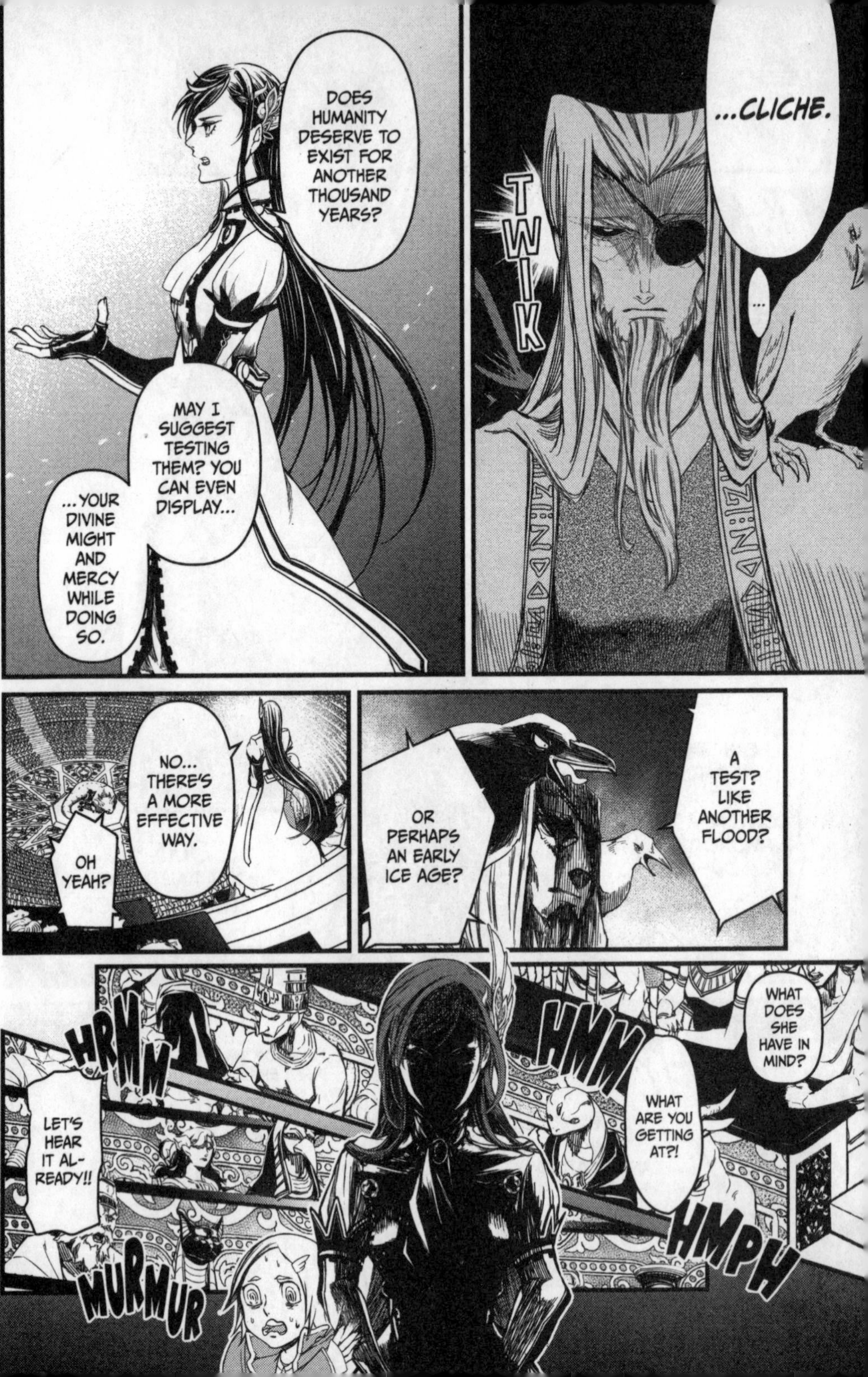
...CLICHE.
TWIK
...
DOES HUMANITY DESERVE TO EXIST FOR ANOTHER THOUSAND YEARS?
MAY I SUGGEST TESTING THEM? YOU CAN EVEN DISPLAY...
...YOUR DIVINE MIGHT AND MERCY WHILE DOING SO.
A TEST? LIKE ANOTHER FLOOD?
OR PERHAPS AN EARLY ICE AGE?
NO... THERE'S A MORE EFFECTIVE WAY.
OH YEAH?
WHAT DOES SHE HAVE IN MIND?
HMM
WHAT ARE YOU GETTING AT?!
HMPH
HRMM
LET'S HEAR IT AL-READY!!
MURMUR

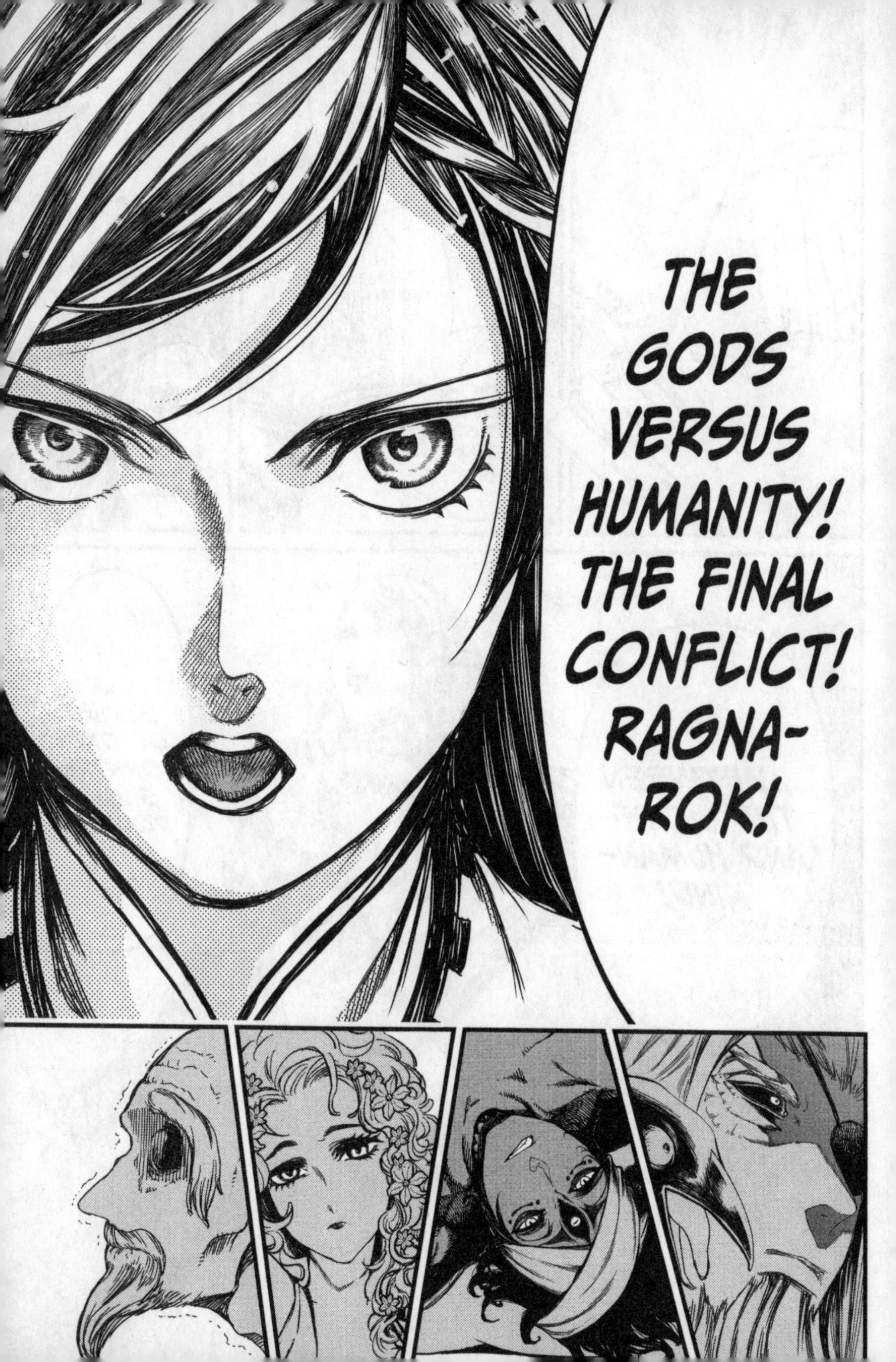
THE GODS VERSUS HUMANITY! THE FINAL CONFLICT! RAGNA-ROK!

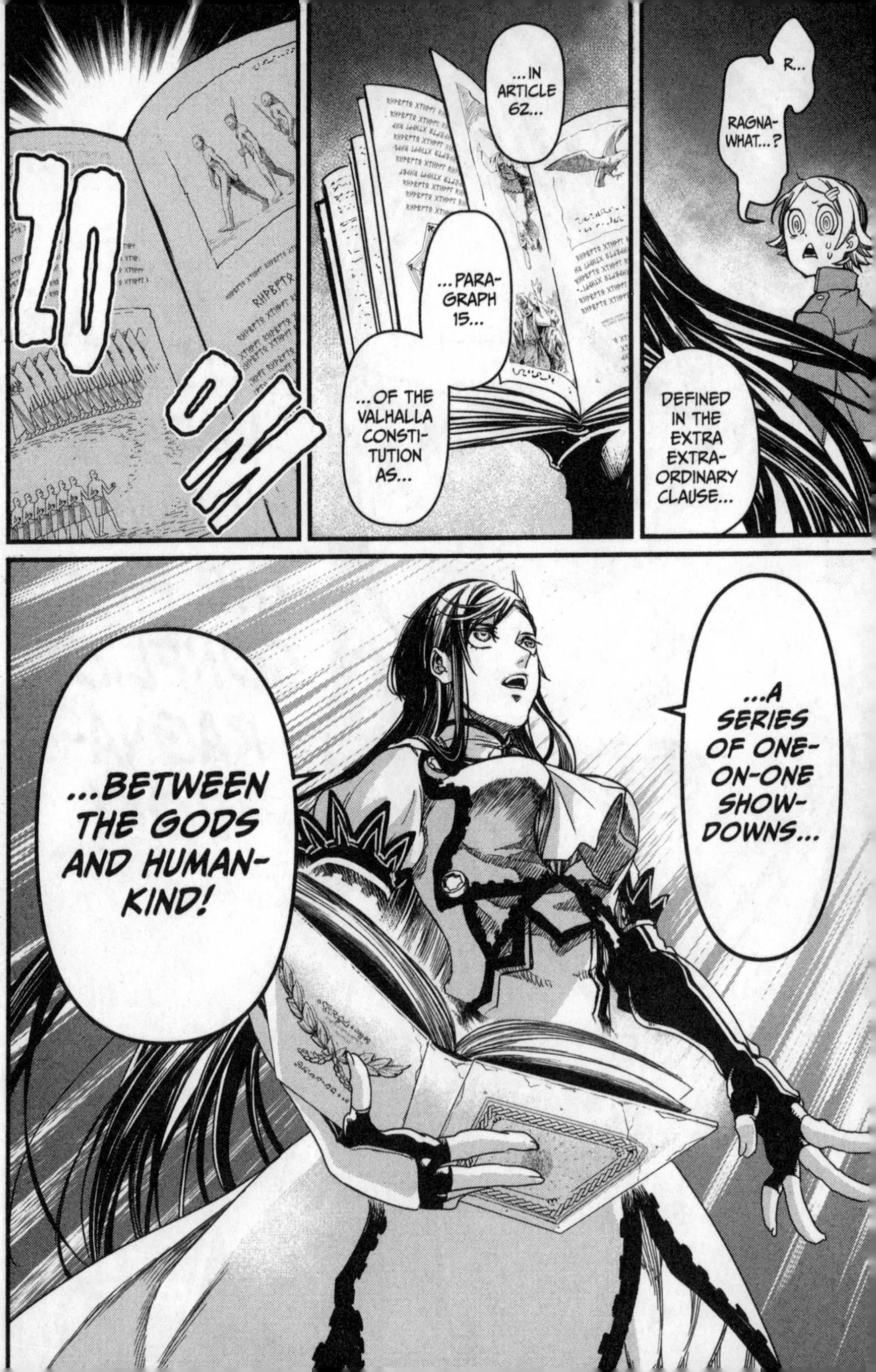
R...
RAGNA-WHAT...?
DEFINED IN THE EXTRA EXTRA-ORDINARY CLAUSE...
...IN ARTICLE 62...
...PARAGRAPH 15...
...OF THE VALHALLA CONSTITUTION AS...
ZOOM
...A SERIES OF ONE-ON-ONE SHOWDOWNS...
...BETWEEN THE GODS AND HUMANKIND!

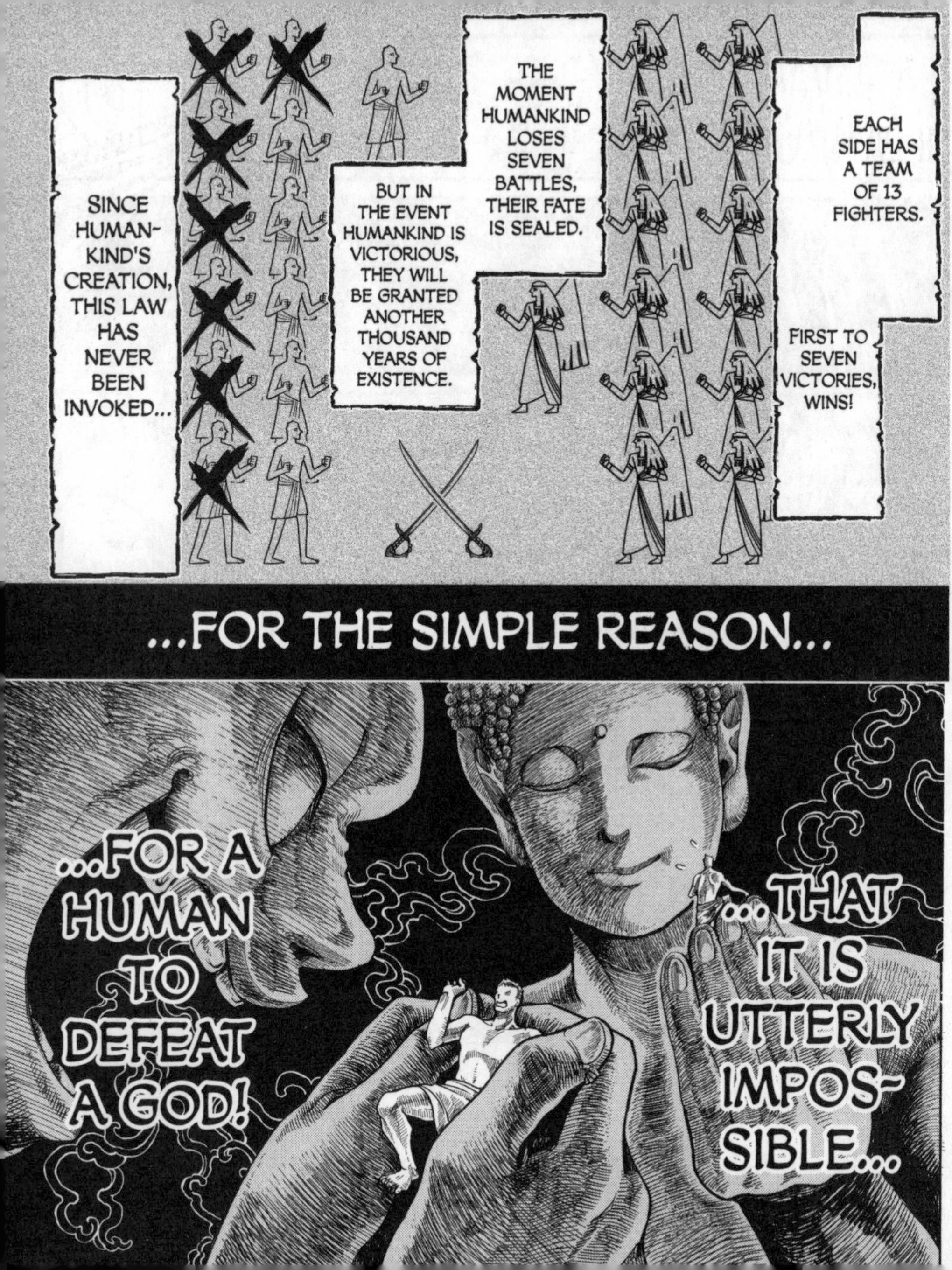
EACH SIDE HAS A TEAM OF 13 FIGHTERS.
FIRST TO SEVEN VICTORIES, WINS!
THE MOMENT HUMANKIND LOSES SEVEN BATTLES, THEIR FATE IS SEALED.
BUT IN THE EVENT HUMANKIND IS VICTORIOUS, THEY WILL BE GRANTED ANOTHER THOUSAND YEARS OF EXISTENCE.
SINCE HUMAN-KIND'S CREATION, THIS LAW HAS NEVER BEEN INVOKED...
...FOR THE SIMPLE REASON...
...THAT IT IS UTTERLY IMPOS-SIBLE...
...FOR A HUMAN TO DEFEAT A GOD!

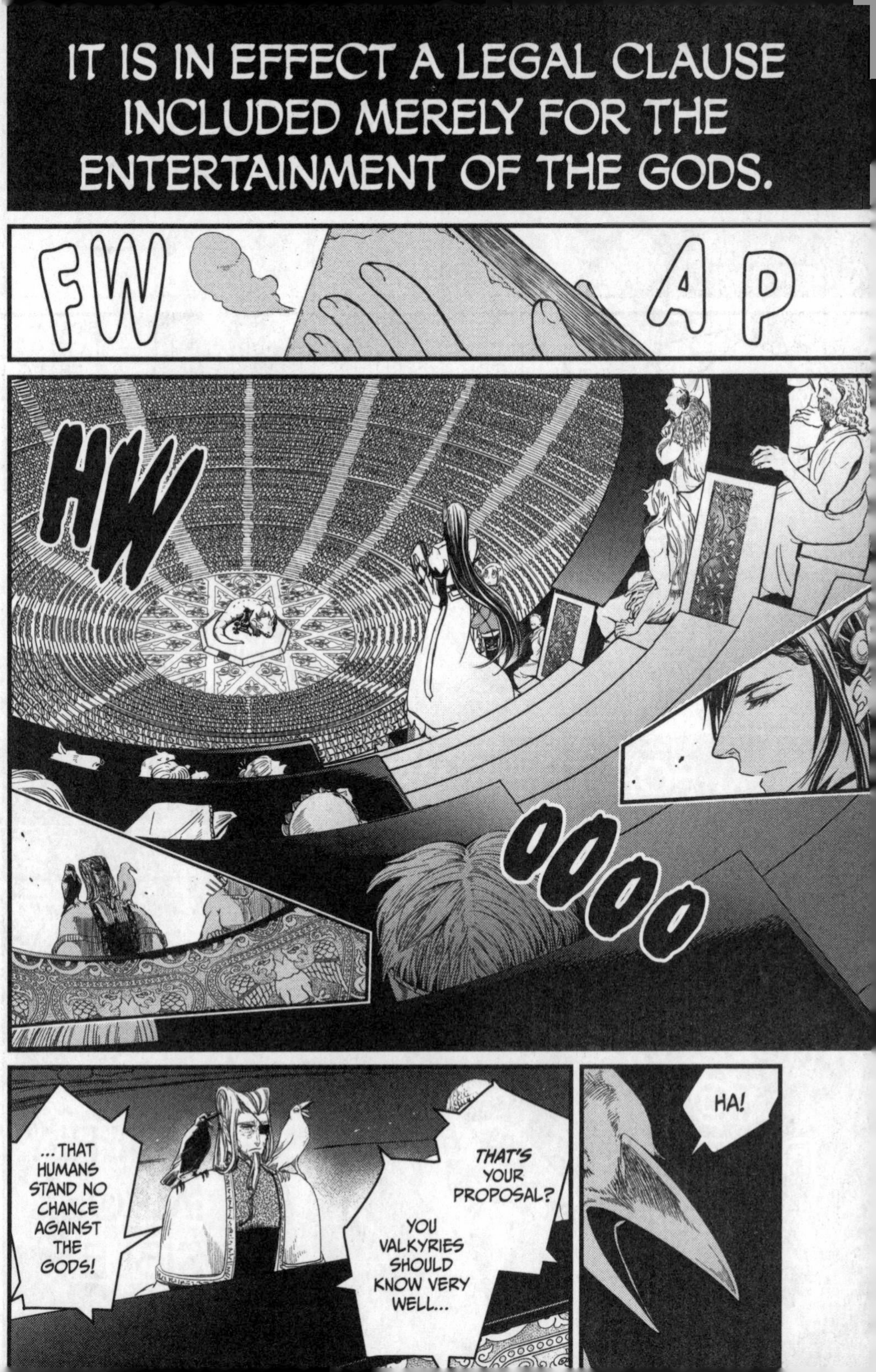
IT IS IN EFFECT A LEGAL CLAUSE INCLUDED MERELY FOR THE ENTERTAINMENT OF THE GODS.
FWAP
HW
OOOO
HA!
THAT'S YOUR PROPOSAL?
YOU VALKYRIES SHOULD KNOW VERY WELL...
...THAT HUMANS STAND NO CHANCE AGAINST THE GODS!

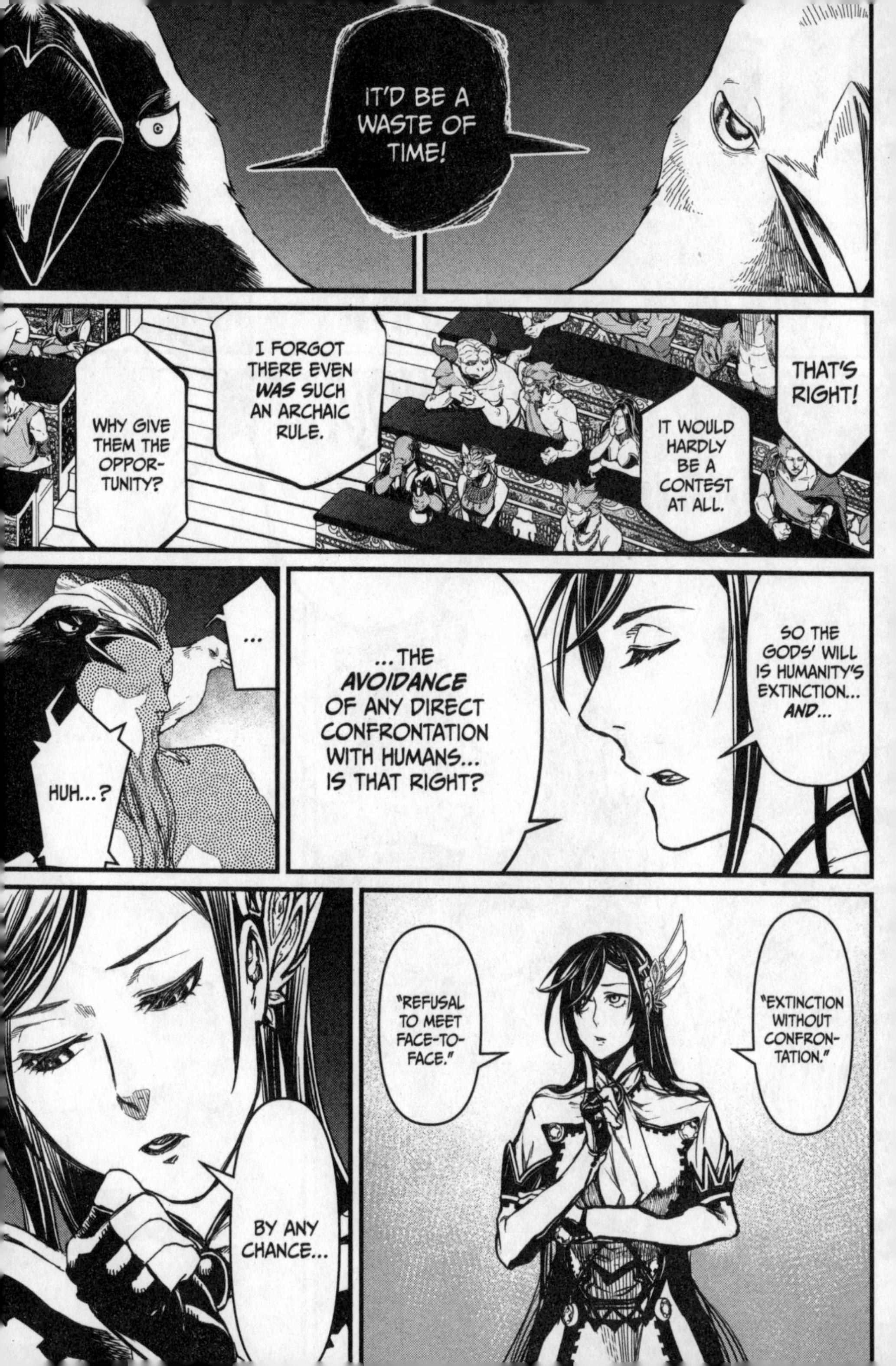
IT'D BE A WASTE OF TIME!
THAT'S RIGHT!
IT WOULD HARDLY BE A CONTEST AT ALL.
I FORGOT THERE EVEN WAS SUCH AN ARCHAIC RULE.
WHY GIVE THEM THE OPPORTUNITY?
SO THE GODS' WILL IS HUMANITY'S EXTINCTION... AND...
...THE AVOIDANCE OF ANY DIRECT CONFRONTATION WITH HUMANS... IS THAT RIGHT?
...
HUH...?
"EXTINCTION WITHOUT CONFRONTATION."
"REFUSAL TO MEET FACE-TO-FACE."
BY ANY CHANCE...

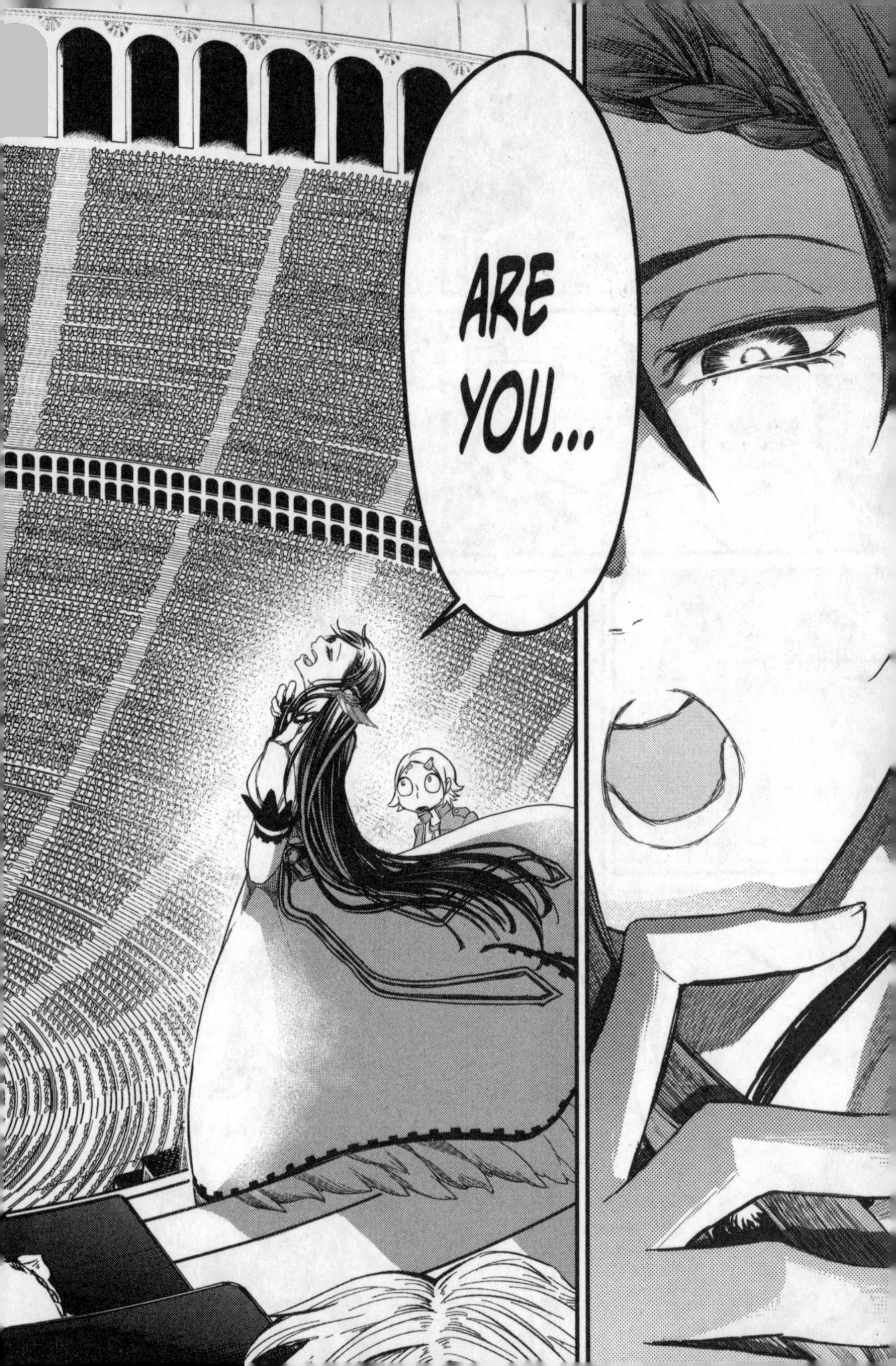
ARE YOU...

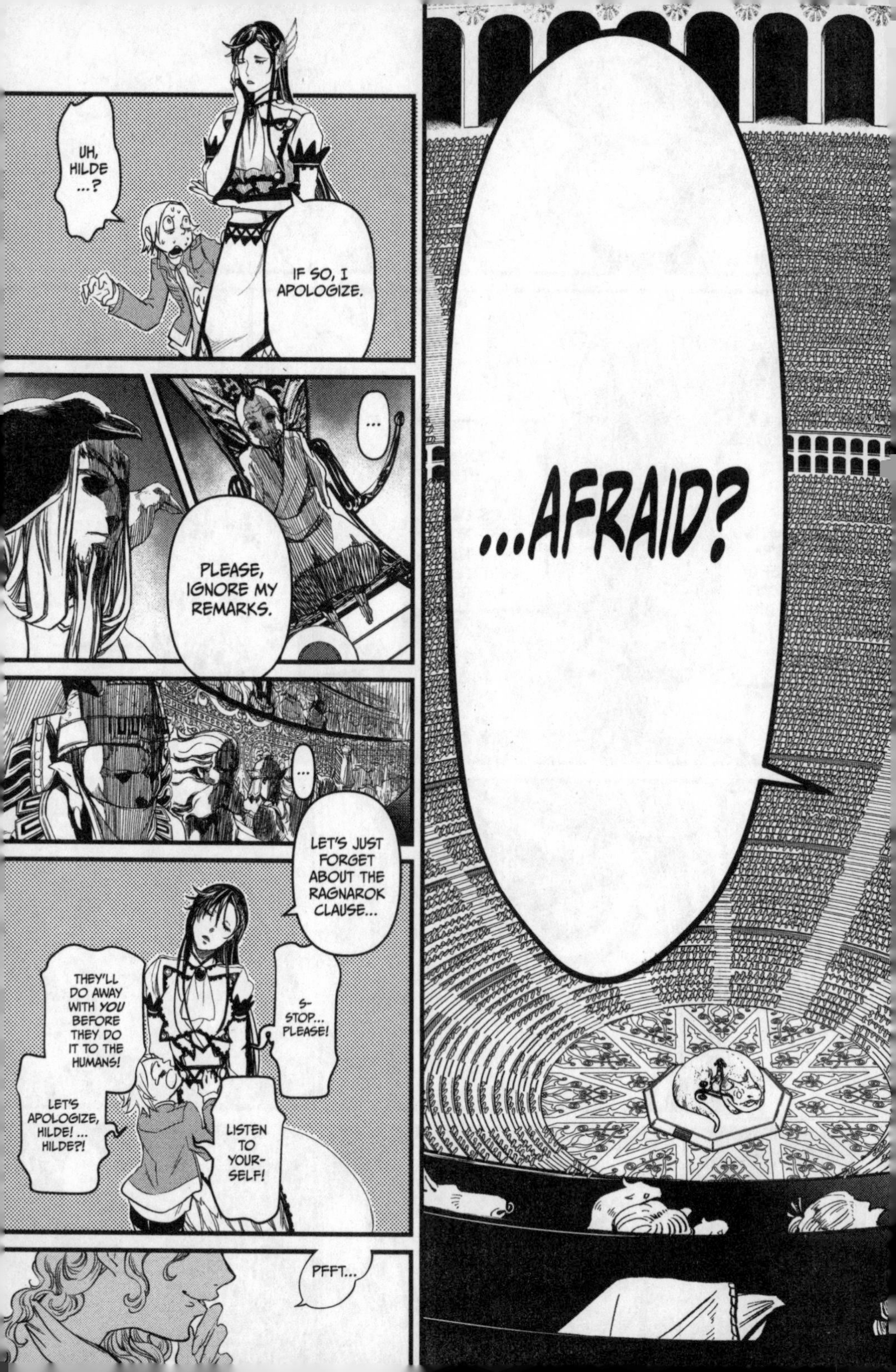
...AFRAID?
IF SO, I APOLOGIZE.
UH, HILDE ...?
...
PLEASE, IGNORE MY REMARKS.
...
LET'S JUST FORGET ABOUT THE RAGNAROK CLAUSE...
S-STOP... PLEASE!
THEY'LL DO AWAY WITH *YOU* BEFORE THEY DO IT TO THE HUMANS!
LISTEN TO YOURSELF!
LET'S APOLOGIZE, HILDE! ... HILDE?!
PFFT...

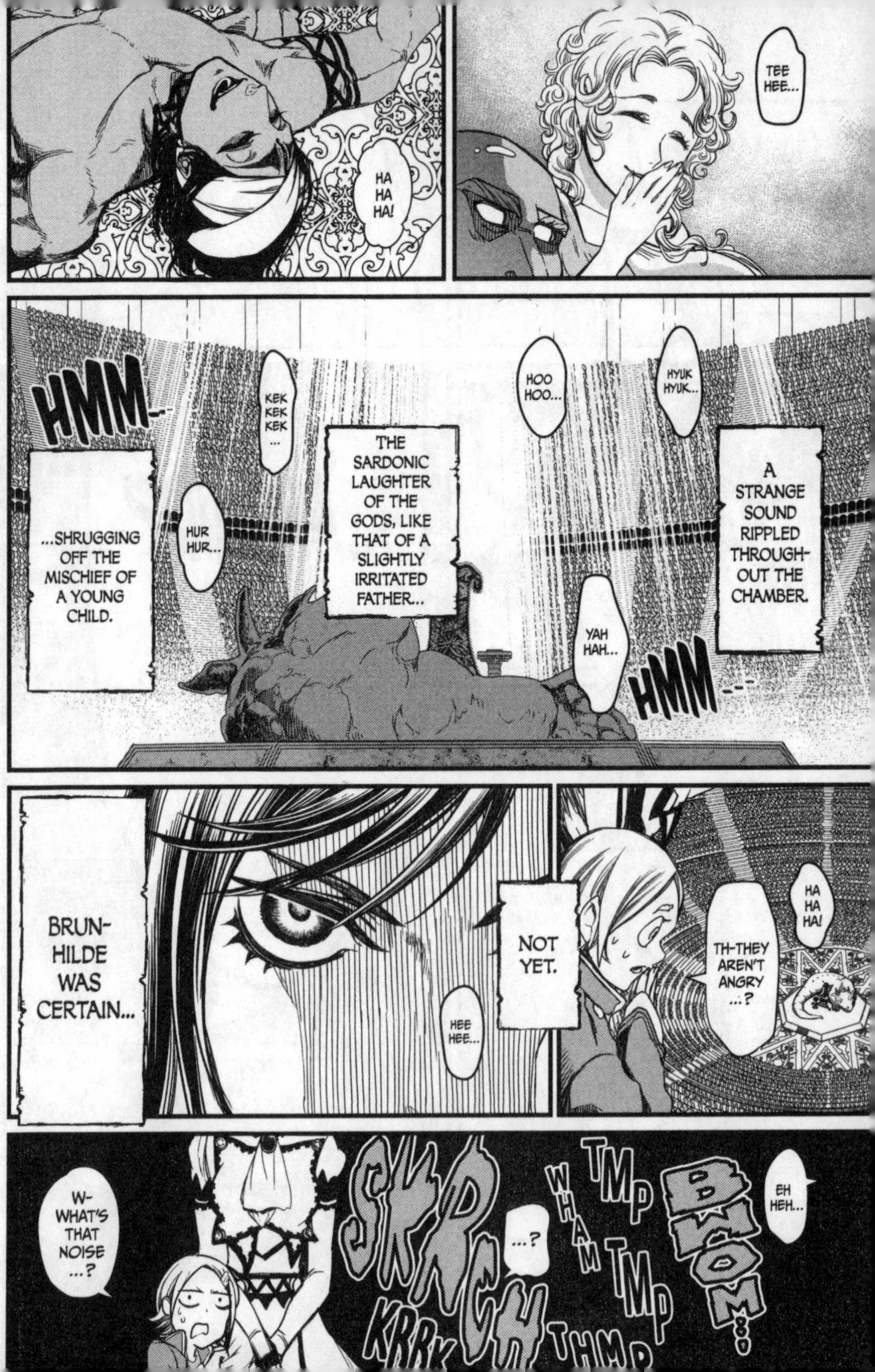
TEE HEE...
HA HA HA!
HYUK HYUK...
HOO HOO...
A STRANGE SOUND RIPPLED THROUGHOUT THE CHAMBER.
YAH HAH...
HMM...
KEK KEK KEK...
THE SARDONIC LAUGHTER OF THE GODS, LIKE THAT OF A SLIGHTLY IRRITATED FATHER...
HMM...
HUR HUR...
...SHRUGGING OFF THE MISCHIEF OF A YOUNG CHILD.
HA HA HA!
TH-THEY AREN'T ANGRY ...?
BRUNHILDE WAS CERTAIN...
NOT YET.
HEE HEE...
EH HEH...
BWOM...
TMP TMP TMP THMP
WHAM
SKRCH
KRRK
...?
W-WHAT'S THAT NOISE ...?

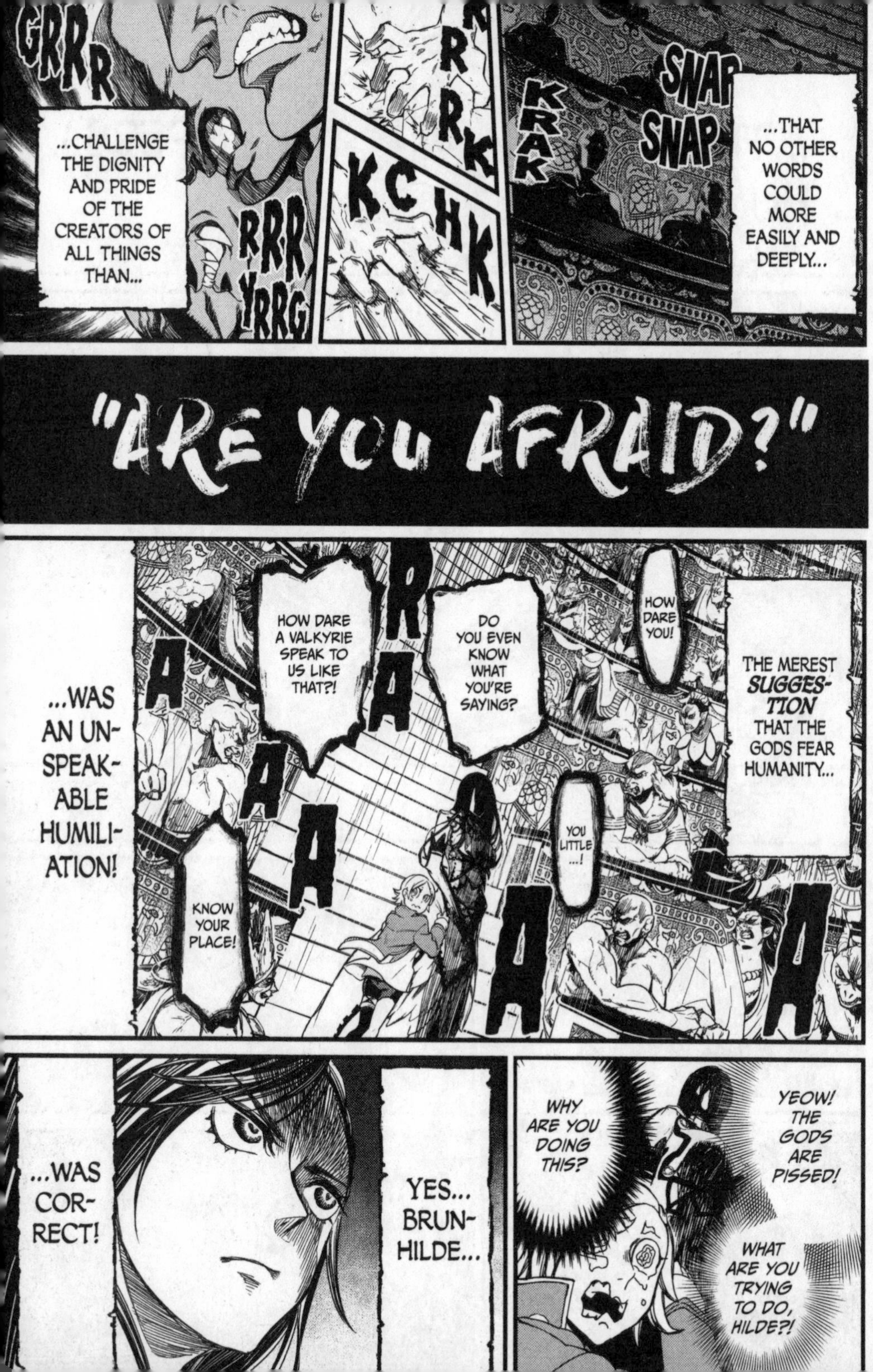

SNAP SNAP
KRAK
...THAT NO OTHER WORDS COULD MORE EASILY AND DEEPLY...
RRRK
KCHK
GRRR
...CHALLENGE THE DIGNITY AND PRIDE OF THE CREATORS OF ALL THINGS THAN...
RRR YRRG
"ARE YOU AFRAID?"
THE MEREST *SUGGES-TION* THAT THE GODS FEAR HUMANITY...
HOW DARE YOU!
DO YOU EVEN KNOW WHAT YOU'RE SAYING?
RAAAAAAA
HOW DARE A VALKYRIE SPEAK TO US LIKE THAT?!
YOU LITTLE ...!
KNOW YOUR PLACE!
...WAS AN UN-SPEAK-ABLE HUMILI-ATION!
YEOW! THE GODS ARE PISSED!
WHY ARE YOU DOING THIS?
WHAT ARE YOU TRYING TO DO, HILDE?!
YES... BRUN-HILDE...
...WAS COR-RECT!

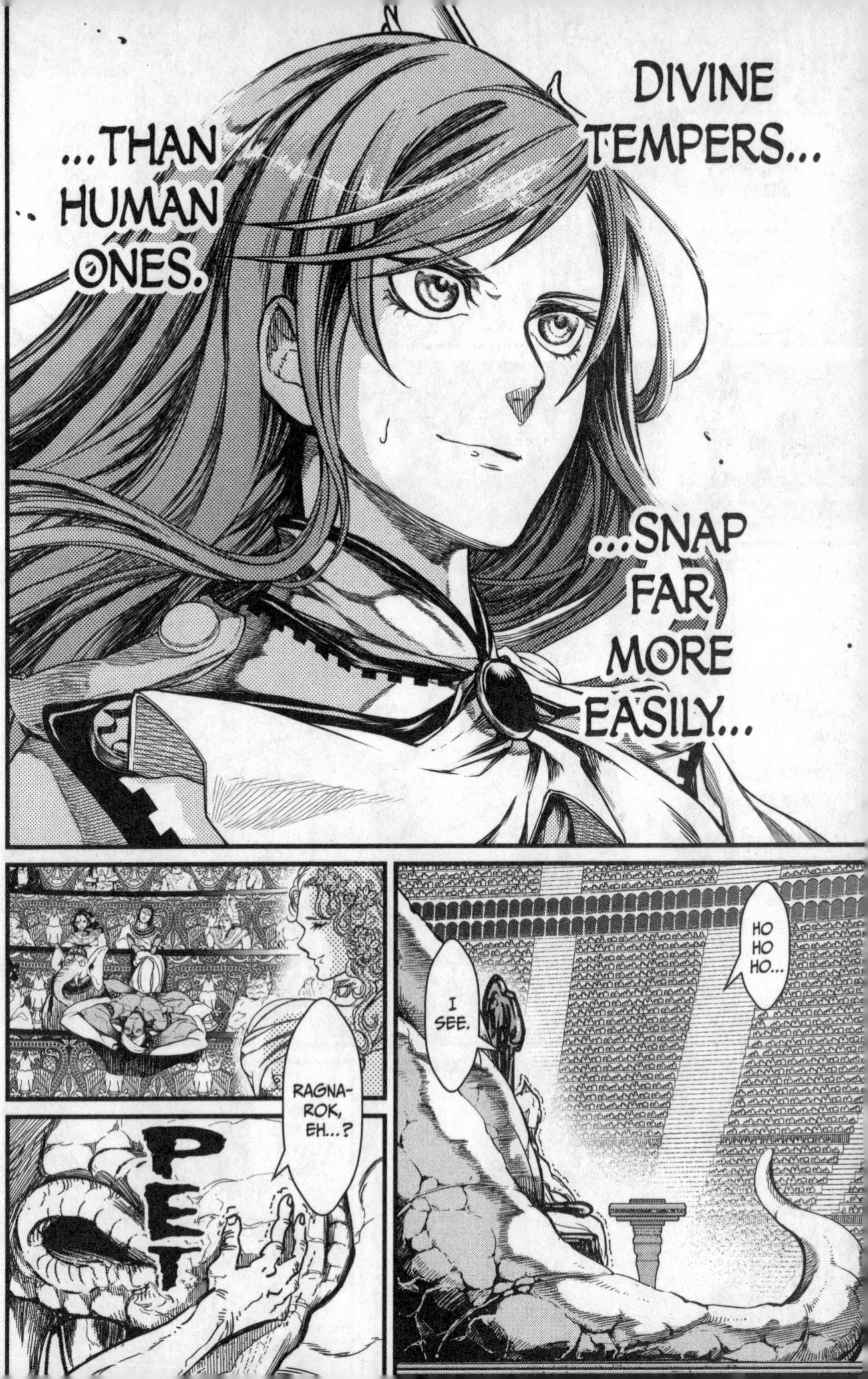
DIVINE TEMPERS...
...SNAP FAR MORE EASILY...
...THAN HUMAN ONES.
HO HO HO...
I SEE.
RAGNAROK, EH...?
PET

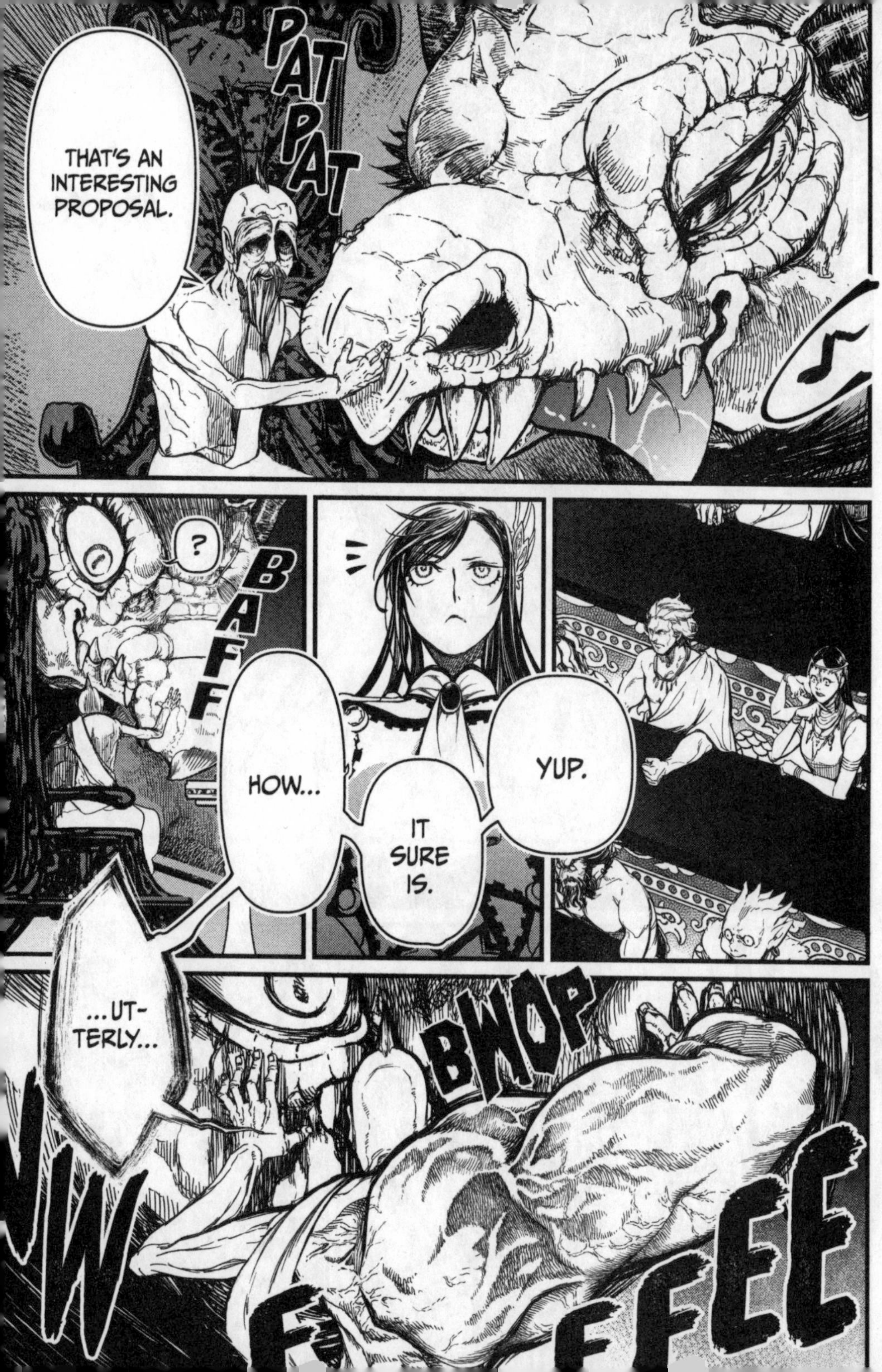
THAT'S AN INTERESTING PROPOSAL.
PAT PAT
YUP.
IT SURE IS.
?
BAFF
HOW...
...UT-TERLY...
BWOP

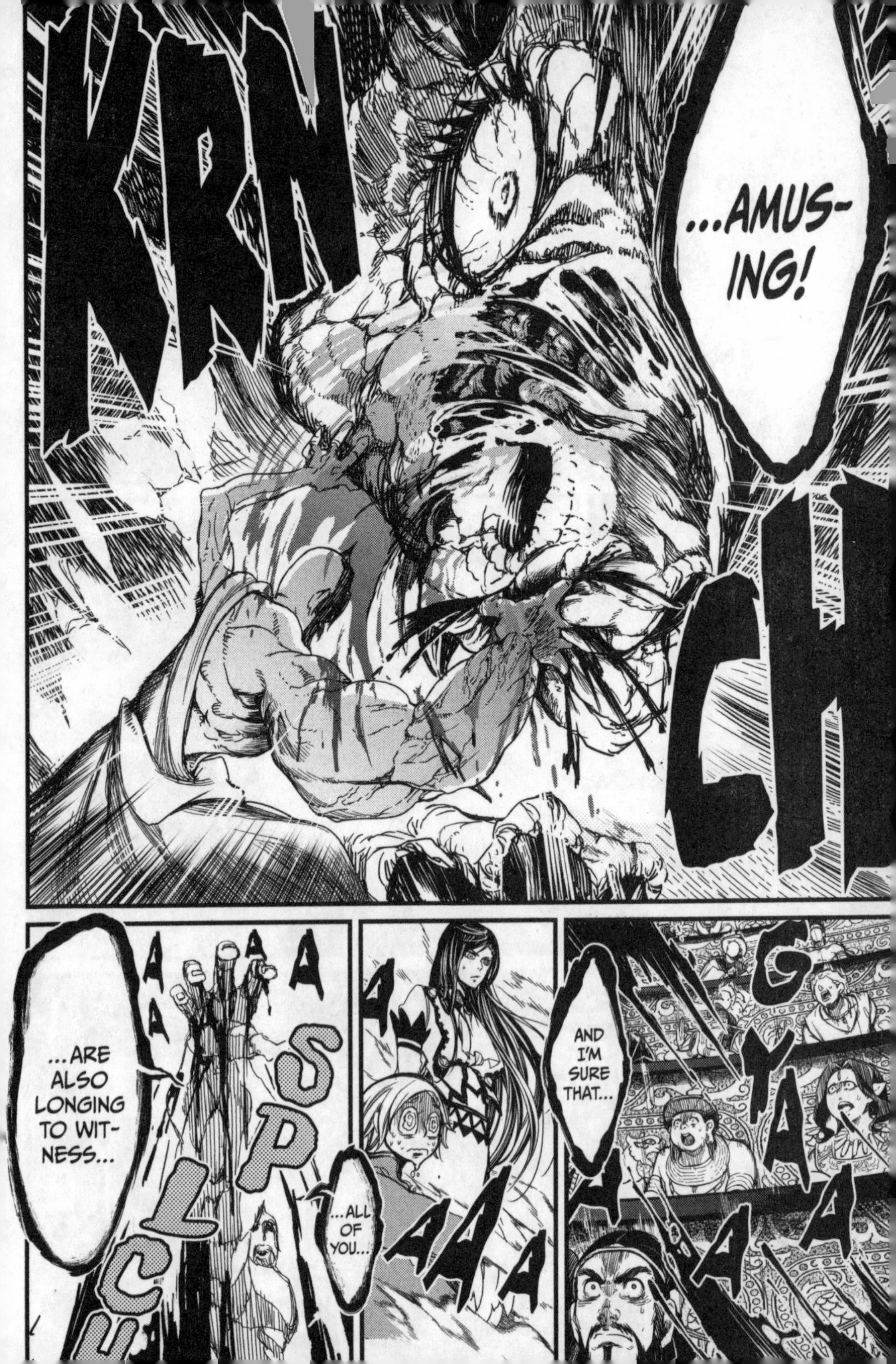
KRA
...AMUS- ING!
CH
GYAAAA
AND I'M SURE THAT...
AAAA
...ALL OF YOU...
AAAA
...ARE ALSO LONGING TO WIT- NESS...
SPLCH

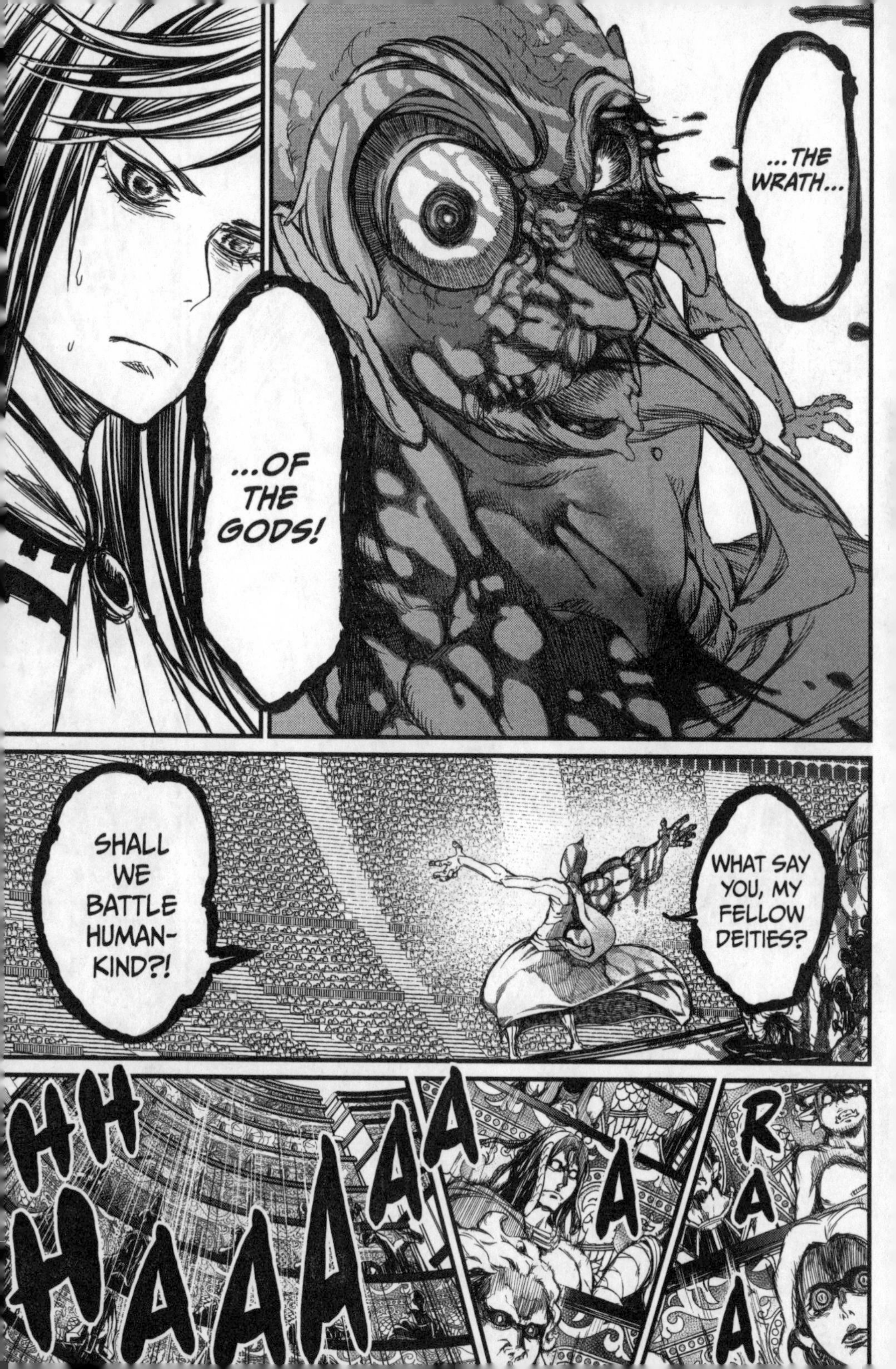
...THE WRATH...
...OF THE GODS!
WHAT SAY YOU, MY FELLOW DEITIES?
SHALL WE BATTLE HUMAN-KIND?!
HHHAAAAAAARAA

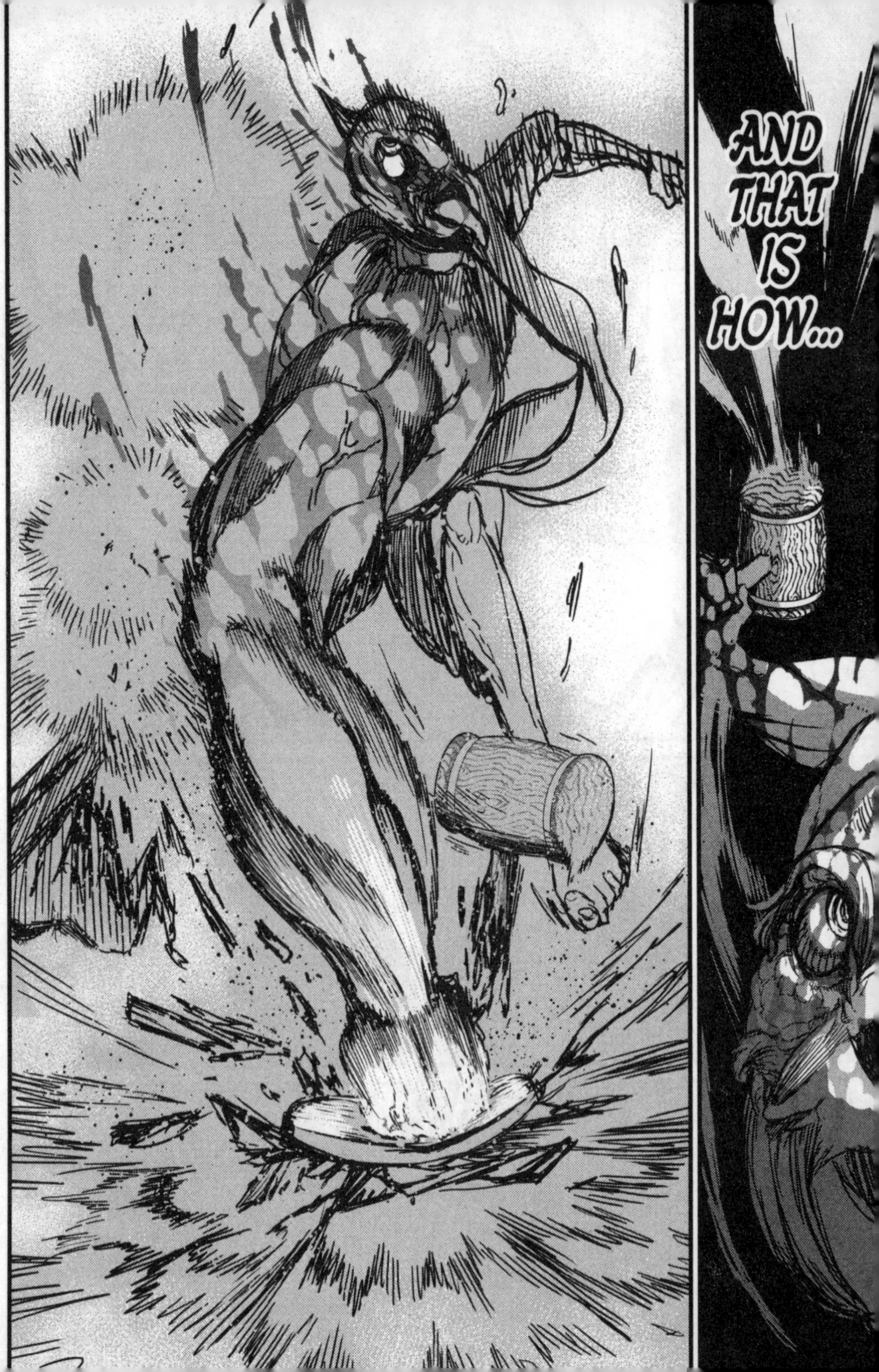
AND THAT IS HOW...

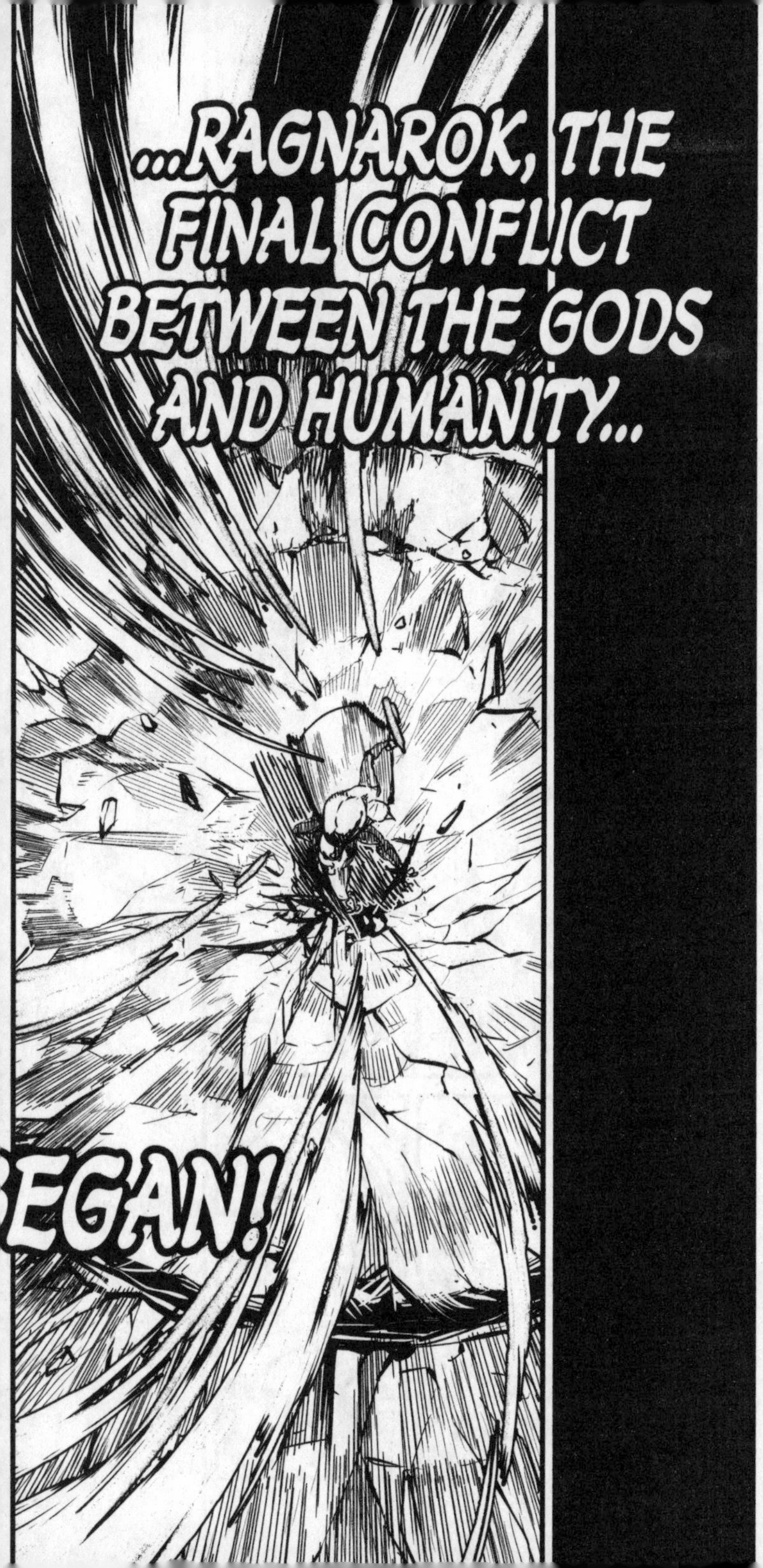
...RAGNAROK, THE FINAL CONFLICT BETWEEN THE GODS AND HUMANITY...
EGAN!

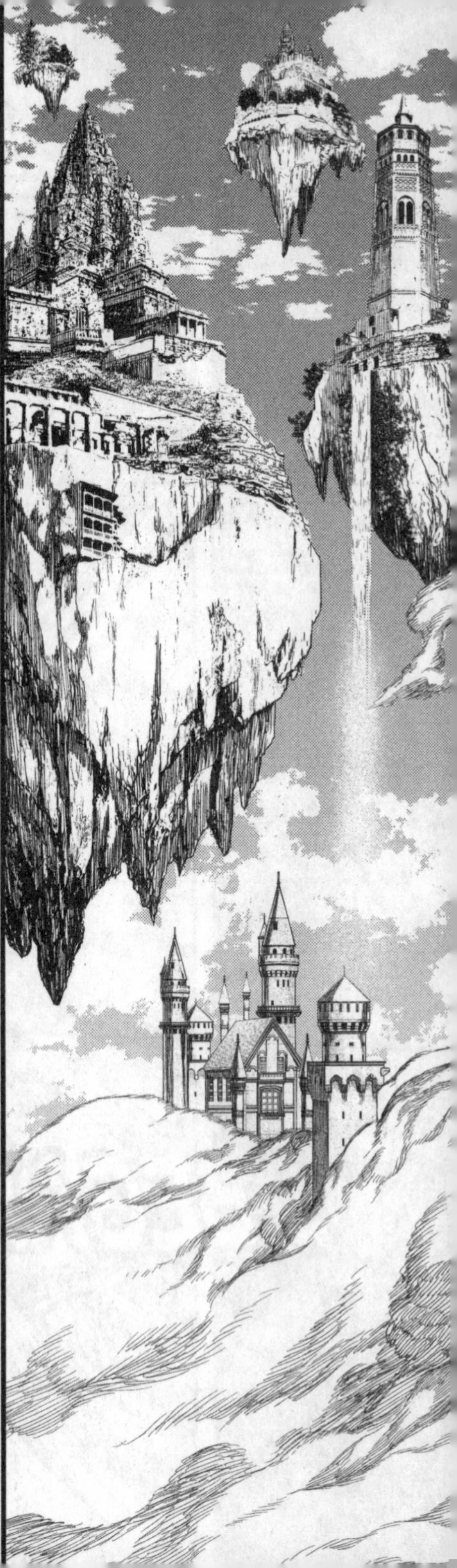

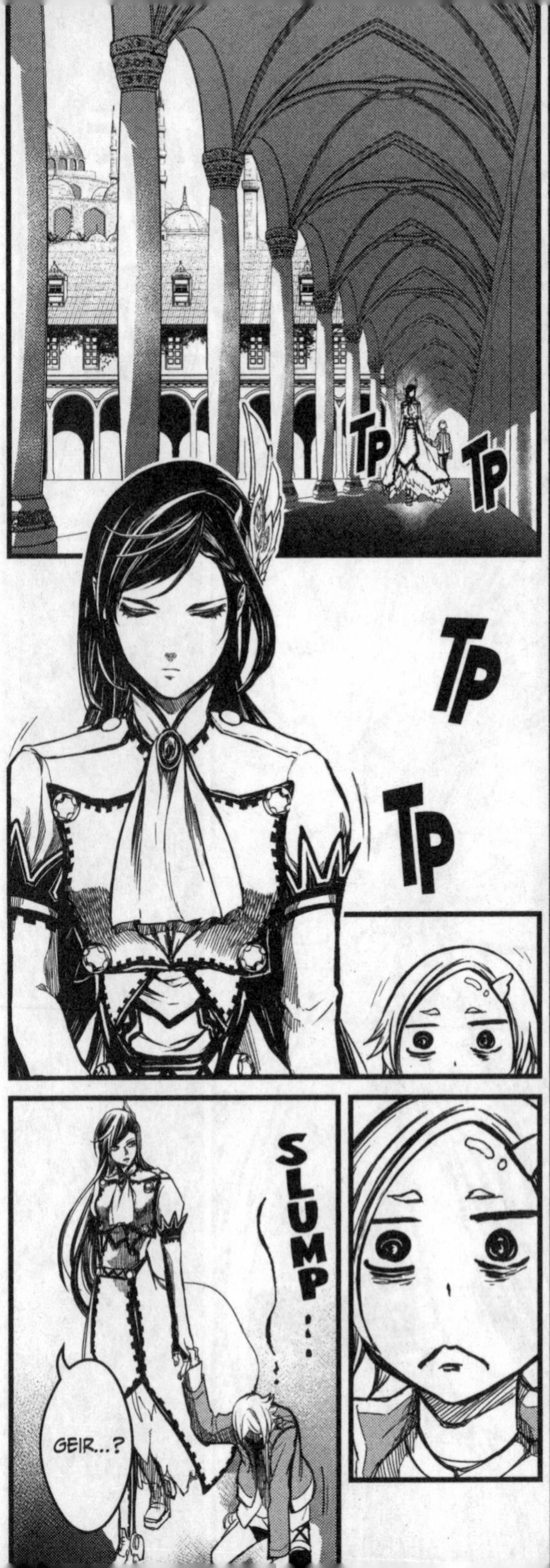
TP
TP
TP
TP
SLUMP...
GEIR...?

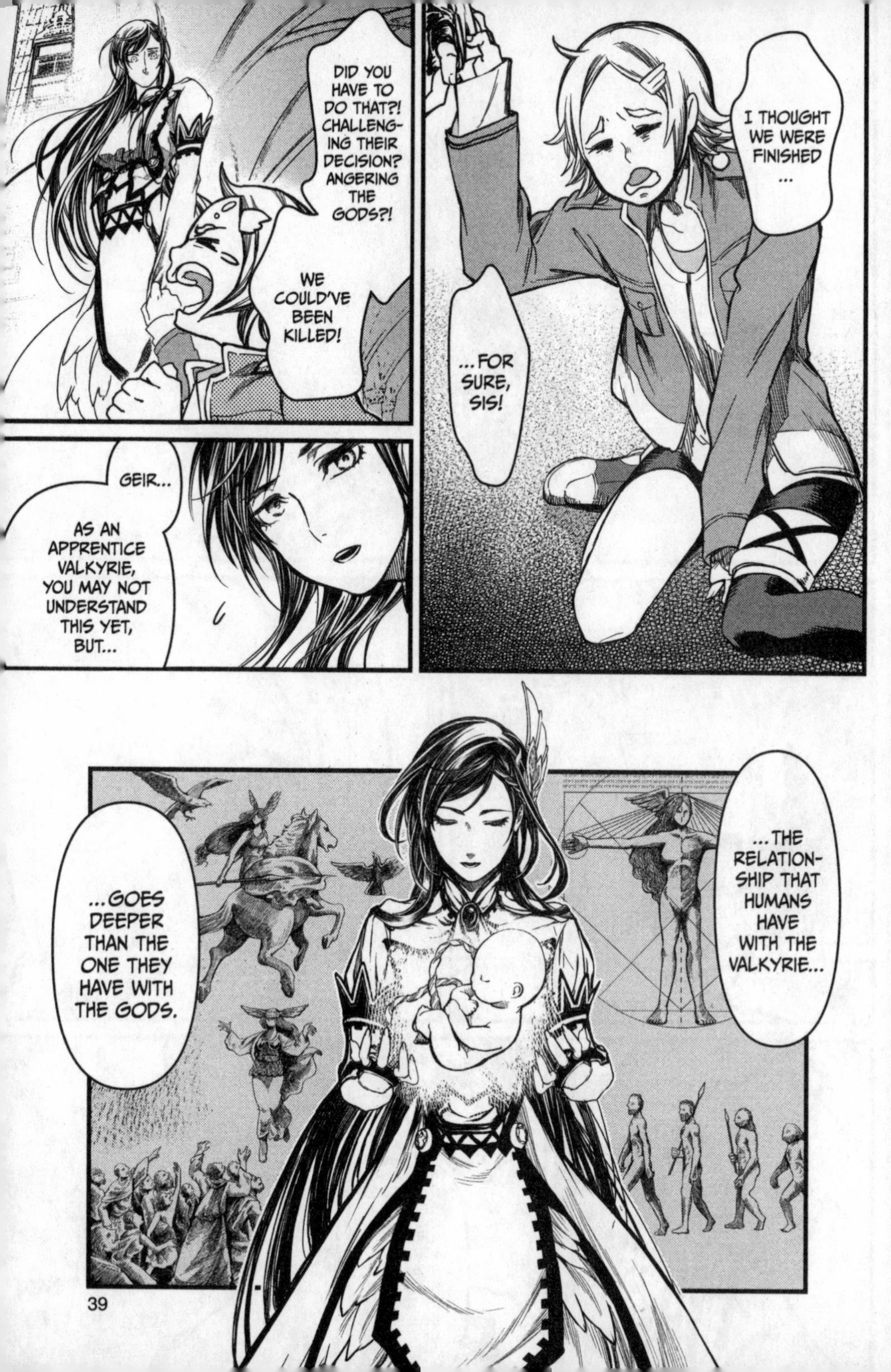
I THOUGHT WE WERE FINISHED ...
...FOR SURE, SIS!
DID YOU HAVE TO DO THAT?! CHALLENGING THEIR DECISION? ANGERING THE GODS?!
WE COULD'VE BEEN KILLED!
GEIR...
AS AN APPRENTICE VALKYRIE, YOU MAY NOT UNDERSTAND THIS YET, BUT...
...THE RELATIONSHIP THAT HUMANS HAVE WITH THE VALKYRIE...
...GOES DEEPER THAN THE ONE THEY HAVE WITH THE GODS.

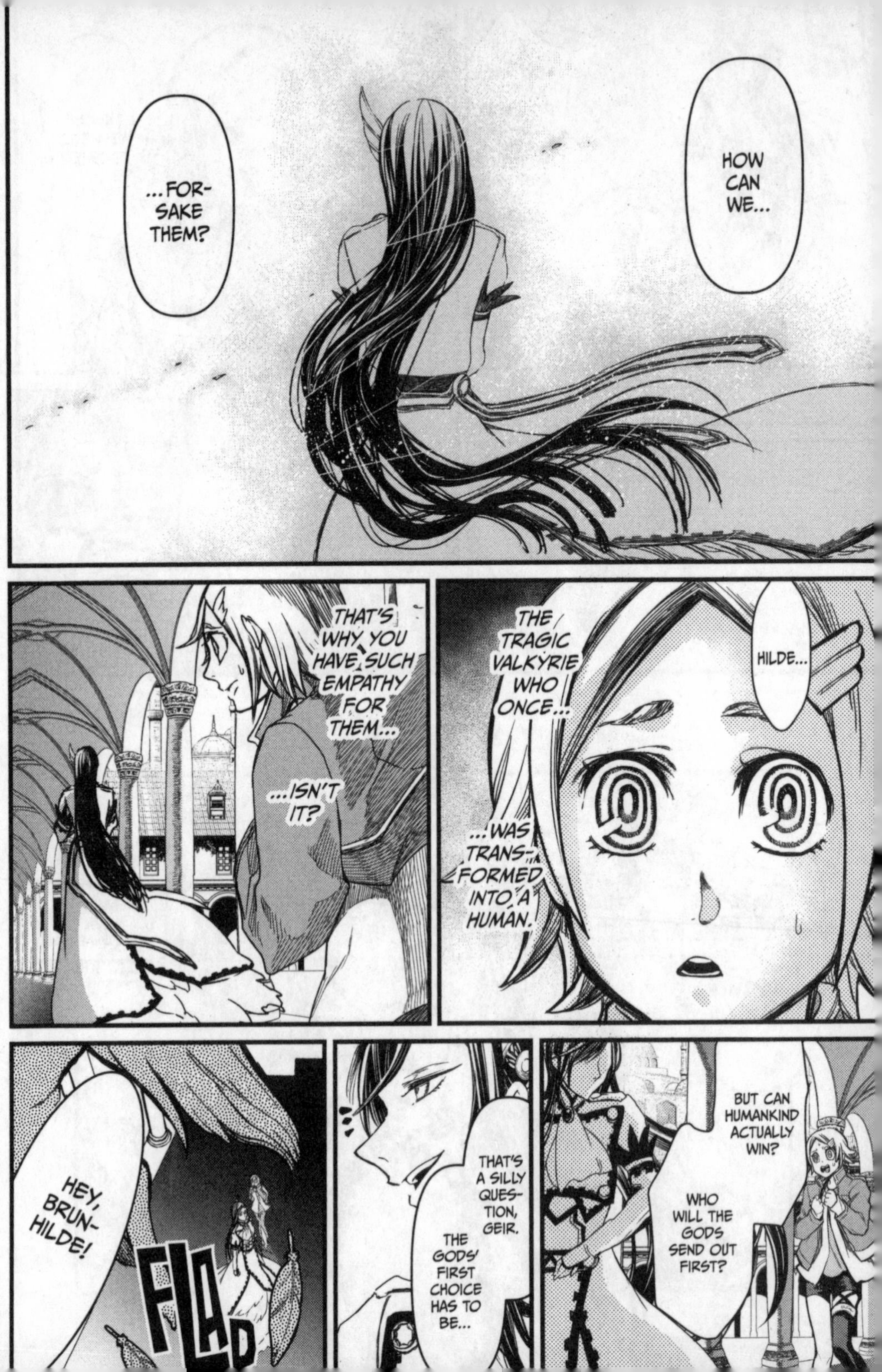
HOW CAN WE...
...FOR-SAKE THEM?
HILDE...
THE TRAGIC VALKYRIE WHO ONCE...
...WAS TRANS-FORMED INTO A HUMAN.
THAT'S WHY YOU HAVE SUCH EMPATHY FOR THEM...
...ISN'T IT?
BUT CAN HUMANKIND ACTUALLY WIN?
WHO WILL THE GODS SEND OUT FIRST?
THAT'S A SILLY QUES-TION, GEIR.
THE GODS' FIRST CHOICE HAS TO BE...
HEY, BRUN-HILDE!
FLAP

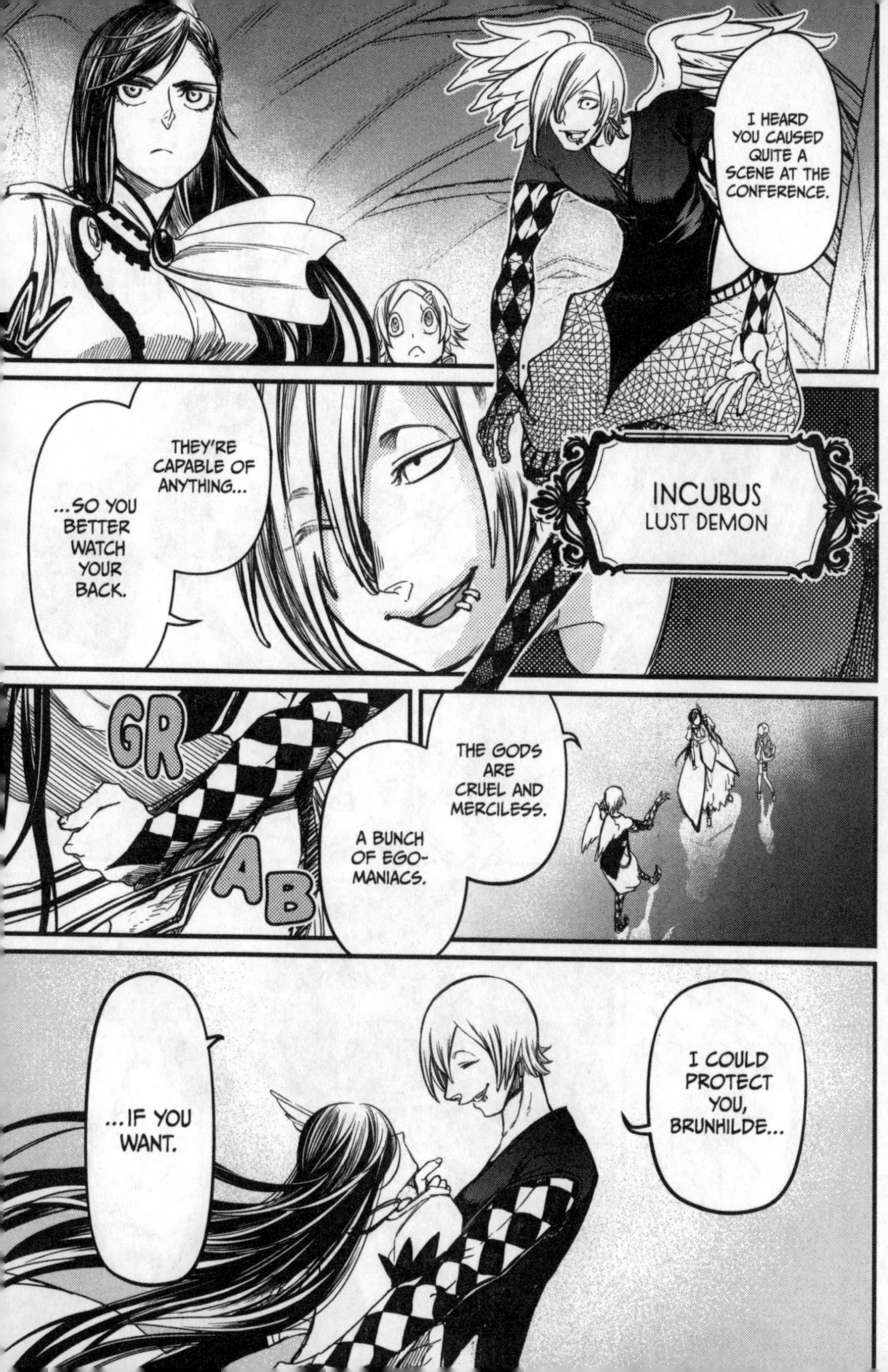
I HEARD YOU CAUSED QUITE A SCENE AT THE CONFERENCE.
INCUBUS
LUST DEMON
THEY'RE CAPABLE OF ANYTHING...
...SO YOU BETTER WATCH YOUR BACK.
THE GODS ARE CRUEL AND MERCILESS.
A BUNCH OF EGO-MANIACS.
GRAB
I COULD PROTECT YOU, BRUNHILDE...
...IF YOU WANT.

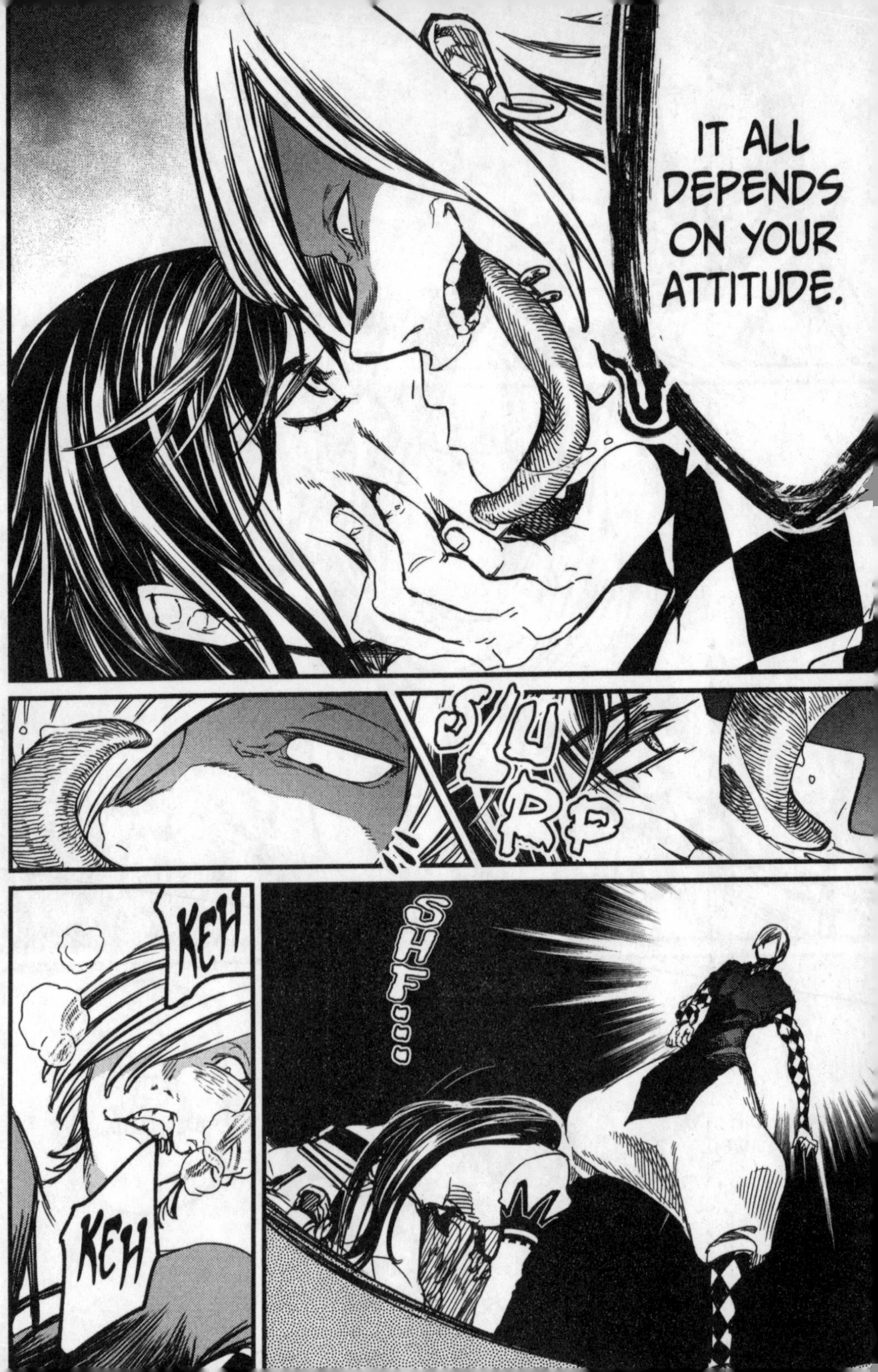
IT ALL DEPENDS ON YOUR ATTITUDE.
SLURP
SHF...
KEH
KEH

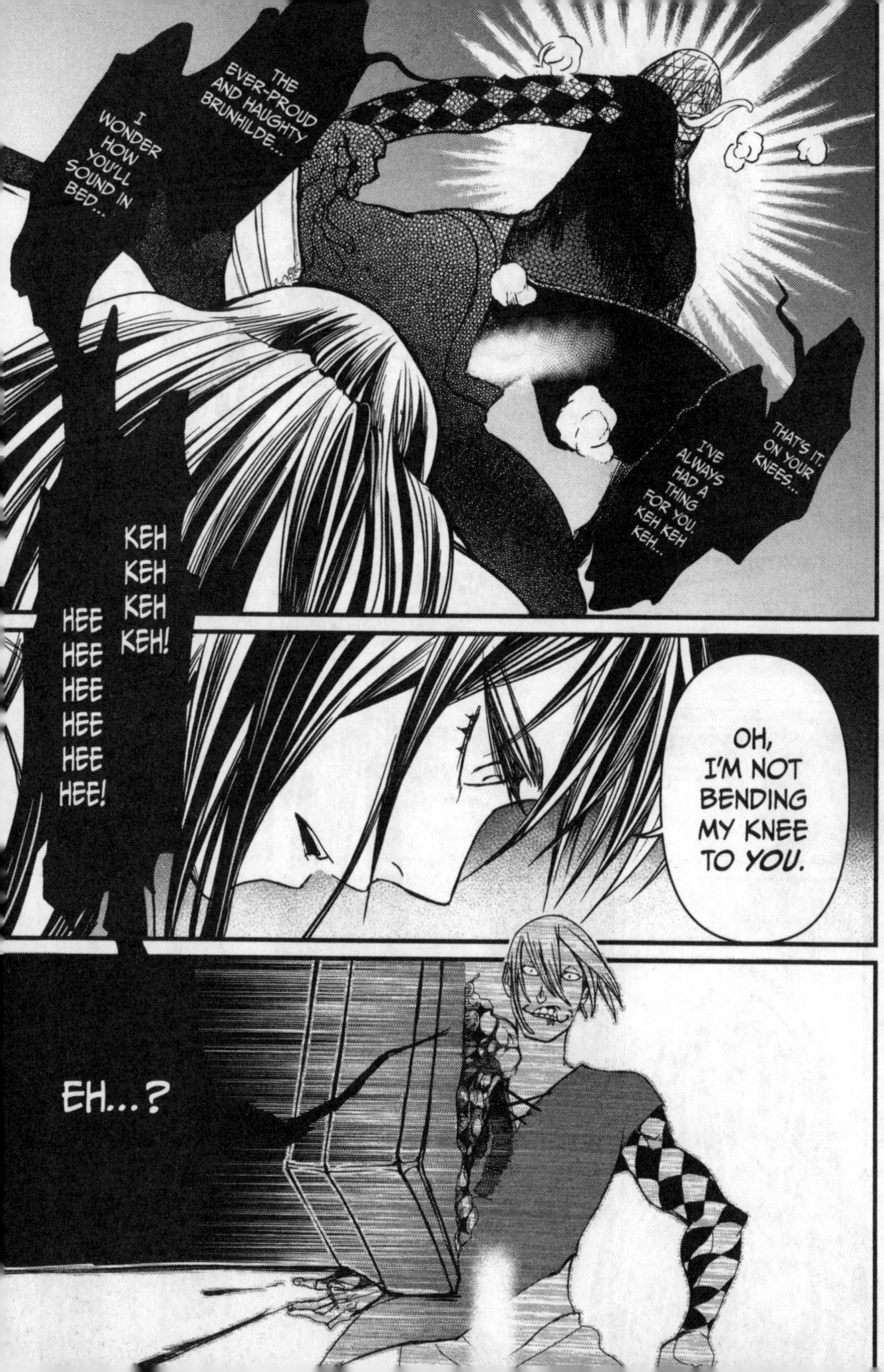
THAT'S IT. ON YOUR KNEES...
I'VE ALWAYS HAD A THING FOR YOU. KEH KEH KEH...
THE EVER-PROUD AND HAUGHTY BRUNHILDE...
I WONDER HOW YOU'LL SOUND IN BED...
KEH KEH KEH KEH!
HEE HEE HEE HEE HEE HEE!
OH, I'M NOT BENDING MY KNEE TO *YOU*.
EH...?

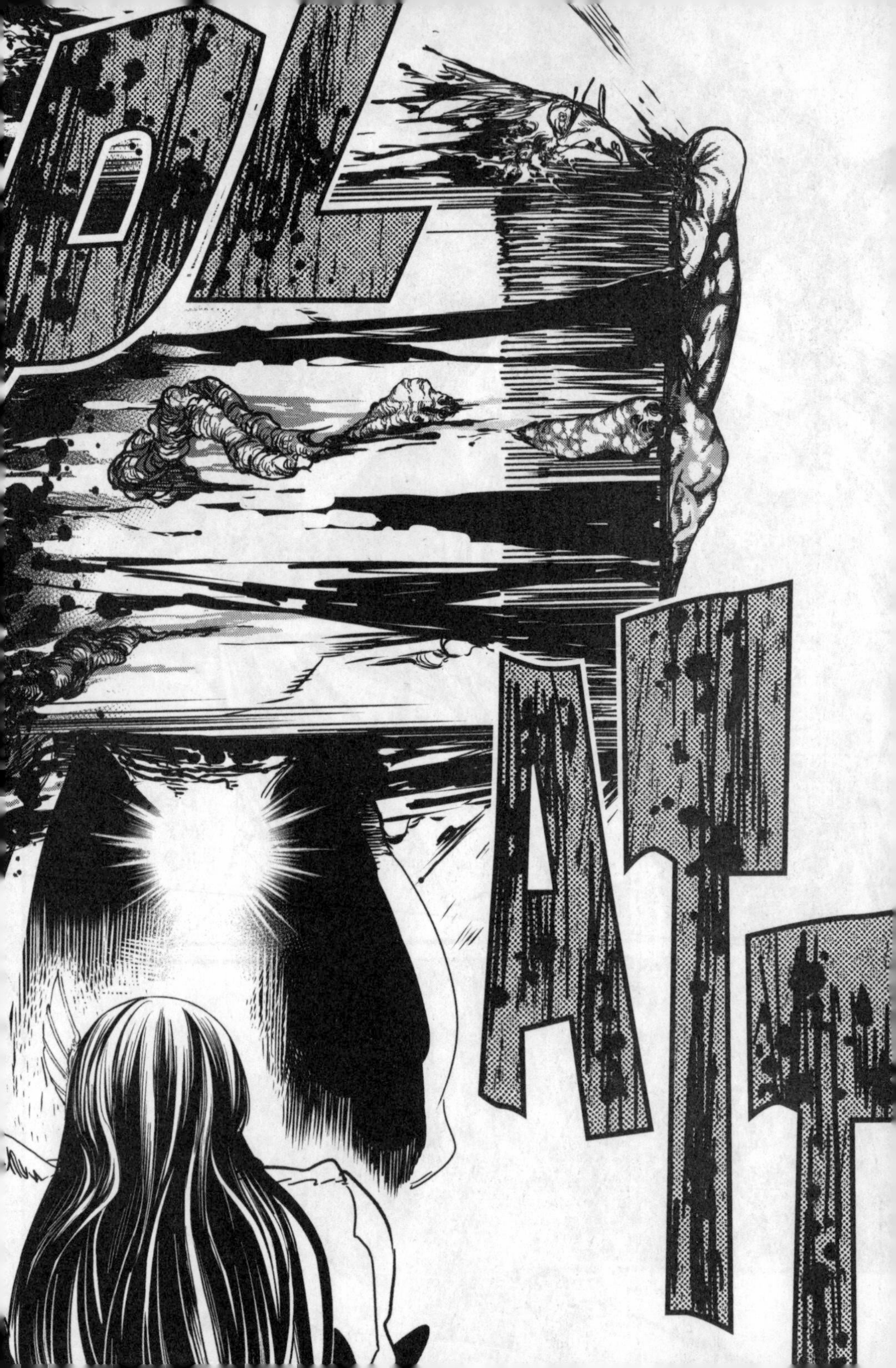

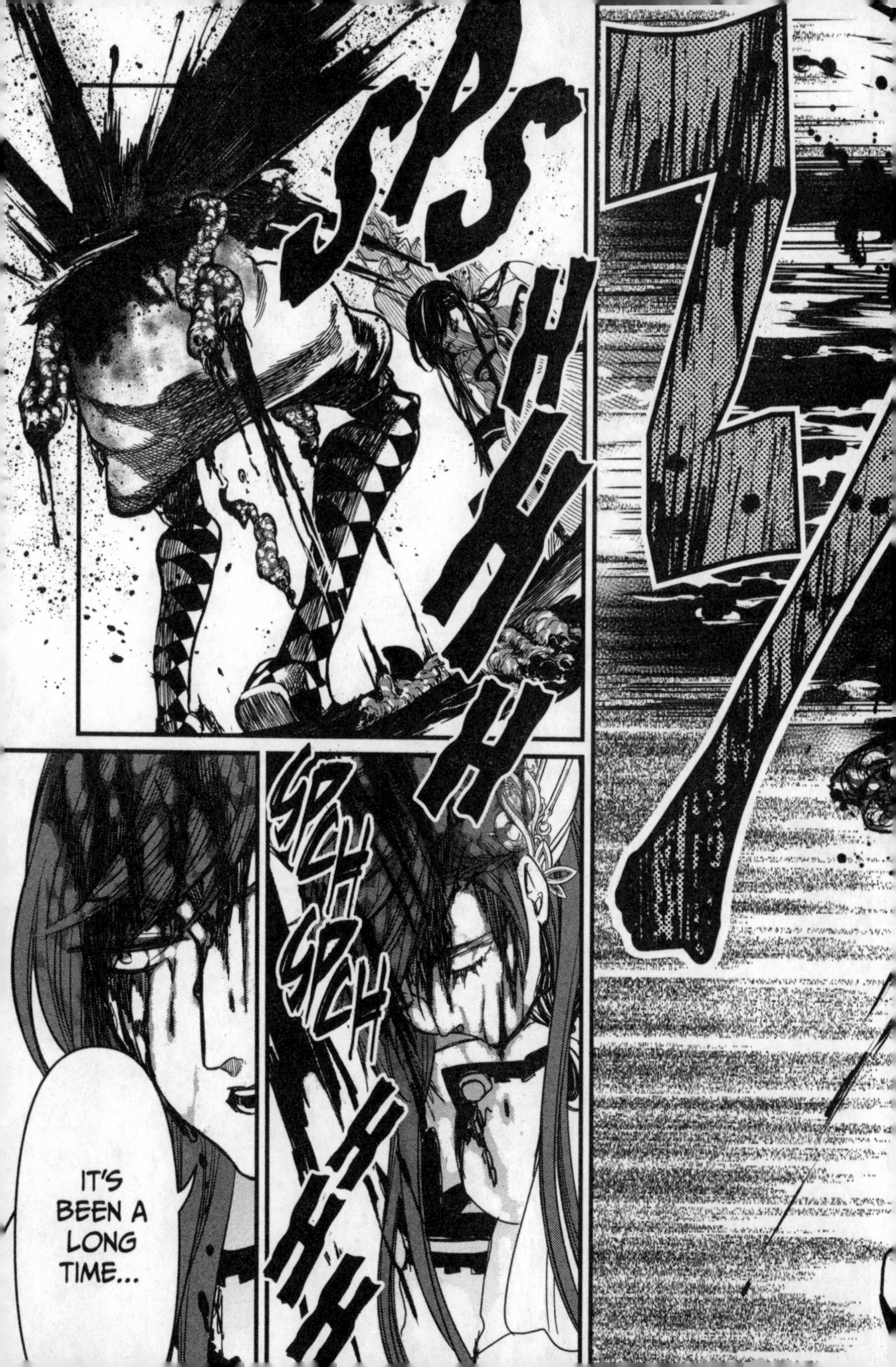
SPSHHHH
SPCH SPCH HHHH
IT'S BEEN A LONG TIME...

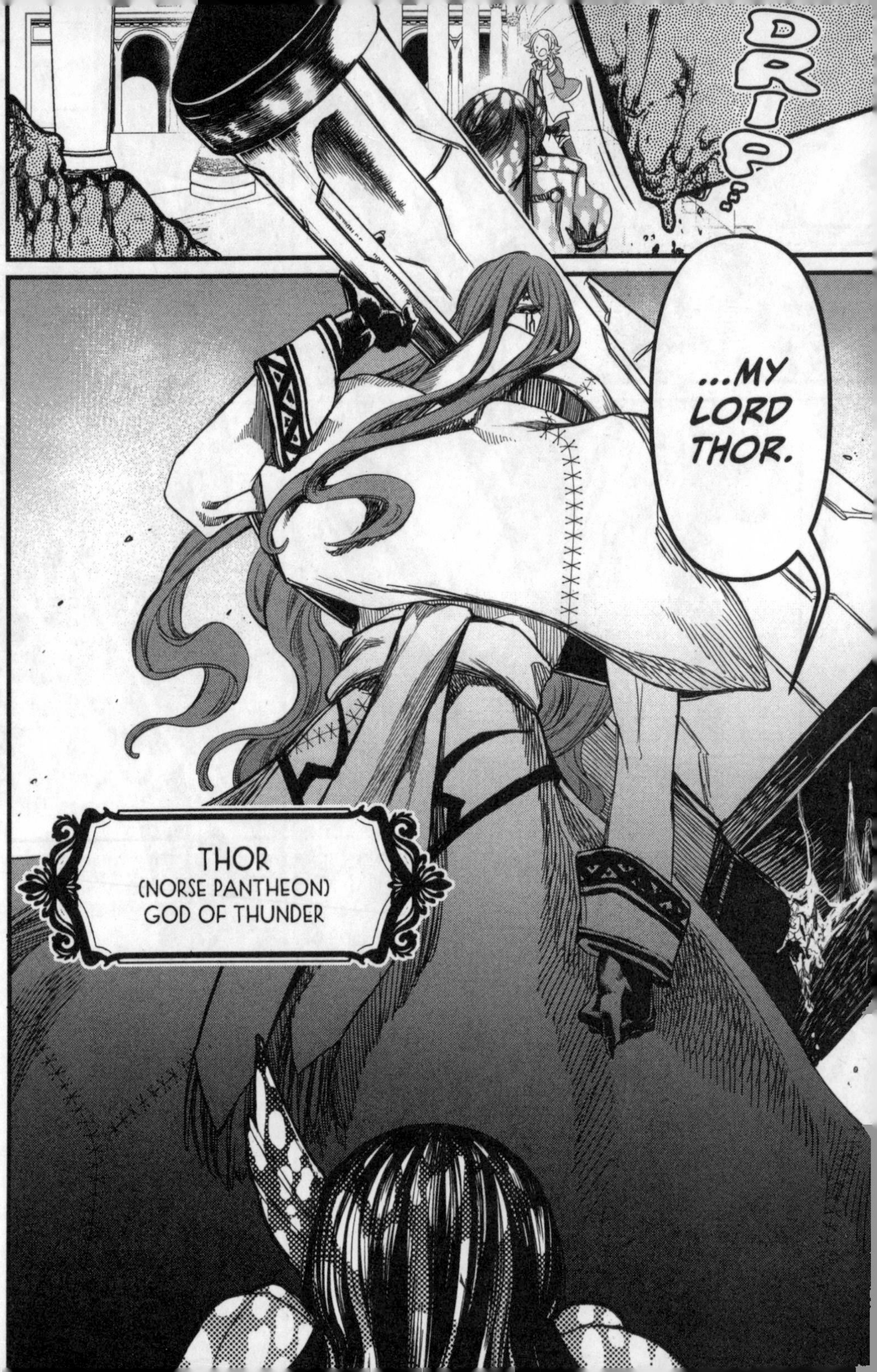
DRIP...
...MY LORD THOR.
THOR
(NORSE PANTHEON)
GOD OF THUNDER

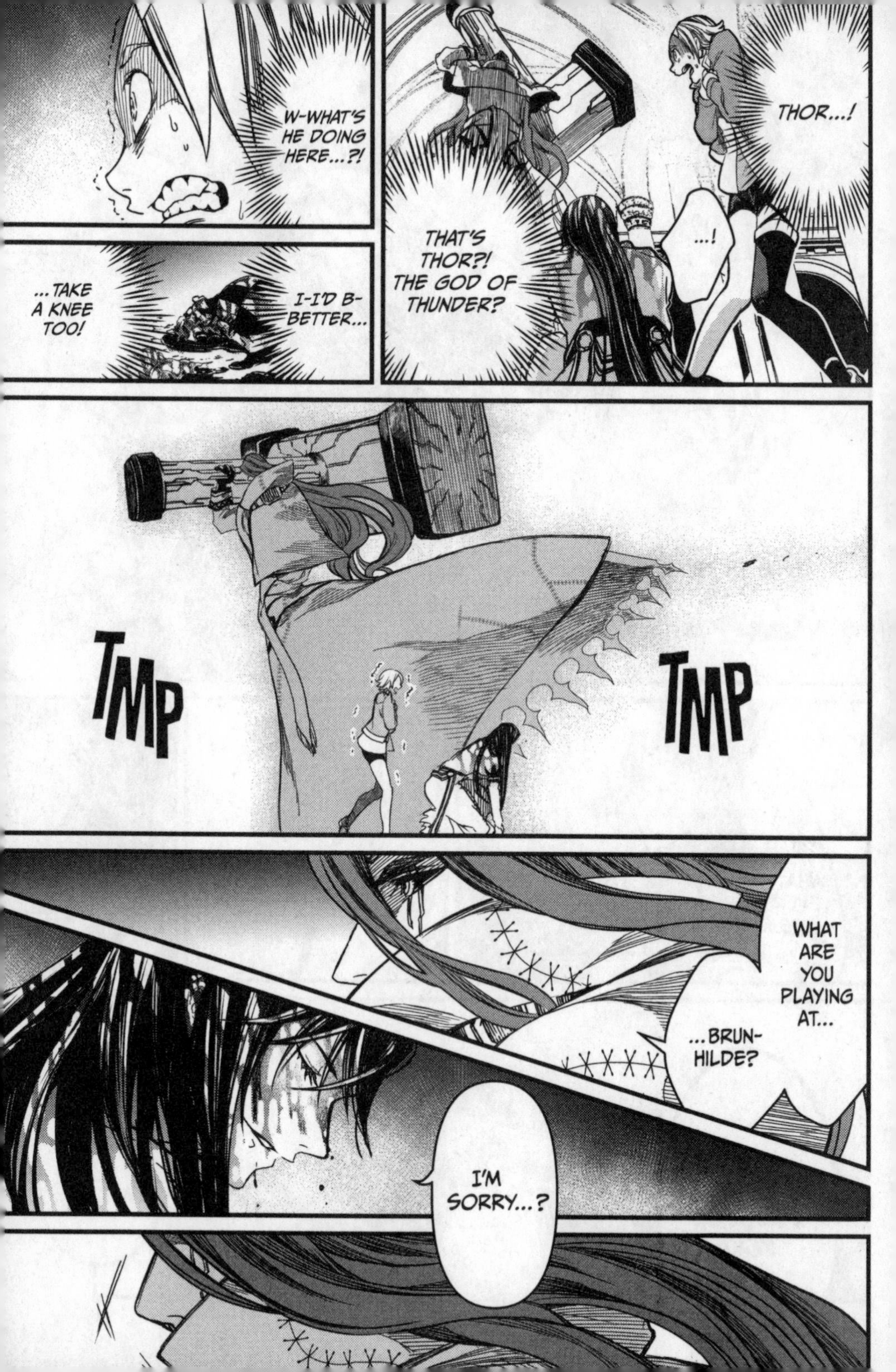
THOR...!
...!
THAT'S THOR?! THE GOD OF THUNDER?
W-WHAT'S HE DOING HERE...?!
I-I'D B-BETTER...
...TAKE A KNEE TOO!
TMP
TMP
WHAT ARE YOU PLAYING AT...
...BRUNHILDE?
I'M SORRY...?

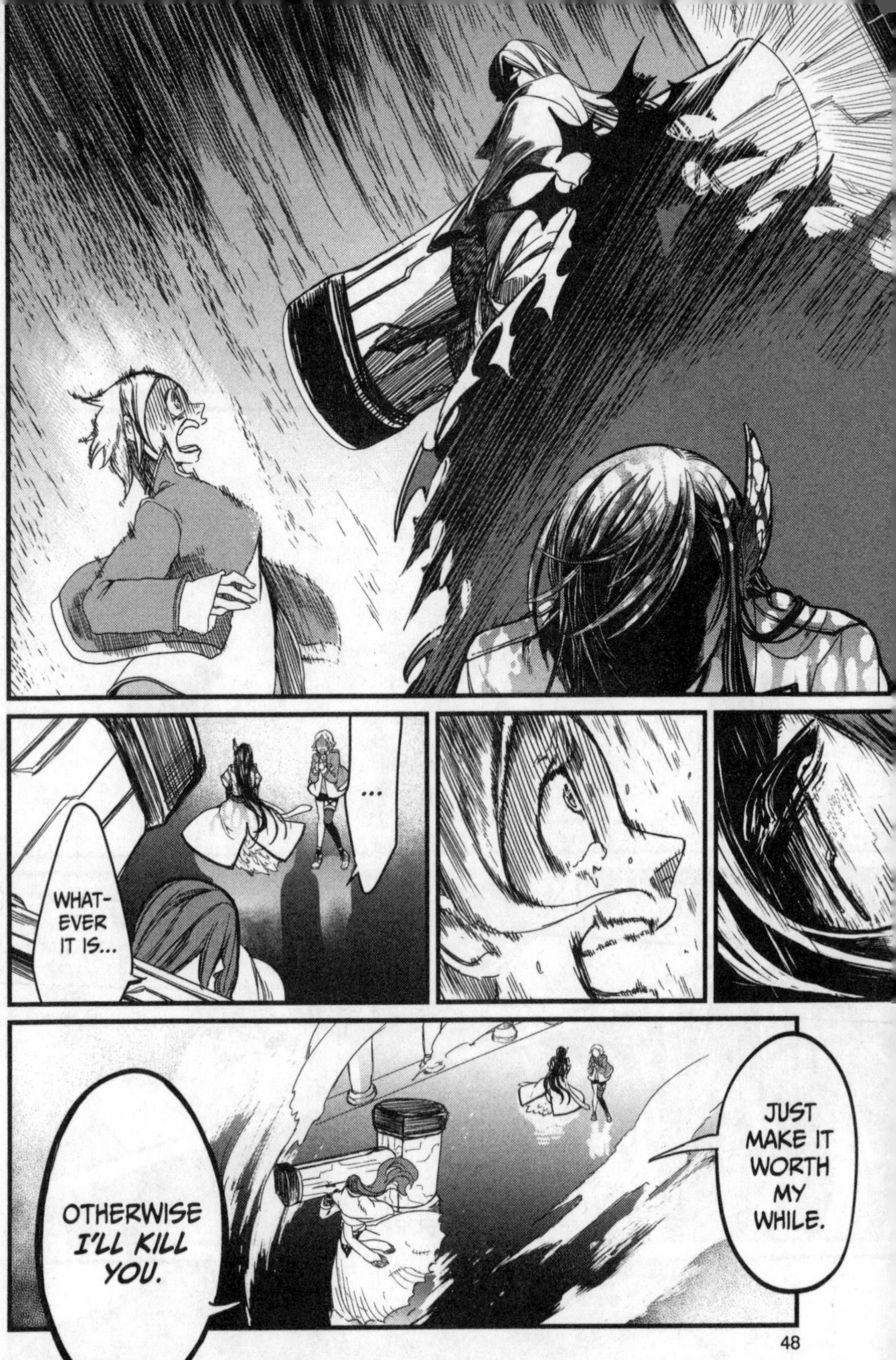
...
WHAT-
EVER
IT IS...
JUST MAKE IT WORTH MY WHILE.
OTHERWISE I'LL KILL YOU.

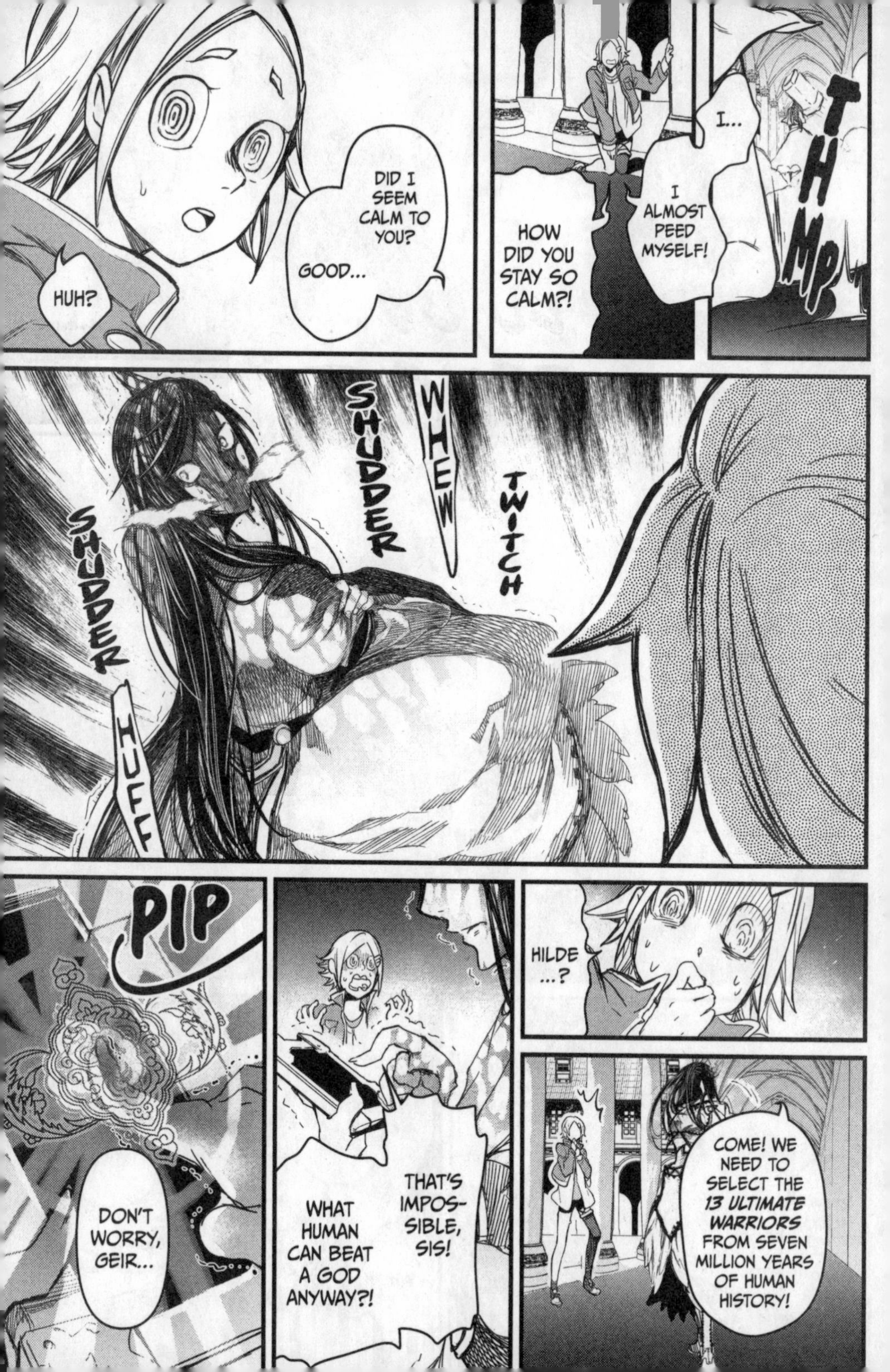
I...
I ALMOST PEED MYSELF!
THMP
HOW DID YOU STAY SO CALM?!
DID I SEEM CALM TO YOU? GOOD...
HUH?
TWITCH
WHEW
SHUDDER
SHUDDER
HUFF
HILDE...?
COME! WE NEED TO SELECT THE *13 ULTIMATE WARRIORS* FROM SEVEN MILLION YEARS OF HUMAN HISTORY!
THAT'S IMPOSSIBLE, SIS!
WHAT HUMAN CAN BEAT A GOD ANYWAY?!
PIP
DON'T WORRY, GEIR...

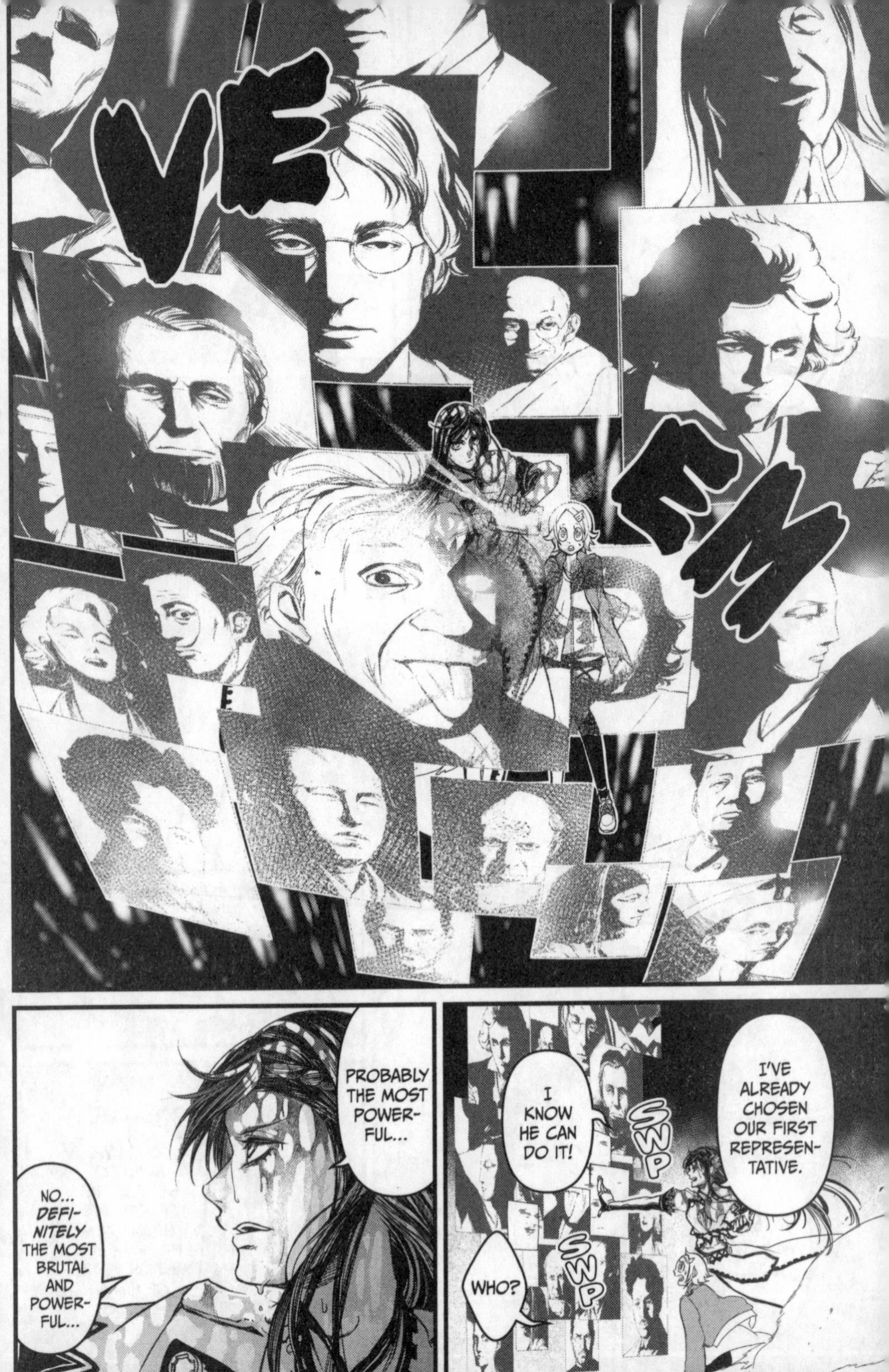
VE
EM
I'VE ALREADY CHOSEN OUR FIRST REPRESENTATIVE.
I KNOW HE CAN DO IT!
SWP
SWP
WHO?
PROBABLY THE MOST POWERFUL...
NO... *DEFINITELY* THE MOST BRUTAL AND POWERFUL...

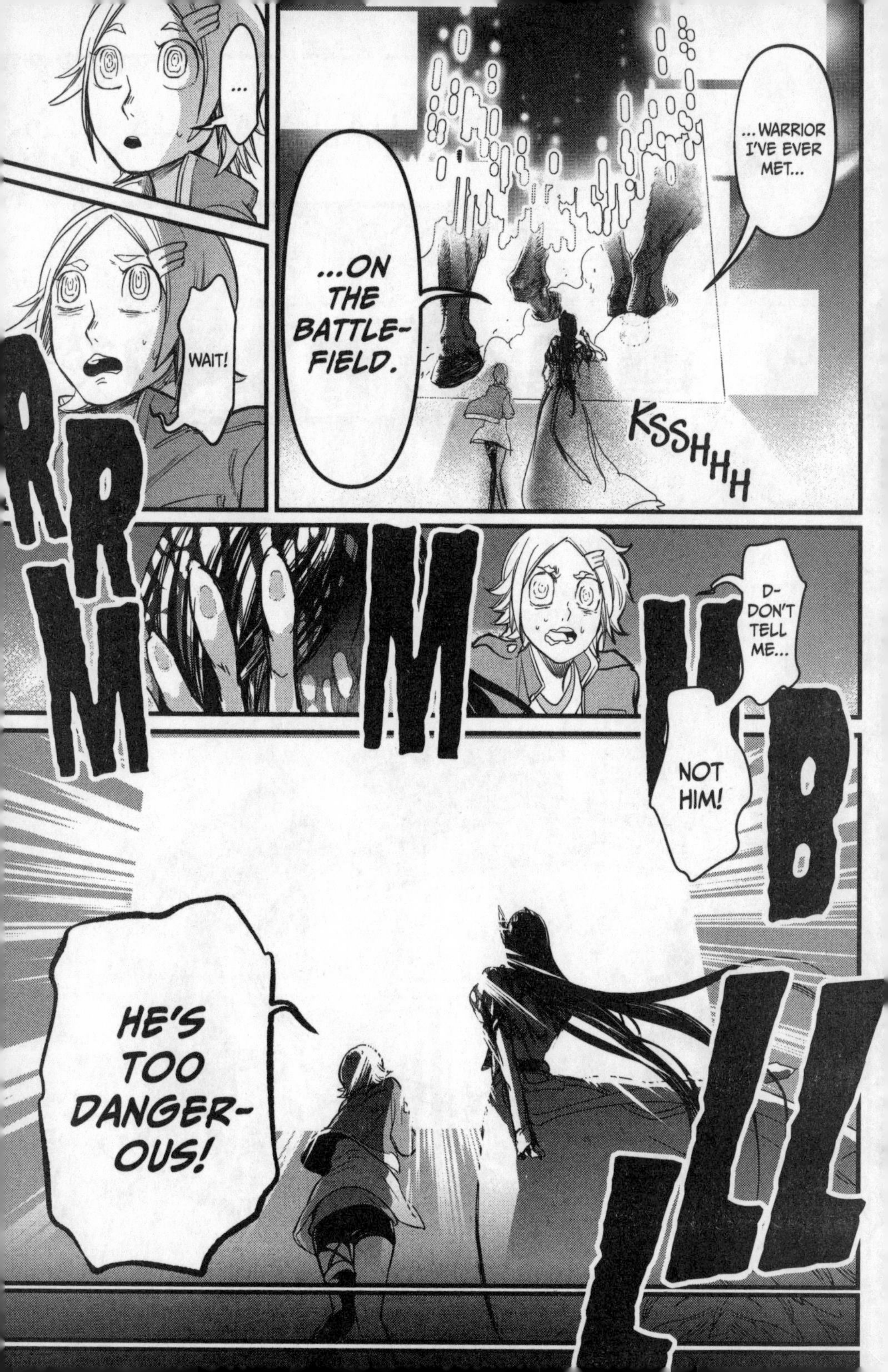
...WARRIOR I'VE EVER MET...
...ON THE BATTLE-FIELD.
KSSHHHH
...
WAIT!
D-DON'T TELL ME...
NOT HIM!
HE'S TOO DANGER-OUS!

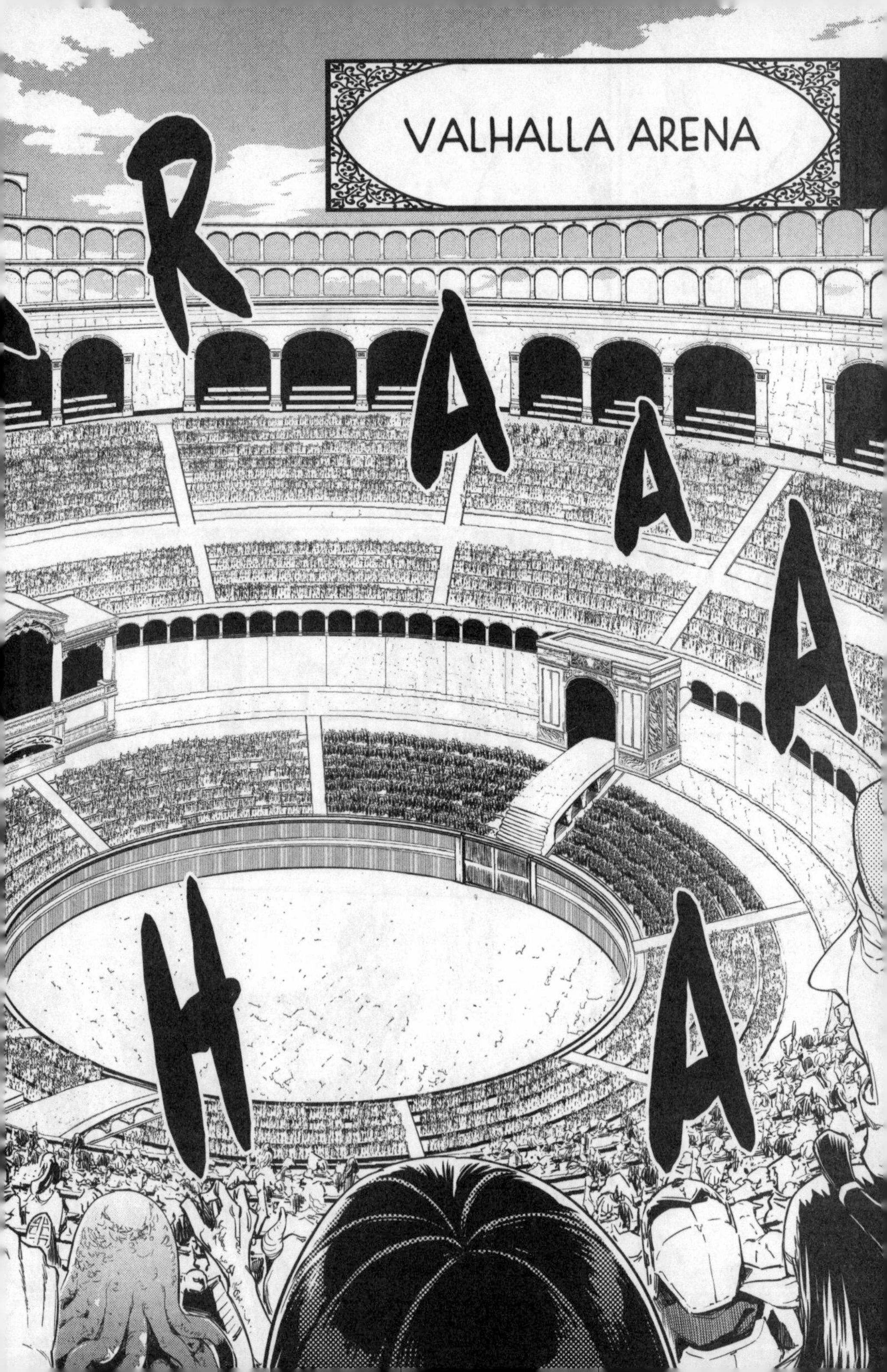
VALHALLA ARENA

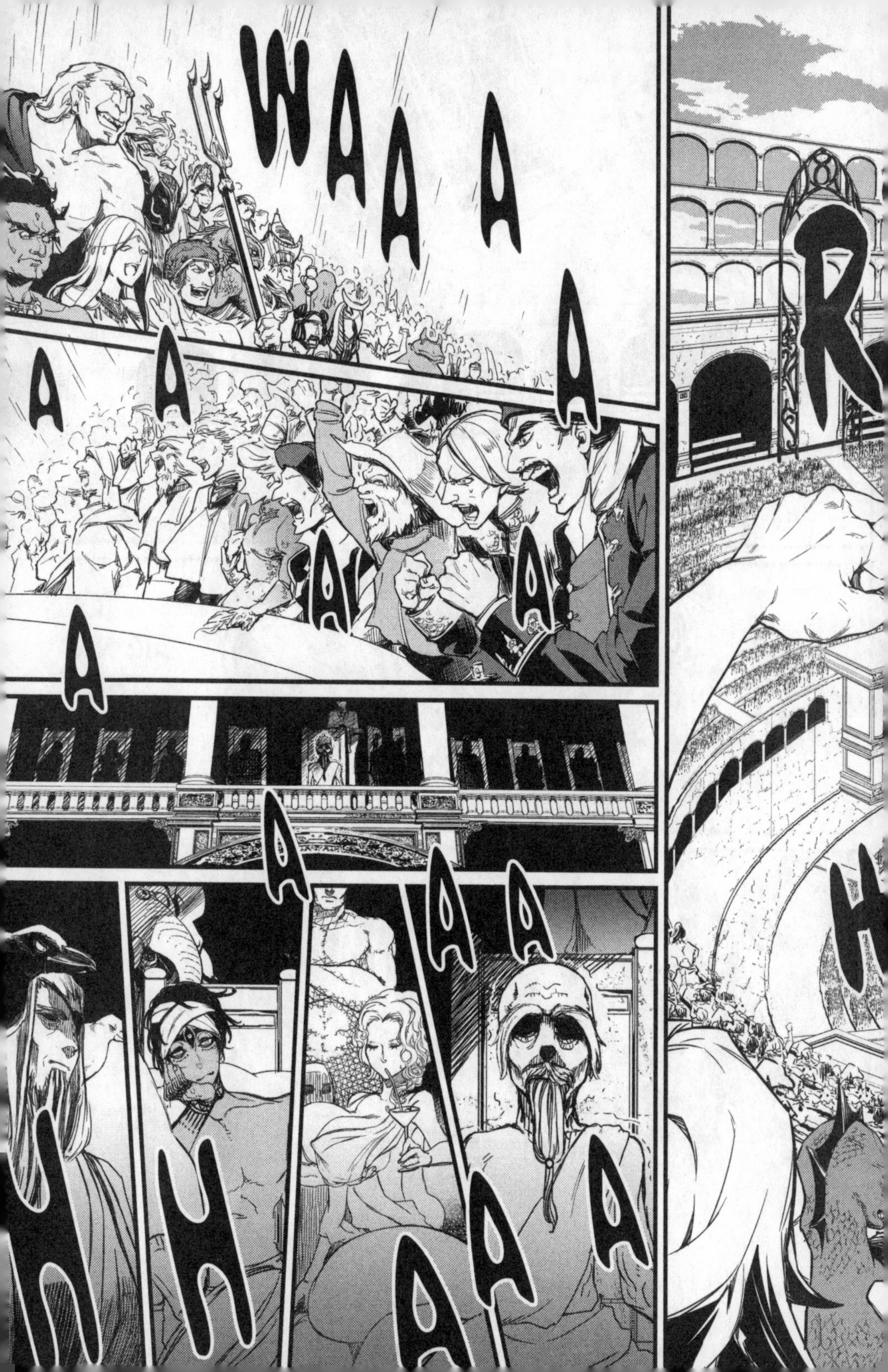

R
H
WAAAA
AAAAAAAAAAAAA
HHHH
AAAAA

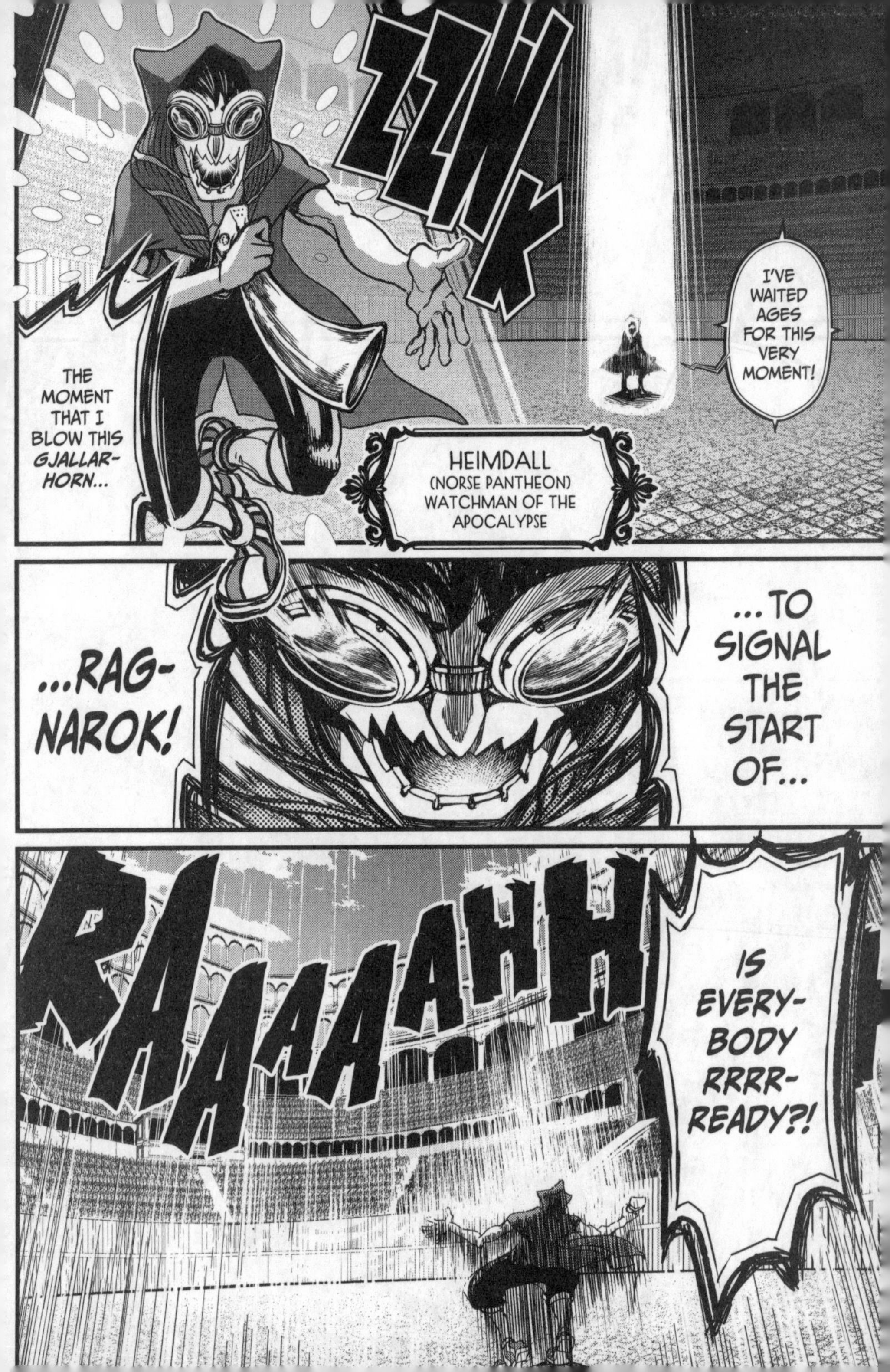
I'VE WAITED AGES FOR THIS VERY MOMENT!
HEIMDALL (NORSE PANTHEON) WATCHMAN OF THE APOCALYPSE
THE MOMENT THAT I BLOW THIS GJALLARHORN...
...TO SIGNAL THE START OF...
...RAG-NAROK!
IS EVERY-BODY RRRR-READY?!

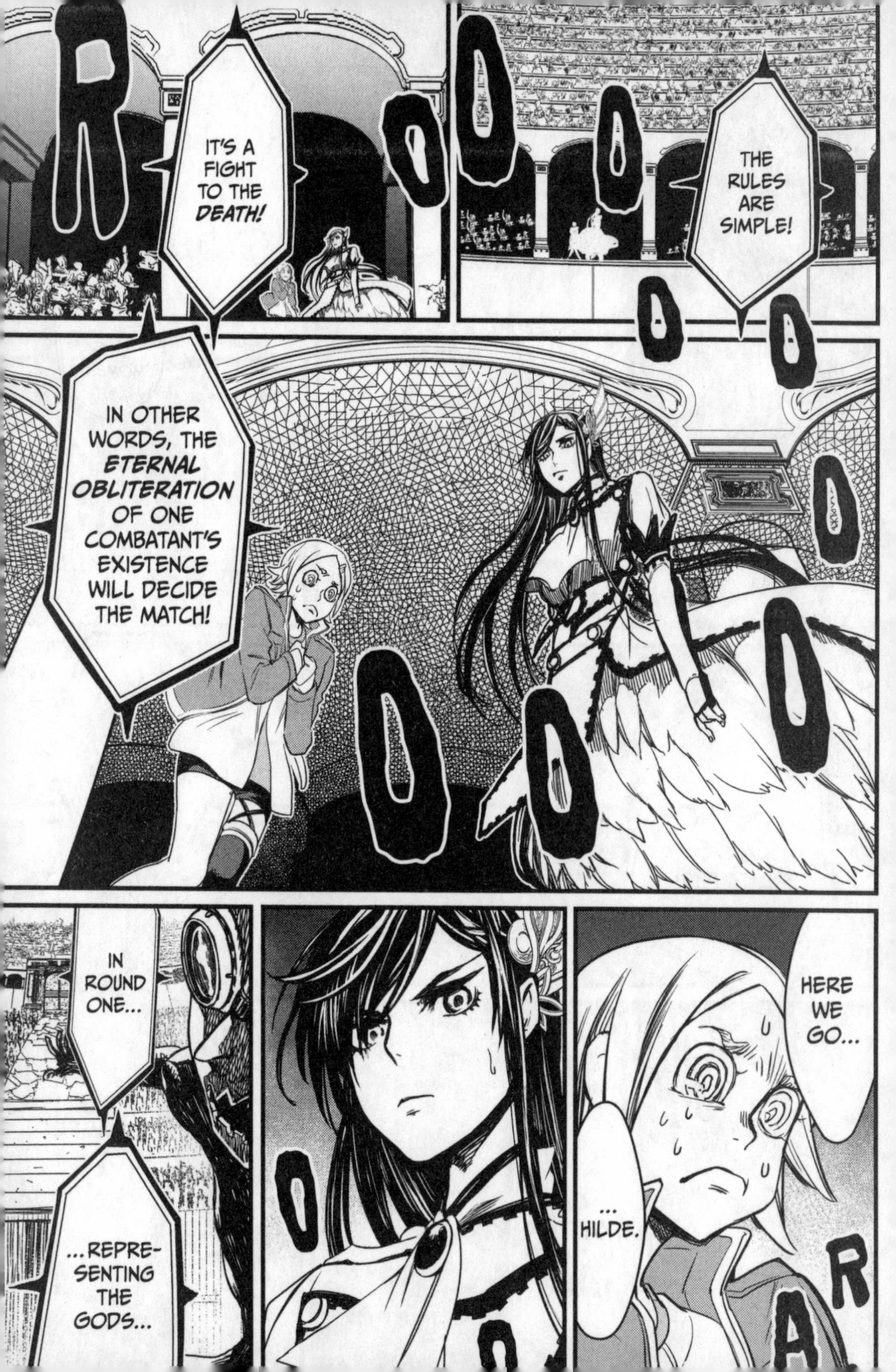
THE RULES ARE SIMPLE!
IT'S A FIGHT TO THE *DEATH!*
IN OTHER WORDS, THE ***ETERNAL OBLITERATION*** OF ONE COMBATANT'S EXISTENCE WILL DECIDE THE MATCH!
HERE WE GO...
...HILDE.
IN ROUND ONE...
...REPRE-SENTING THE GODS...

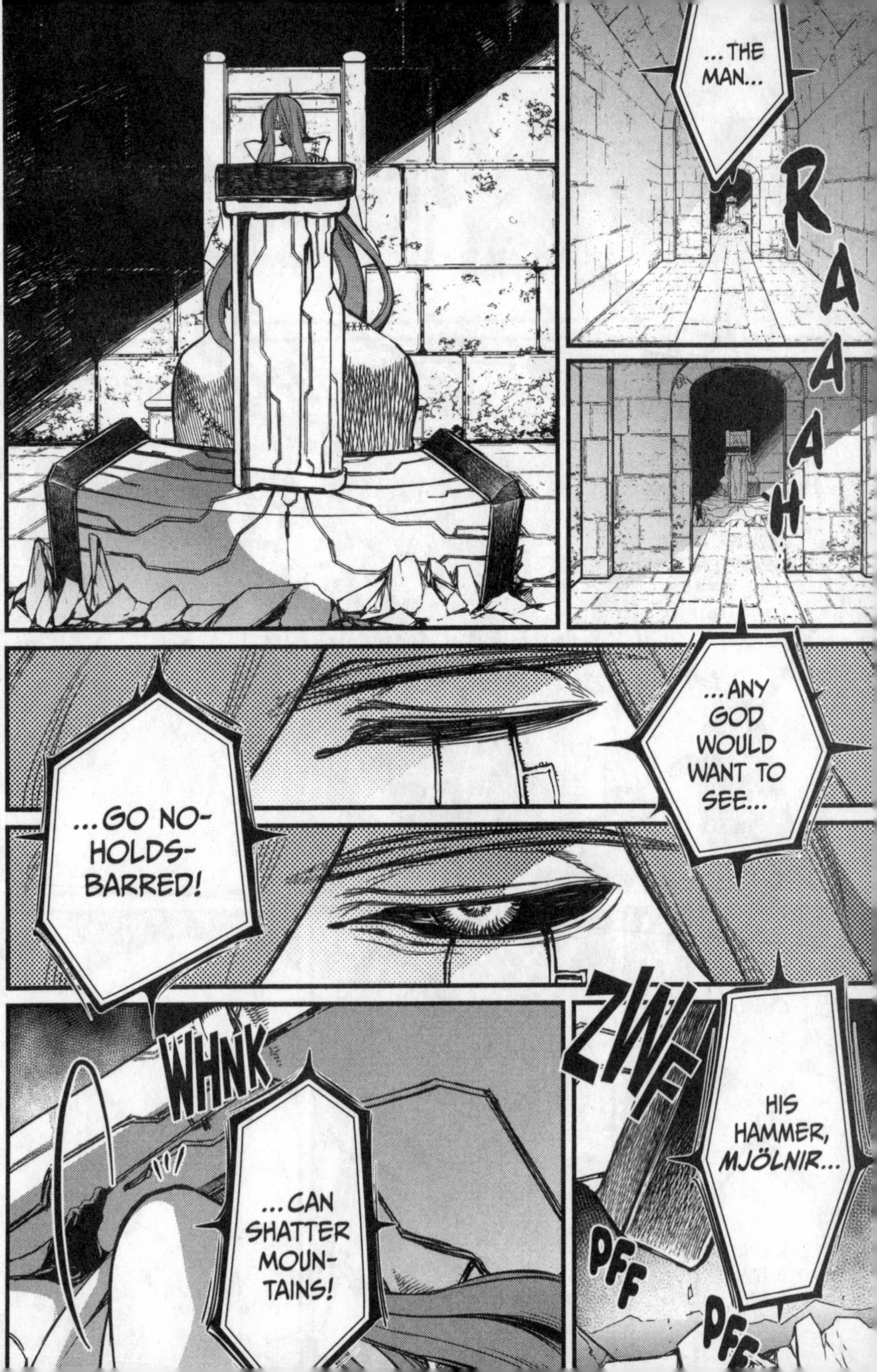
...THE MAN...
RAAAH
...ANY GOD WOULD WANT TO SEE...
...GO NO-HOLDS-BARRED!
ZWF
HIS HAMMER, MJÖLNIR...
PFF
PFF
WHNK
...CAN SHATTER MOUN-TAINS!

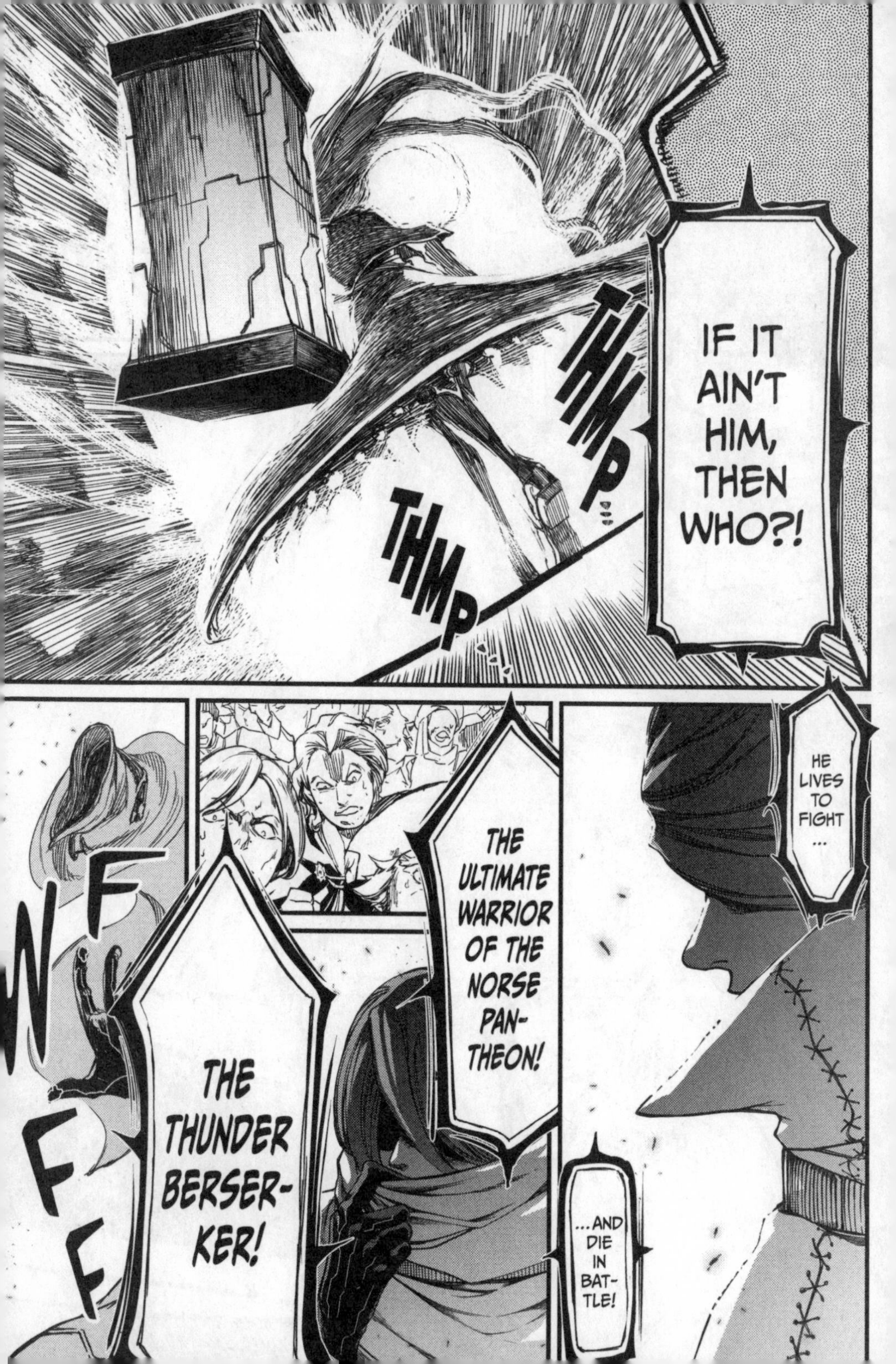
IF IT AIN'T HIM, THEN WHO?!
THMP
THMP
HE LIVES TO FIGHT...
...AND DIE IN BAT-TLE!
THE ULTIMATE WARRIOR OF THE NORSE PAN-THEON!
THE THUNDER BERSER-KER!
WFFF

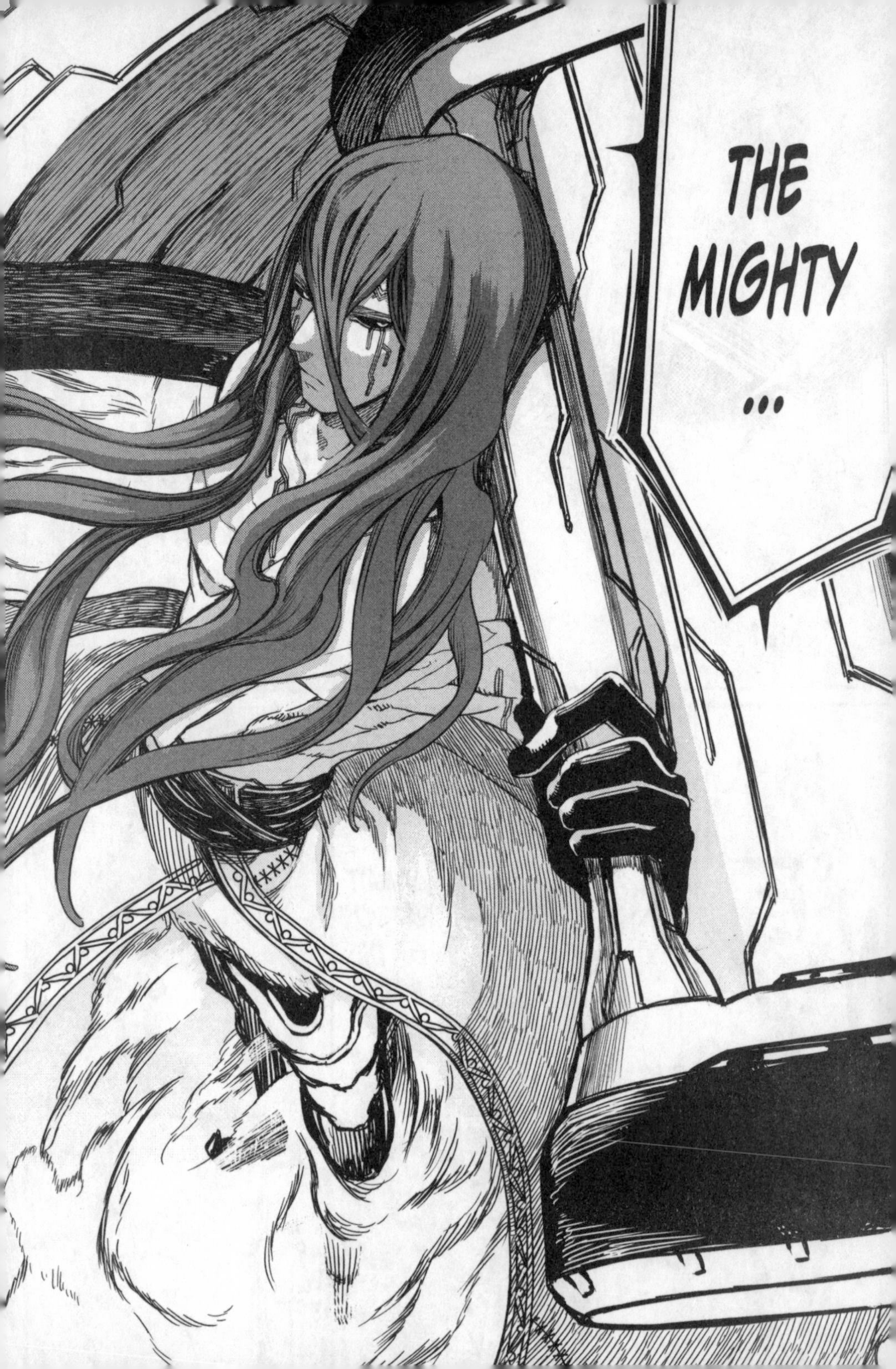
THE MIGHTY ...

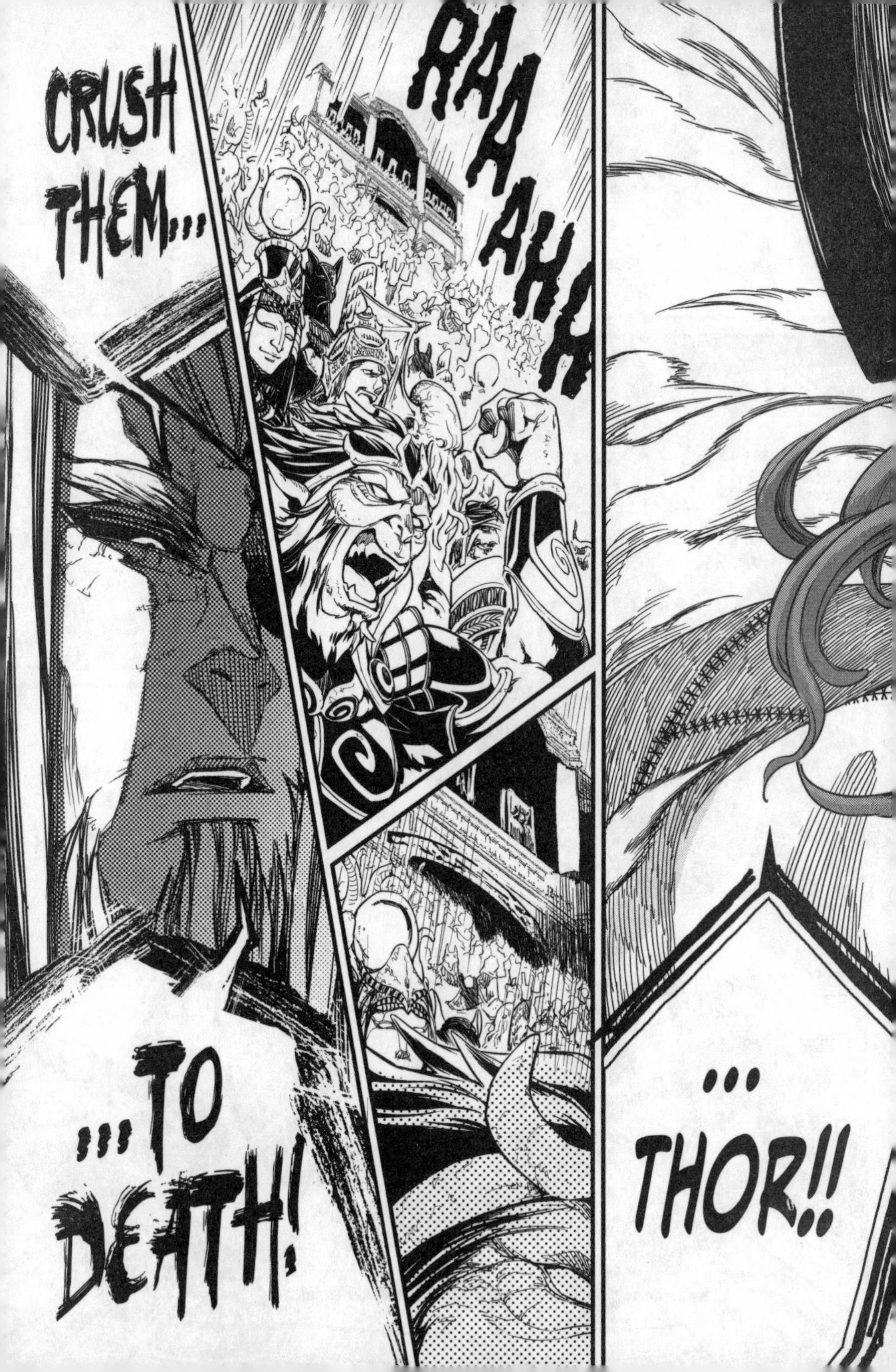
... THOR!!
RAAAHH
CRUSH THEM...
...TO DEATH!

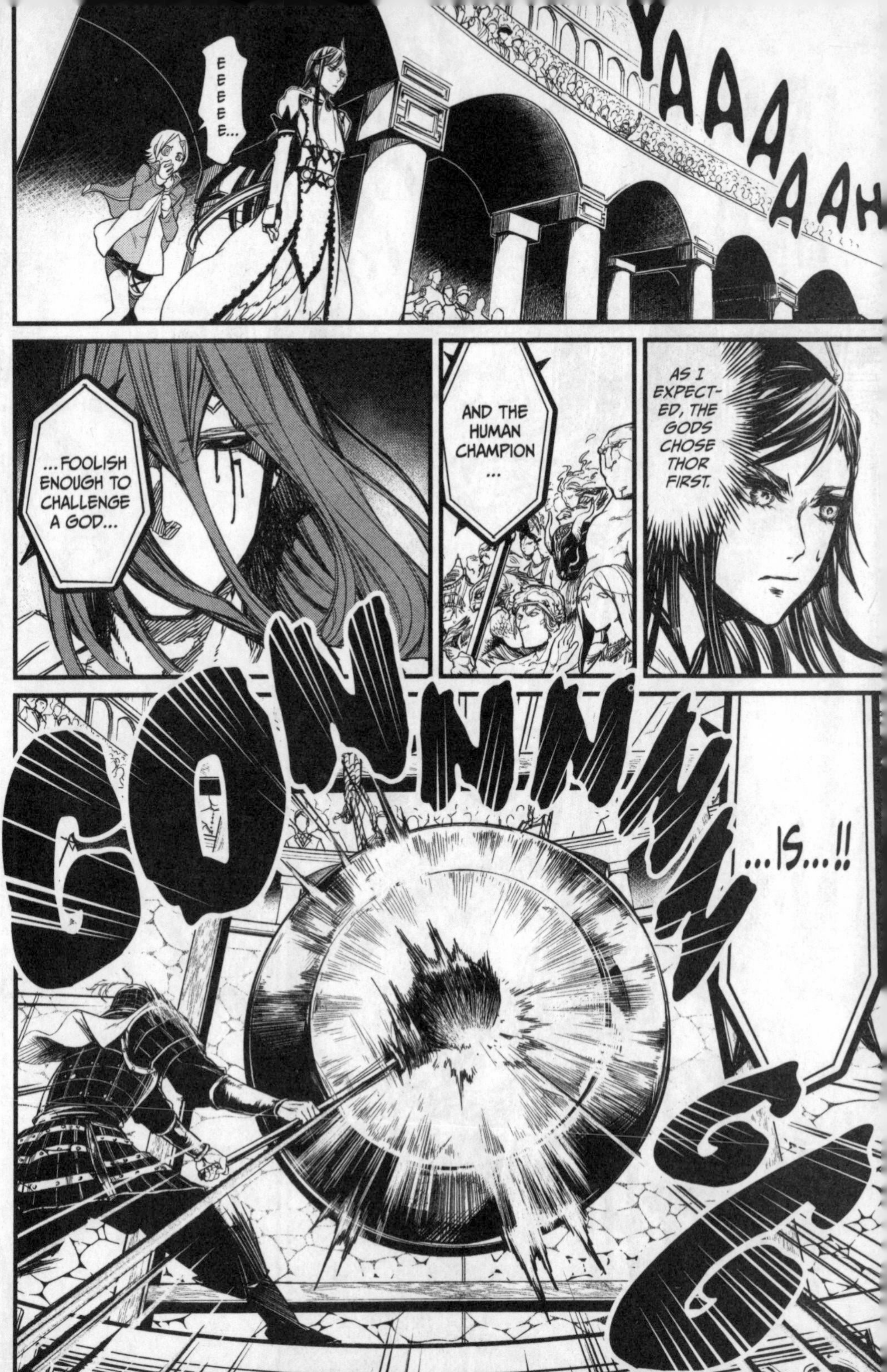
YAAAAAH
EEEEE...
AS I EXPECTED, THE GODS CHOSE THOR FIRST.
AND THE HUMAN CHAMPION...
...FOOLISH ENOUGH TO CHALLENGE A GOD...
...IS...!!

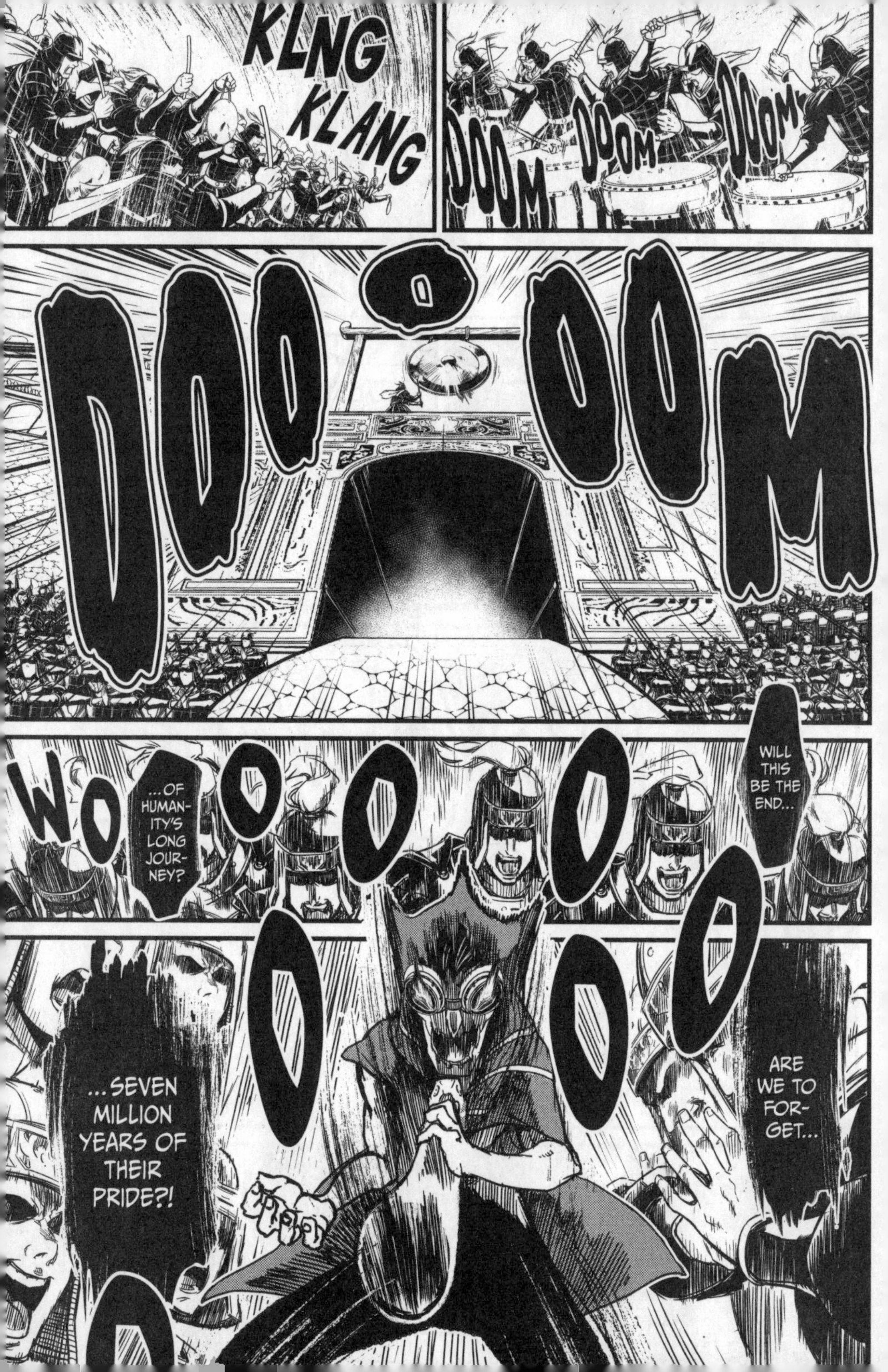
DOOM DOOM DOOM
KLNG KLANG
DOO-O-OOOM
WILL THIS BE THE END...
...OF HUMANITY'S LONG JOURNEY?
WOOOOOO
ARE WE TO FORGET...
...SEVEN MILLION YEARS OF THEIR PRIDE?!

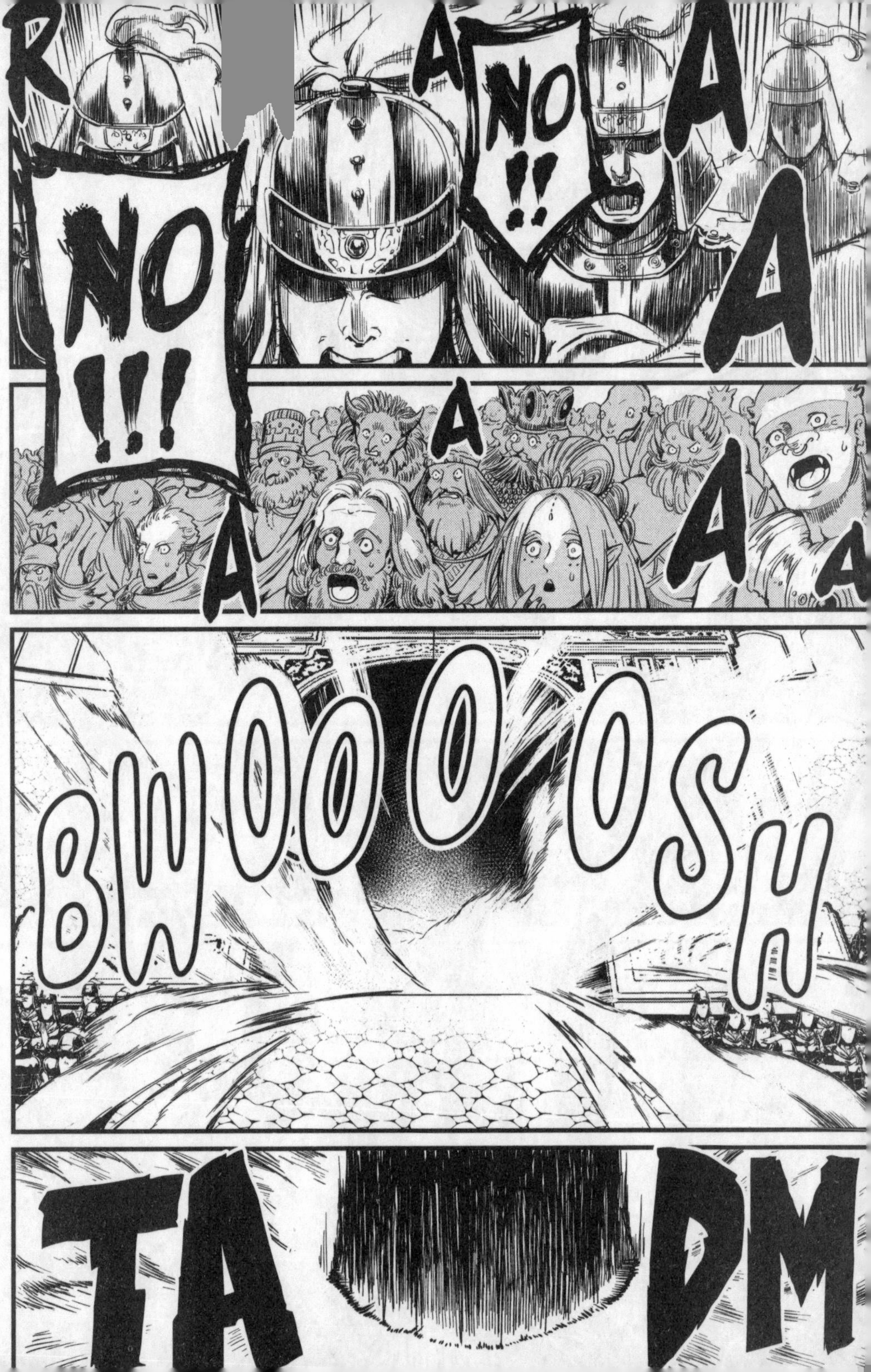
NO!!
NO!!!
RAAAAAAAA
BWOOOOSH
TA DM

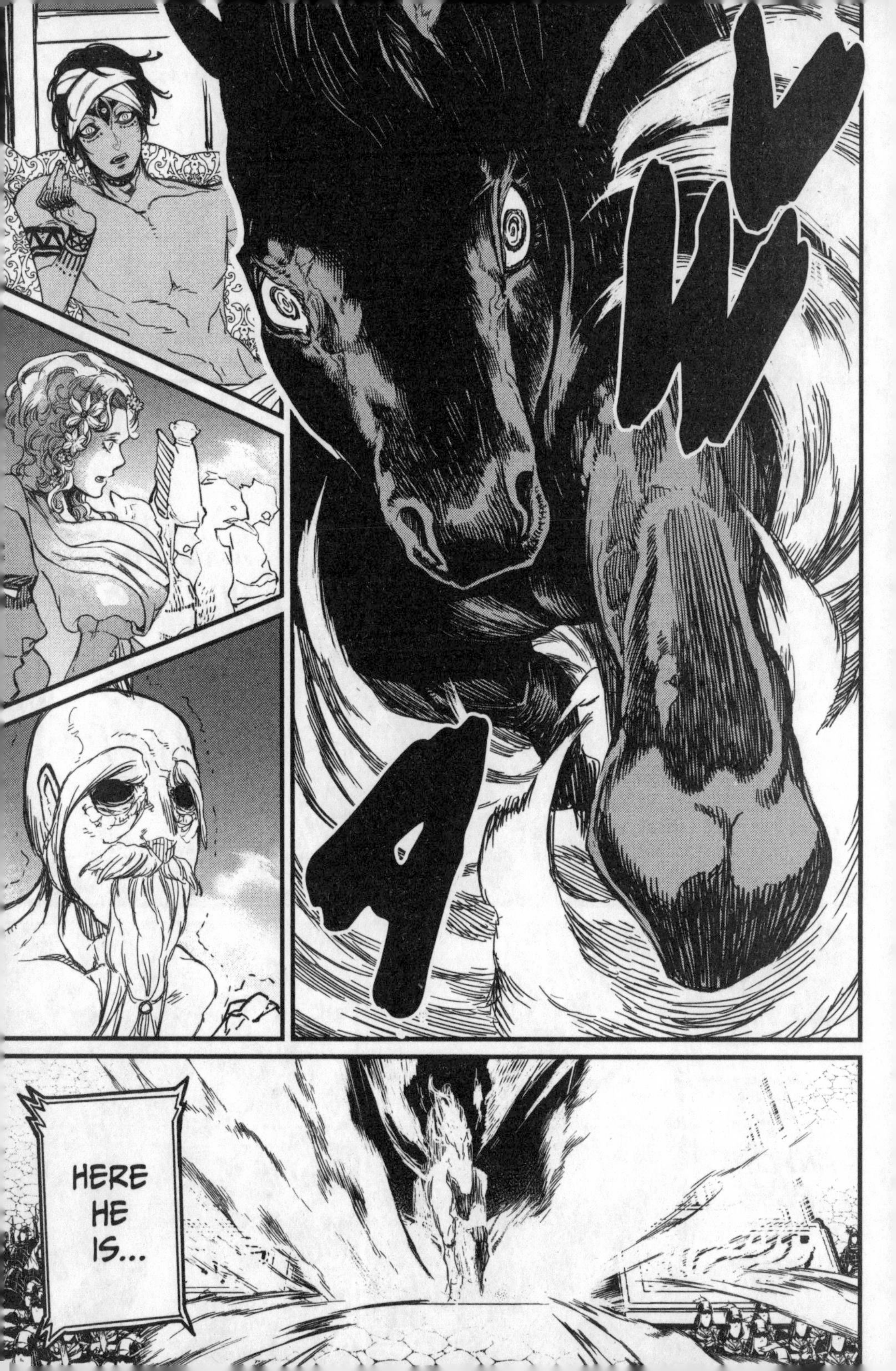
HERE HE IS...

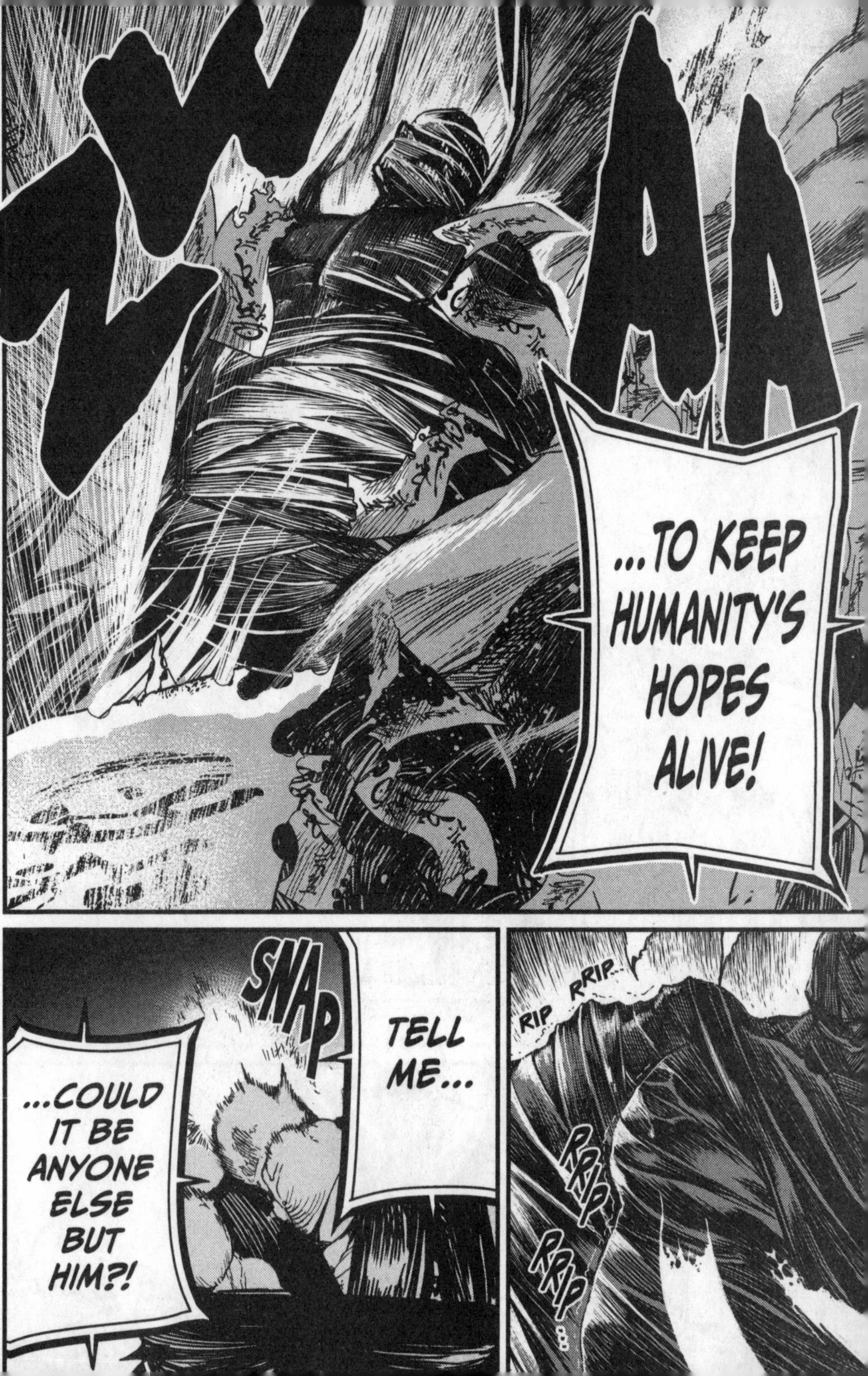
...TO KEEP HUMANITY'S HOPES ALIVE!
RIP
RRIP...
RRIP
RRIP...
TELL ME...
SNAP
...COULD IT BE ANYONE ELSE BUT HIM?!

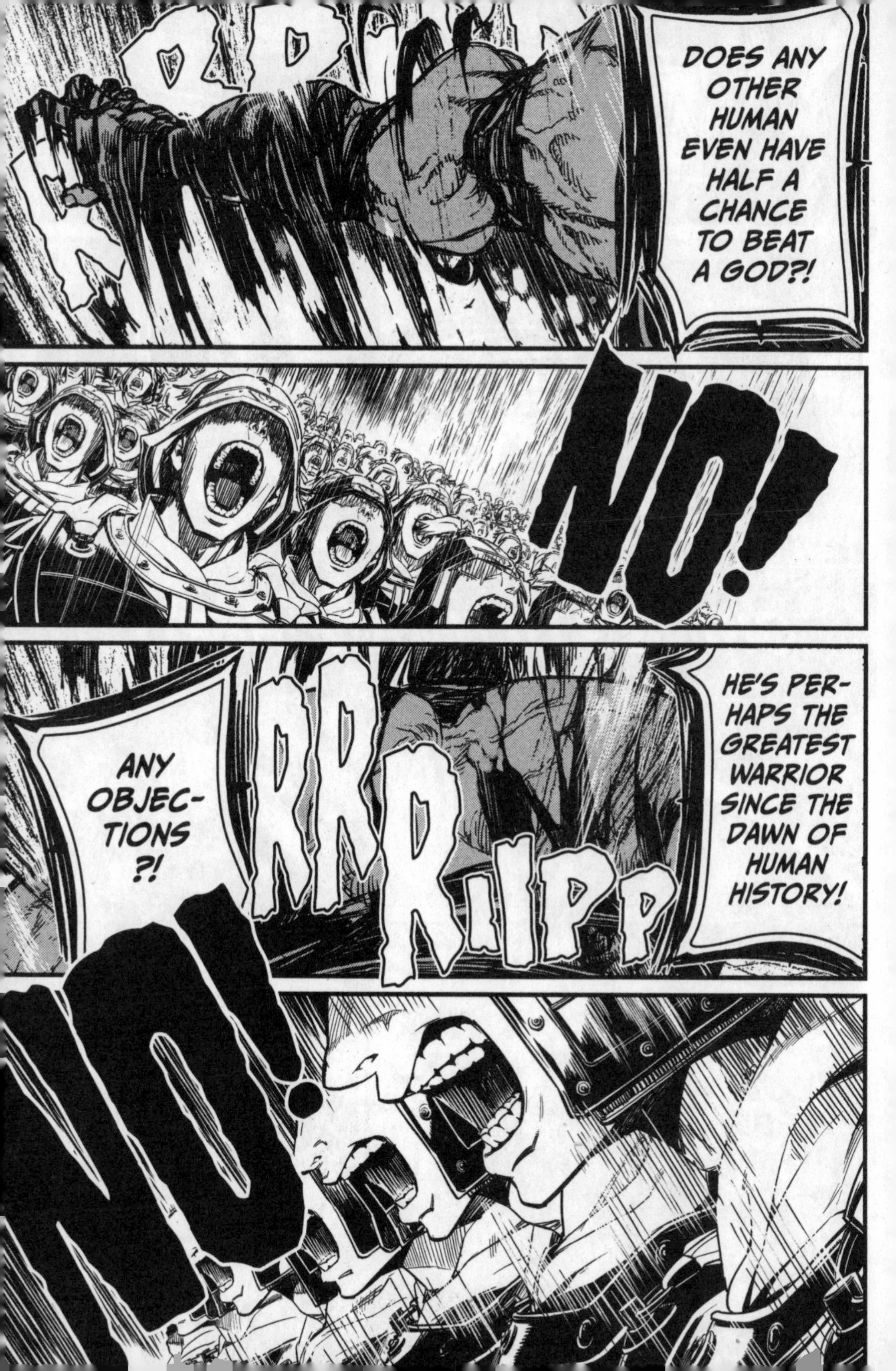
DOES ANY OTHER HUMAN EVEN HAVE HALF A CHANCE TO BEAT A GOD?!
NO!
HE'S PER-HAPS THE GREATEST WARRIOR SINCE THE DAWN OF HUMAN HISTORY!
ANY OBJEC-TIONS ?!
RRRIPP
NO!

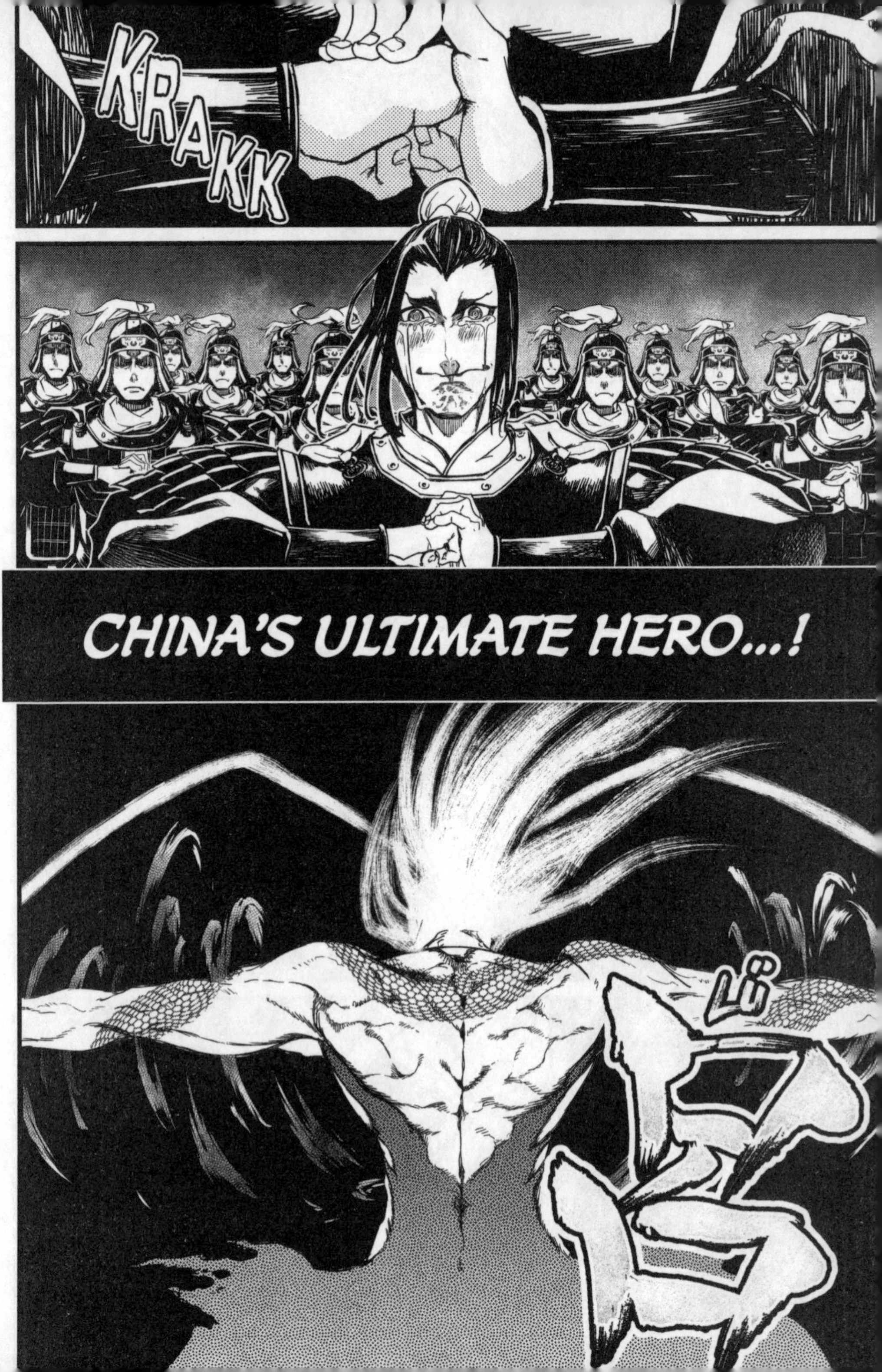
KRAKK
CHINA'S ULTIMATE HERO...!

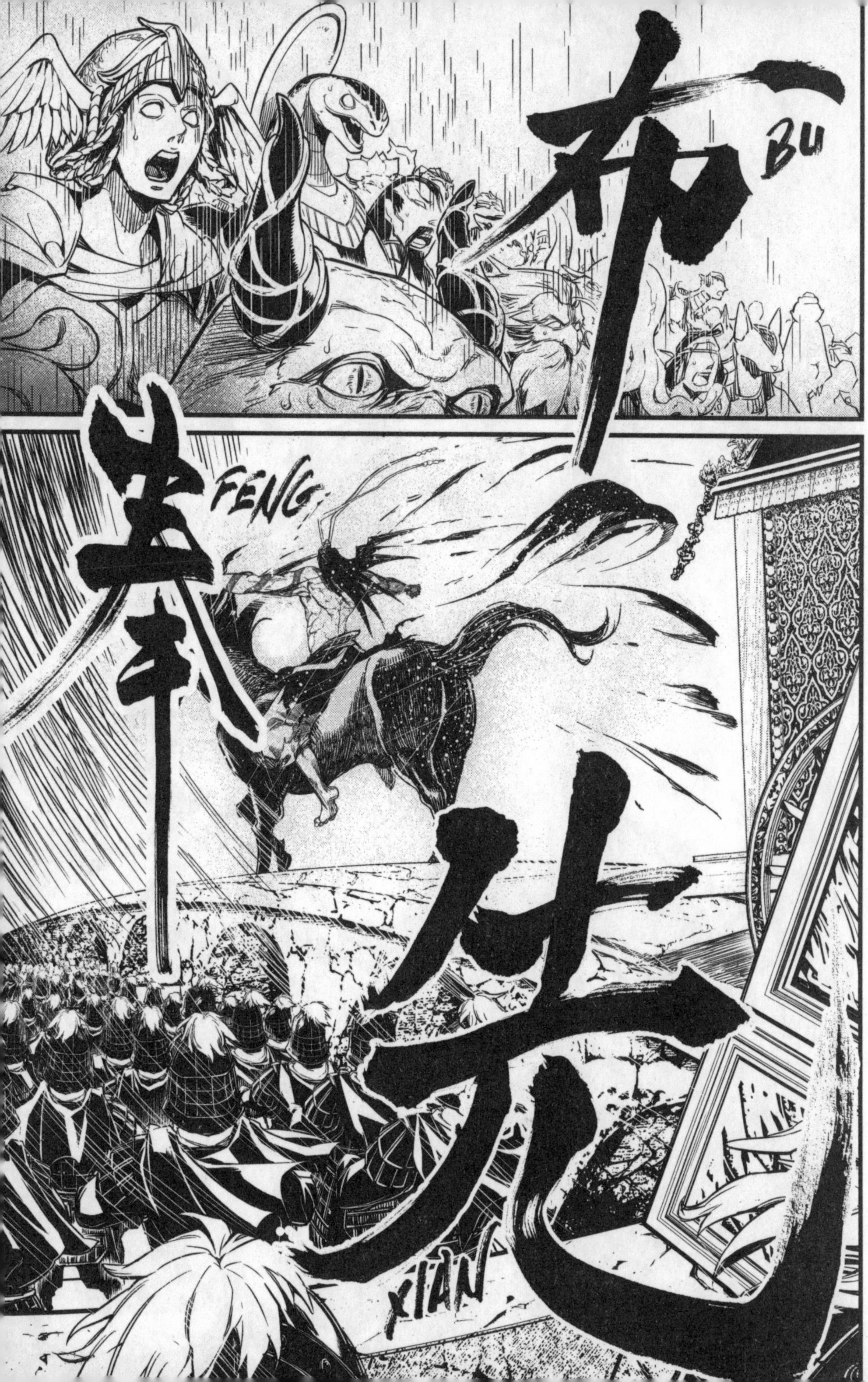

布
BU
奉
FENG
先
XIAN

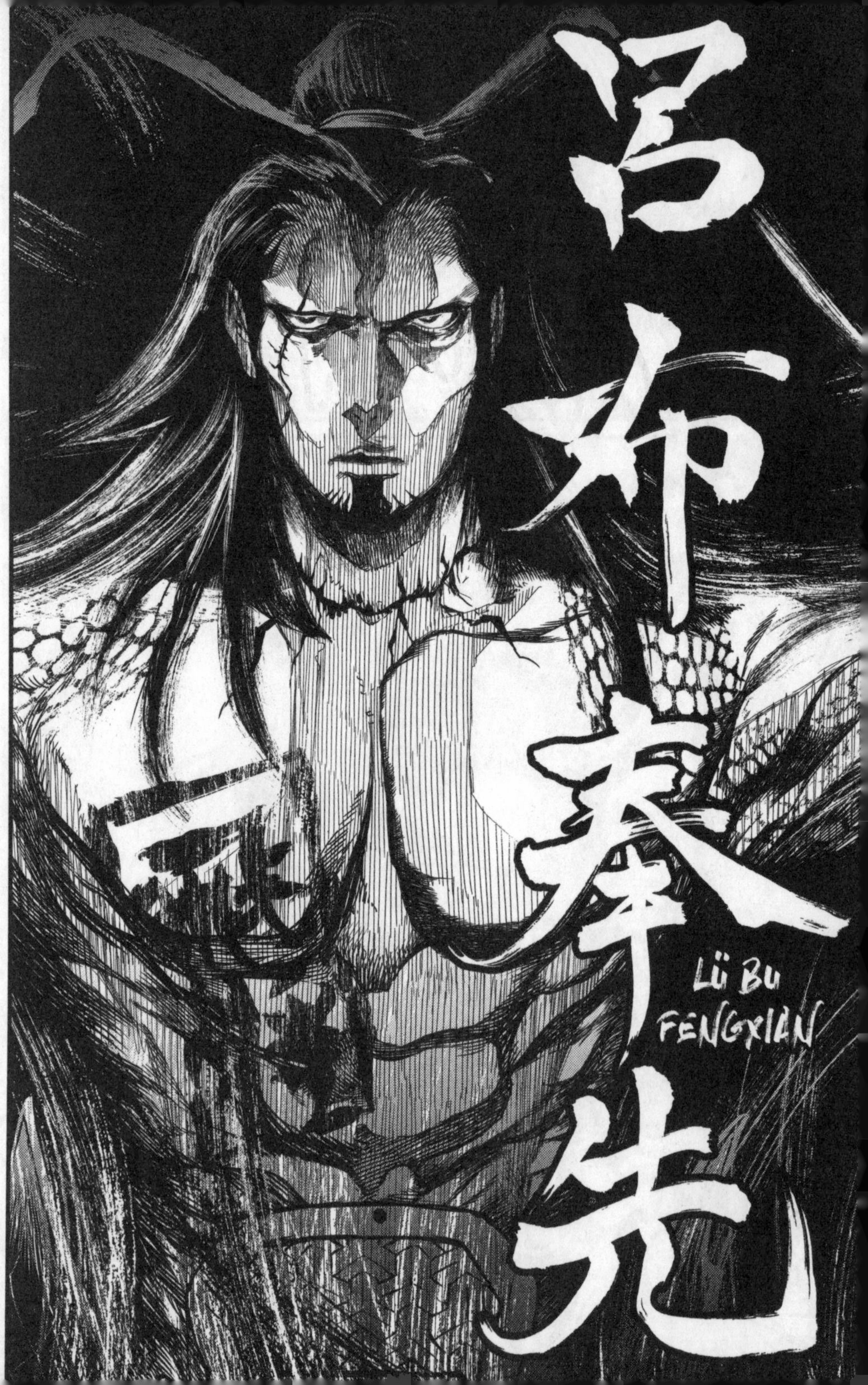

呂布奉先
LÜ BU FENGXIAN

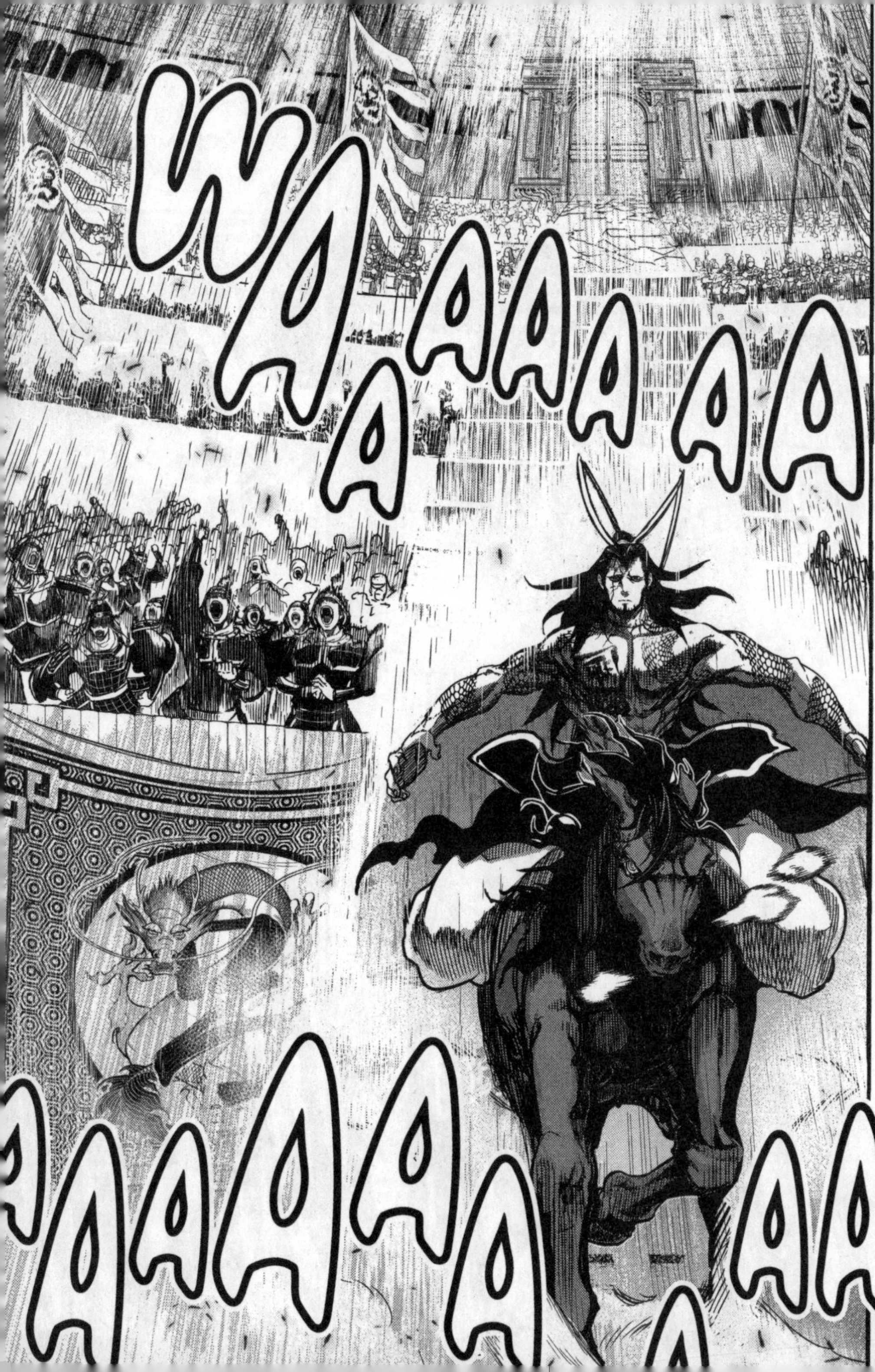
WAAAAAAAA
AAAAAAAAAAAAAA

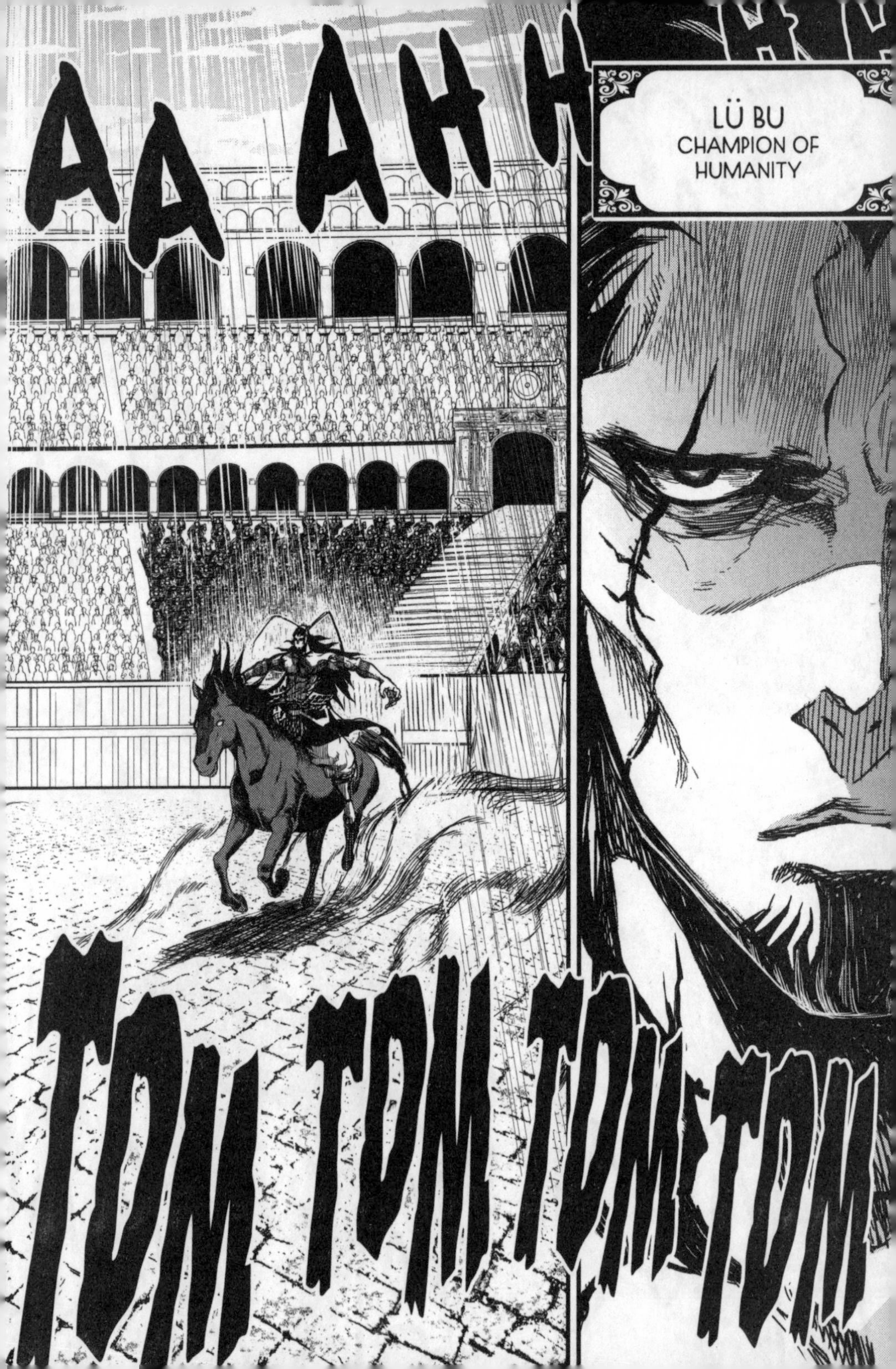
LÜ BU
CHAMPION OF HUMANITY
AAAHH

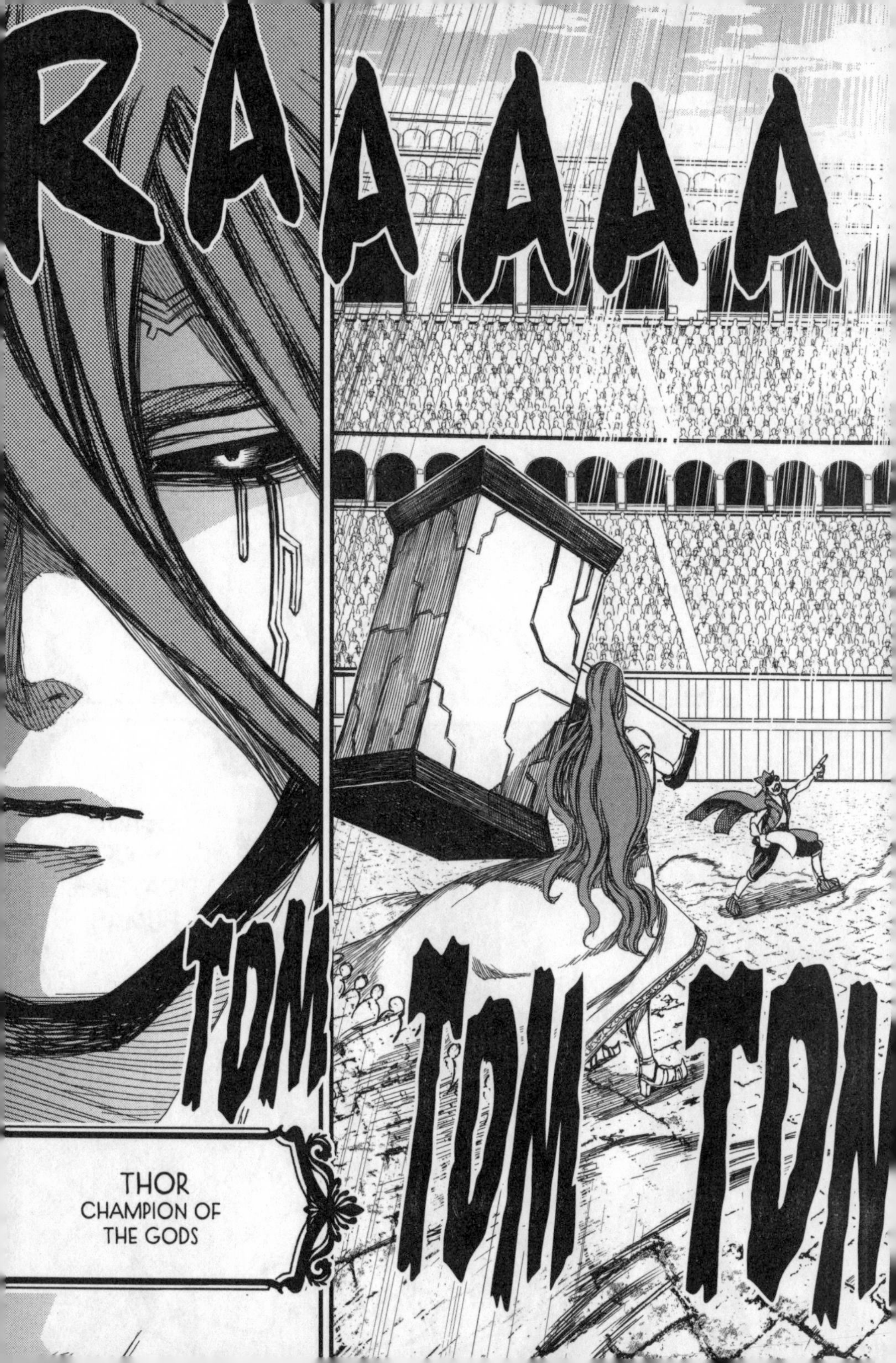
RAAAAA
TOM TOM TOM TOM
THOR
CHAMPION OF THE GODS

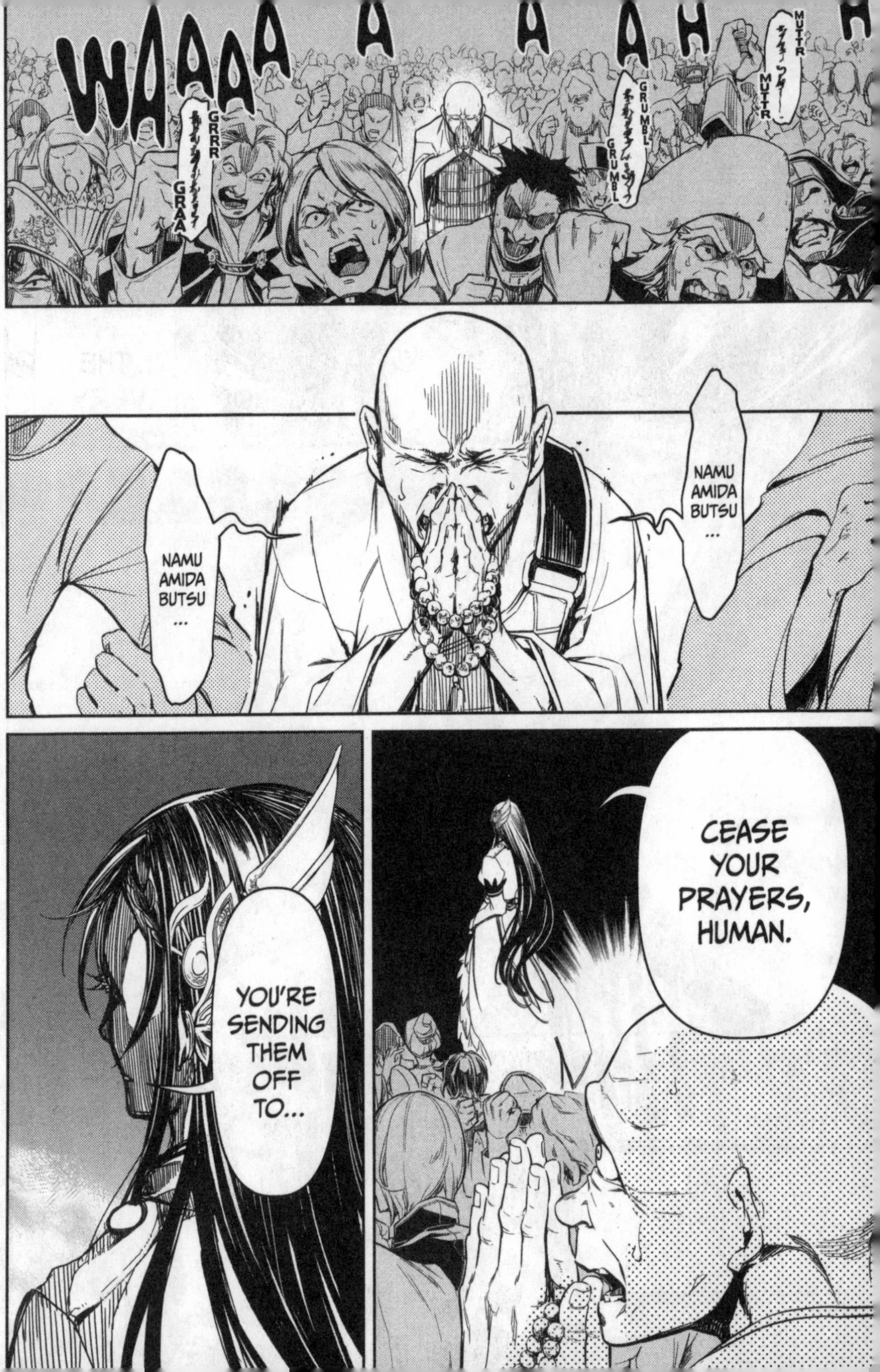
WAAAA A A A H H
MUTTR
MUTTR
GRUMBL
GRUMBL
GRRR
GRAA
NAMU AMIDA BUTSU ...
NAMU AMIDA BUTSU ...
CEASE YOUR PRAYERS, HUMAN.
YOU'RE SENDING THEM OFF TO...

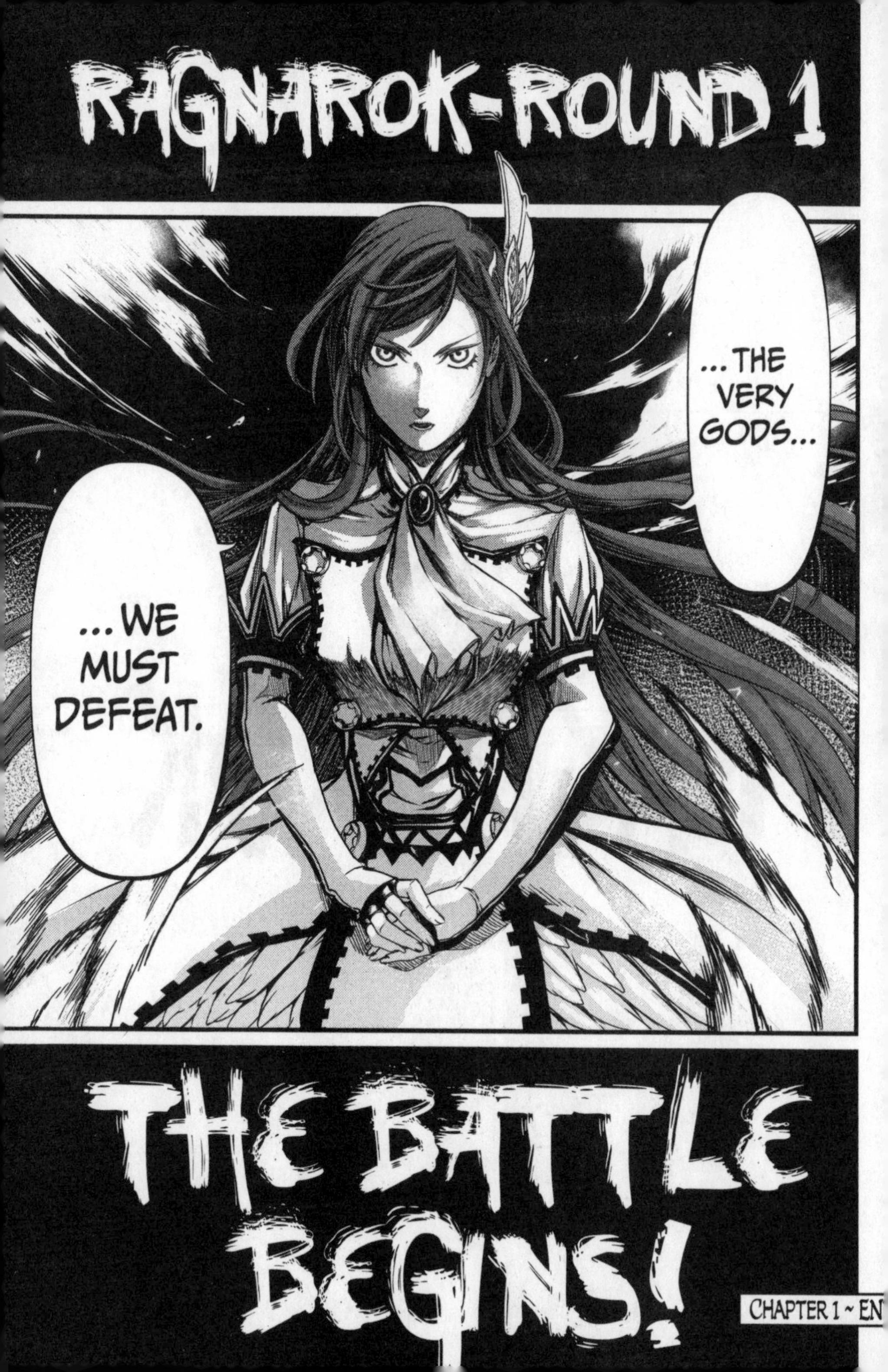
RAGNAROK-ROUND 1
...THE VERY GODS...
...WE MUST DEFEAT.
THE BATTLE BEGINS!
CHAPTER 1 ~ EN

RECORD OF RAGNAROK

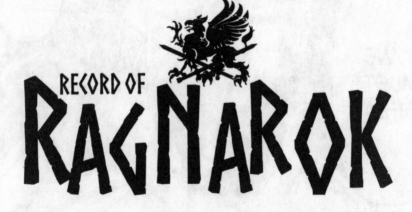

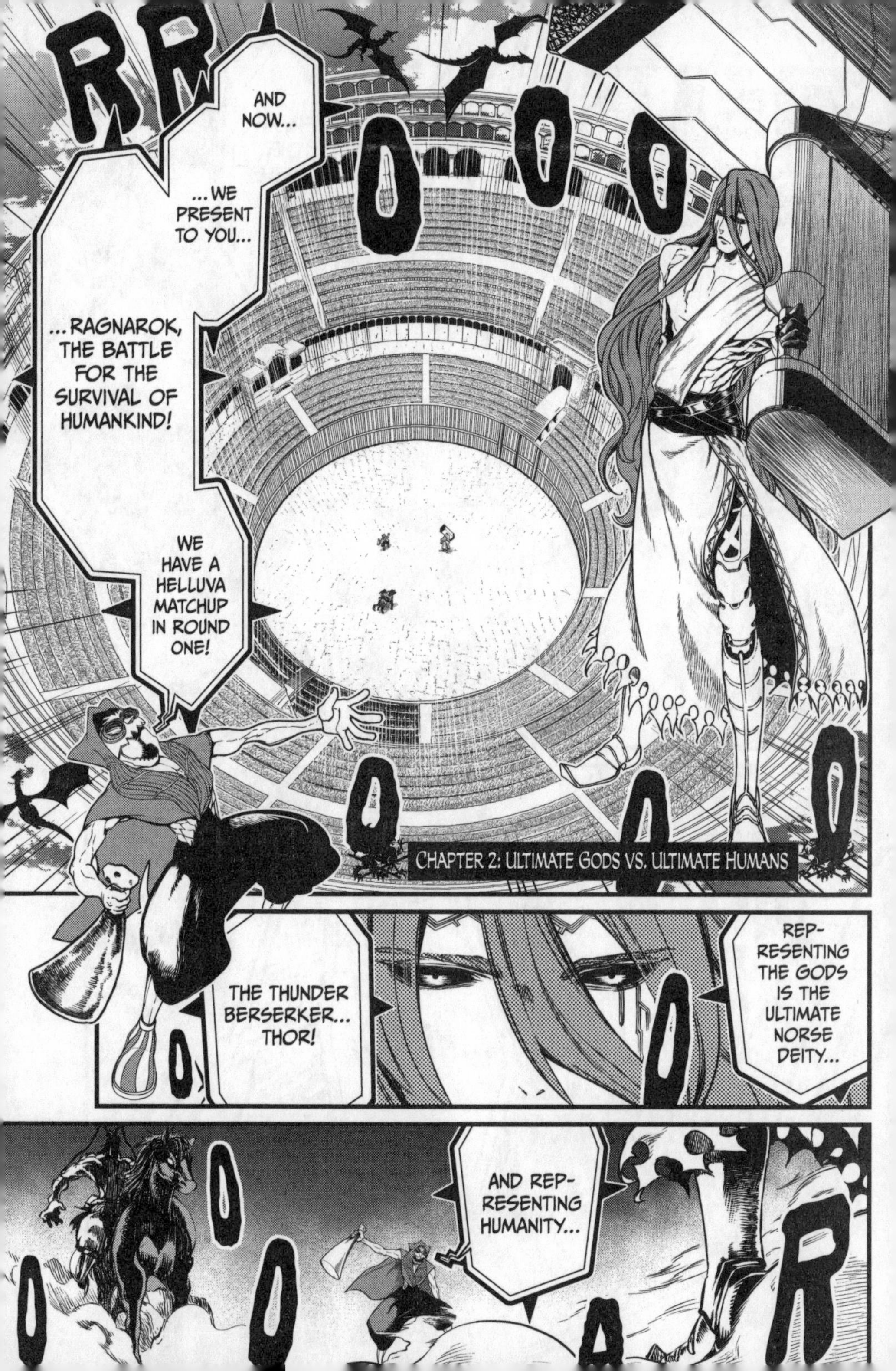
RROOOO
AND NOW...
...WE PRESENT TO YOU...
...RAGNAROK, THE BATTLE FOR THE SURVIVAL OF HUMANKIND!
WE HAVE A HELLUVA MATCHUP IN ROUND ONE!
OOOO
CHAPTER 2: ULTIMATE GODS VS. ULTIMATE HUMANS
REP-RESENTING THE GODS IS THE ULTIMATE NORSE DEITY...
THE THUNDER BERSERKER... THOR!
OO
AND REP-RESENTING HUMANITY...
RAOOOO

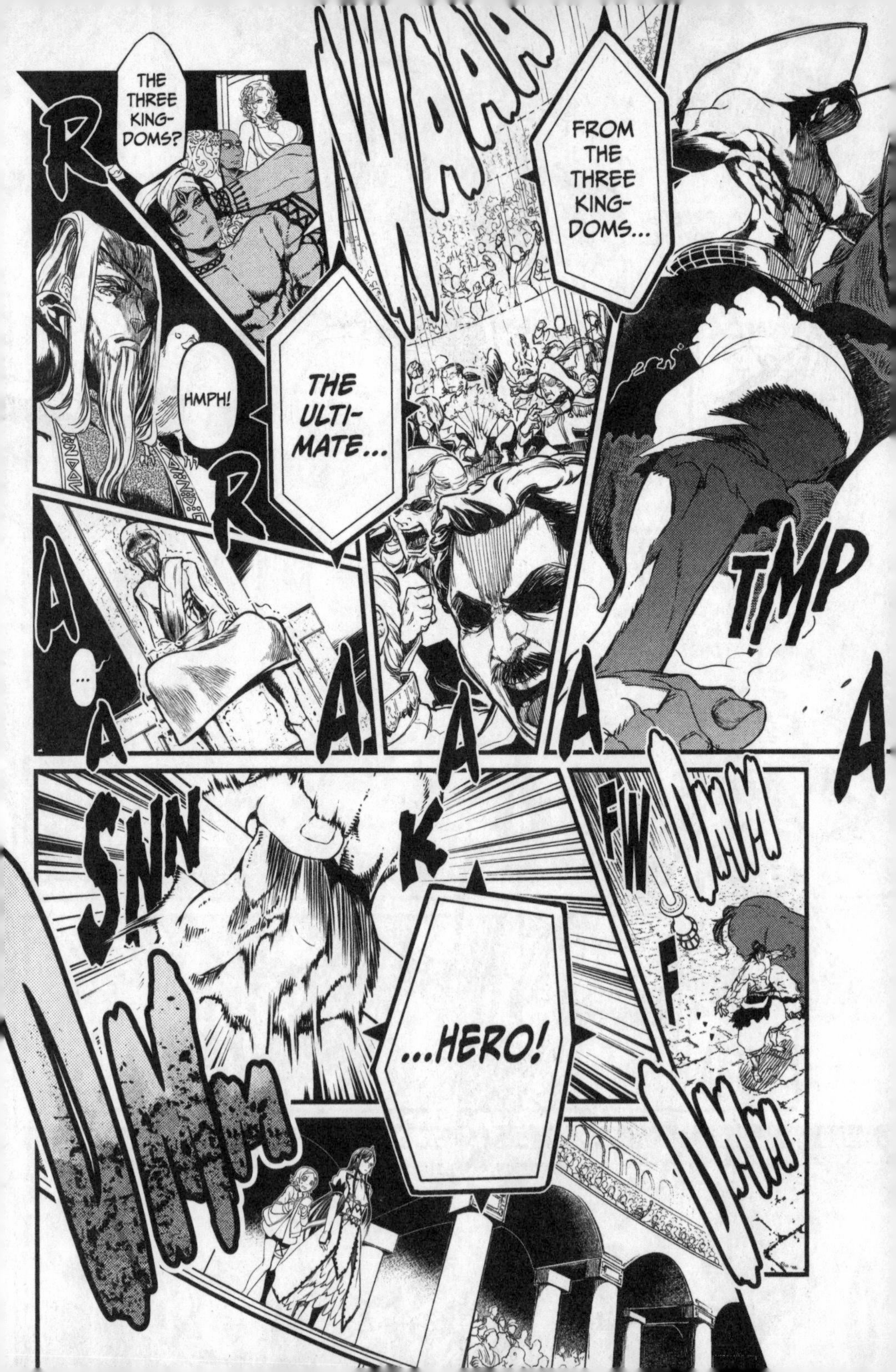
FROM THE THREE KING- DOMS...
TMP
THE ULTI- MATE...
THE THREE KING- DOMS?
HMPH!
...
...HERO!
K
SNN

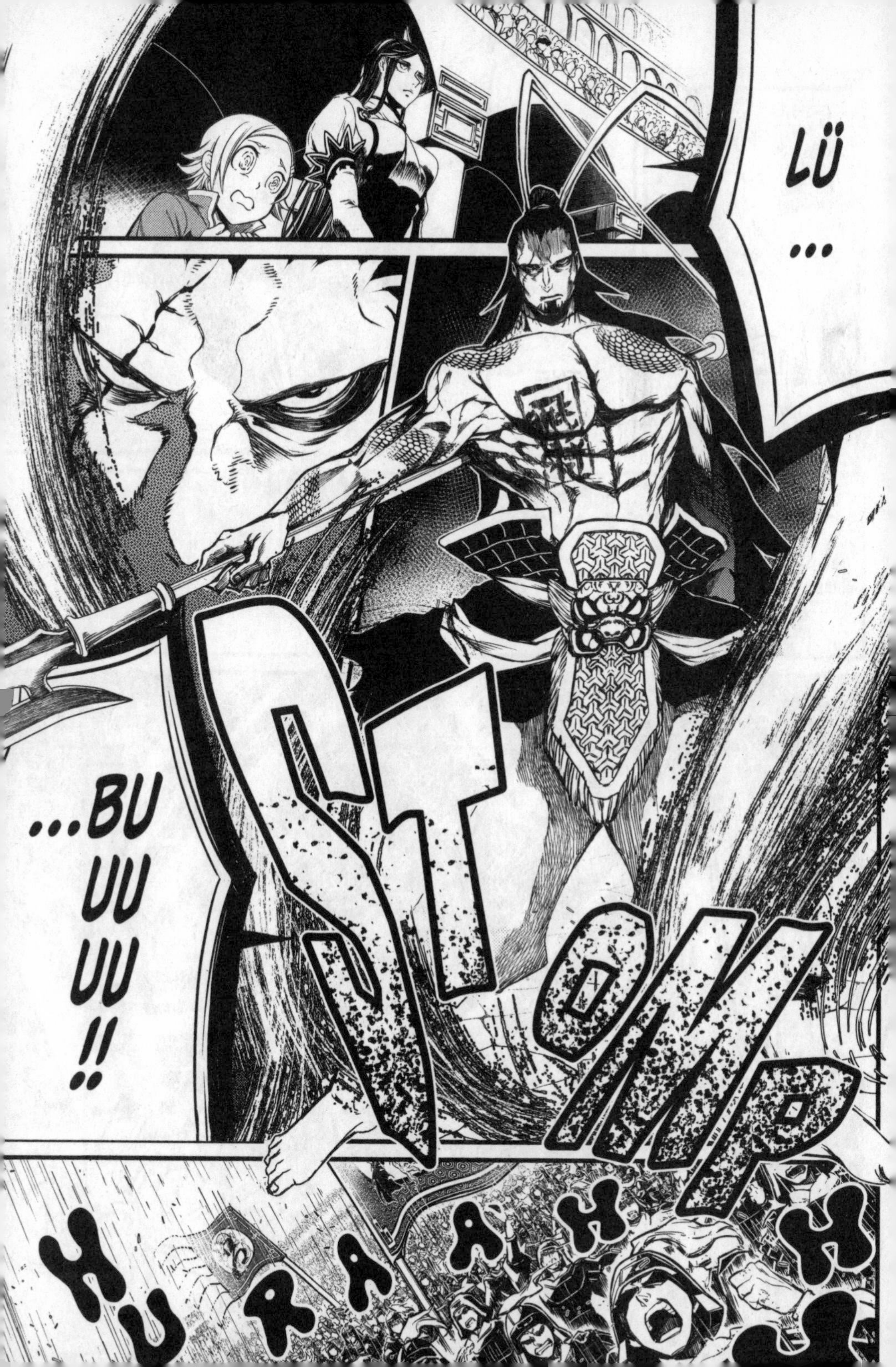
LÜ ...
...BUUUUUU!!
STOMP
HURAAHHS

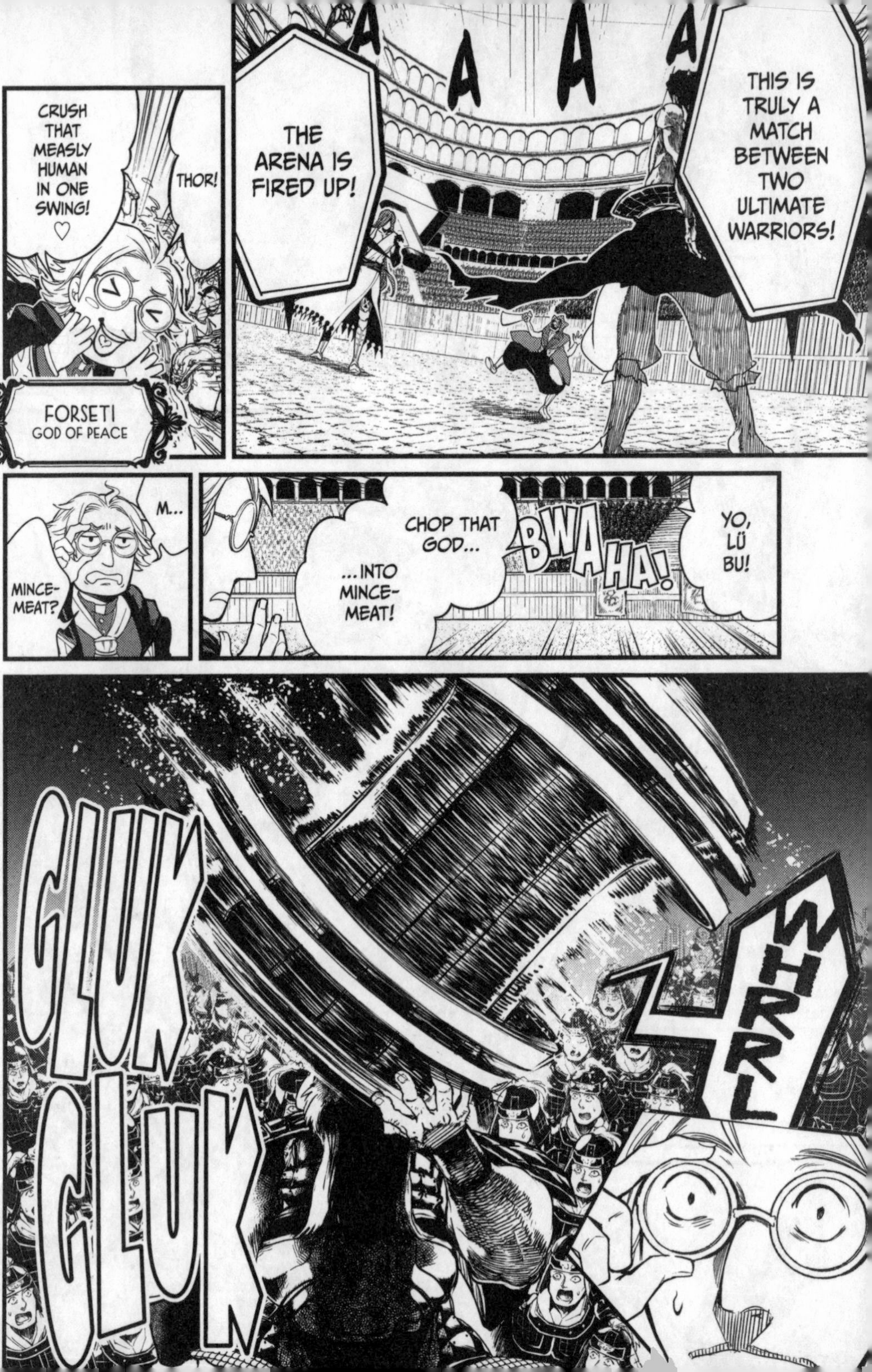
AAAA
THIS IS TRULY A MATCH BETWEEN TWO ULTIMATE WARRIORS!
THE ARENA IS FIRED UP!
THOR!
CRUSH THAT MEASLY HUMAN IN ONE SWING! ♡
FORSETI
GOD OF PEACE
YO, LÜ BU!
BWAHA!
CHOP THAT GOD...
...INTO MINCE-MEAT!
M...
MINCE-MEAT?
WHRRL
CLUK CLUK

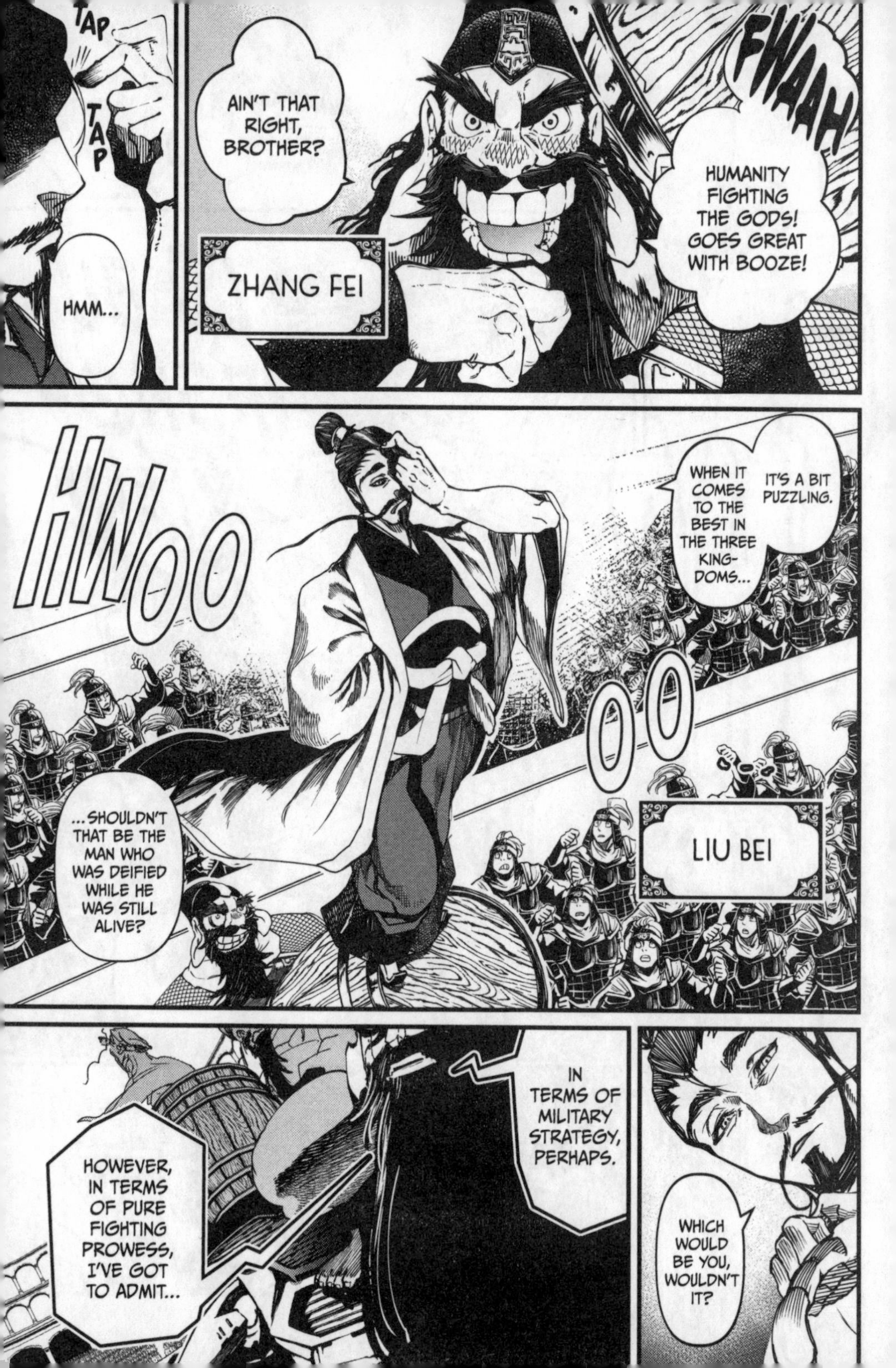
FWAAH
HUMANITY FIGHTING THE GODS! GOES GREAT WITH BOOZE!
AIN'T THAT RIGHT, BROTHER?
ZHANG FEI
TAP
TAP
TAP
HMM...
IT'S A BIT PUZZLING.
WHEN IT COMES TO THE BEST IN THE THREE KING-DOMS...
HWOOOO
LIU BEI
...SHOULDN'T THAT BE THE MAN WHO WAS DEIFIED WHILE HE WAS STILL ALIVE?
WHICH WOULD BE YOU, WOULDN'T IT?
IN TERMS OF MILITARY STRATEGY, PERHAPS.
HOWEVER, IN TERMS OF PURE FIGHTING PROWESS, I'VE GOT TO ADMIT...

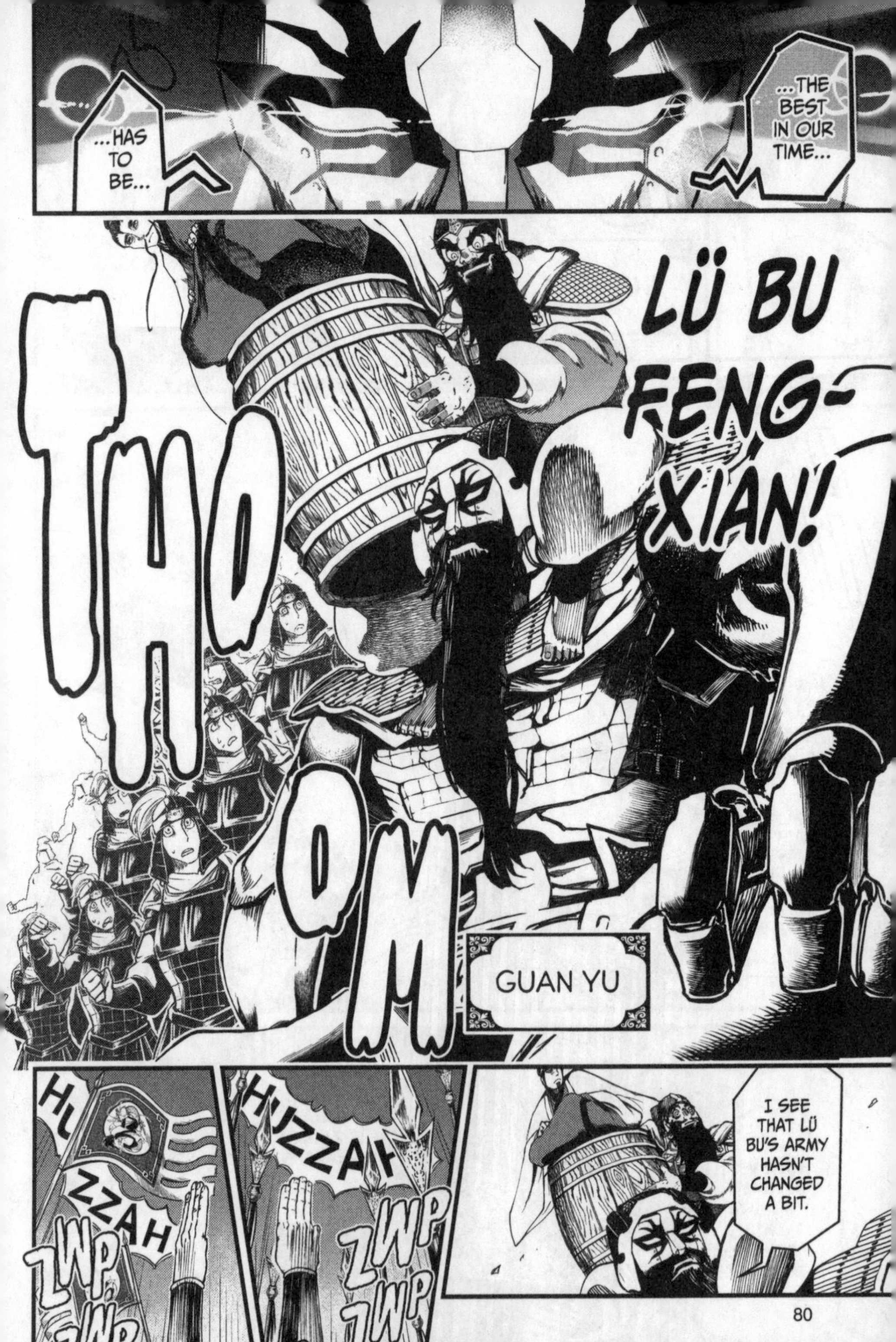
...THE BEST IN OUR TIME...
...HAS TO BE...
LÜ BU FENG-XIAN!
THOOM
GUAN YU
I SEE THAT LÜ BU'S ARMY HASN'T CHANGED A BIT.
HUZZAH
ZWP ZWP ZWP
HU ZZAH
ZWP ZWP

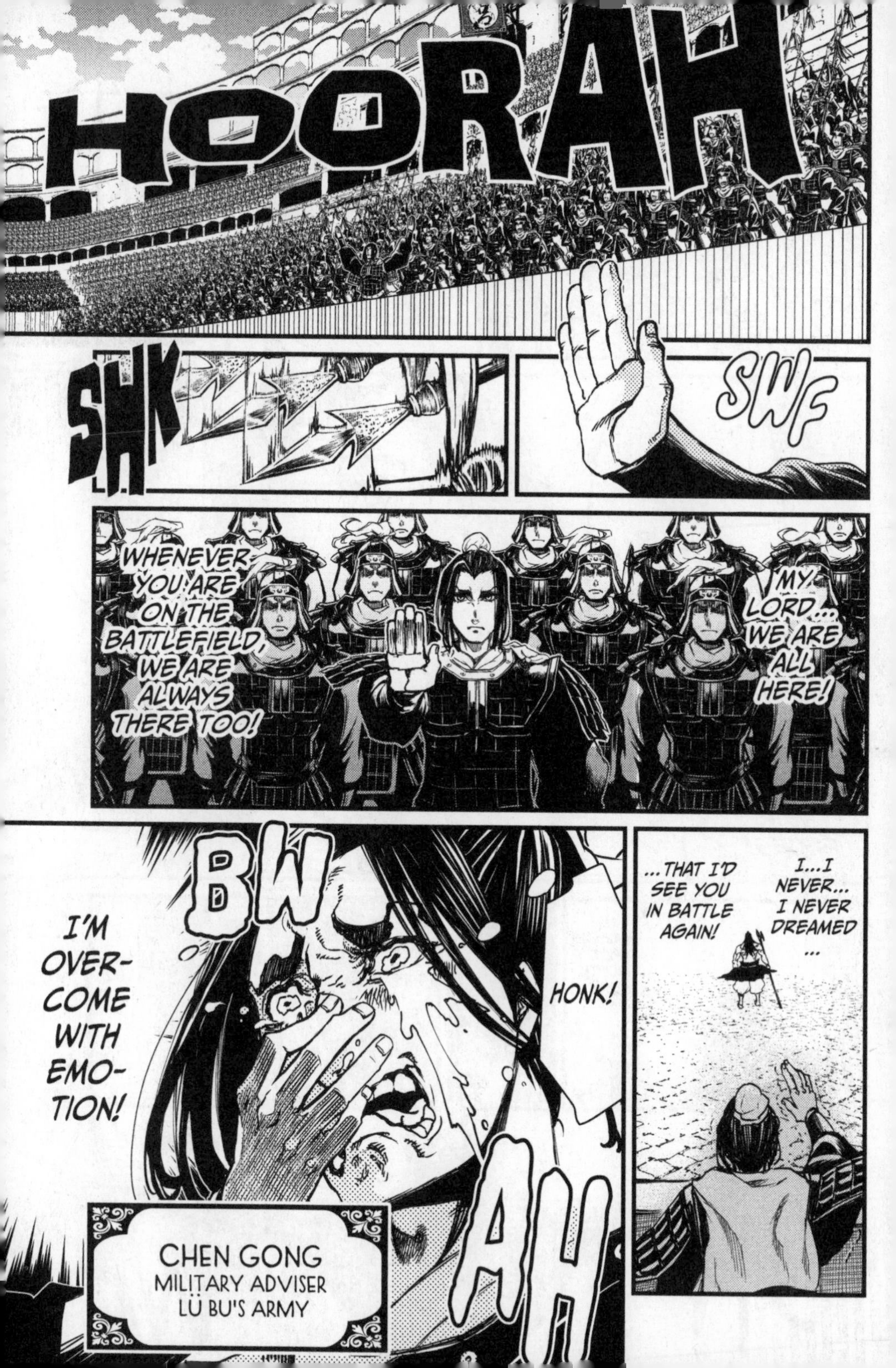
HOORAH
SWF
SHK
MY LORD... WE ARE ALL HERE!
WHENEVER YOU ARE ON THE BATTLEFIELD, WE ARE ALWAYS THERE TOO!
I...I NEVER... I NEVER DREAMED ...
...THAT I'D SEE YOU IN BATTLE AGAIN!
BWAH
HONK!
I'M OVER-COME WITH EMO-TION!
CHEN GONG
MILITARY ADVISER
LÜ BU'S ARMY

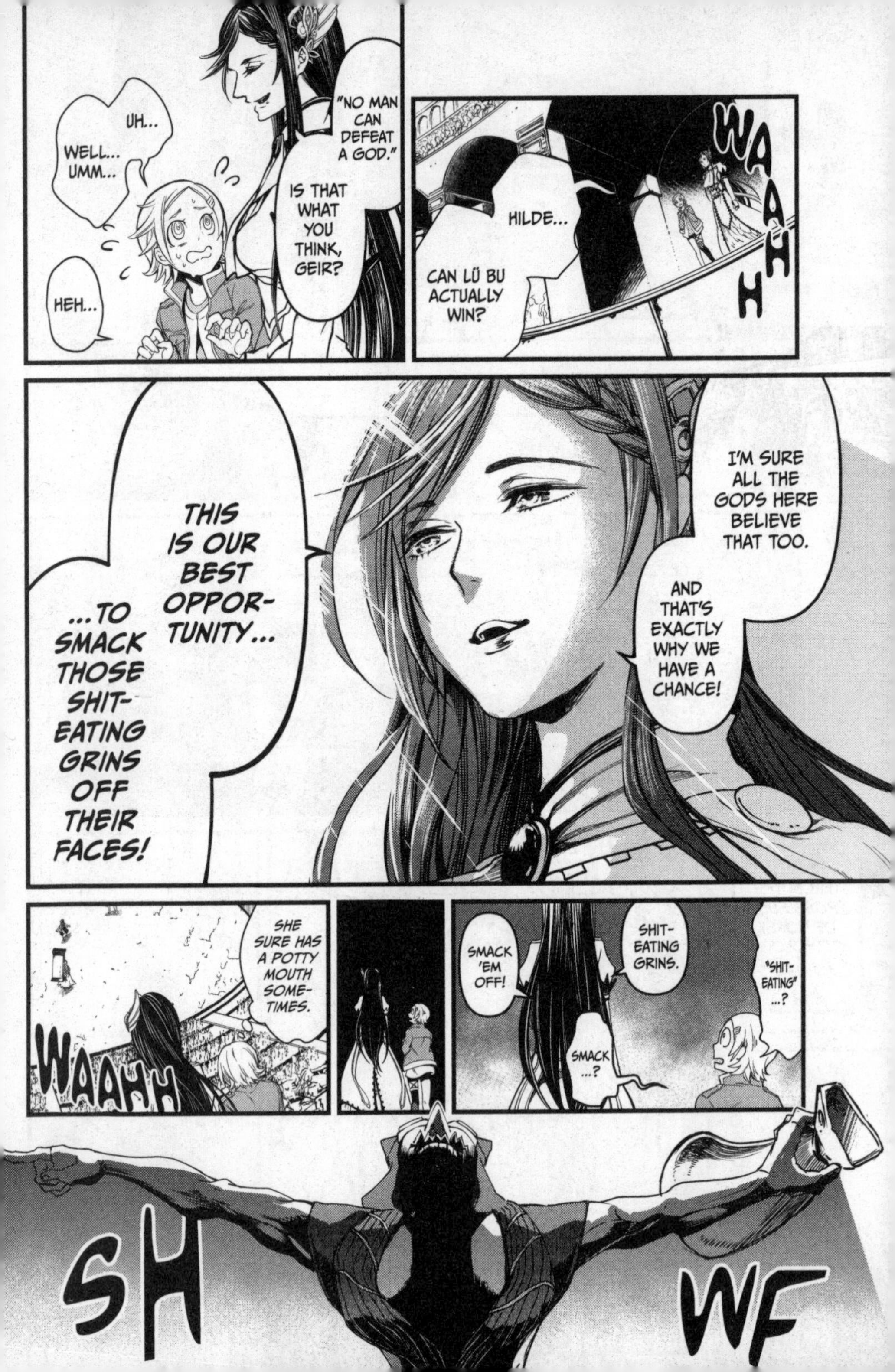
WAAHHH
HILDE...
CAN LÜ BU ACTUALLY WIN?
"NO MAN CAN DEFEAT A GOD."
IS THAT WHAT YOU THINK, GEIR?
UH...
WELL... UMM...
HEH...
I'M SURE ALL THE GODS HERE BELIEVE THAT TOO.
AND THAT'S EXACTLY WHY WE HAVE A CHANCE!
THIS IS OUR BEST OPPOR-TUNITY...
...TO SMACK THOSE SHIT-EATING GRINS OFF THEIR FACES!
"SHIT-EATING" ...?
SHIT-EATING GRINS.
SMACK 'EM OFF!
SMACK ...?
SHE SURE HAS A POTTY MOUTH SOME-TIMES.
WAAHH
SH WF

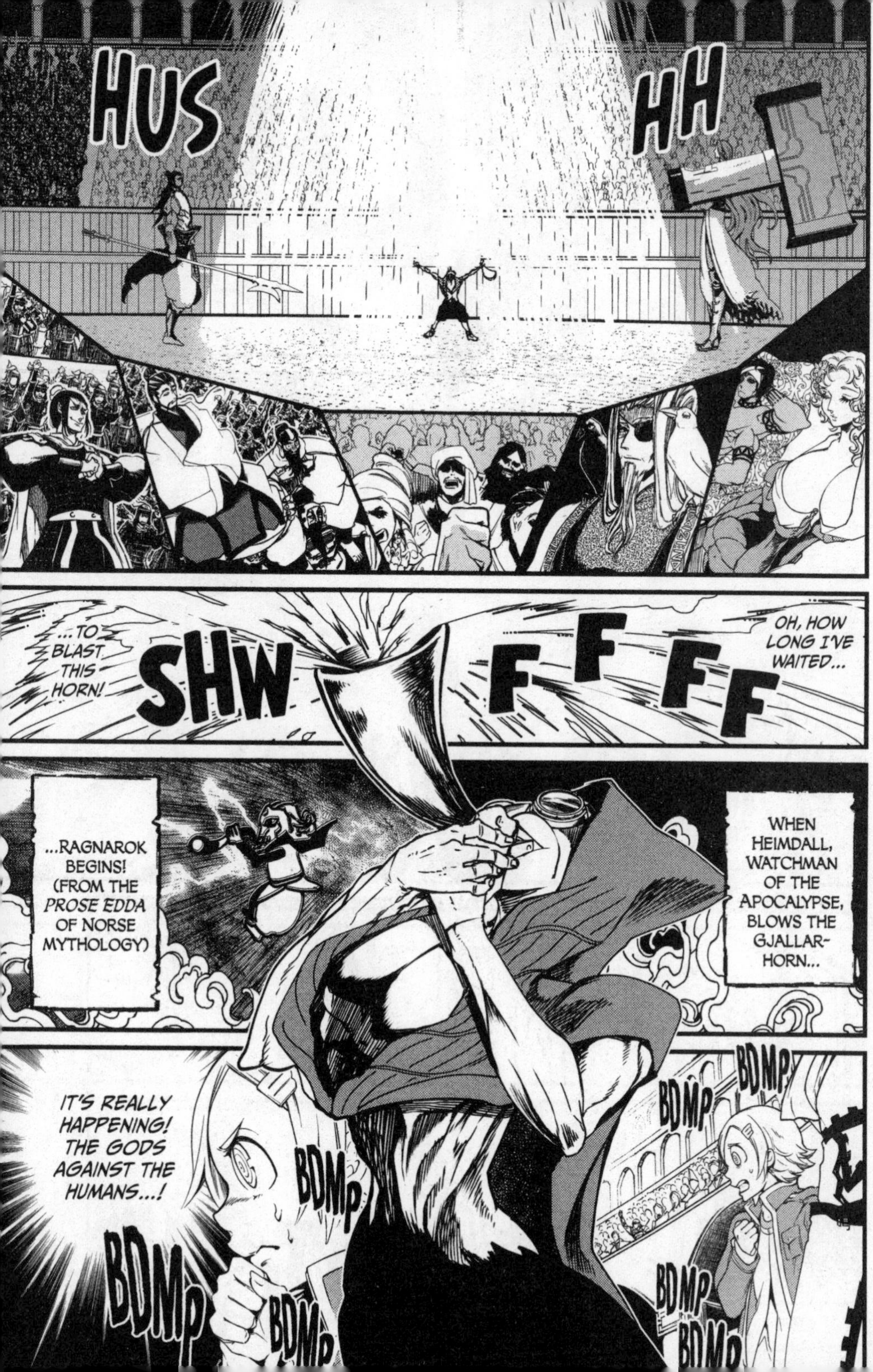

HUSHH
OH, HOW LONG I'VE WAITED...
SHW
FFFFF
...TO BLAST THIS HORN!
WHEN HEIMDALL, WATCHMAN OF THE APOCALYPSE, BLOWS THE GJALLARHORN...
...RAGNAROK BEGINS! (FROM THE *PROSE EDDA* OF NORSE MYTHOLOGY)
BDMP
BDMP
BDMP
BDMP
IT'S REALLY HAPPENING! THE GODS AGAINST THE HUMANS...!
BDMP
BDMP
BDMP

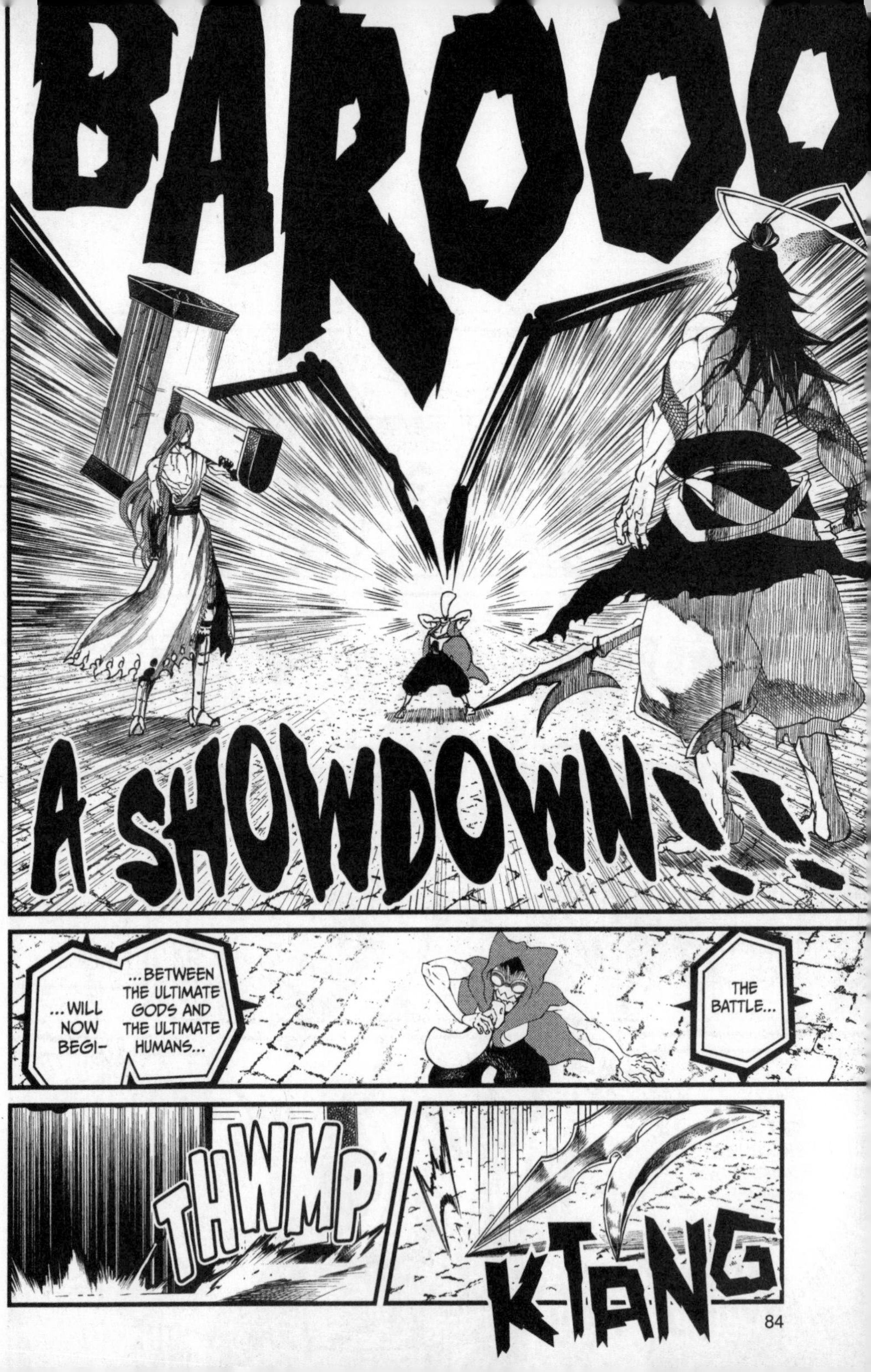
BAROOO
A SHOWDOWN...!!
THE BATTLE...
...BETWEEN THE ULTIMATE GODS AND THE ULTIMATE HUMANS...
...WILL NOW BEGI-
KTANG
THWMP

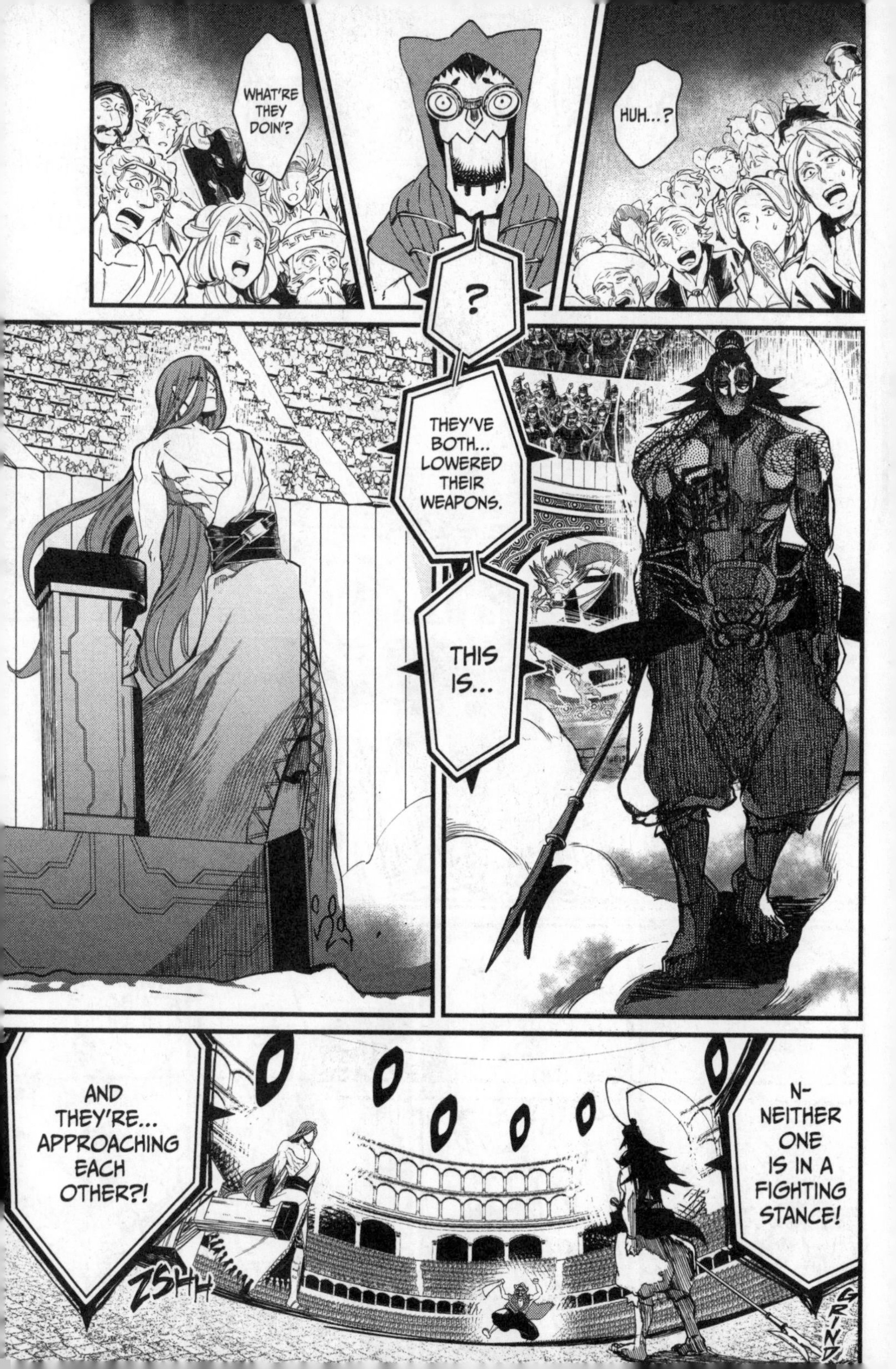
HUH...?
?
WHAT'RE THEY DOIN'?
THEY'VE BOTH... LOWERED THEIR WEAPONS.
THIS IS...
N-NEITHER ONE IS IN A FIGHTING STANCE!
GRIND
AND THEY'RE... APPROACHING EACH OTHER?!
ZSHH

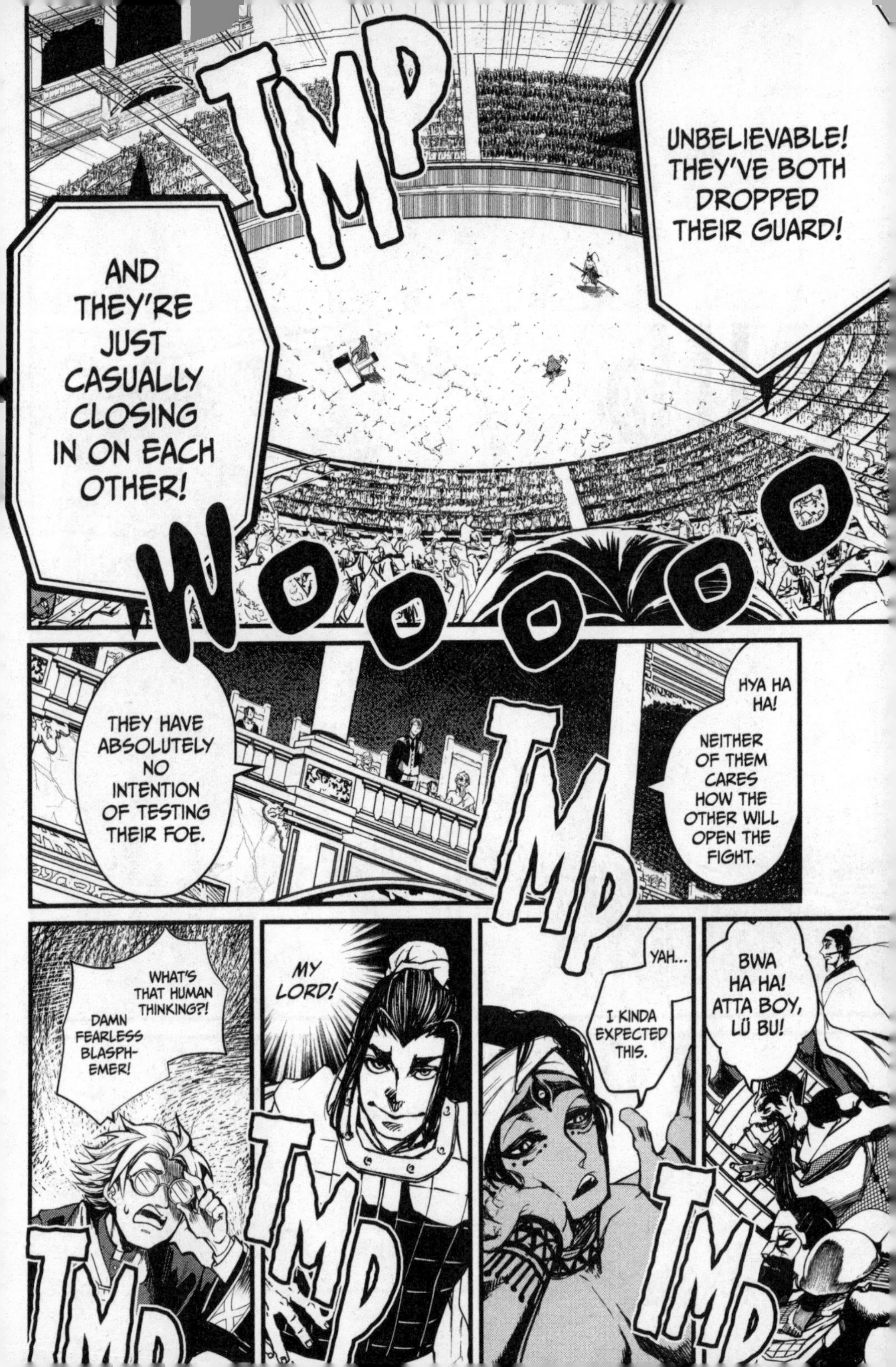
TMP
UNBELIEVABLE! THEY'VE BOTH DROPPED THEIR GUARD!
AND THEY'RE JUST CASUALLY CLOSING IN ON EACH OTHER!
WOOOOOO
HYA HA HA!
NEITHER OF THEM CARES HOW THE OTHER WILL OPEN THE FIGHT.
TMP
THEY HAVE ABSOLUTELY NO INTENTION OF TESTING THEIR FOE.
BWA HA HA! ATTA BOY, LÜ BU!
TMP
YAH...
I KINDA EXPECTED THIS.
MY LORD!
TMP
WHAT'S THAT HUMAN THINKING?!
DAMN FEARLESS BLASPH-EMER!
TMP

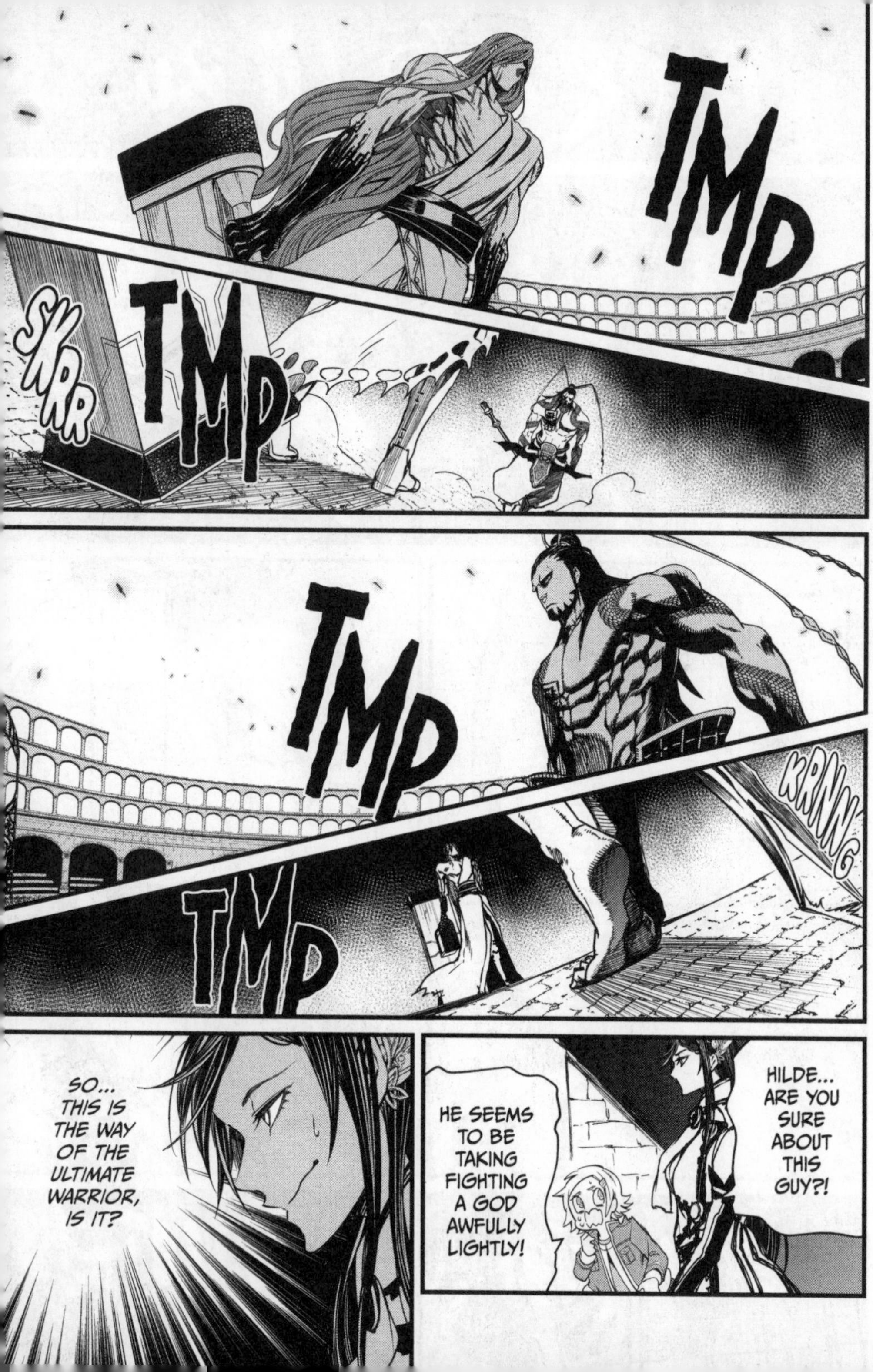
TMP
TMP
SKRR
TMP
KRNNG
TMP
HILDE... ARE YOU SURE ABOUT THIS GUY?!
HE SEEMS TO BE TAKING FIGHTING A GOD AWFULLY LIGHTLY!
SO... THIS IS THE WAY OF THE ULTIMATE WARRIOR, IS IT?

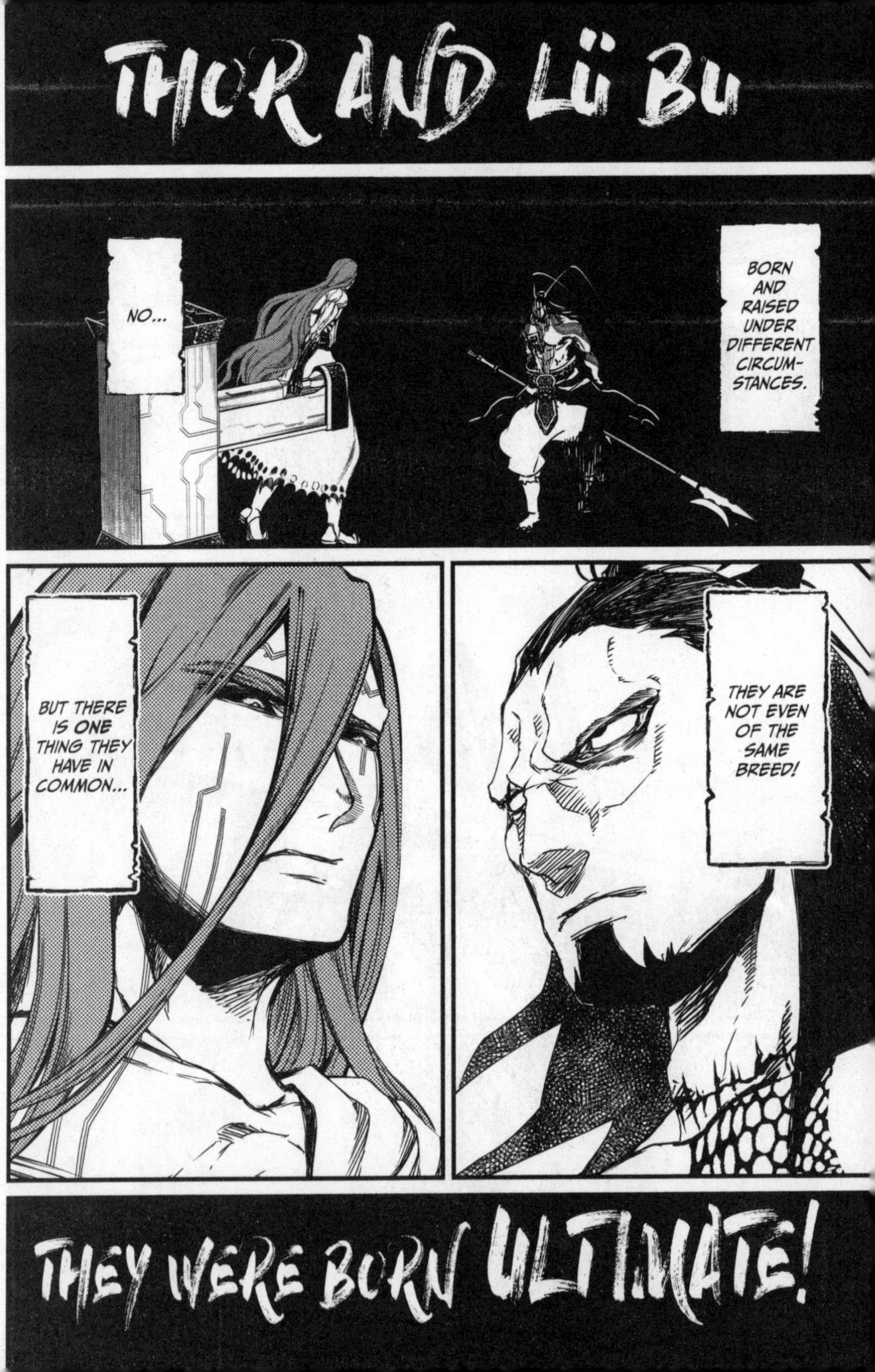
THOR AND LÜ BU
BORN AND RAISED UNDER DIFFERENT CIRCUM-STANCES.
NO...
THEY ARE NOT EVEN OF THE SAME BREED!
BUT THERE IS ONE THING THEY HAVE IN COMMON...
THEY WERE BORN ULTIMATE!

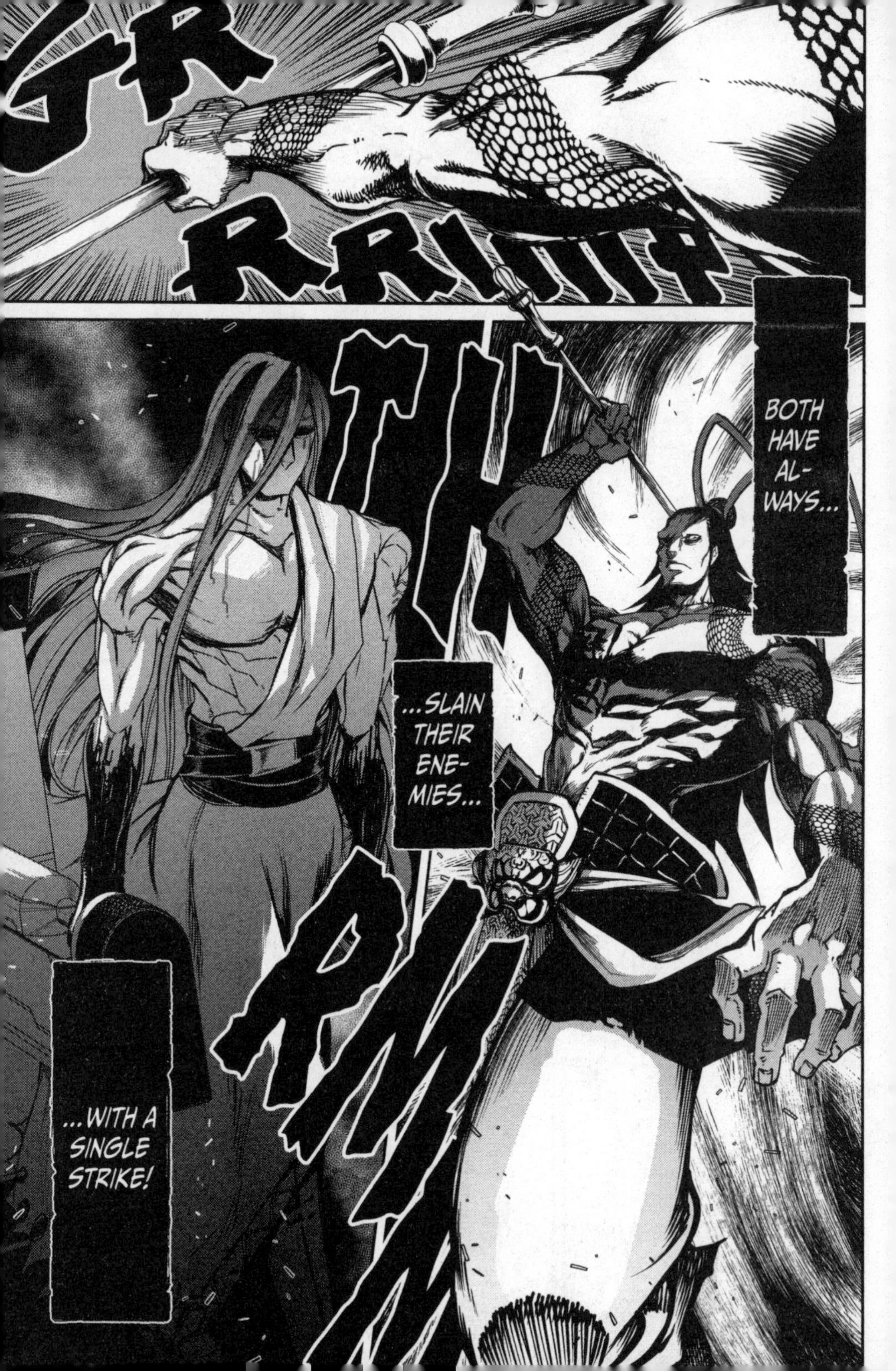
BOTH HAVE AL-WAYS...
...SLAIN THEIR ENE-MIES...
...WITH A SINGLE STRIKE!

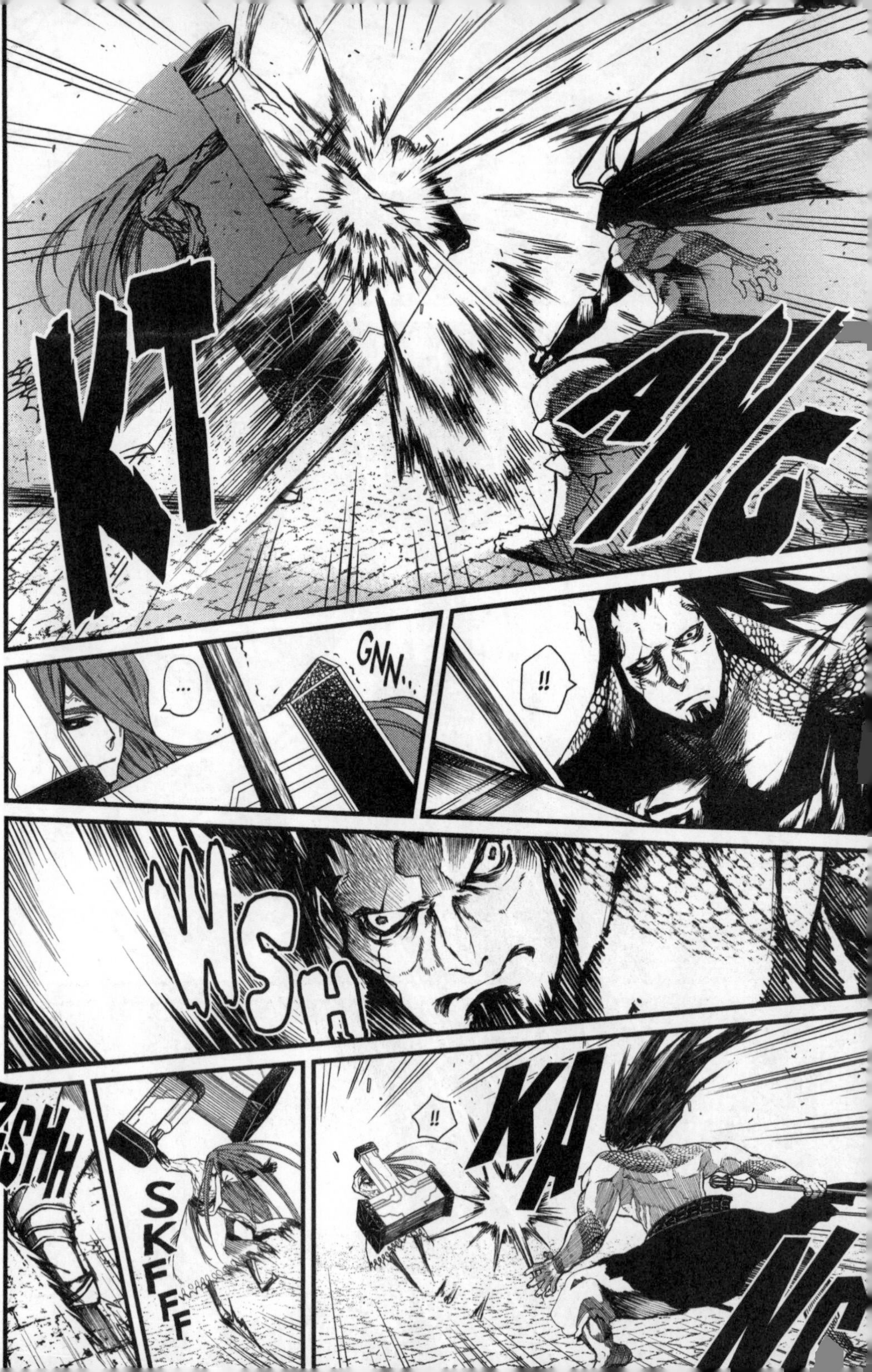
KT
ANG
!!
GNN...
...
WSH
!!
KA
NG
SKFFF
ZSHH

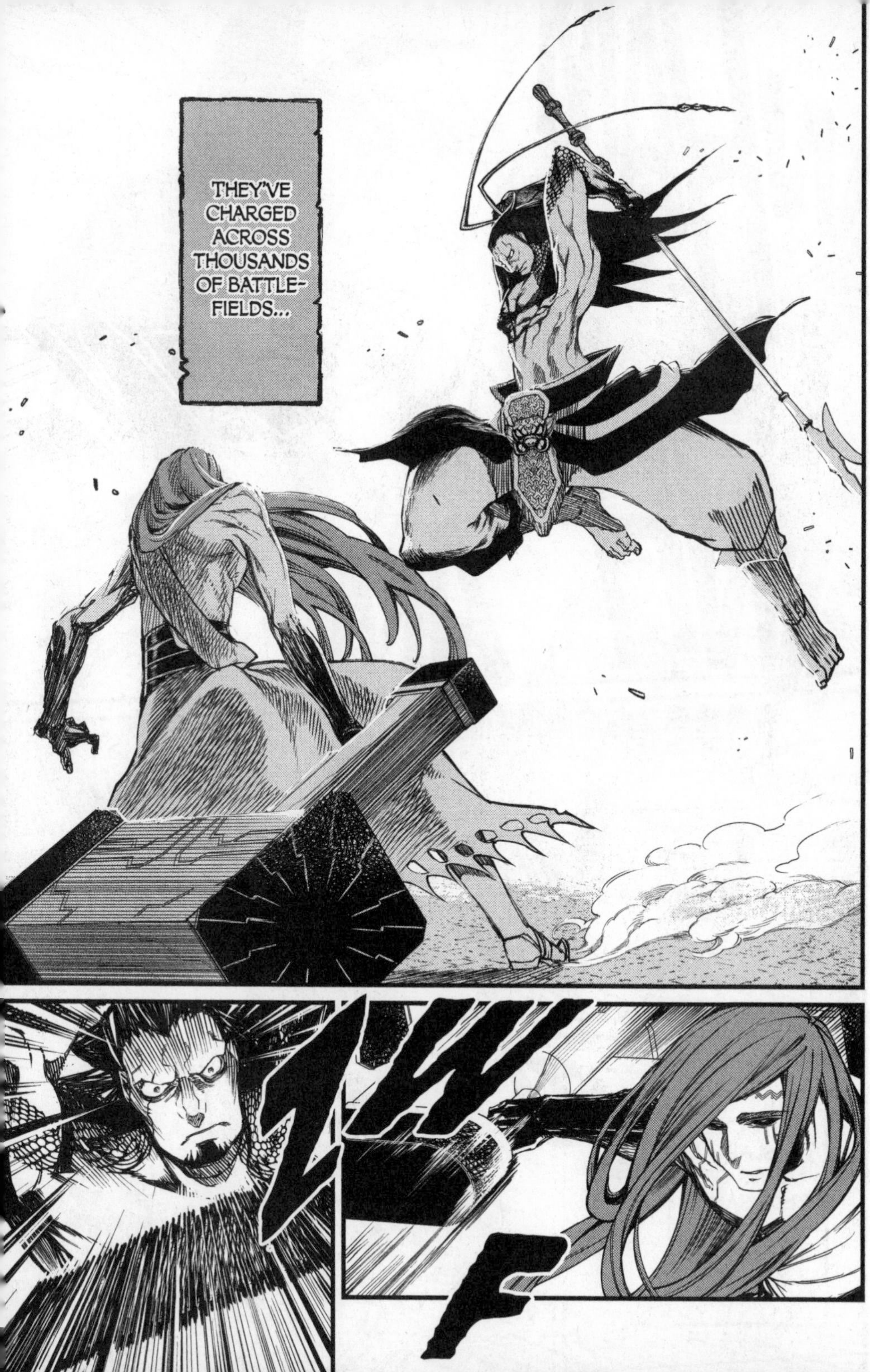
THEY'VE CHARGED ACROSS THOUSANDS OF BATTLE-FIELDS...

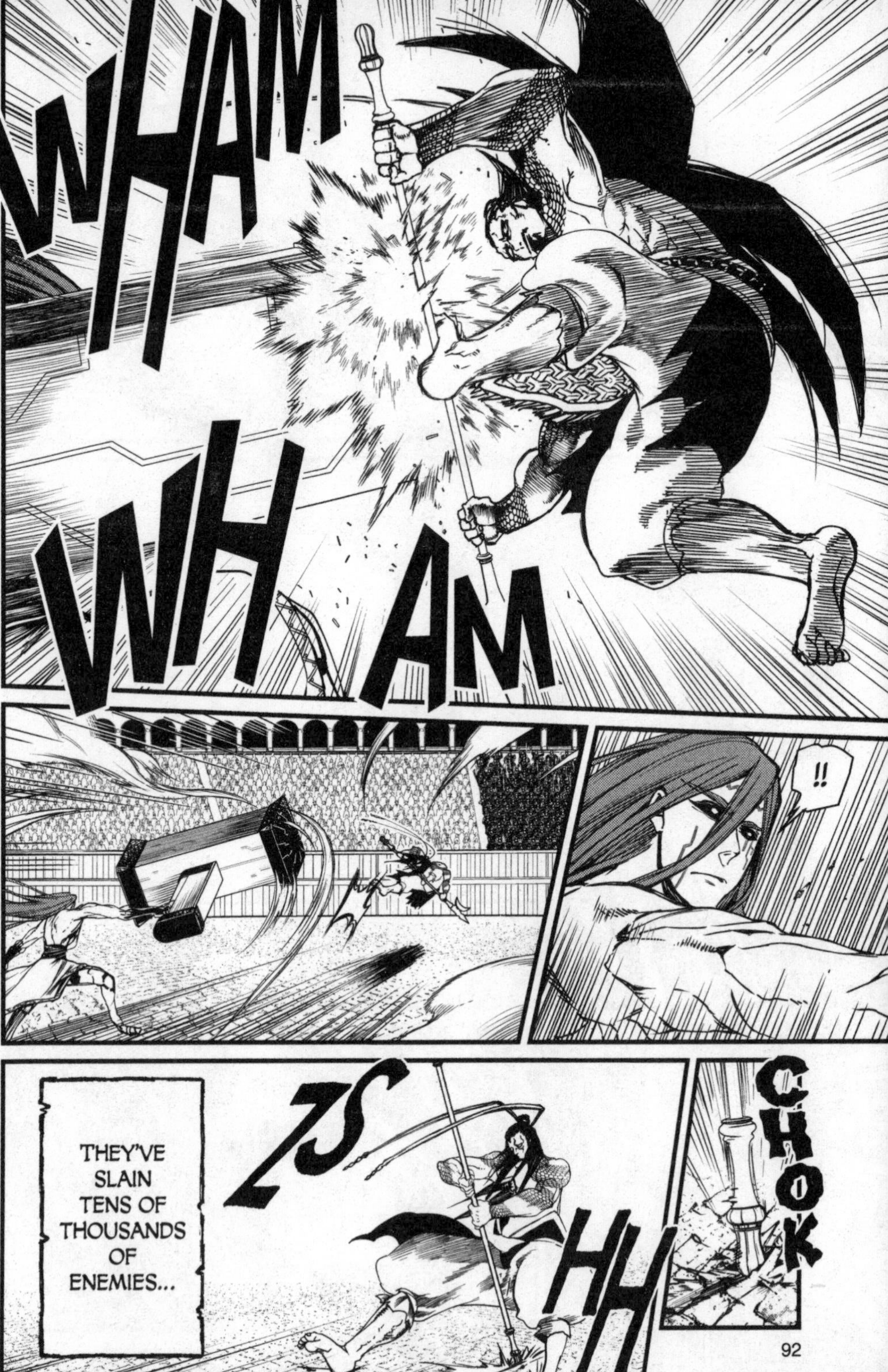
WHAM
WHAM
!!
CHOK
THEY'VE SLAIN TENS OF THOUSANDS OF ENEMIES...
ZSHH

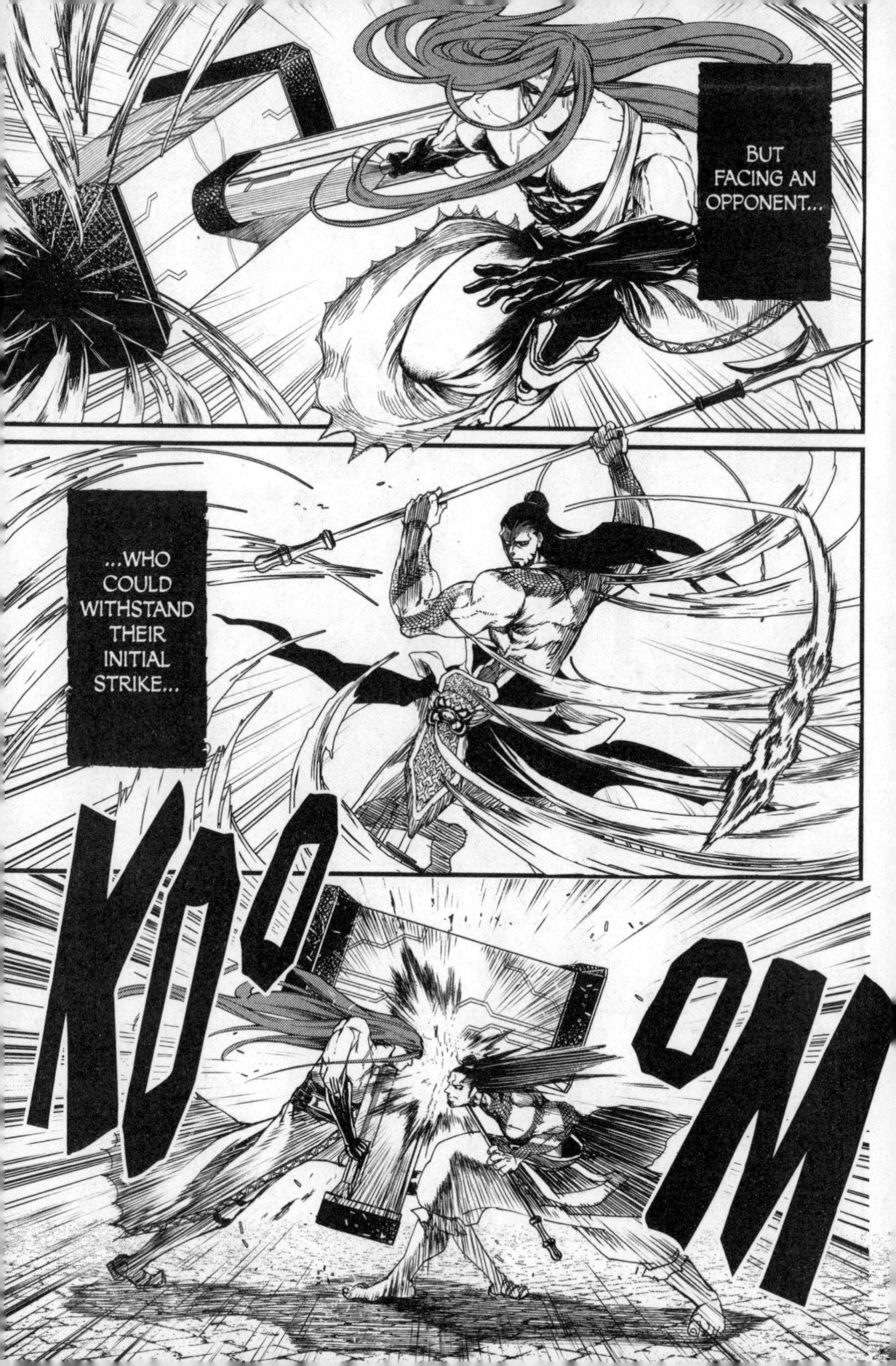
BUT FACING AN OPPONENT...
...WHO COULD WITHSTAND THEIR INITIAL STRIKE...
KDOOM

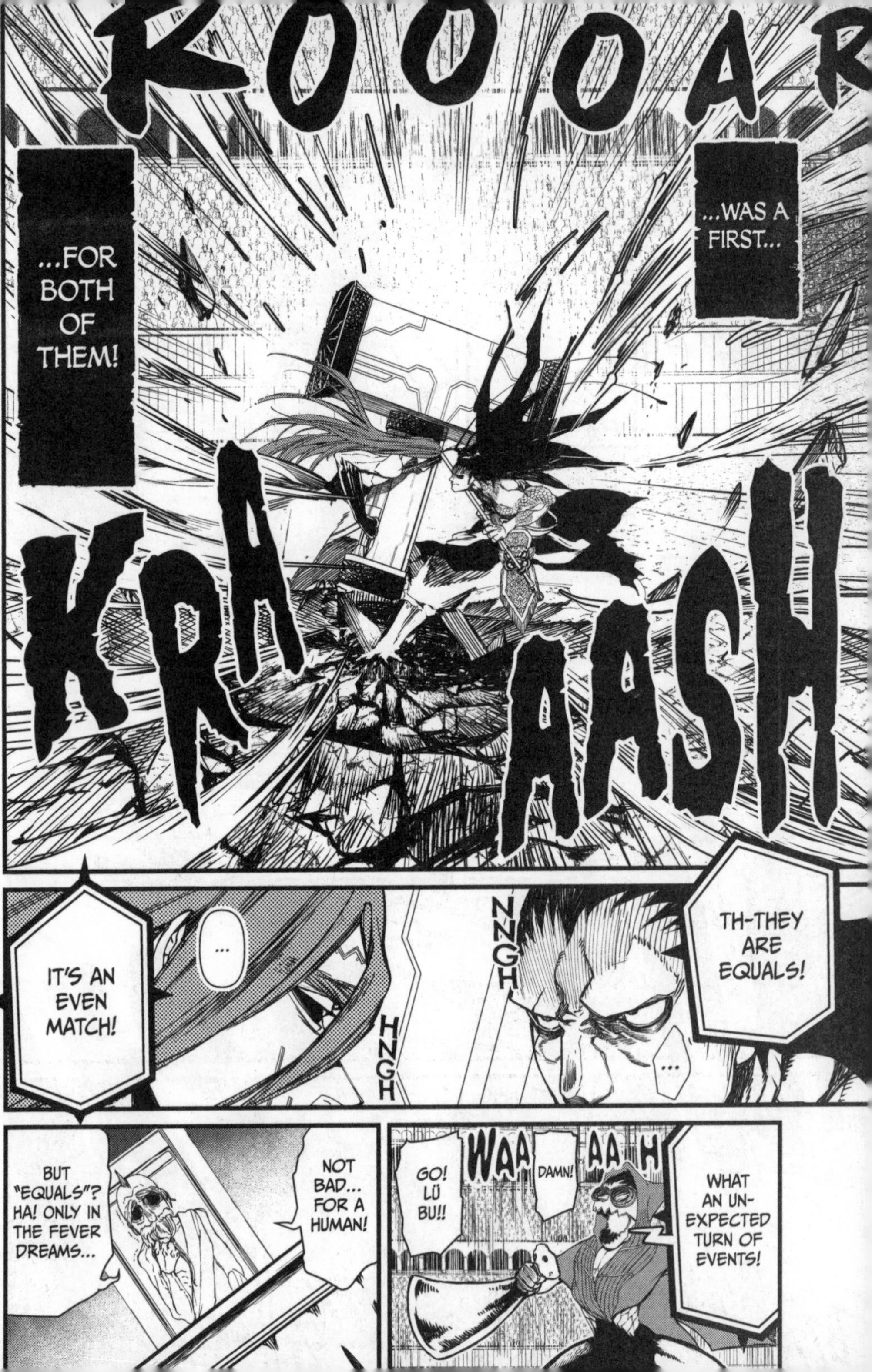
KOOOAR
...WAS A FIRST...
...FOR BOTH OF THEM!
KRAASH
TH-THEY ARE EQUALS!
NNGH
...
...
IT'S AN EVEN MATCH!
HNGH
WHAT AN UN-EXPECTED TURN OF EVENTS!
WAA AA H
DAMN!
GO! LÜ BU!!
NOT BAD... FOR A HUMAN!
BUT "EQUALS"? HA! ONLY IN THE FEVER DREAMS...

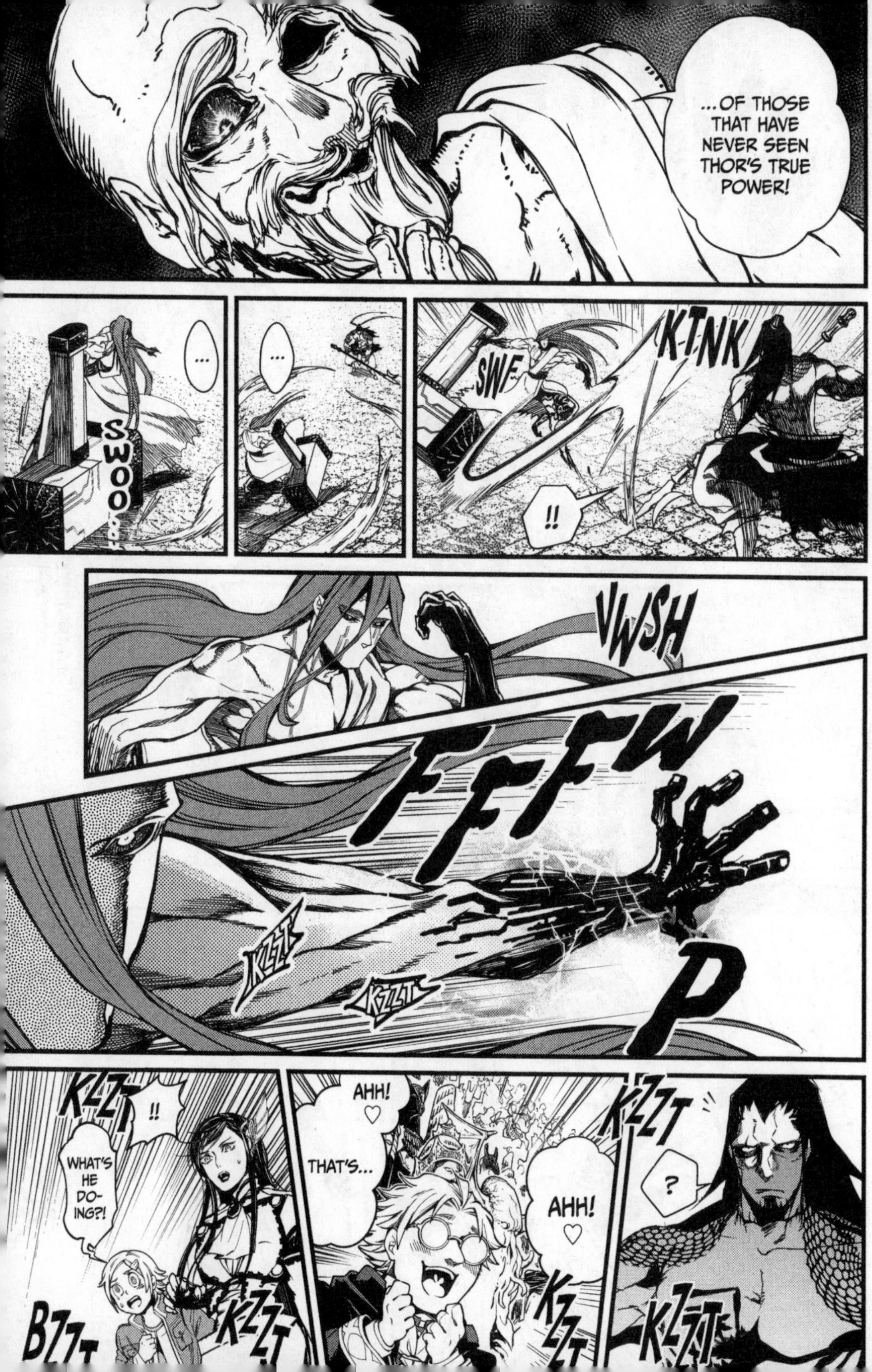
...OF THOSE THAT HAVE NEVER SEEN THOR'S TRUE POWER!
KTNK
SWF
!!
...
...
SWOO...
VWSH
FFFWP
KZZT
KZZT
KZZT
?
KZZZT
AHH! ♡
THAT'S...
AHH! ♡
KZZT
KZZT
!!
WHAT'S HE DOING?!
BZZT
KZZZT

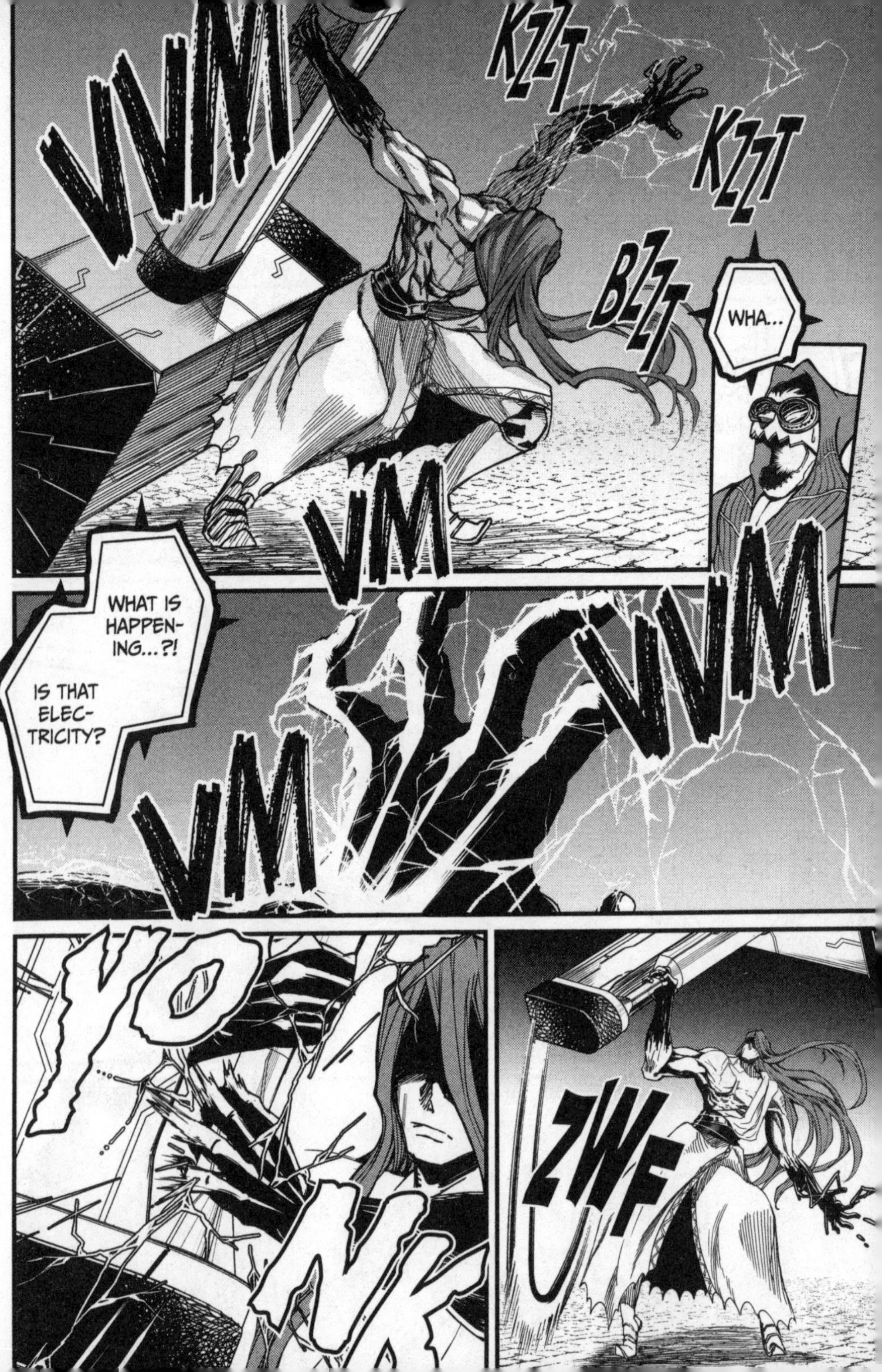
KZZT
KZZT
BZZT
WHA...
VVVM
VM
WHAT IS HAPPEN-ING...?!
IS THAT ELEC-TRICITY?
VVVM
VM
ZWF
YO
...
...

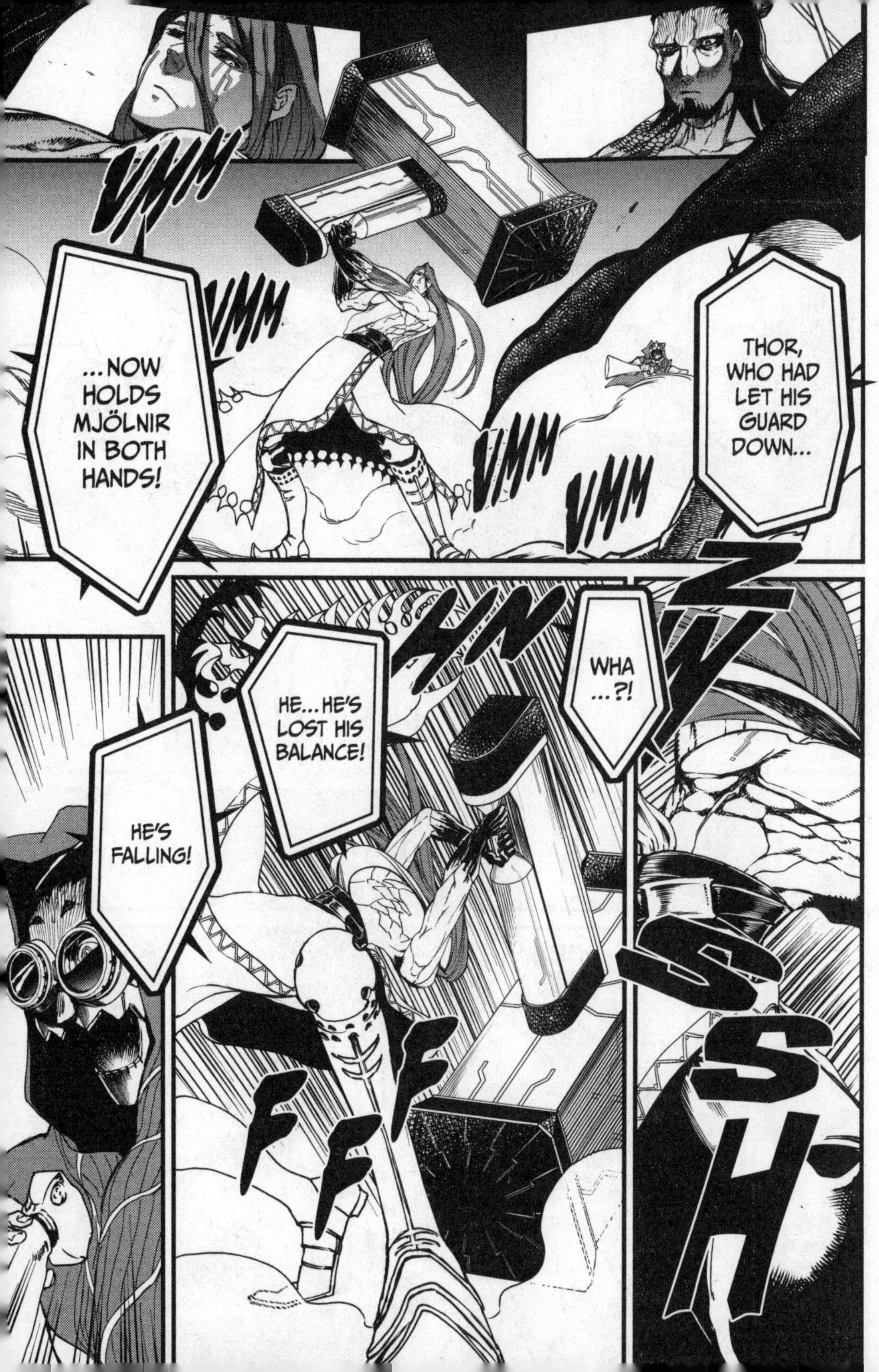
VMM
THOR, WHO HAD LET HIS GUARD DOWN...
VMM
VMM
VMM
...NOW HOLDS MJÖLNIR IN BOTH HANDS!
WHA ...?!
HE...HE'S LOST HIS BALANCE!
HE'S FALLING!
FFF

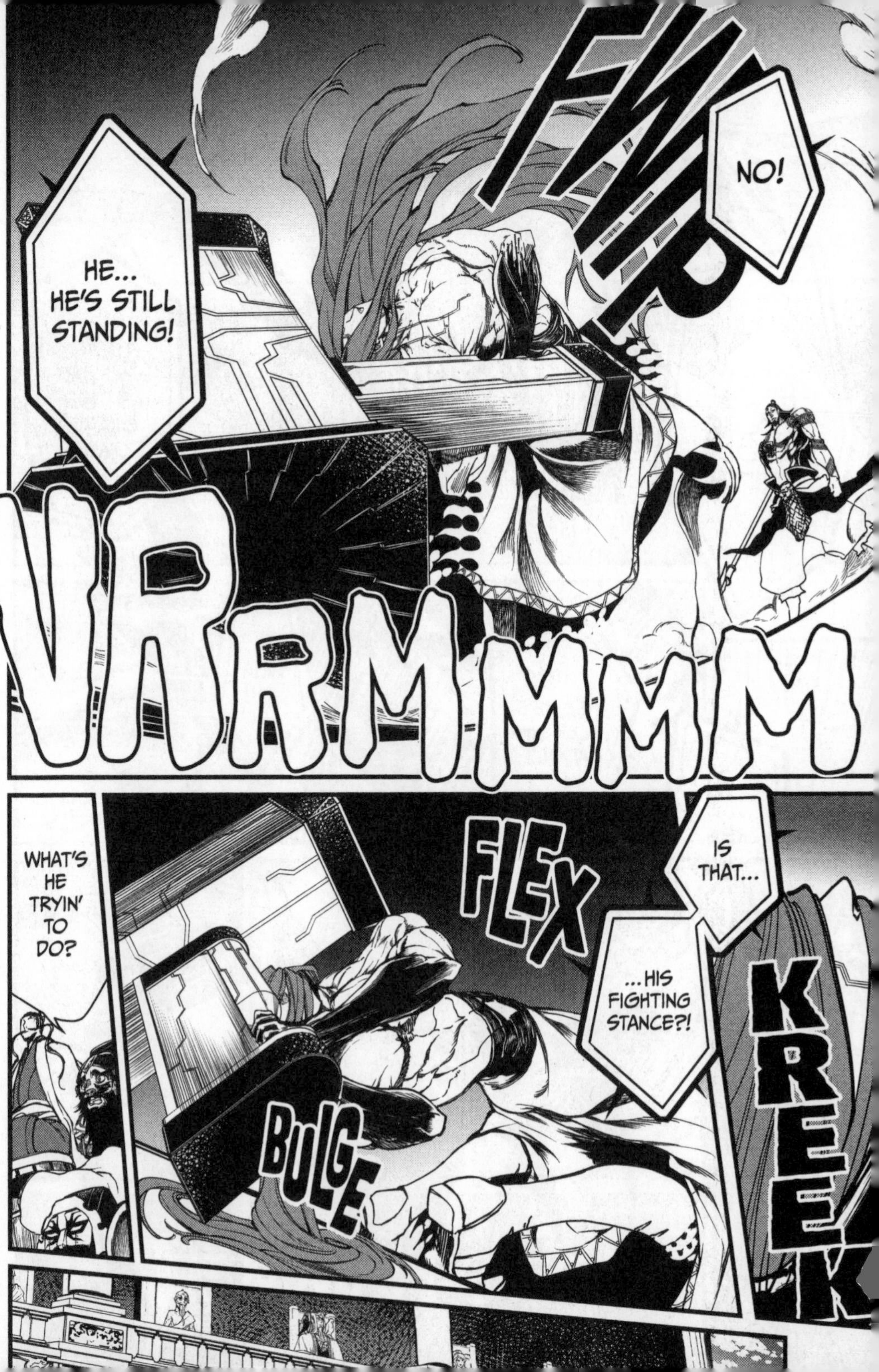
FWIP
NO!
HE... HE'S STILL STANDING!
VRMMMM
IS THAT...
...HIS FIGHTING STANCE?!
KREEK
FLEX
BULGE
WHAT'S HE TRYIN' TO DO?

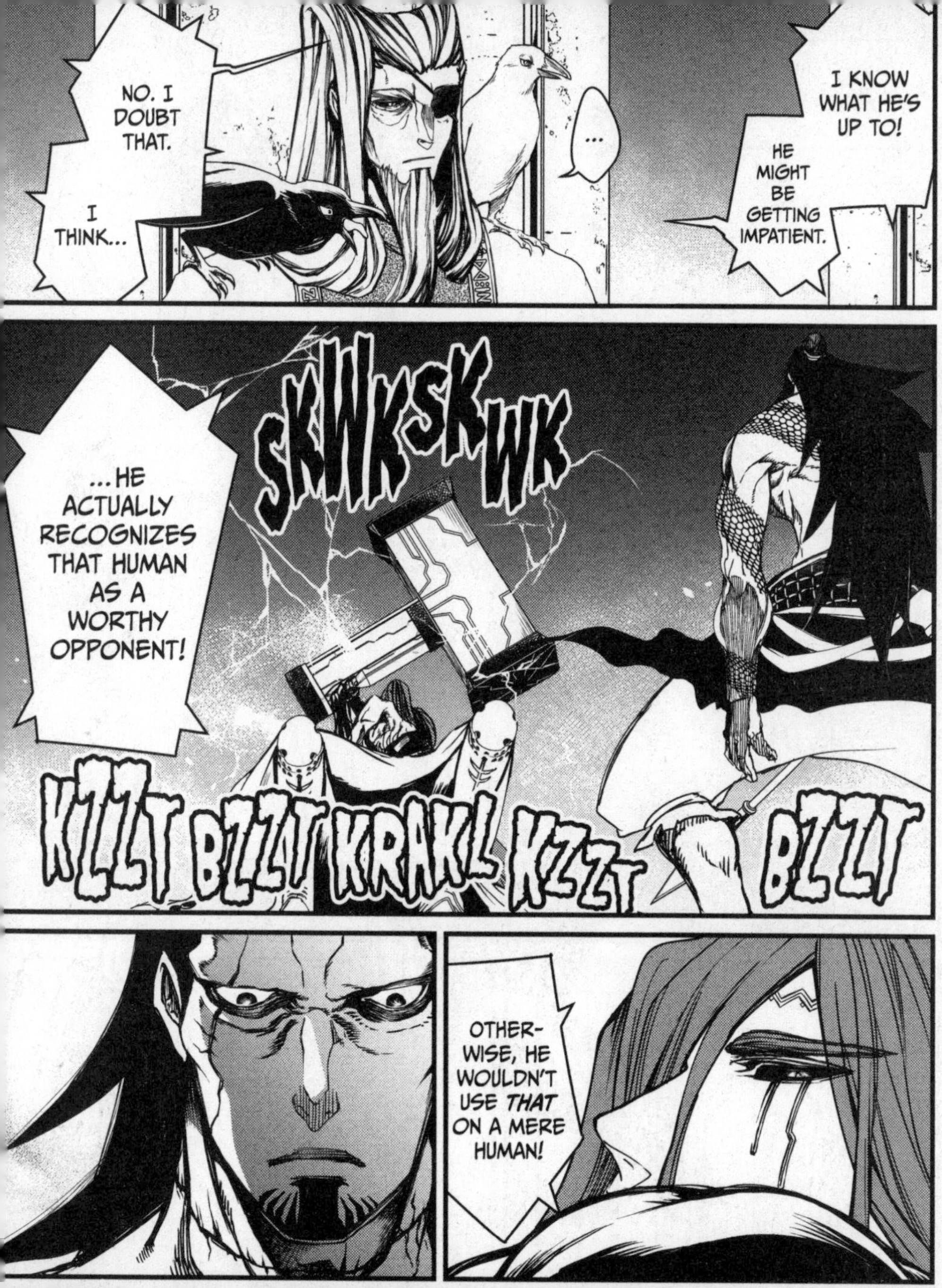
I KNOW WHAT HE'S UP TO!
HE MIGHT BE GETTING IMPATIENT.
...
NO. I DOUBT THAT.
I THINK...
SKWKSKWK
...HE ACTUALLY RECOGNIZES THAT HUMAN AS A WORTHY OPPONENT!
KZZT BZZT KRAKL KZZT BZZT
OTHERWISE, HE WOULDN'T USE *THAT* ON A MERE HUMAN!

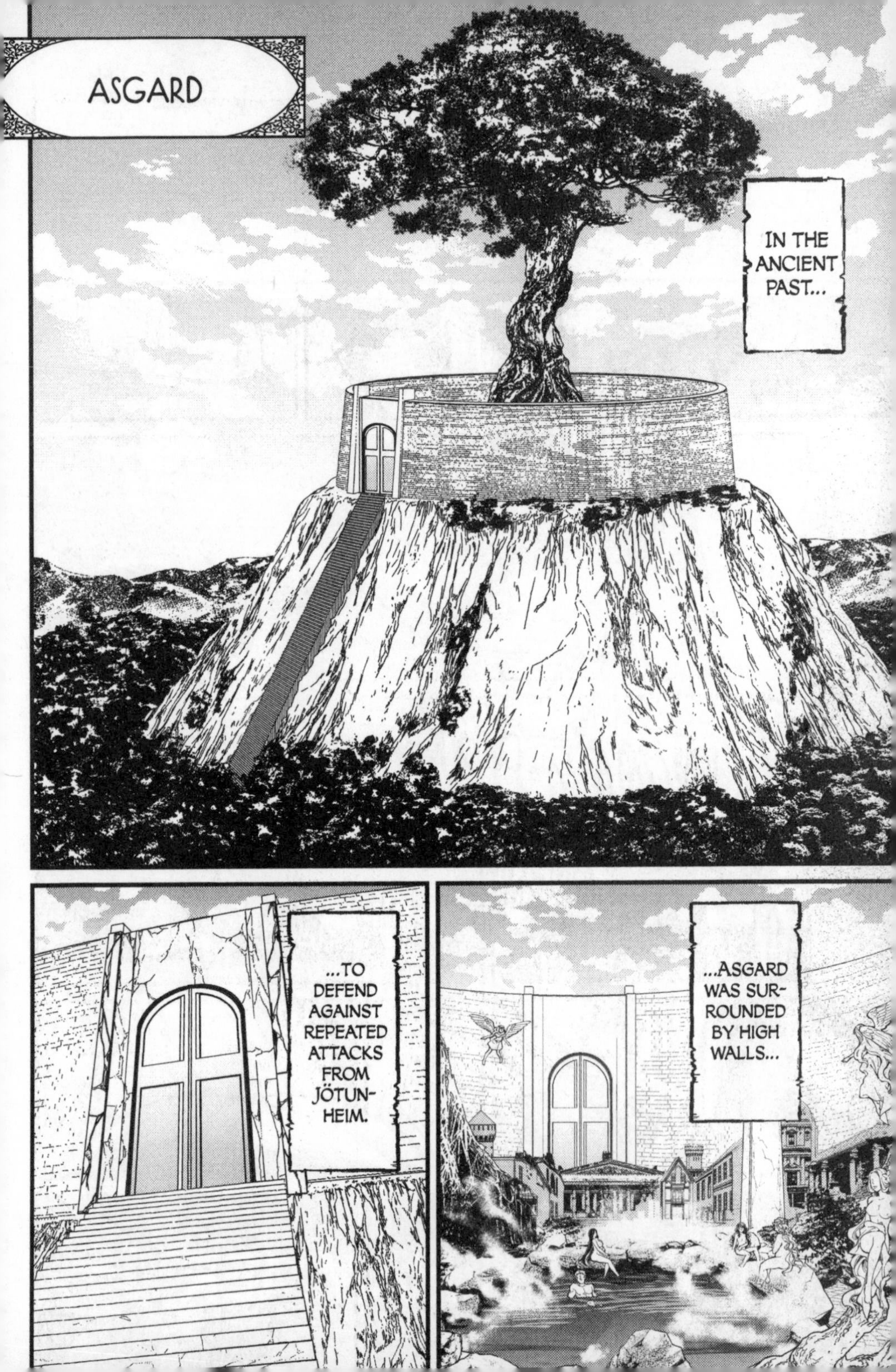
ASGARD
IN THE ANCIENT PAST...
...ASGARD WAS SURROUNDED BY HIGH WALLS...
...TO DEFEND AGAINST REPEATED ATTACKS FROM JÖTUNHEIM.

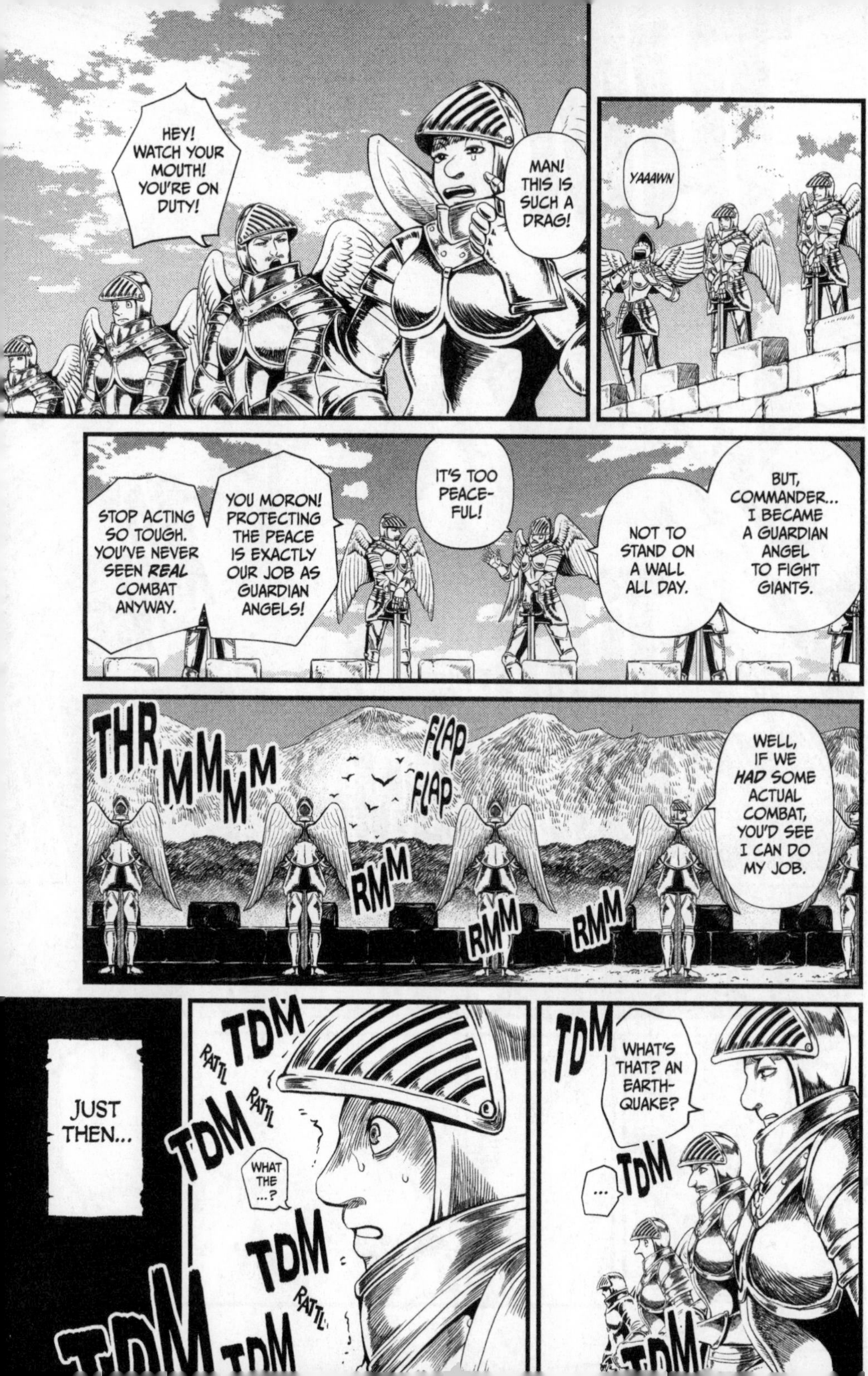
YAAAWN
MAN! THIS IS SUCH A DRAG!
HEY! WATCH YOUR MOUTH! YOU'RE ON DUTY!
BUT, COMMANDER... I BECAME A GUARDIAN ANGEL TO FIGHT GIANTS.
NOT TO STAND ON A WALL ALL DAY.
IT'S TOO PEACE-FUL!
YOU MORON! PROTECTING THE PEACE IS EXACTLY OUR JOB AS GUARDIAN ANGELS!
STOP ACTING SO TOUGH. YOU'VE NEVER SEEN *REAL* COMBAT ANYWAY.
WELL, IF WE *HAD* SOME ACTUAL COMBAT, YOU'D SEE I CAN DO MY JOB.
FLAP FLAP
THRMMMM
RMM
RMM
RMM
TDM
WHAT'S THAT? AN EARTH-QUAKE?
...
TDM
TDM
TDM
RATTL
TDM
RATTL
WHAT THE ...?
TDM
RATTL
TDM
TDM
TDM
JUST THEN...

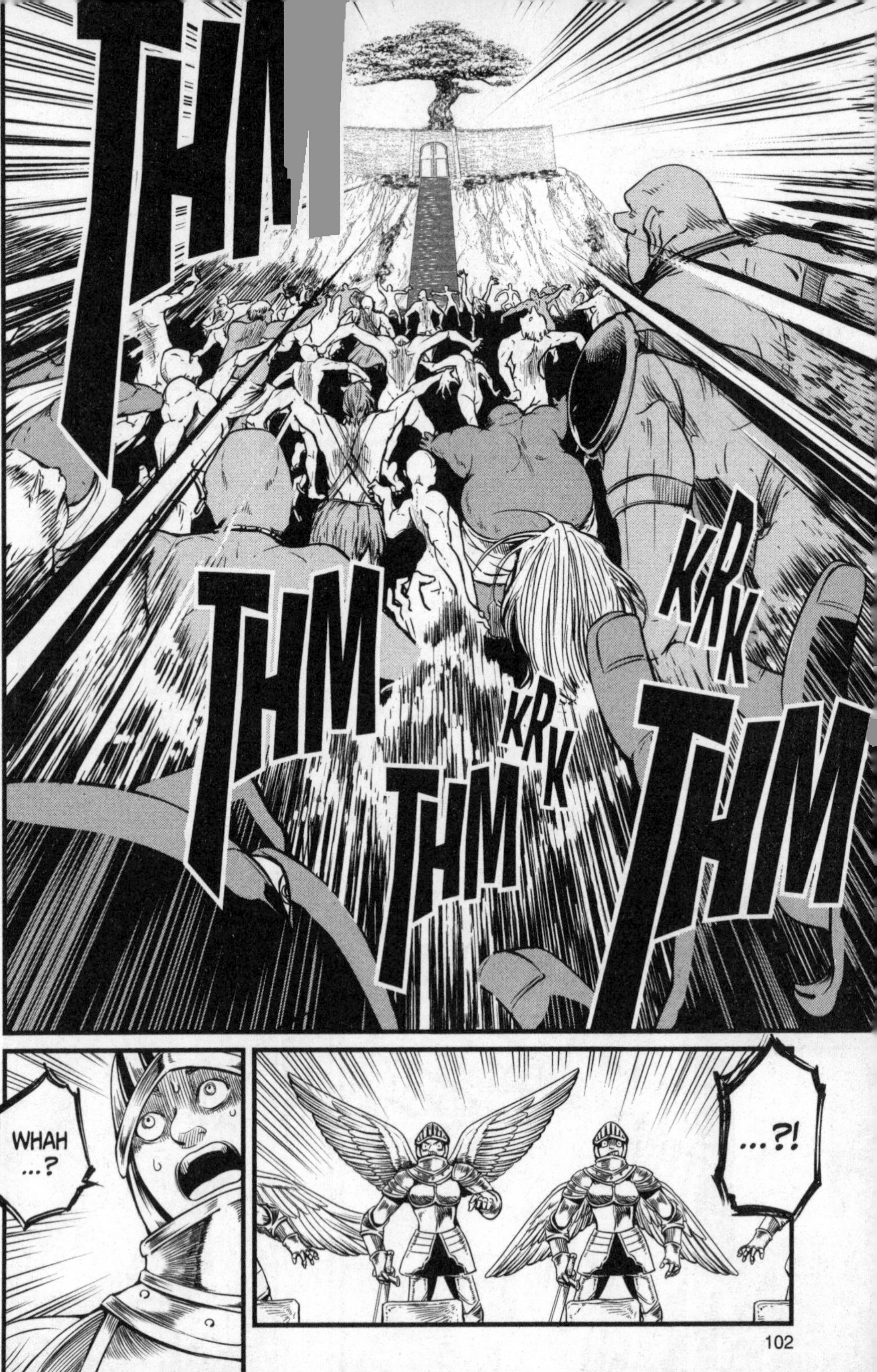
THM
KRK
THM
KRK
THM
THM
...?!
WHAH ...?

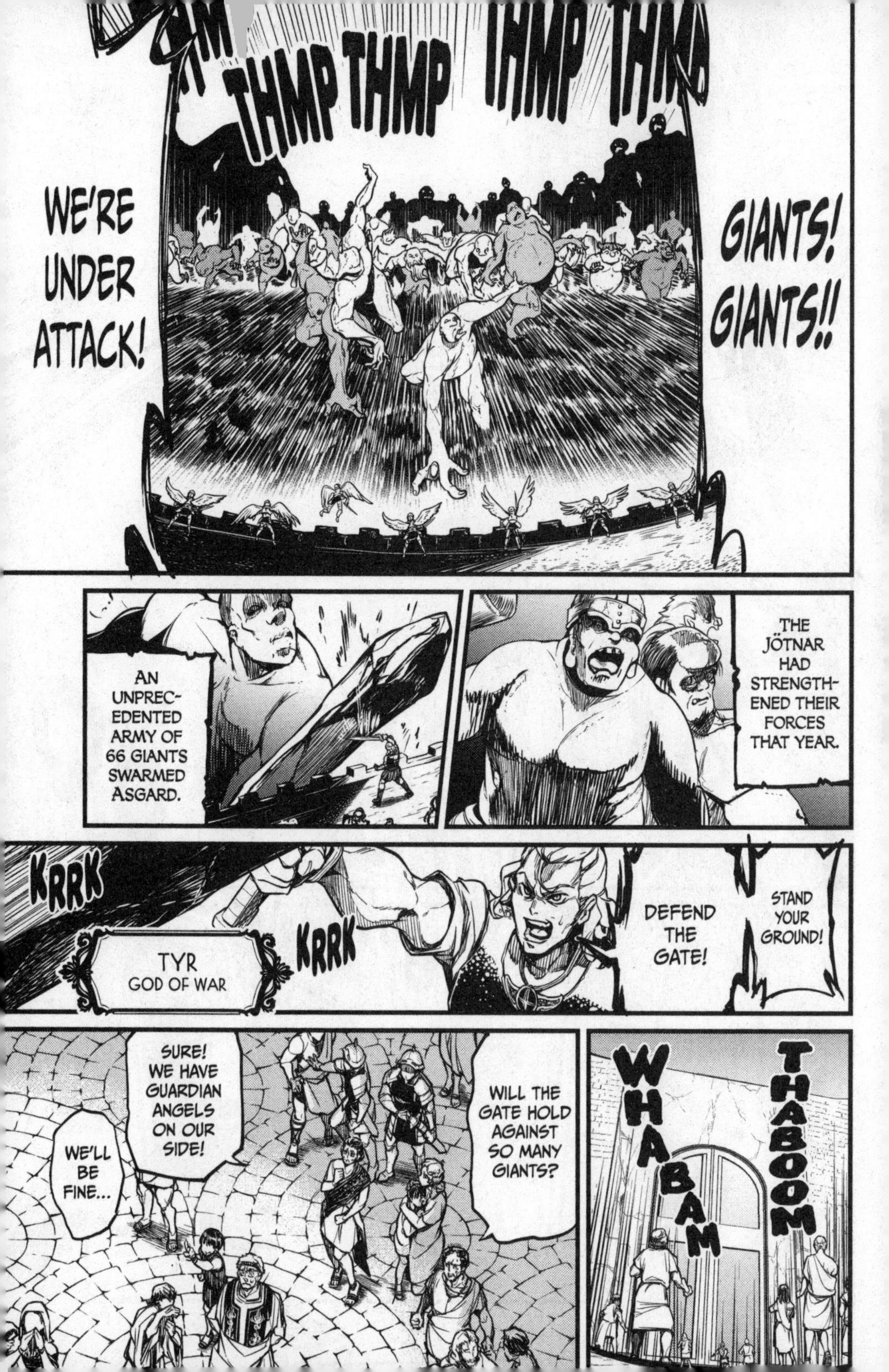
THMP THMP
THMP THMP
GIANTS! GIANTS!!
WE'RE UNDER ATTACK!
THE JÖTNAR HAD STRENGTHENED THEIR FORCES THAT YEAR.
AN UNPRECEDENTED ARMY OF 66 GIANTS SWARMED ASGARD.
STAND YOUR GROUND!
DEFEND THE GATE!
KRRK
TYR
GOD OF WAR
KRRK
THABOOM
WHABAM
WILL THE GATE HOLD AGAINST SO MANY GIANTS?
SURE! WE HAVE GUARDIAN ANGELS ON OUR SIDE!
WE'LL BE FINE...

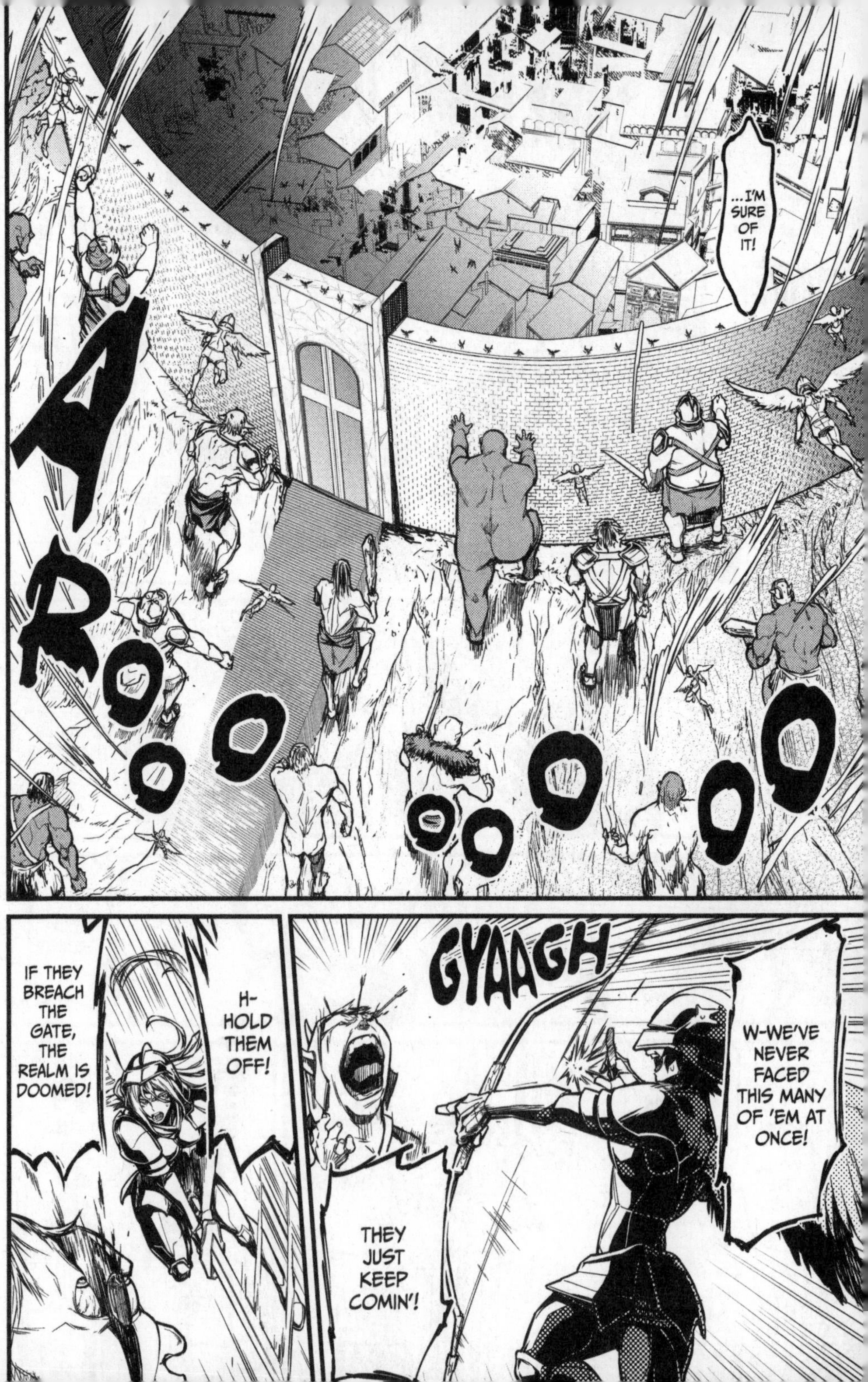
...I'M SURE OF IT!
AROOOOOOOO
GYAAGH
W-WE'VE NEVER FACED THIS MANY OF 'EM AT ONCE!
THEY JUST KEEP COMIN'!
H-HOLD THEM OFF!
IF THEY BREACH THE GATE, THE REALM IS DOOMED!

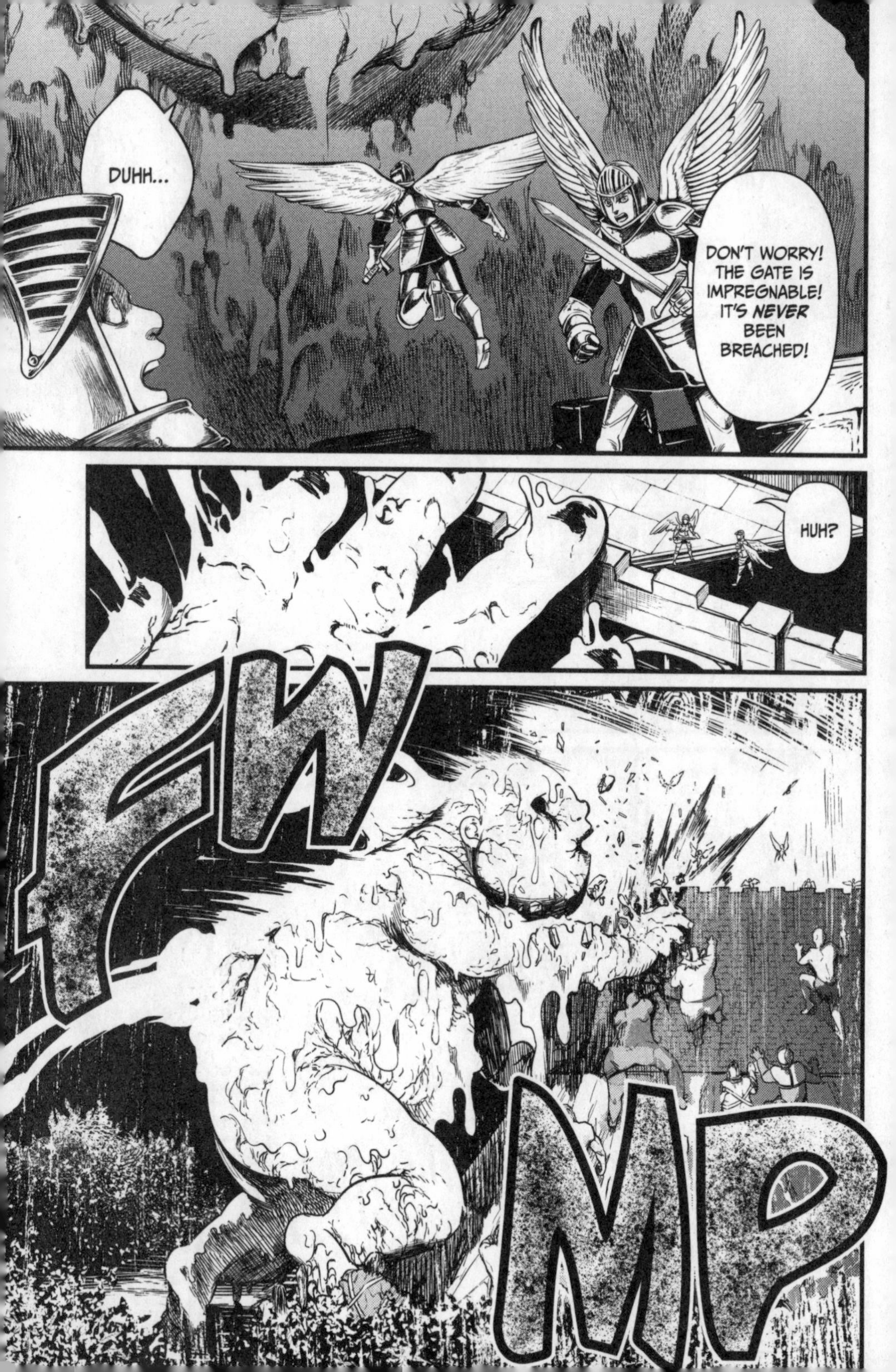
DON'T WORRY! THE GATE IS IMPREGNABLE! IT'S ***NEVER*** BEEN BREACHED!
DUHH...
HUH?
FW
MP

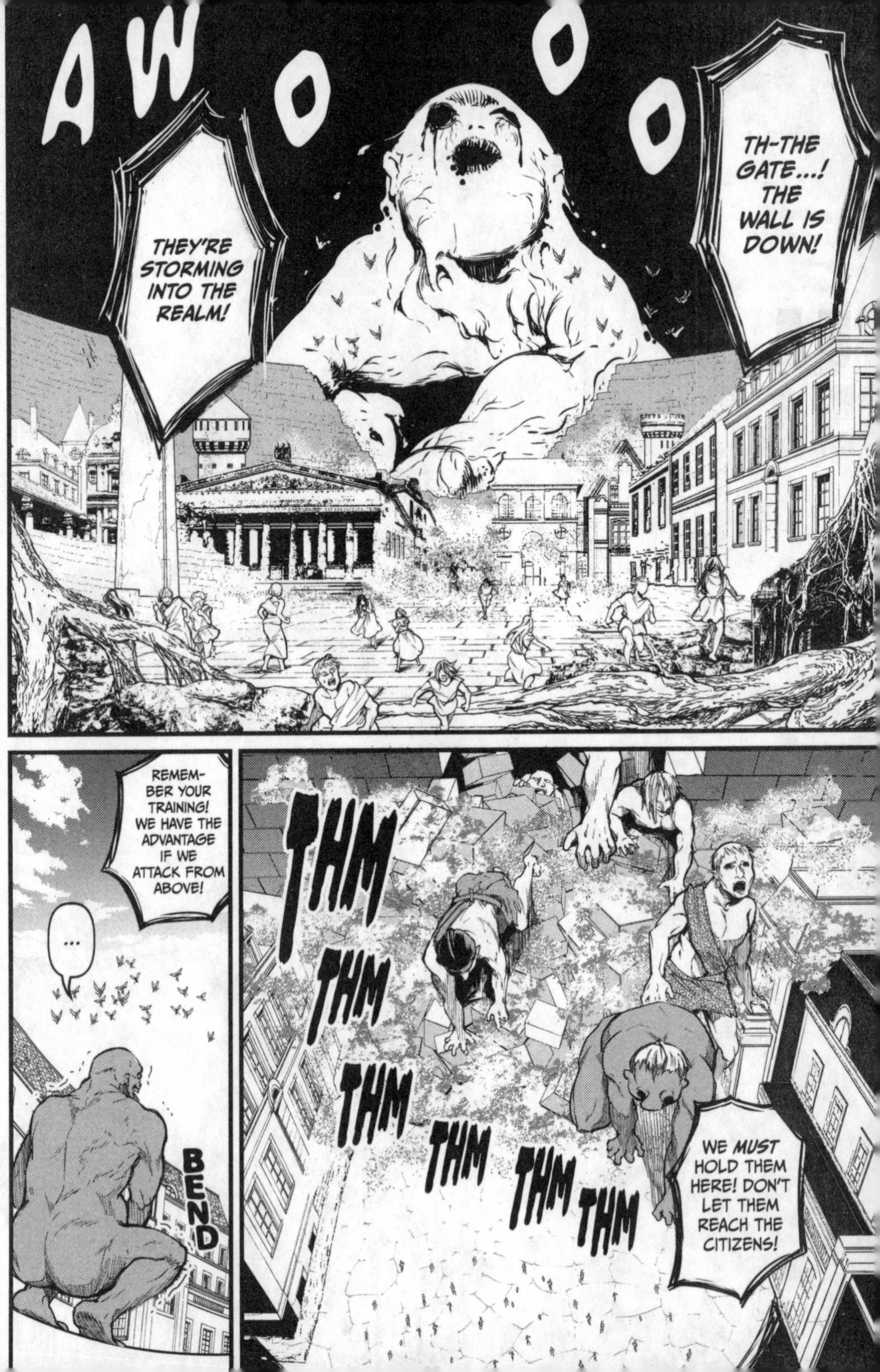
AWOOOO
TH-THE GATE...! THE WALL IS DOWN!
THEY'RE STORMING INTO THE REALM!
THM THM THM THM THM THM
WE MUST HOLD THEM HERE! DON'T LET THEM REACH THE CITIZENS!
REMEMBER YOUR TRAINING! WE HAVE THE ADVANTAGE IF WE ATTACK FROM ABOVE!
...
BEND

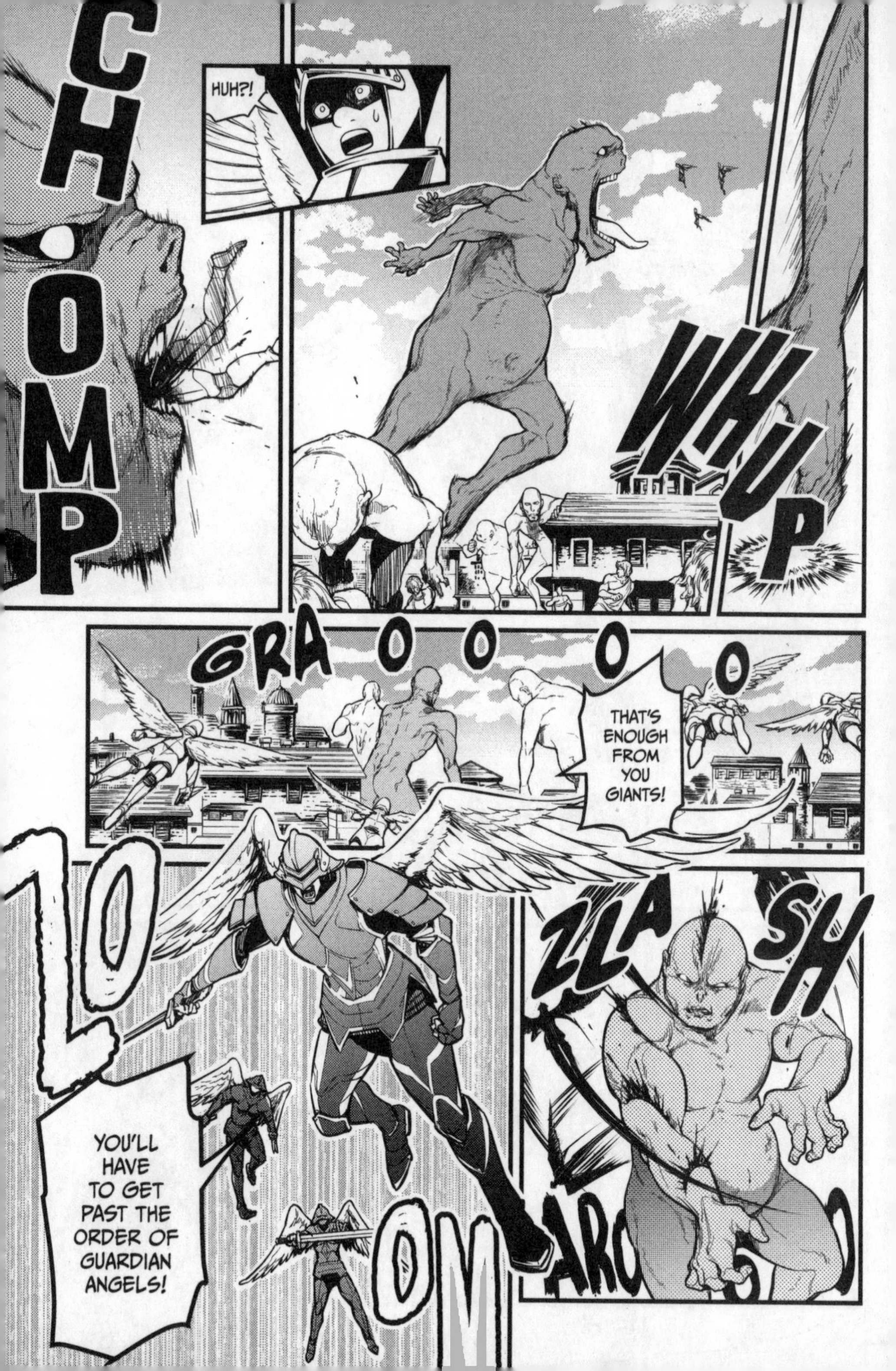
WHUP
HUH?!
CHOMP
GRAOOOOO
THAT'S ENOUGH FROM YOU GIANTS!
ZZLASH
AROOO
ZOOM
YOU'LL HAVE TO GET PAST THE ORDER OF GUARDIAN ANGELS!

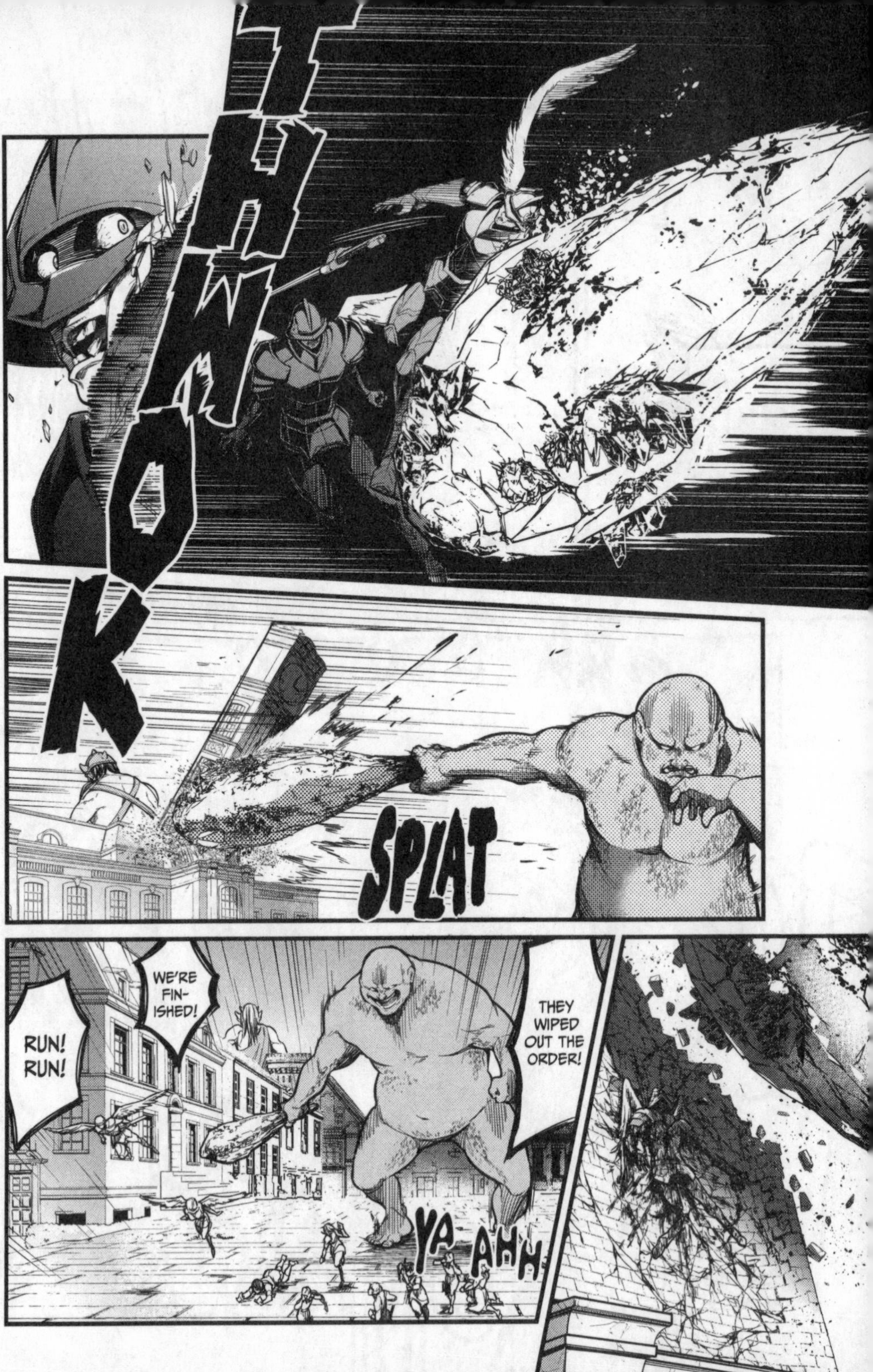
THWOK
SPLAT
THEY WIPED OUT THE ORDER!
WE'RE FINISHED!
RUN! RUN!
YAAHH

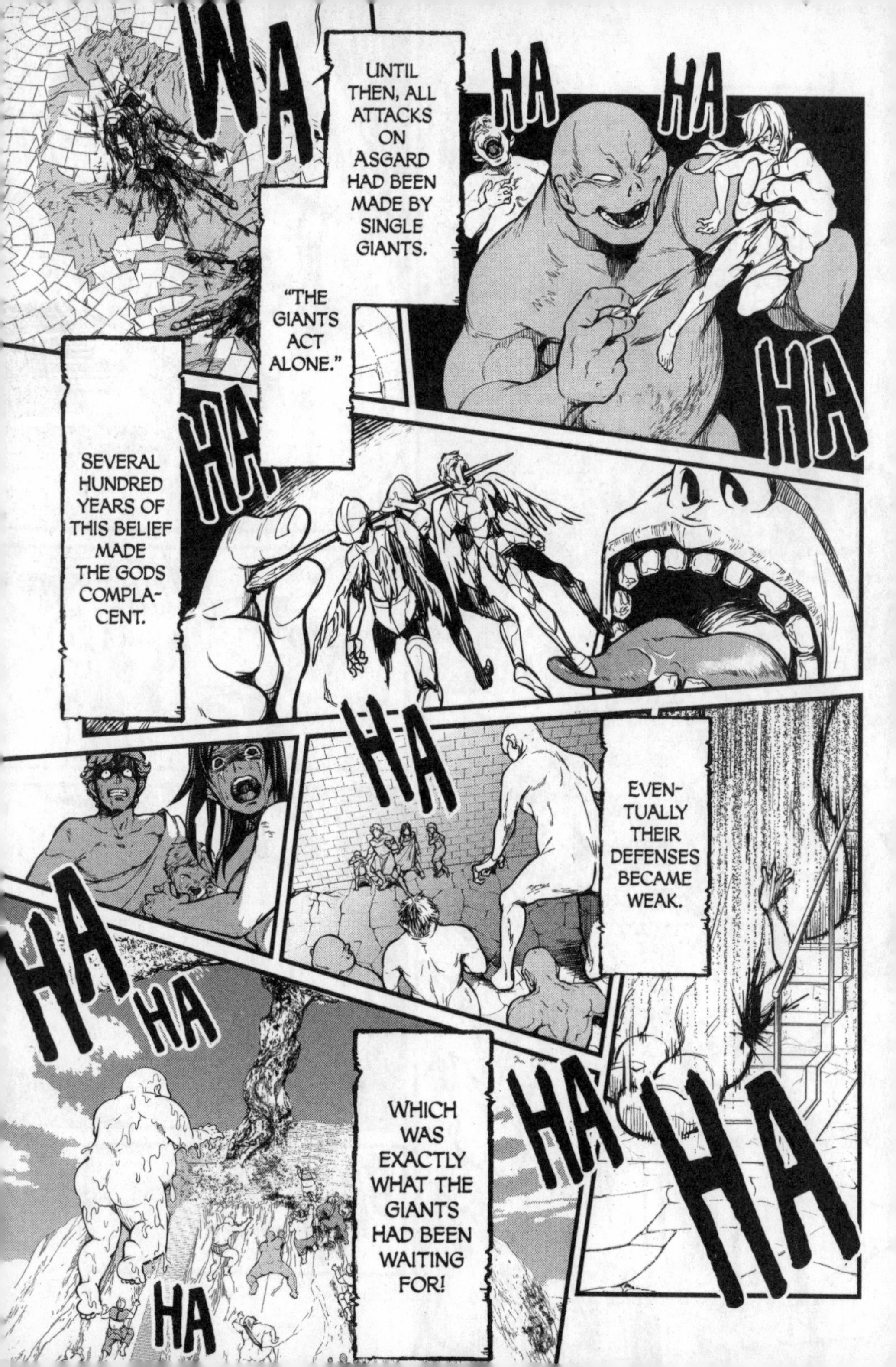
HA
HA
UNTIL THEN, ALL ATTACKS ON ASGARD HAD BEEN MADE BY SINGLE GIANTS.
"THE GIANTS ACT ALONE."
HA
WA
HA
SEVERAL HUNDRED YEARS OF THIS BELIEF MADE THE GODS COMPLACENT.
EVENTUALLY THEIR DEFENSES BECAME WEAK.
HA
HA
HA
HA
HA
WHICH WAS EXACTLY WHAT THE GIANTS HAD BEEN WAITING FOR!
HA
HA

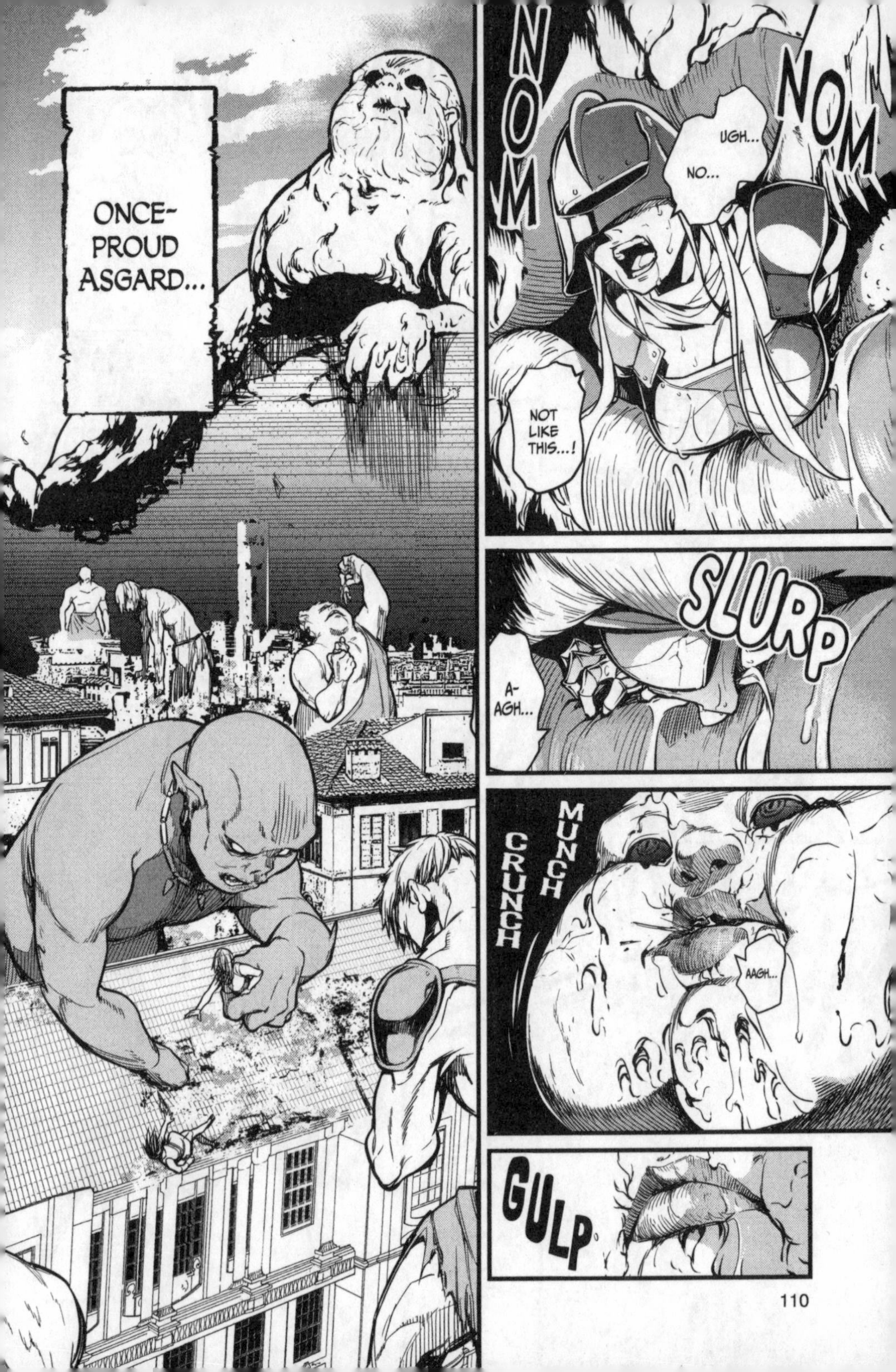
NOM
NOM
UGH...
NO...
NOT LIKE THIS...!
SLURP
A-AGH...
MUNCH
CRUNCH
AAGH...
GULP
ONCE-PROUD ASGARD...

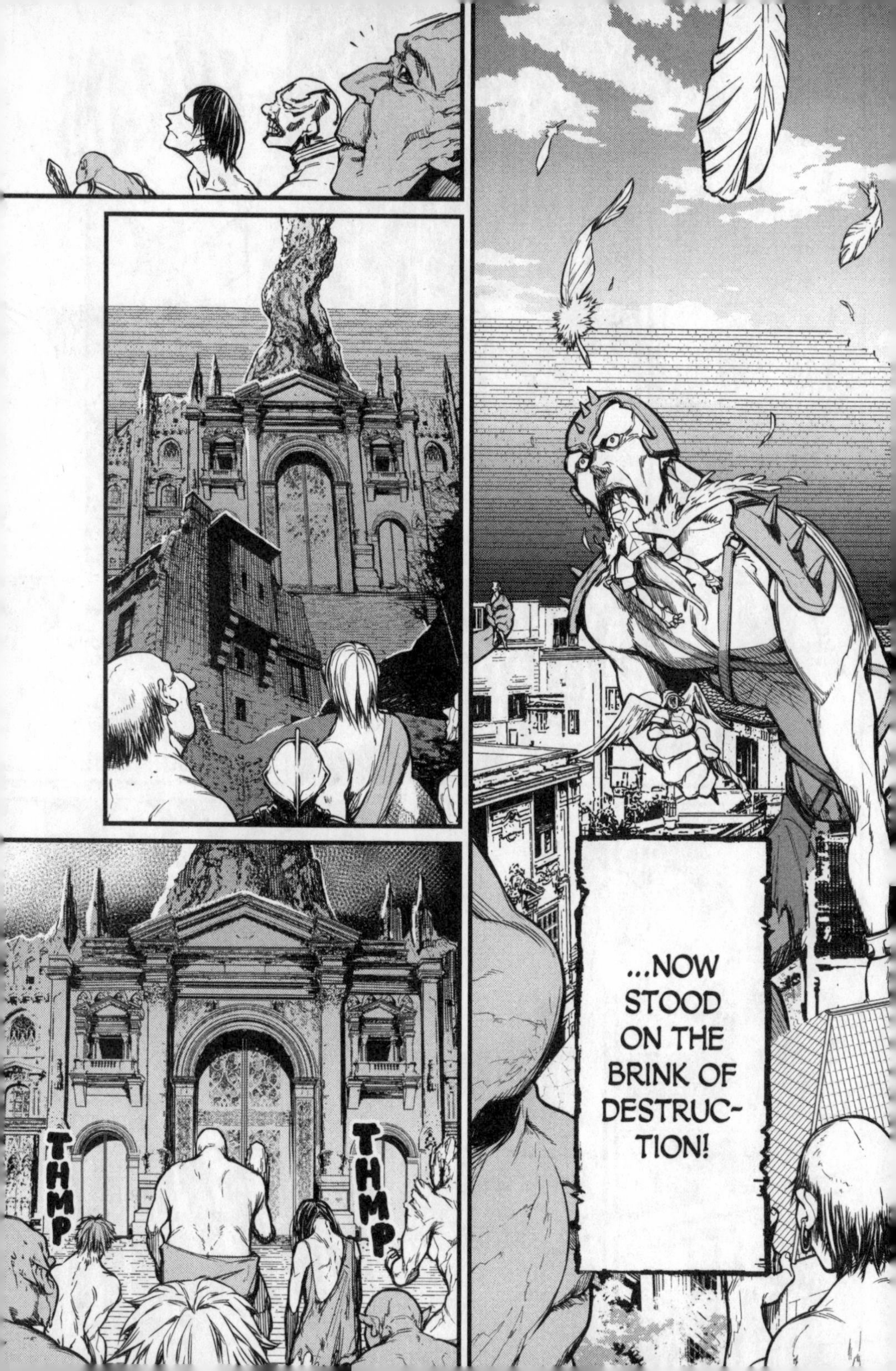
...NOW STOOD ON THE BRINK OF DESTRUCTION!
THMP
THMP

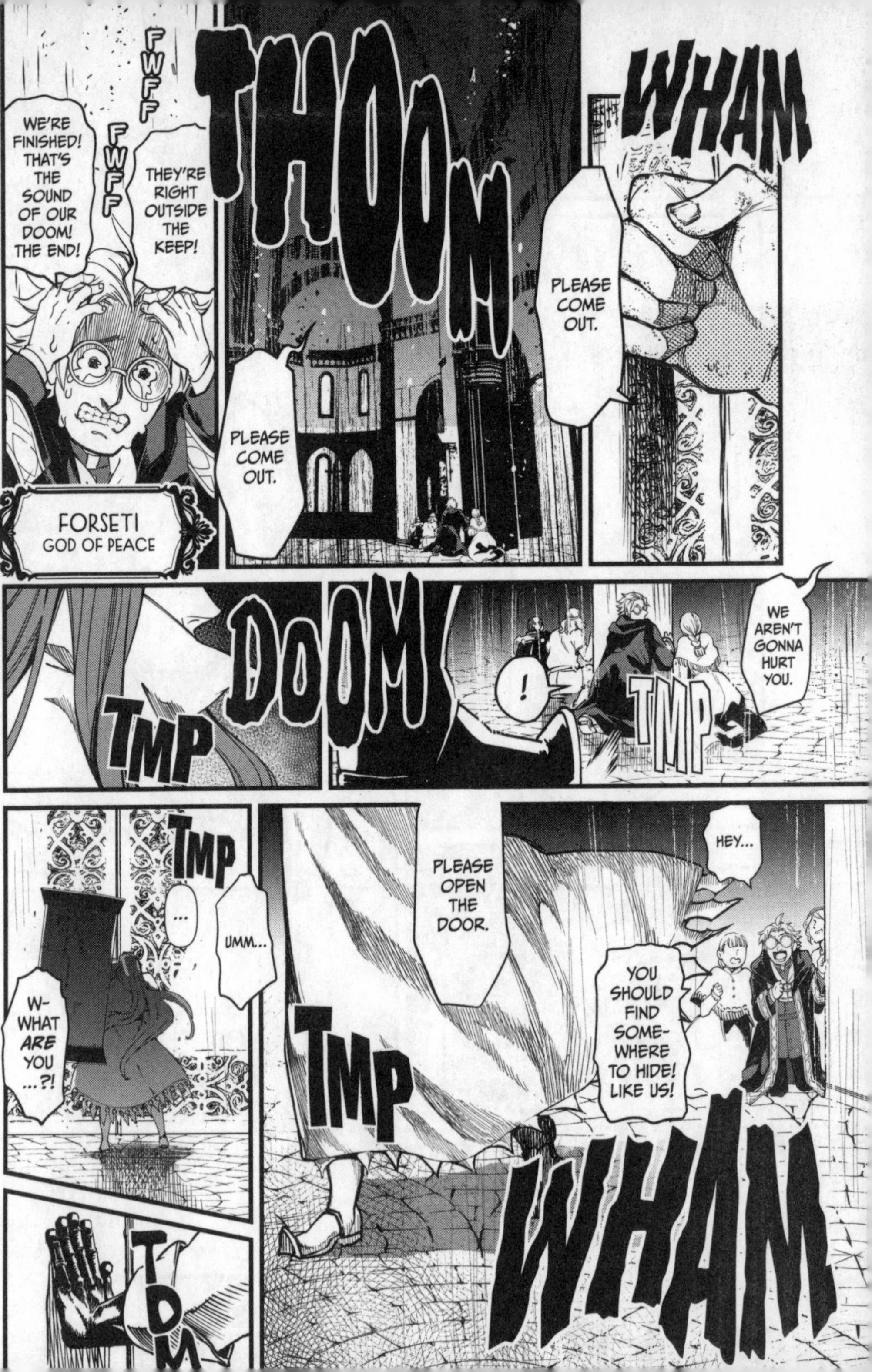
WHAM
PLEASE COME OUT.
THOOM
PLEASE COME OUT.
FWFF
THEY'RE RIGHT OUTSIDE THE KEEP!
FWFF
WE'RE FINISHED! THAT'S THE SOUND OF OUR DOOM! THE END!
FORSETI
GOD OF PEACE
WE AREN'T GONNA HURT YOU.
TMP
!
DOOM
TMP
HEY...
YOU SHOULD FIND SOME-WHERE TO HIDE! LIKE US!
PLEASE OPEN THE DOOR.
TMP
WHAM
TMP
...
UMM...
W-WHAT ARE YOU ...?!
TDM

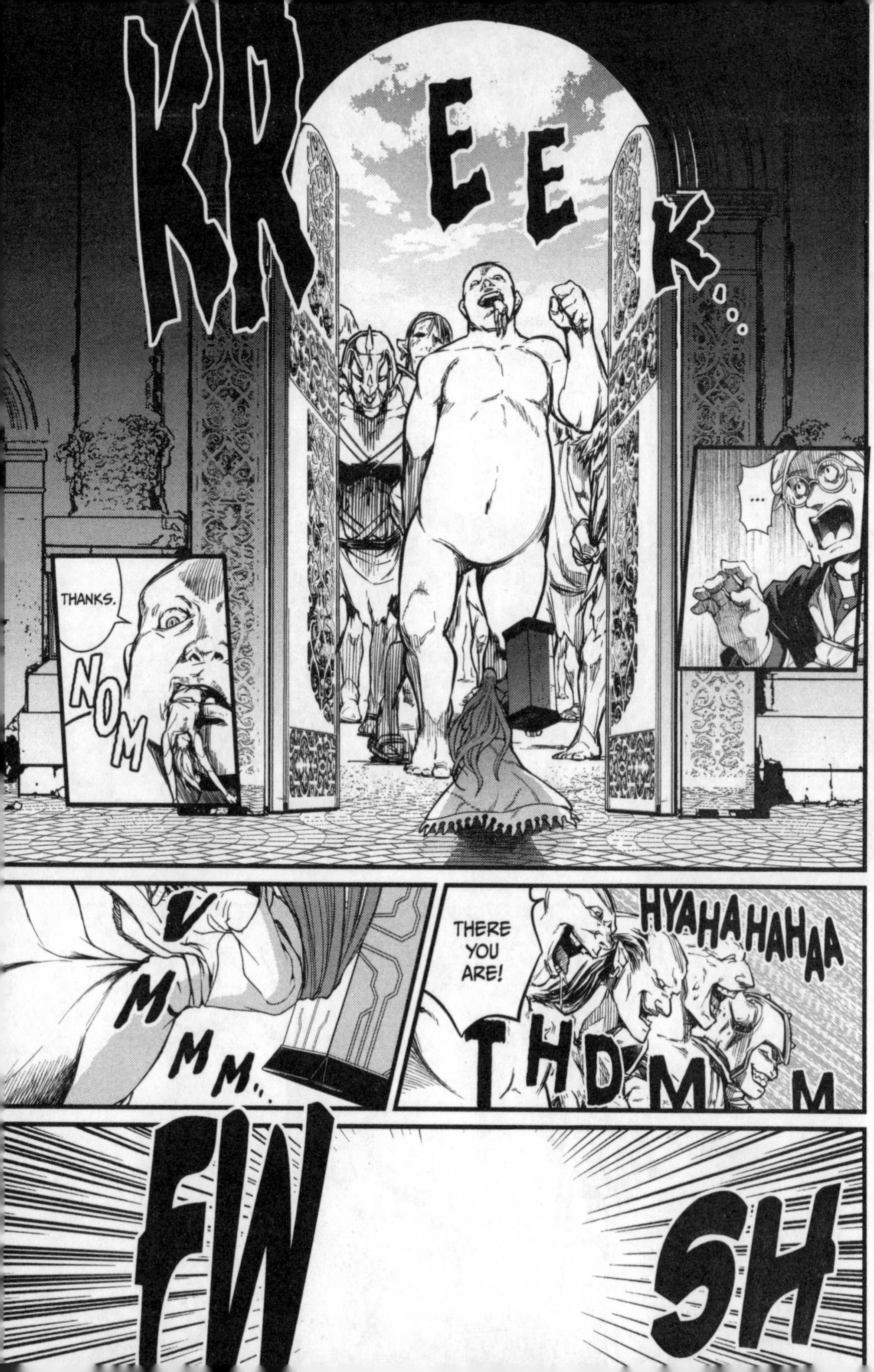
KREEK...
...
THANKS.
NOM
HYAHA HAHAA
THERE YOU ARE!
THDMM M
MMM...
FWSH

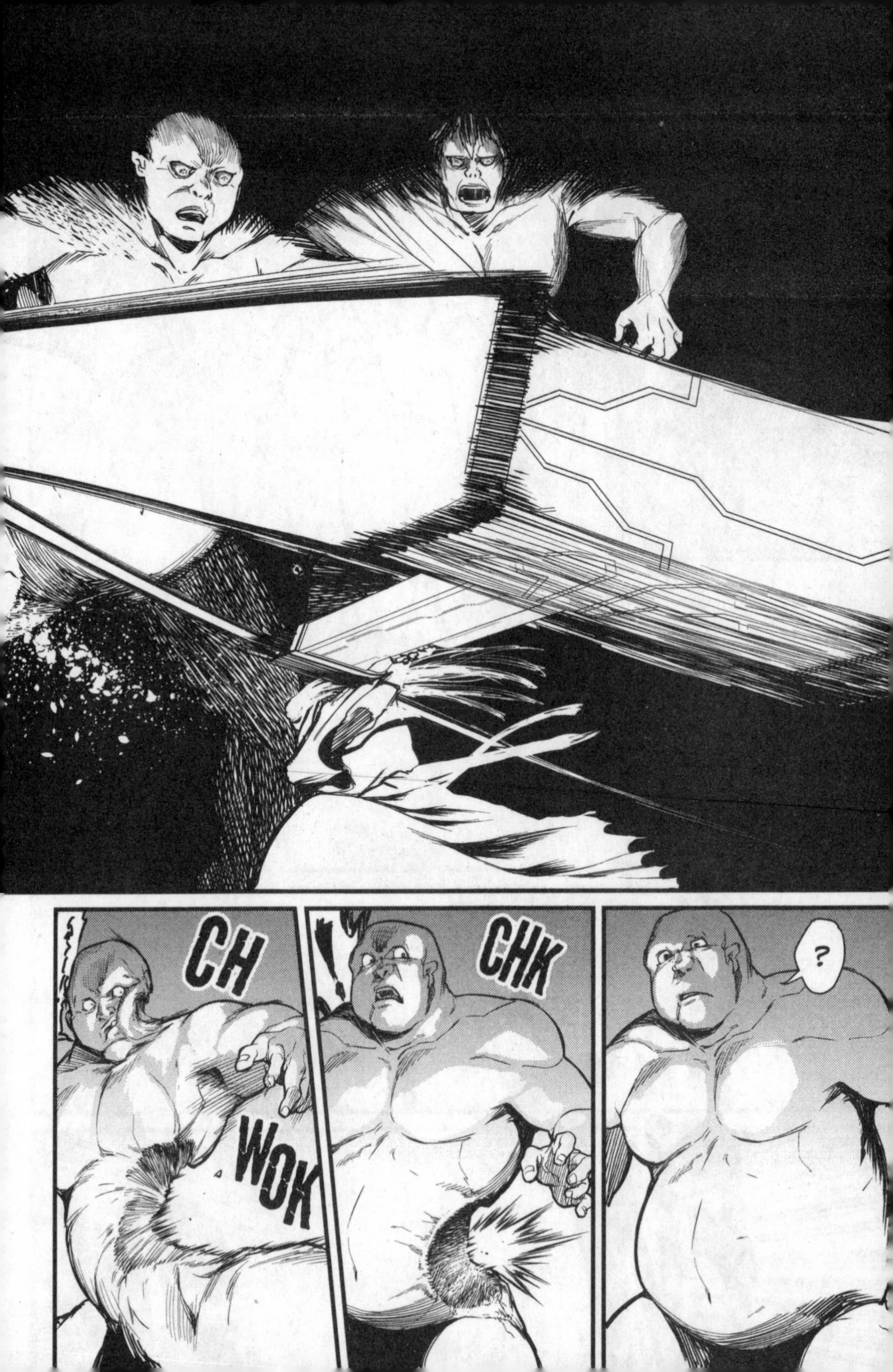
?
CHK
CH
WOK

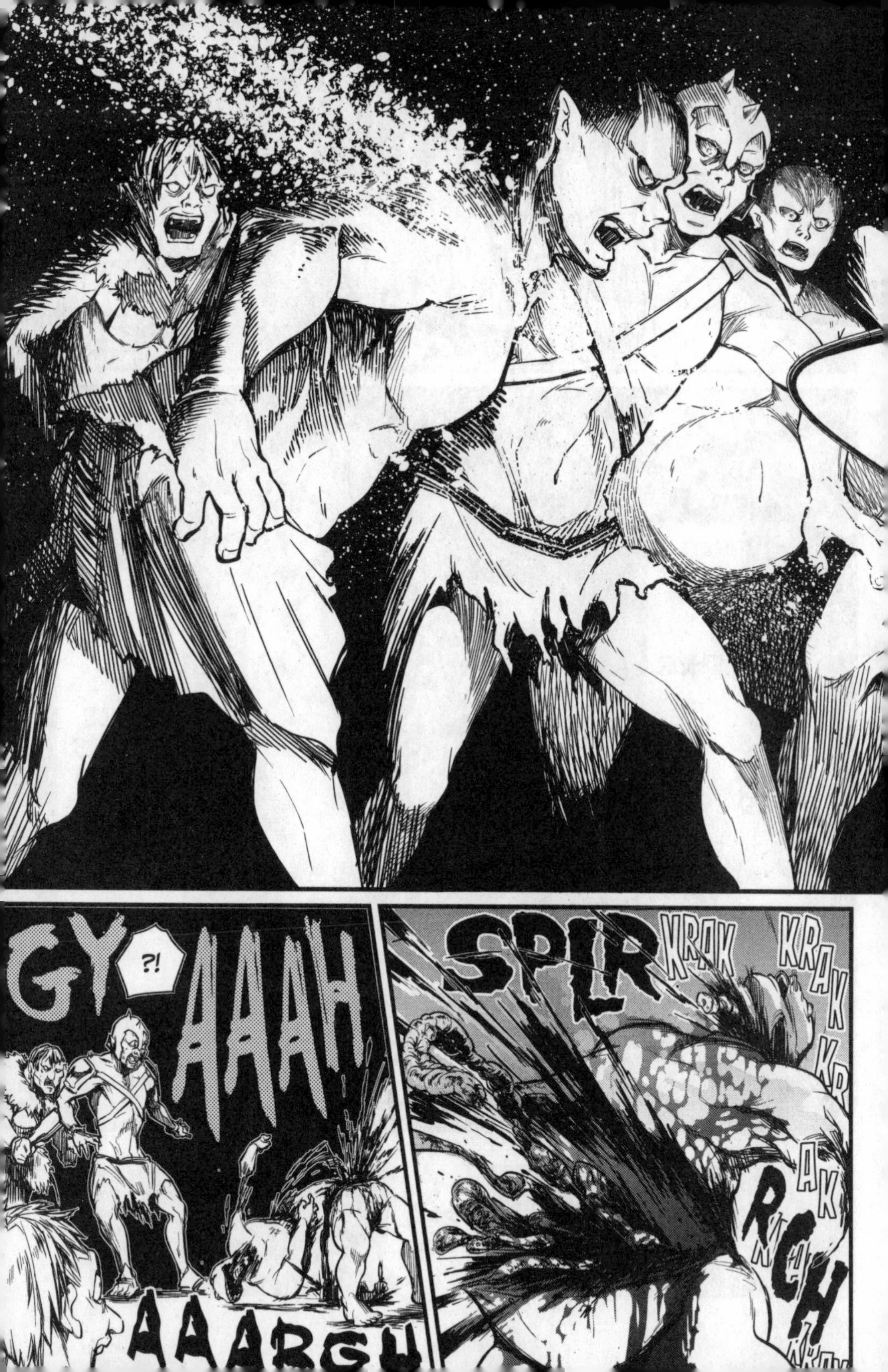
SPLR
KRAK
KRAK
KRAK
KR
AK
RRCH
GY
?!
AAAH
AAARGH

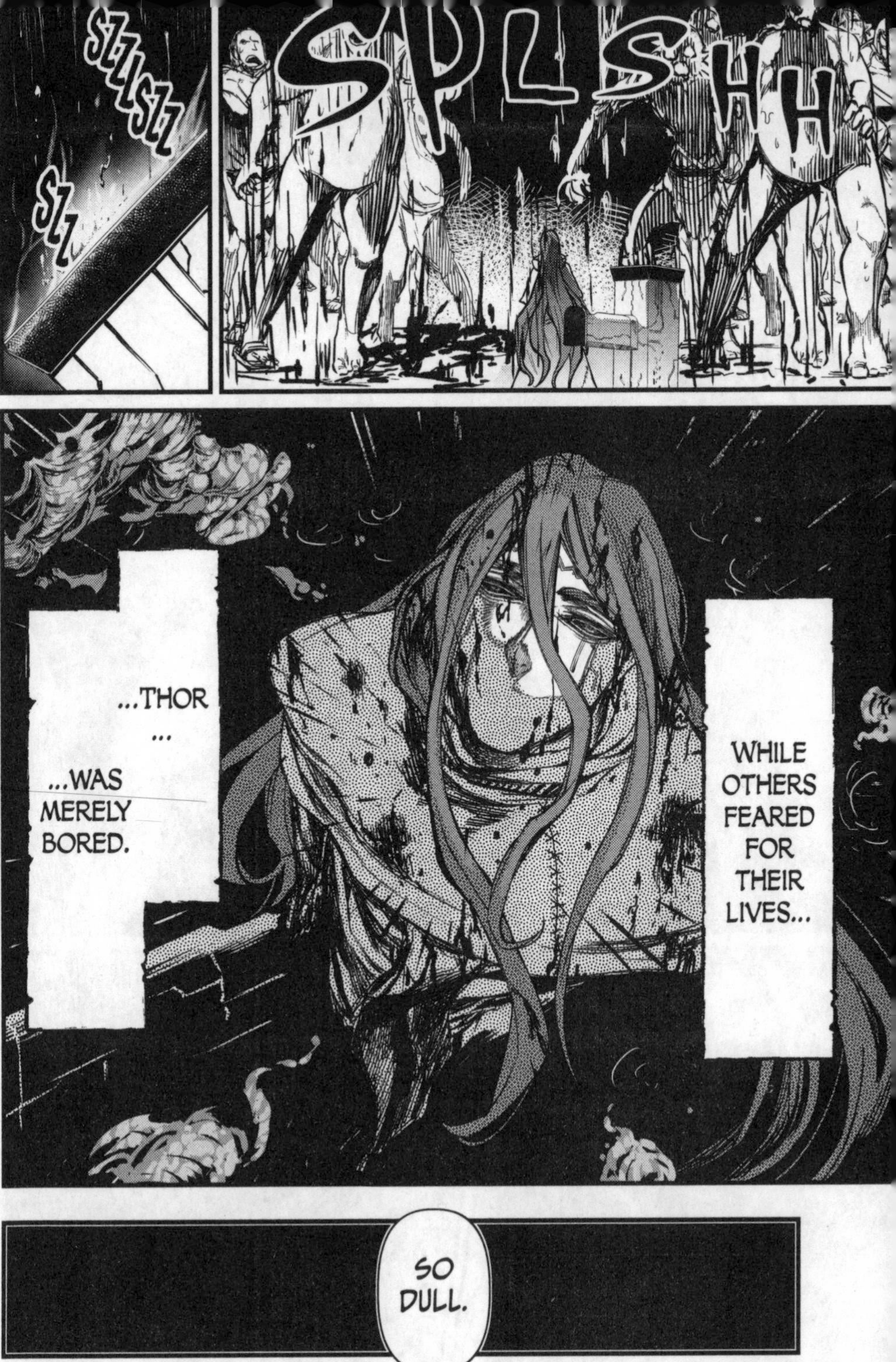
SPLSHH
SZZ SZZ SZZ
SZZ
WHILE OTHERS FEARED FOR THEIR LIVES...
...THOR
...
...WAS MERELY BORED.
SO DULL.

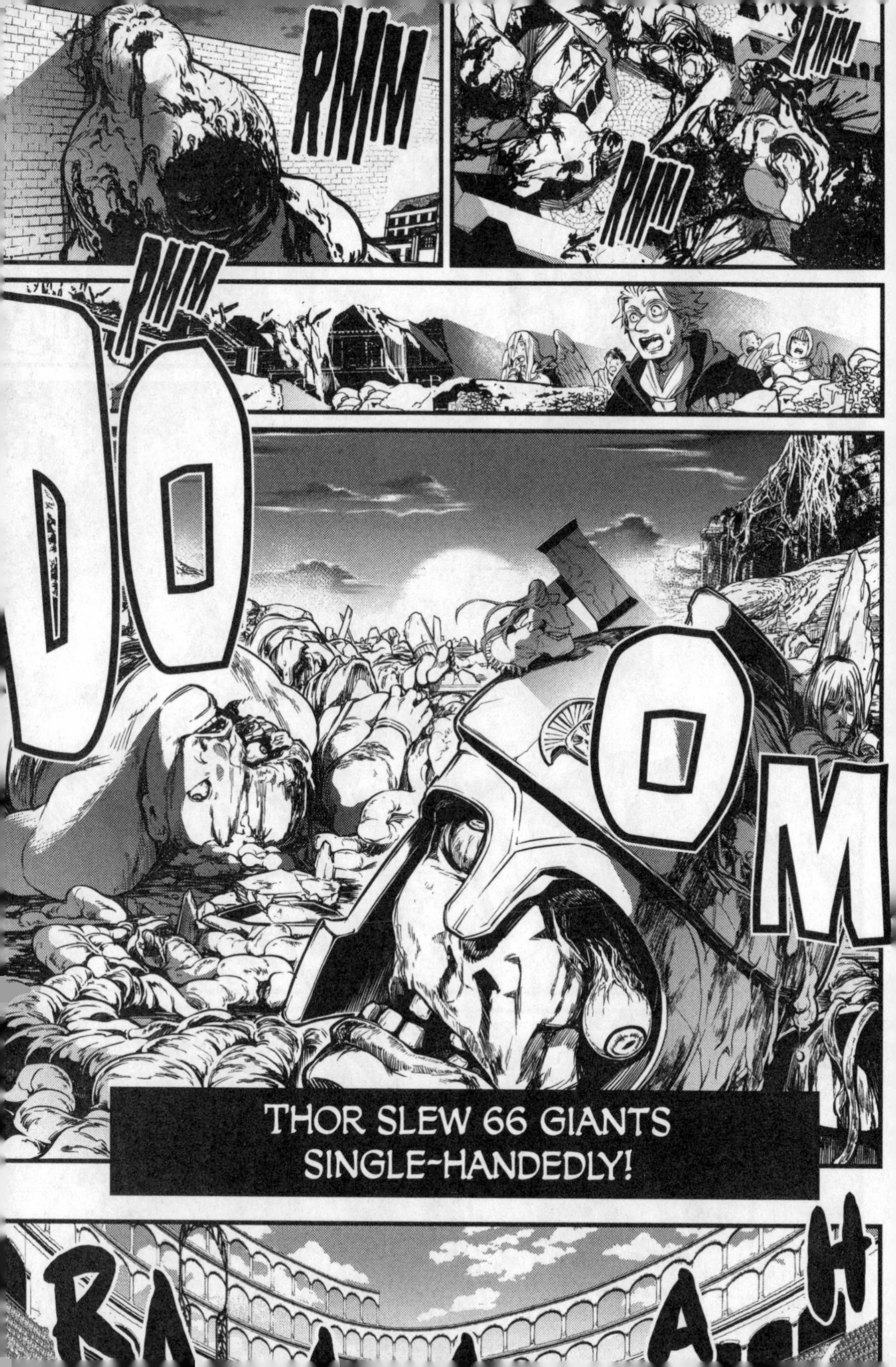

RMM
RMM
RMM
RMM
DOOM
THOR SLEW 66 GIANTS SINGLE-HANDEDLY!

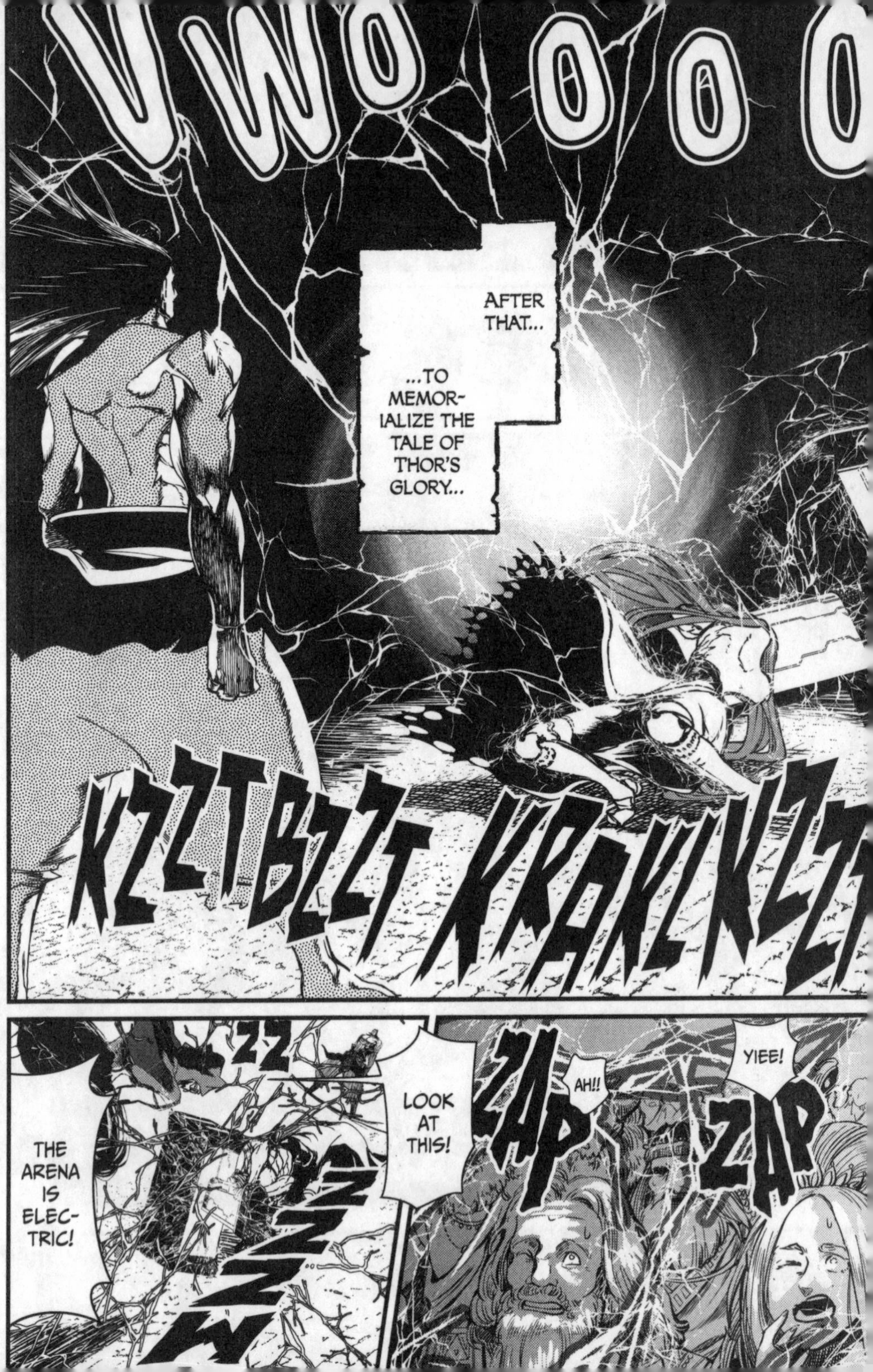
VWOOOO
AFTER THAT...
...TO MEMORIALIZE THE TALE OF THOR'S GLORY...
KZZT BZZT KRAK KZZT
YIEE!
ZAP
AH!!
ZAP
LOOK AT THIS!
ZZ
THE ARENA IS ELECTRIC!

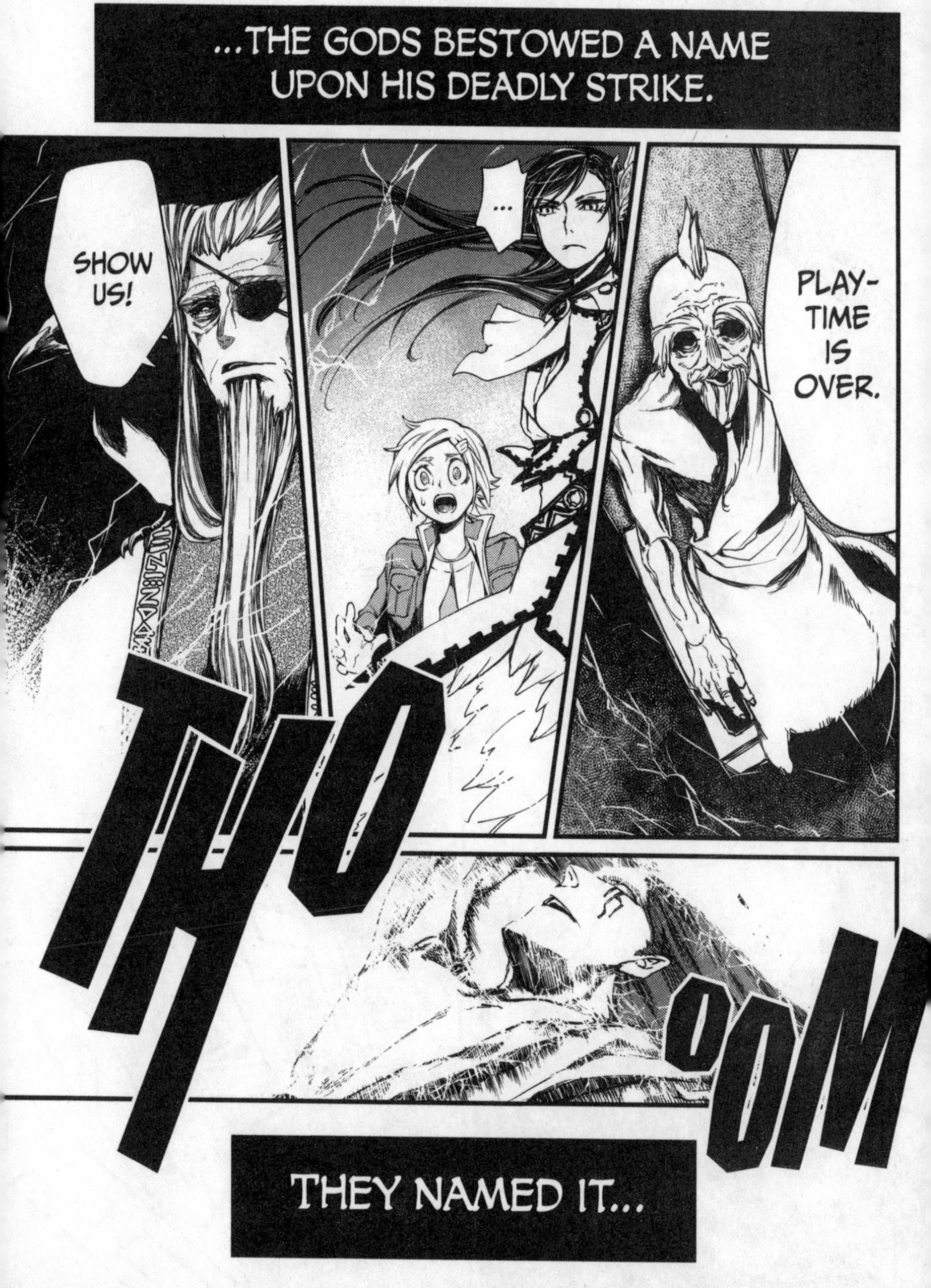
...THE GODS BESTOWED A NAME UPON HIS DEADLY STRIKE.
PLAY-TIME IS OVER.
...
SHOW US!
THOOOM
THEY NAMED IT...

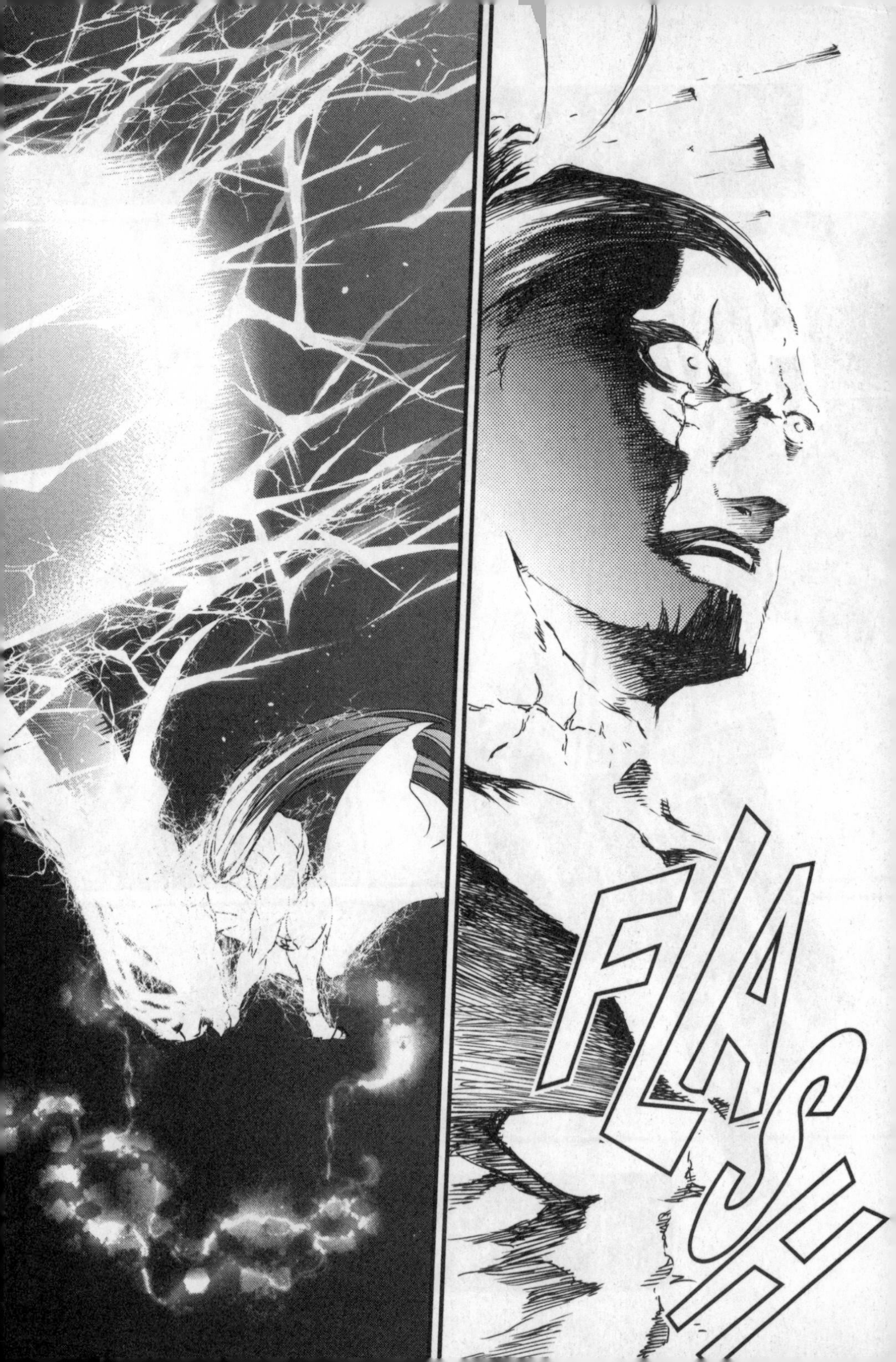
FLASH

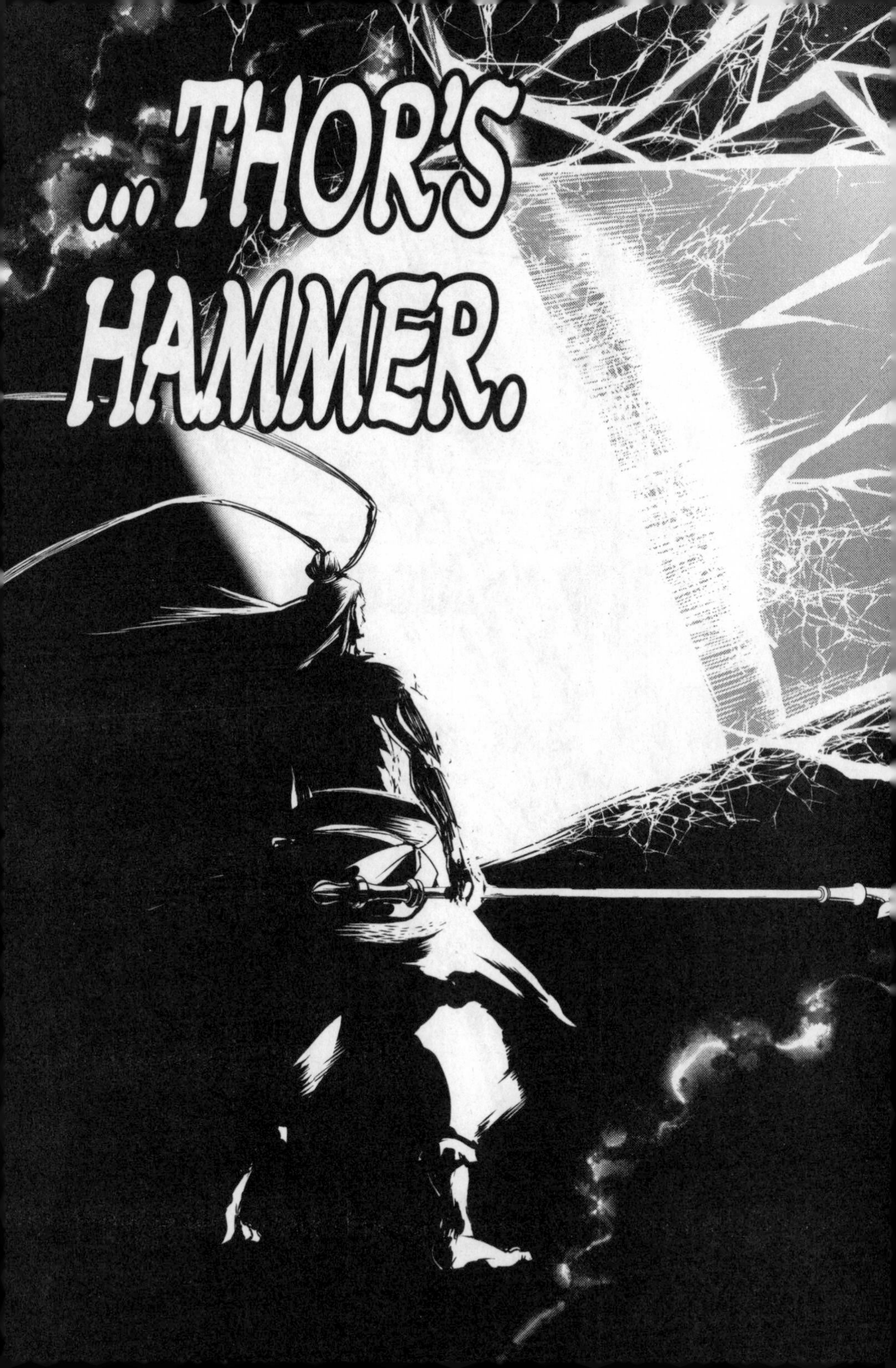
...THOR'S HAMMER.

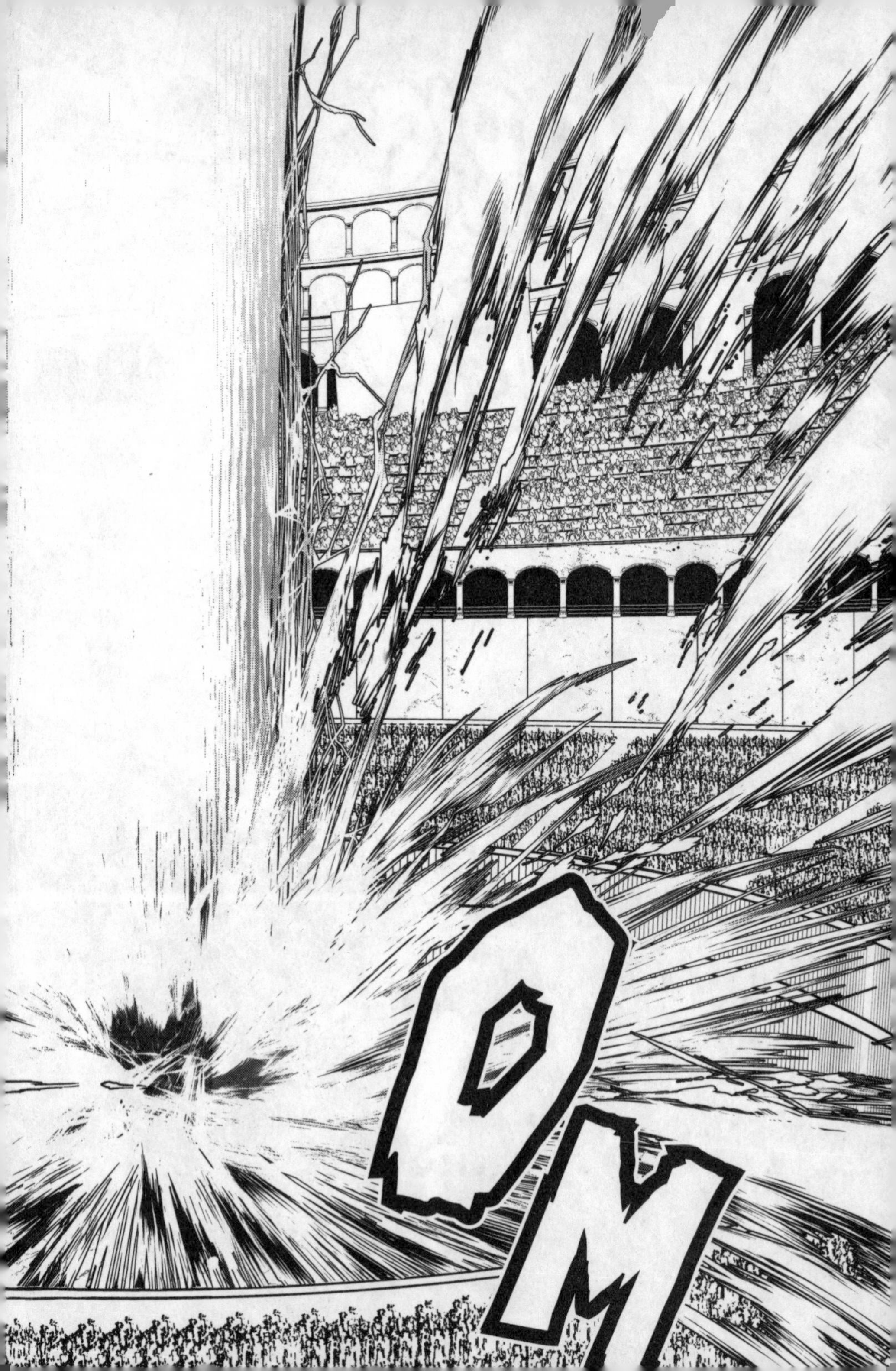
OM

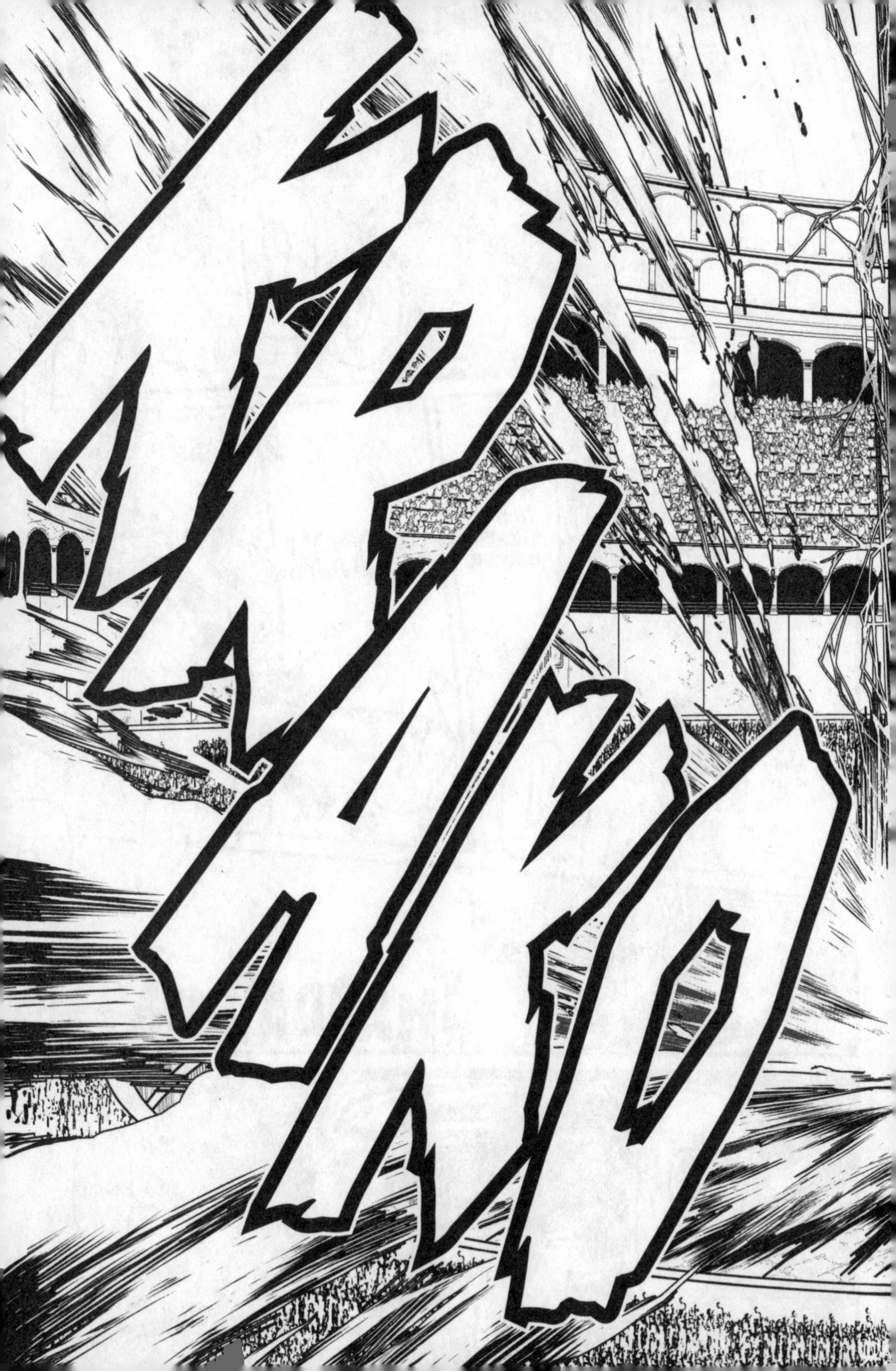

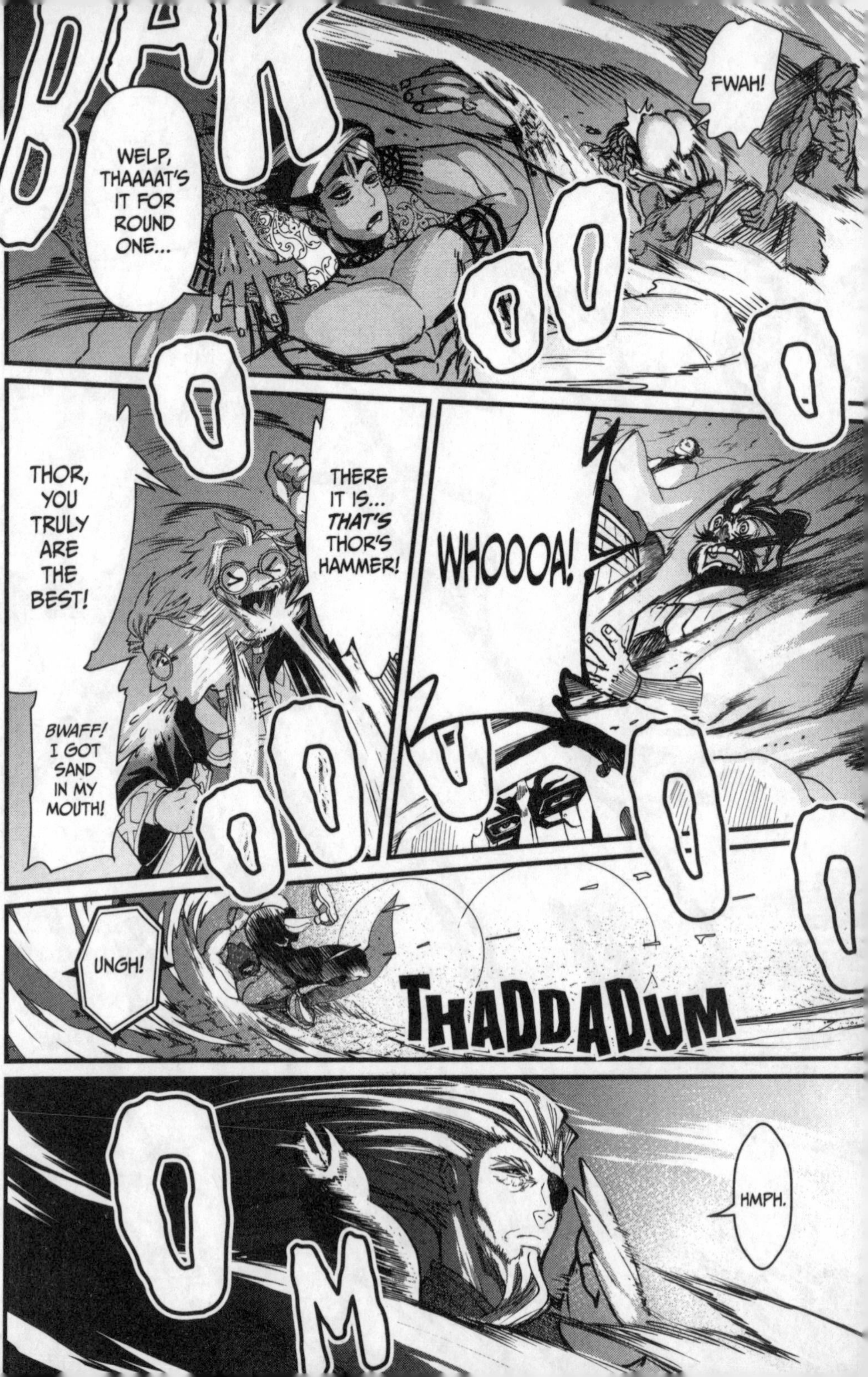
FWAH!
WELP, THAAAAT'S IT FOR ROUND ONE...
WHOOOA!
THERE IT IS... *THAT'S* THOR'S HAMMER!
THOR, YOU TRULY ARE THE BEST!
BWAFF! I GOT SAND IN MY MOUTH!
UNGH!
THADDADUM
HMPH.

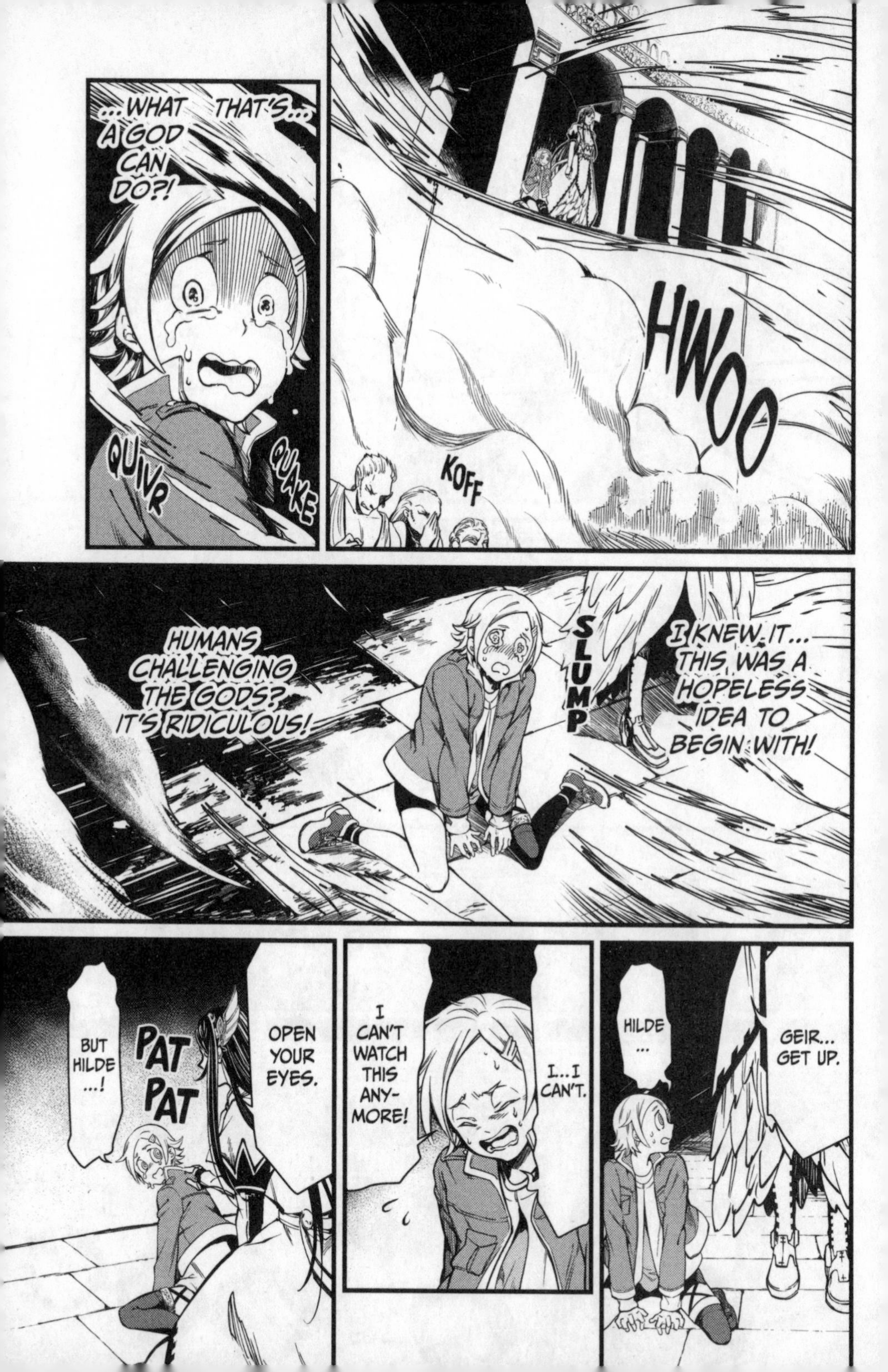
HWOO
KOFF
THAT'S...
...WHAT A GOD CAN DO?!
QUIVR
QUAKE
I KNEW IT... THIS WAS A HOPELESS IDEA TO BEGIN WITH!
SLUMP
HUMANS CHALLENGING THE GODS? IT'S RIDICULOUS!
GEIR... GET UP.
HILDE ...
I...I CAN'T.
I CAN'T WATCH THIS ANYMORE!
OPEN YOUR EYES.
PAT PAT
BUT HILDE ...!

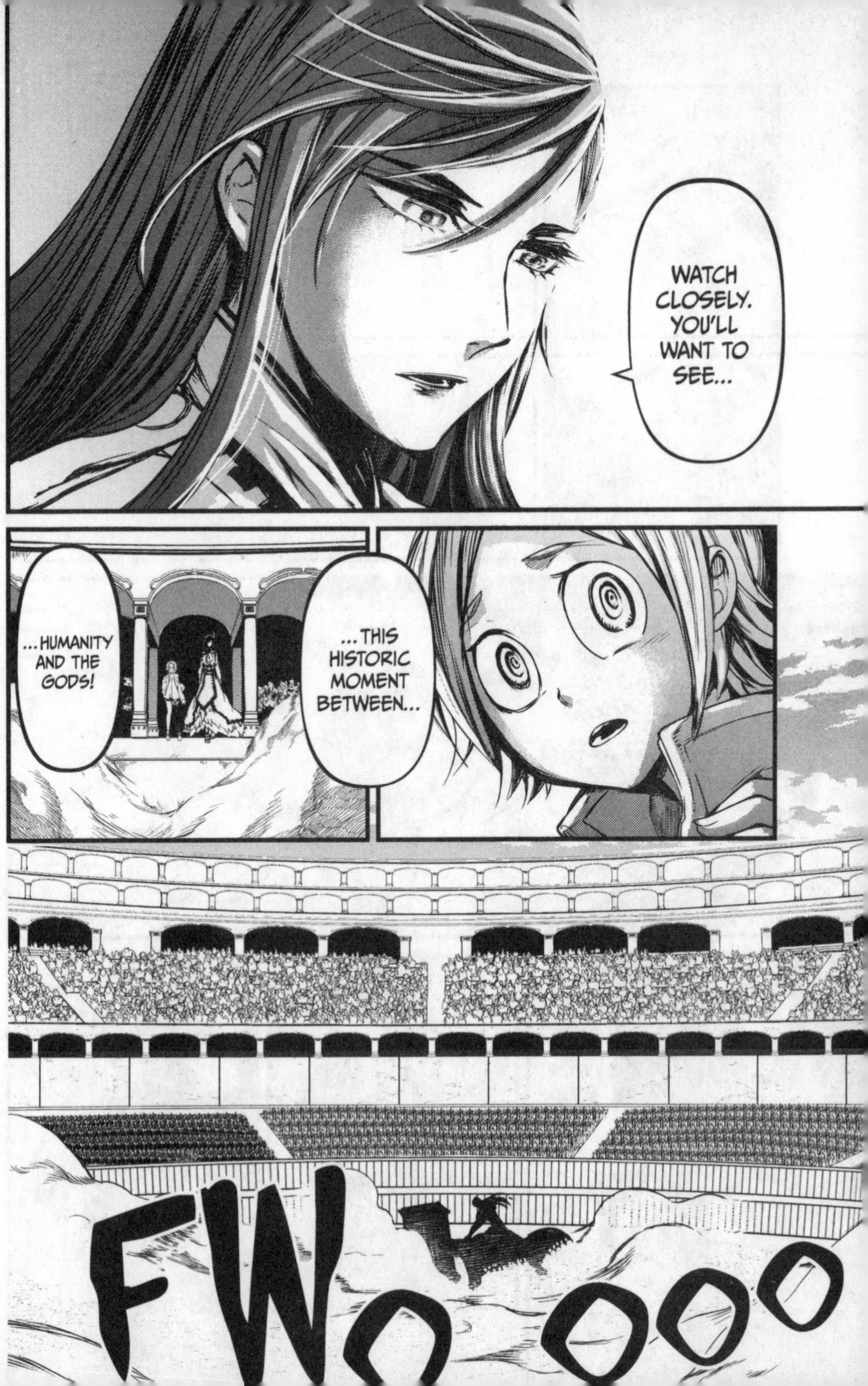
WATCH CLOSELY. YOU'LL WANT TO SEE...
...THIS HISTORIC MOMENT BETWEEN...
...HUMANITY AND THE GODS!
FWOOOO

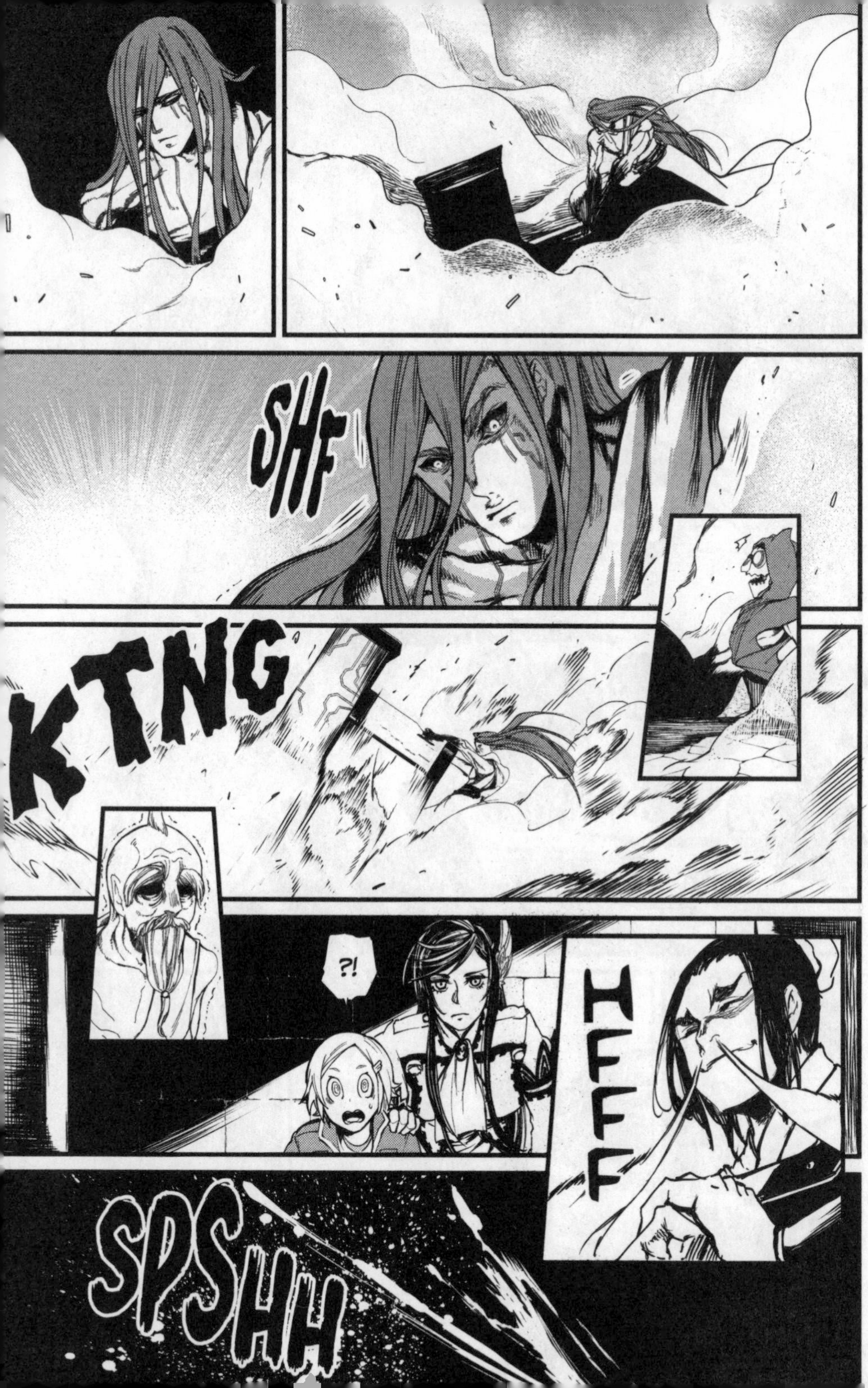
SHF
KTNG
HFFF
?!
SPSHH

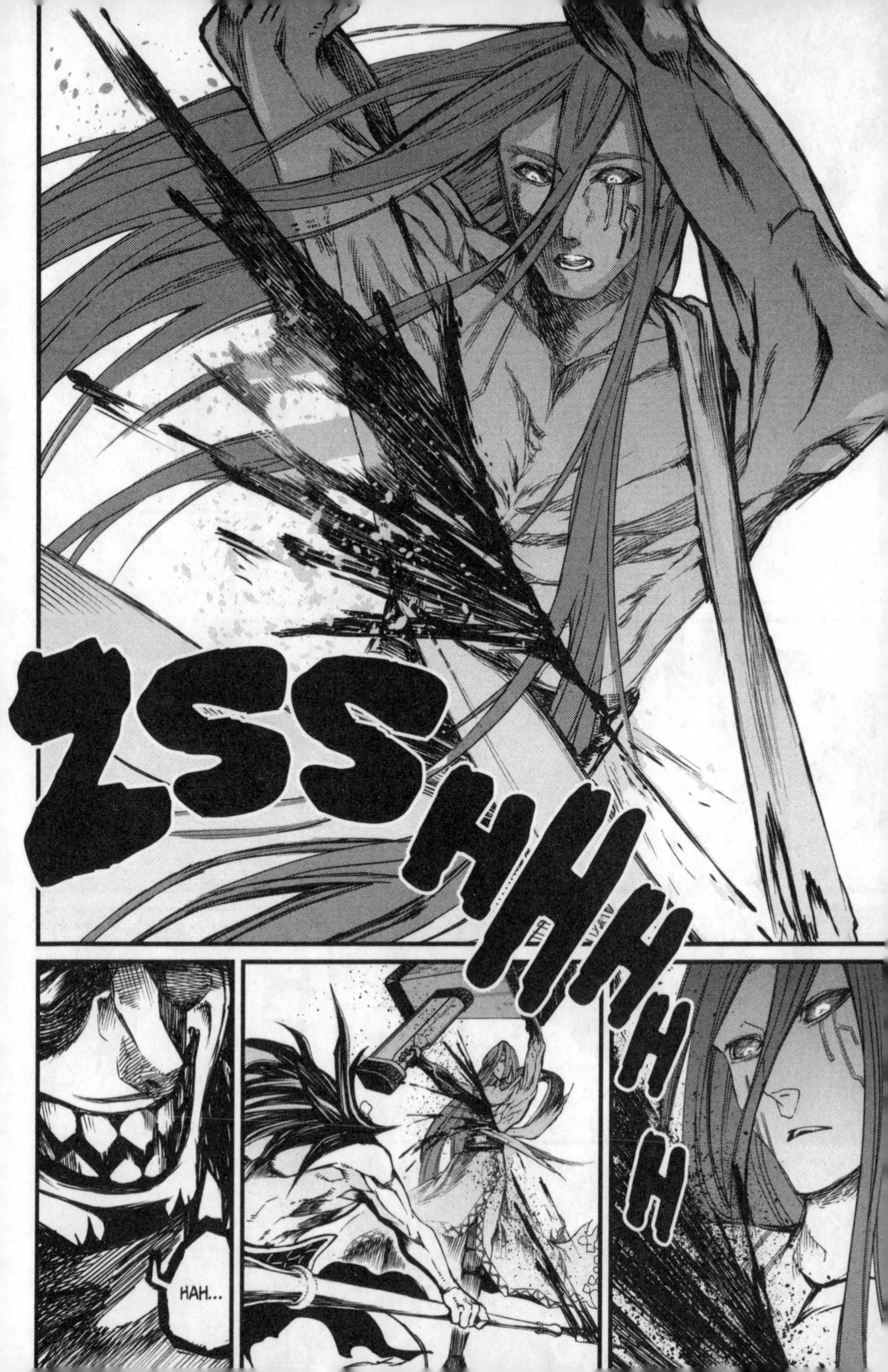
ZSSHHHHHHH
HAH...

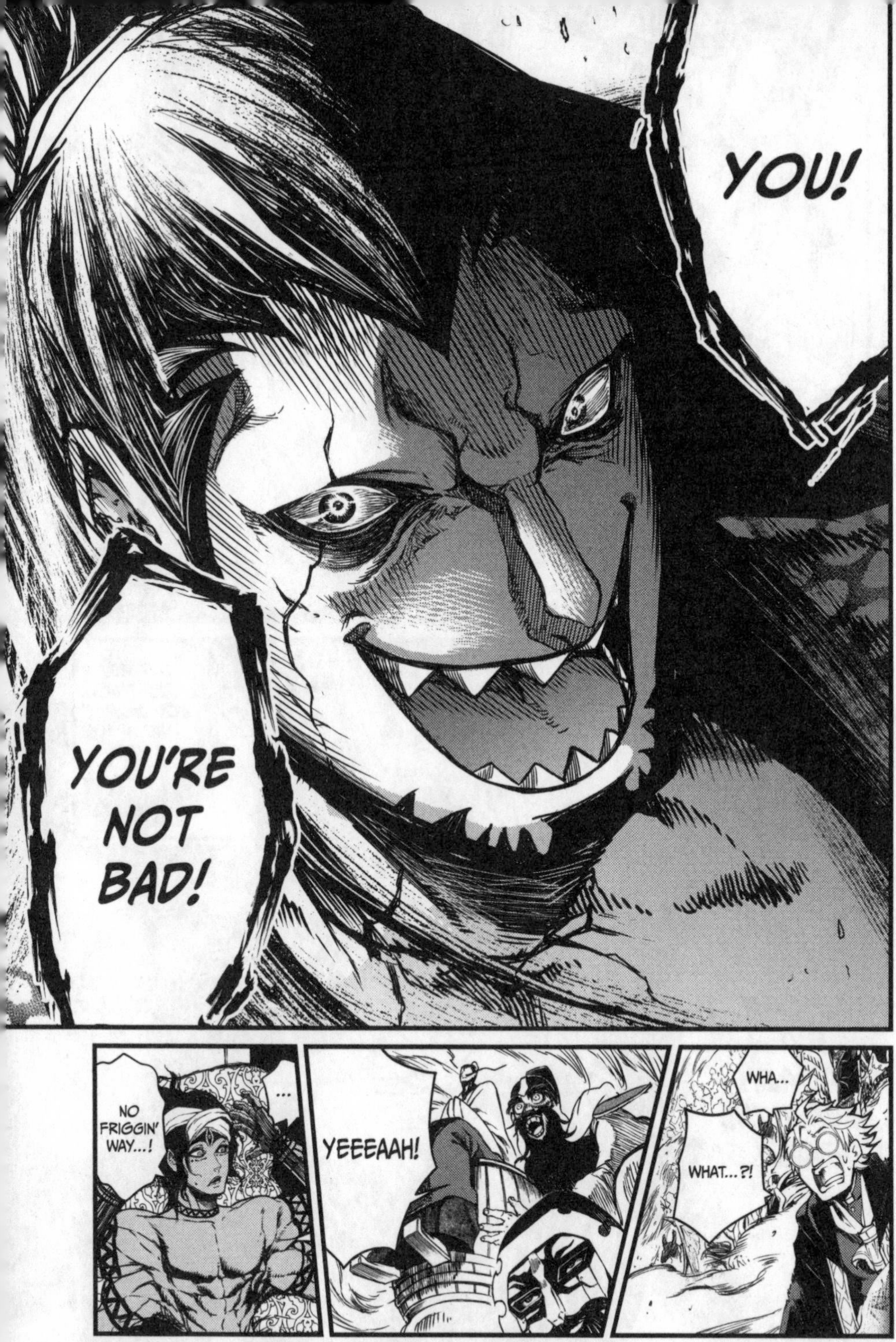
YOU!
YOU'RE NOT BAD!
WHA...
WHAT...?!
YEEEAAH!
...
NO FRIGGIN' WAY...!

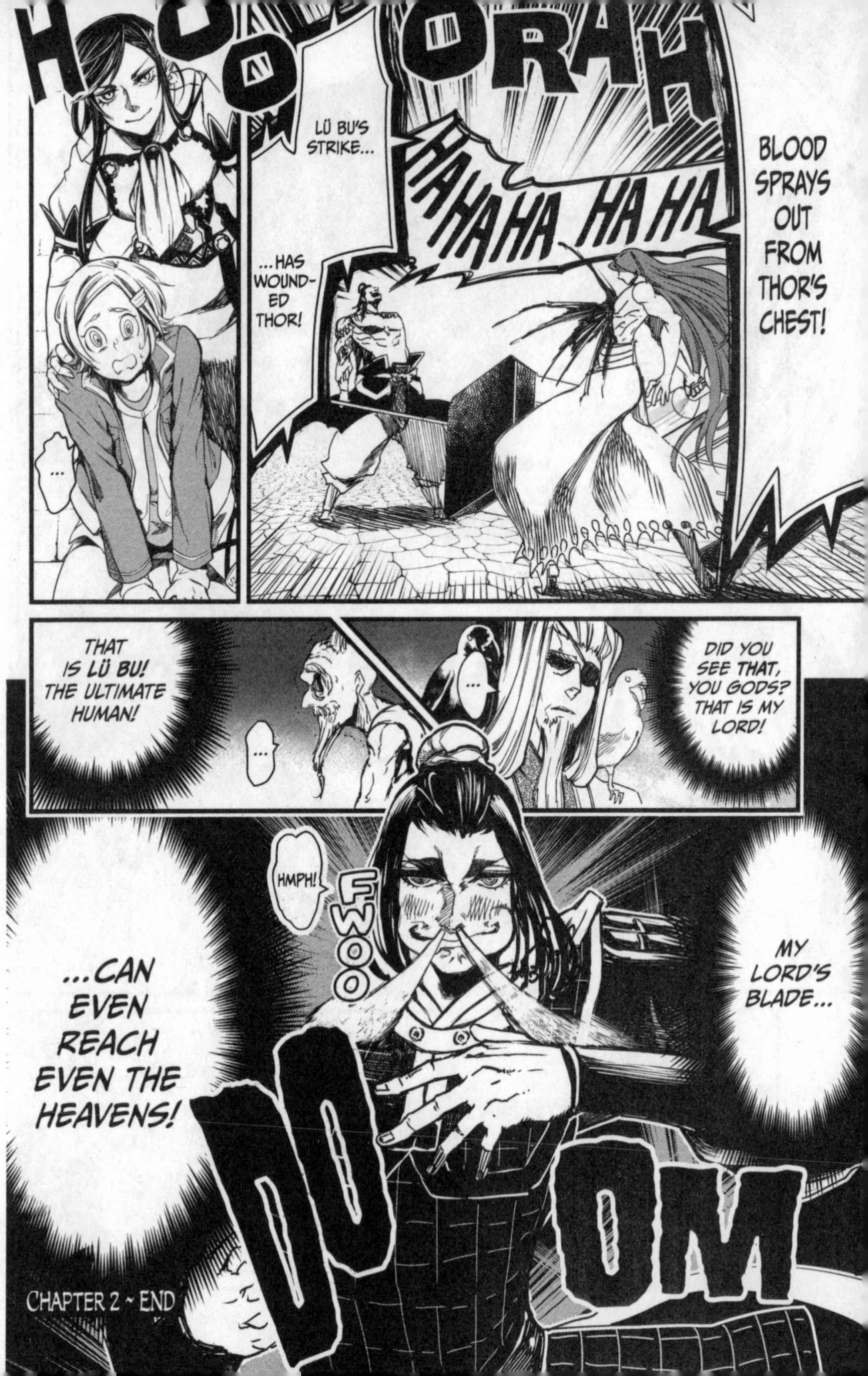
HOOORAH
BLOOD SPRAYS OUT FROM THOR'S CHEST!
HAHAHA HA HA
LÜ BU'S STRIKE...
...HAS WOUND-ED THOR!
...
DID YOU SEE THAT, YOU GODS? THAT IS MY LORD!
...
...
THAT IS LÜ BU! THE ULTIMATE HUMAN!
MY LORD'S BLADE...
HMPH!
FWOO
...CAN EVEN REACH EVEN THE HEAVENS!
DOOM
CHAPTER 2 ~ END

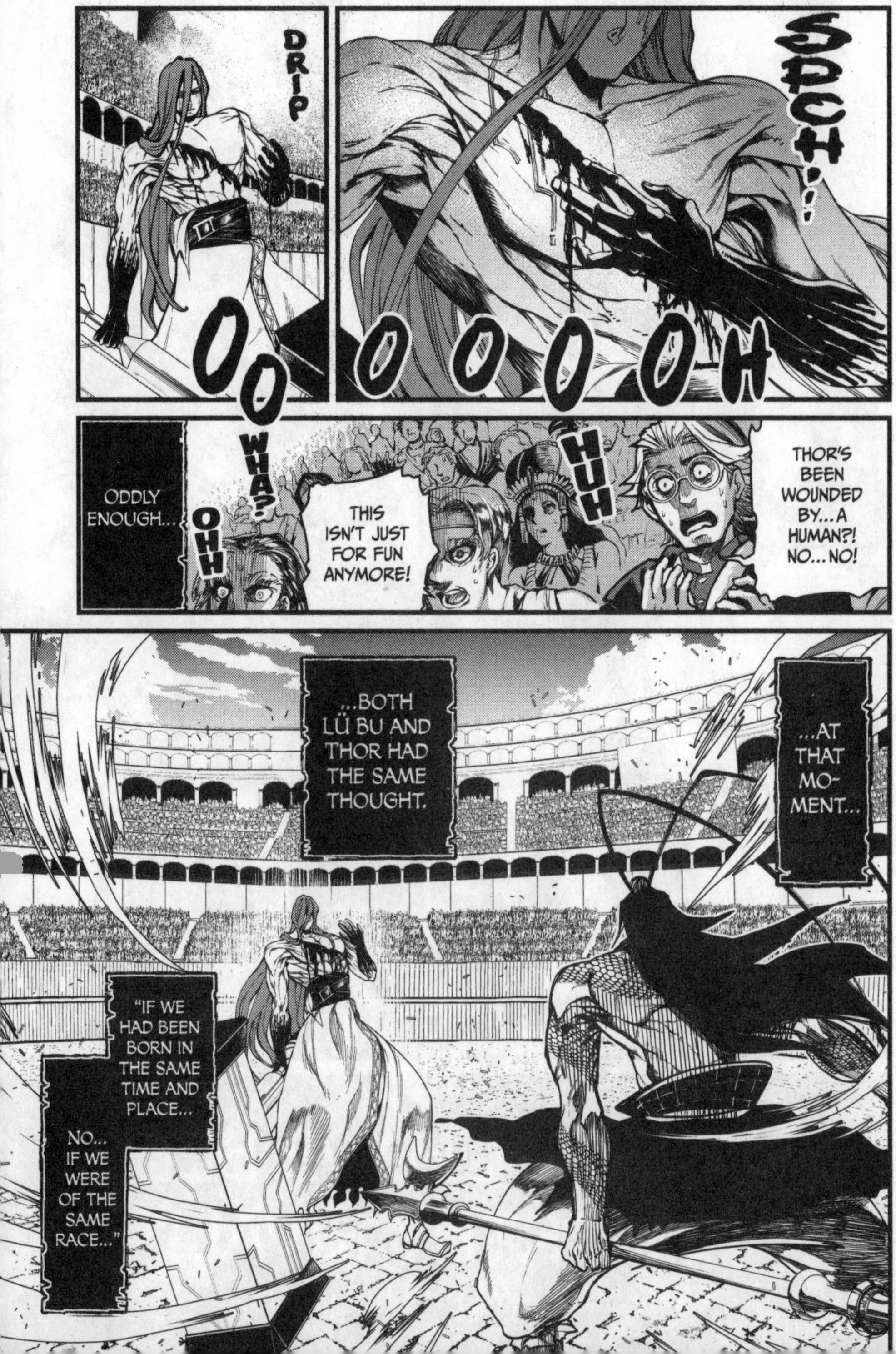
SPCH!!!
OOOOOOOH
DRIP
THOR'S BEEN WOUNDED BY...A HUMAN?! NO...NO!
HUH
THIS ISN'T JUST FOR FUN ANYMORE!
WHA?
OHH
ODDLY ENOUGH...
...AT THAT MO-MENT...
...BOTH LÜ BU AND THOR HAD THE SAME THOUGHT.
"IF WE HAD BEEN BORN IN THE SAME TIME AND PLACE...
NO... IF WE WERE OF THE SAME RACE..."

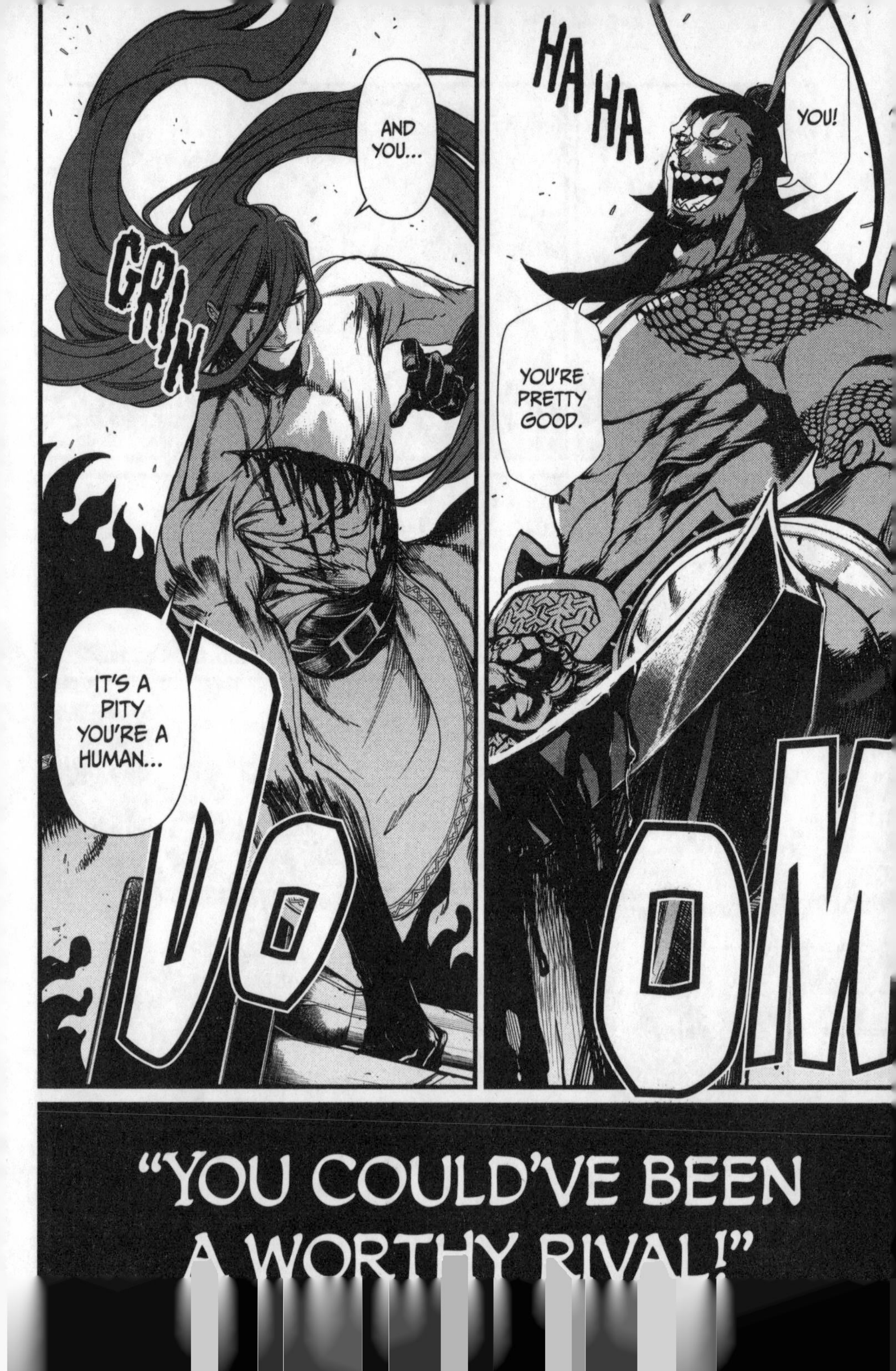
HA HA
YOU!
YOU'RE PRETTY GOOD.
OM
AND YOU...
GRIN
IT'S A PITY YOU'RE A HUMAN...
DO

"YOU COULD'VE BEEN A WORTHY RIVAL!"

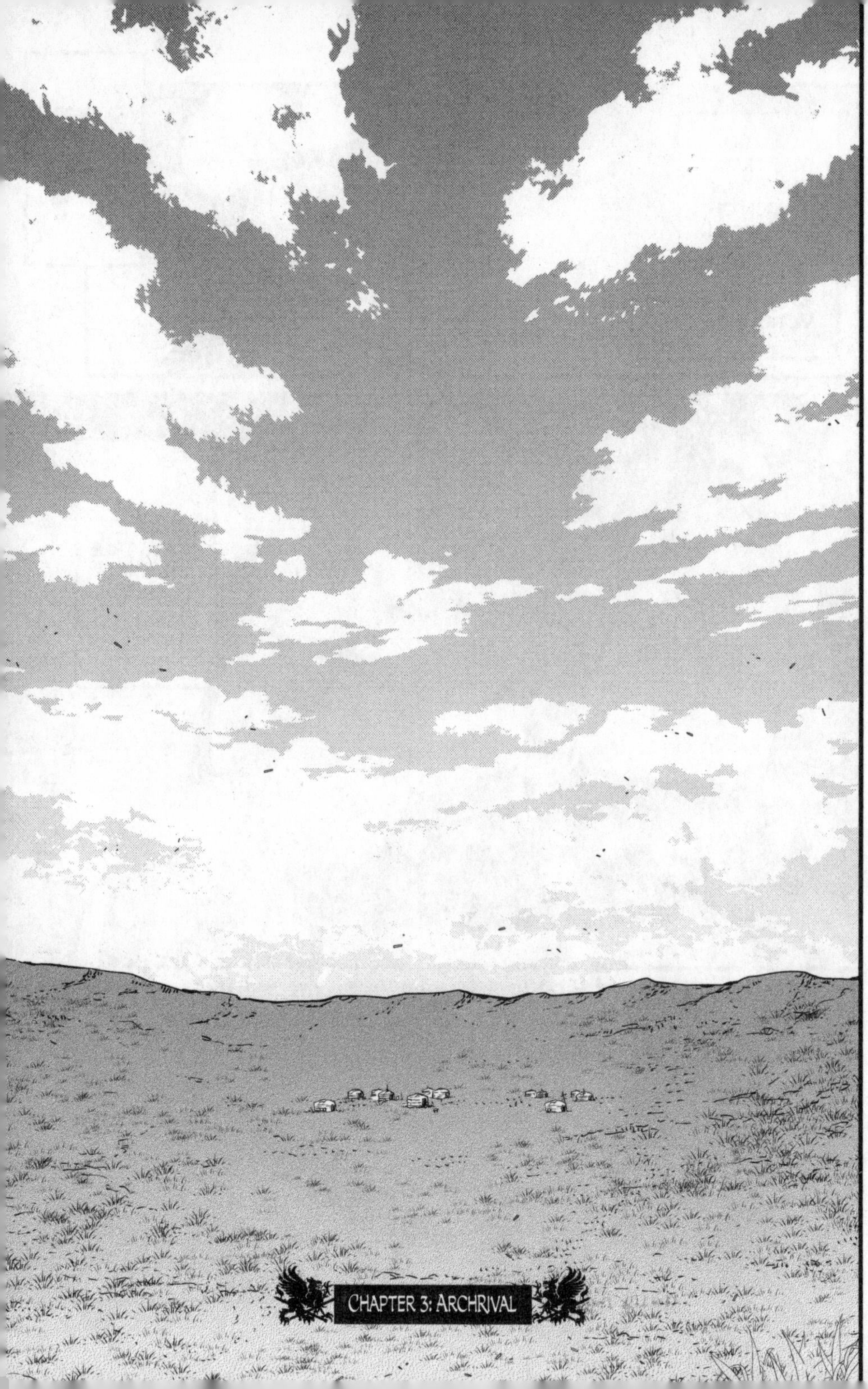
CHAPTER 3: ARCHRIVAL

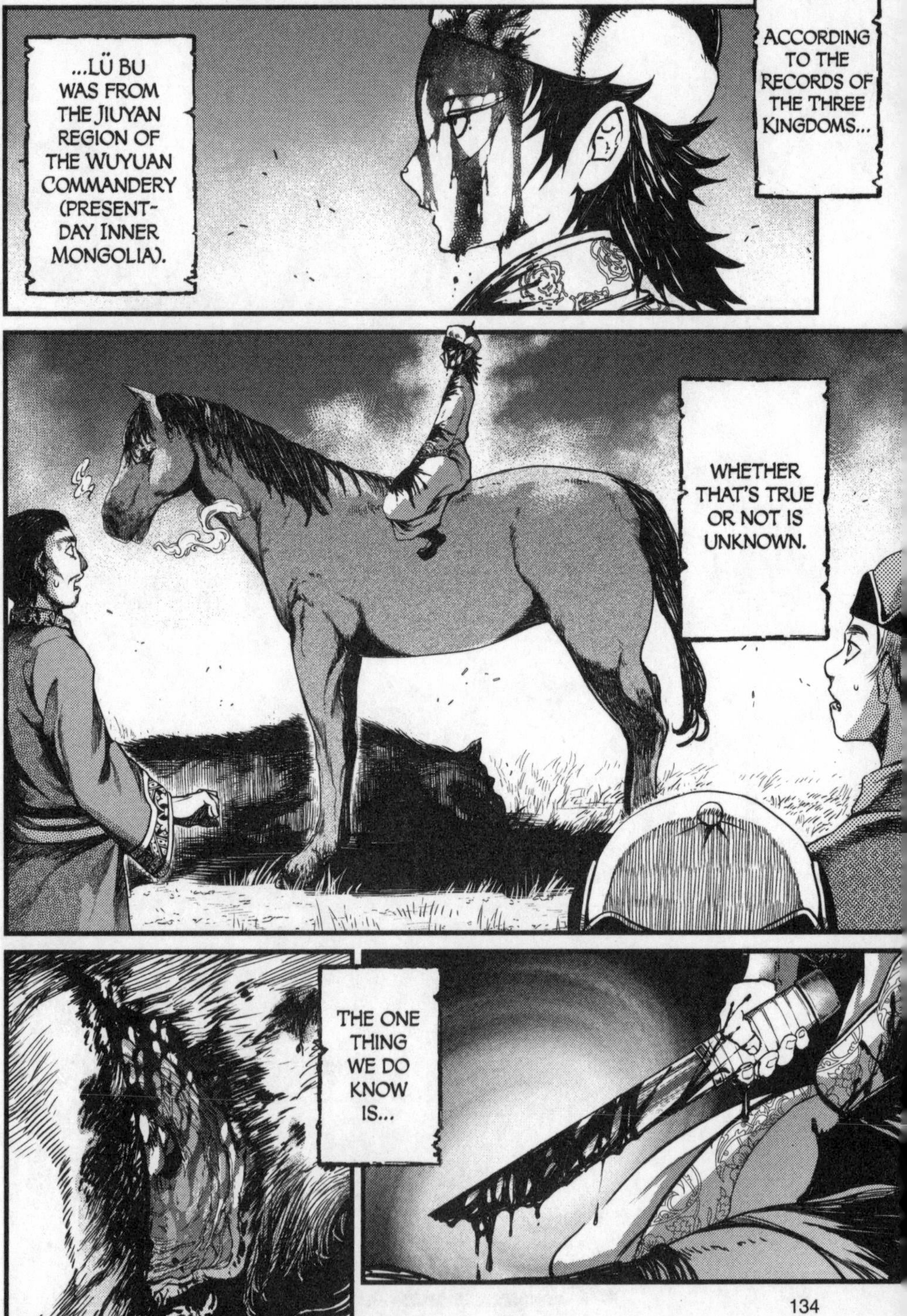
ACCORDING TO THE RECORDS OF THE THREE KINGDOMS...
...LÜ BU WAS FROM THE JIUYAN REGION OF THE WUYUAN COMMANDERY (PRESENT-DAY INNER MONGOLIA).
WHETHER THAT'S TRUE OR NOT IS UNKNOWN.
THE ONE THING WE DO KNOW IS...

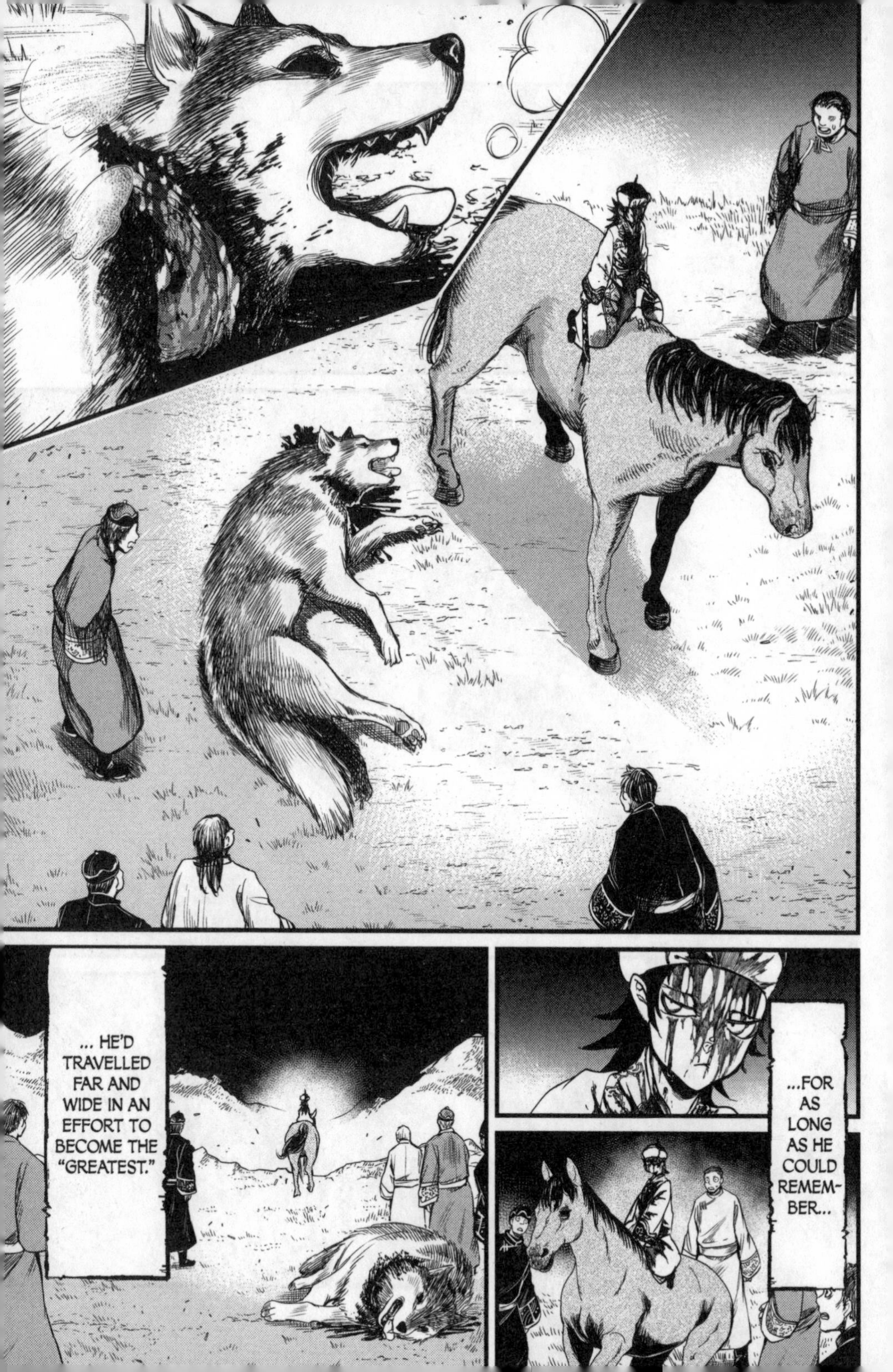
...FOR AS LONG AS HE COULD REMEMBER...
... HE'D TRAVELLED FAR AND WIDE IN AN EFFORT TO BECOME THE "GREATEST."

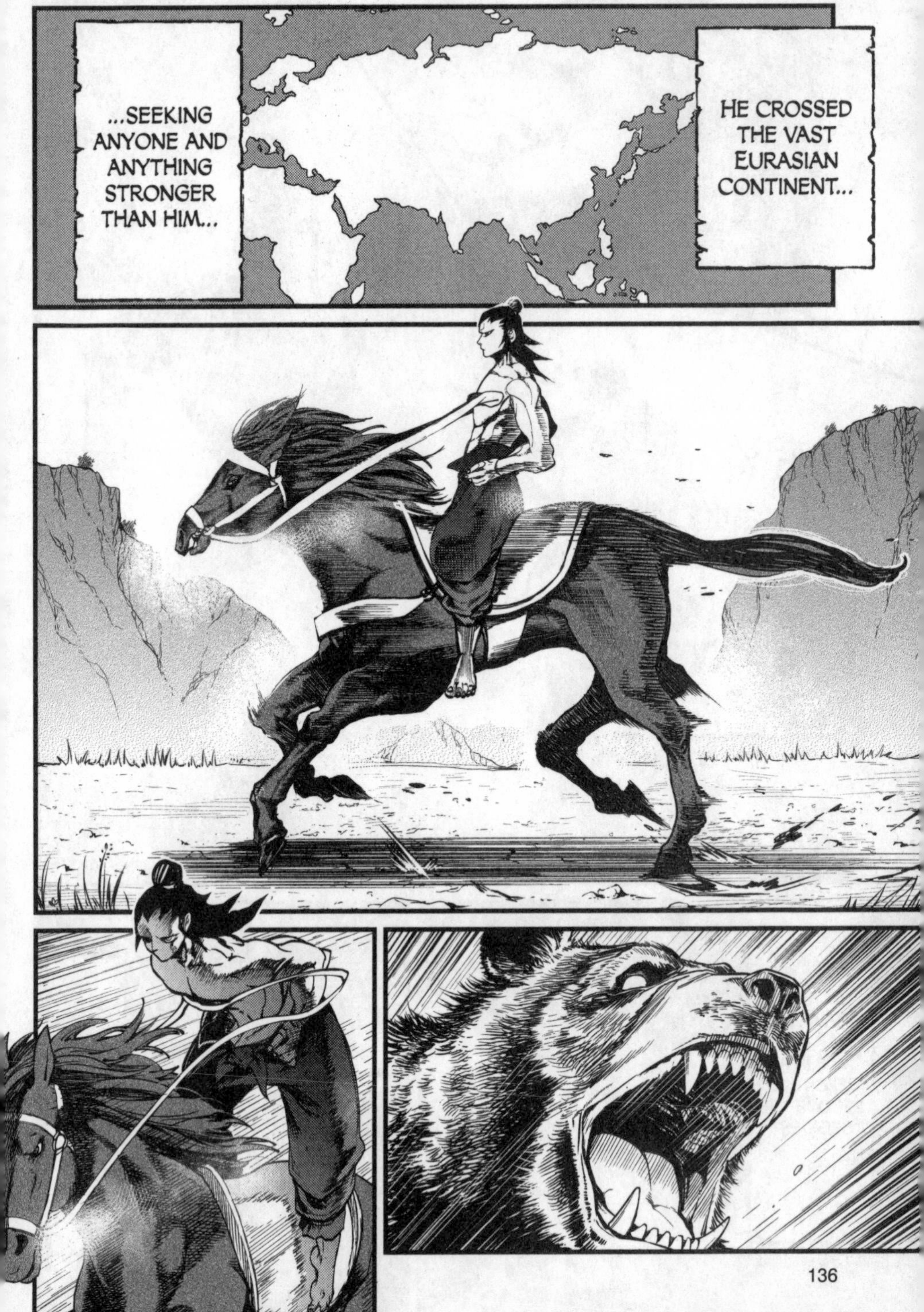
HE CROSSED THE VAST EURASIAN CONTINENT...
...SEEKING ANYONE AND ANYTHING STRONGER THAN HIM...

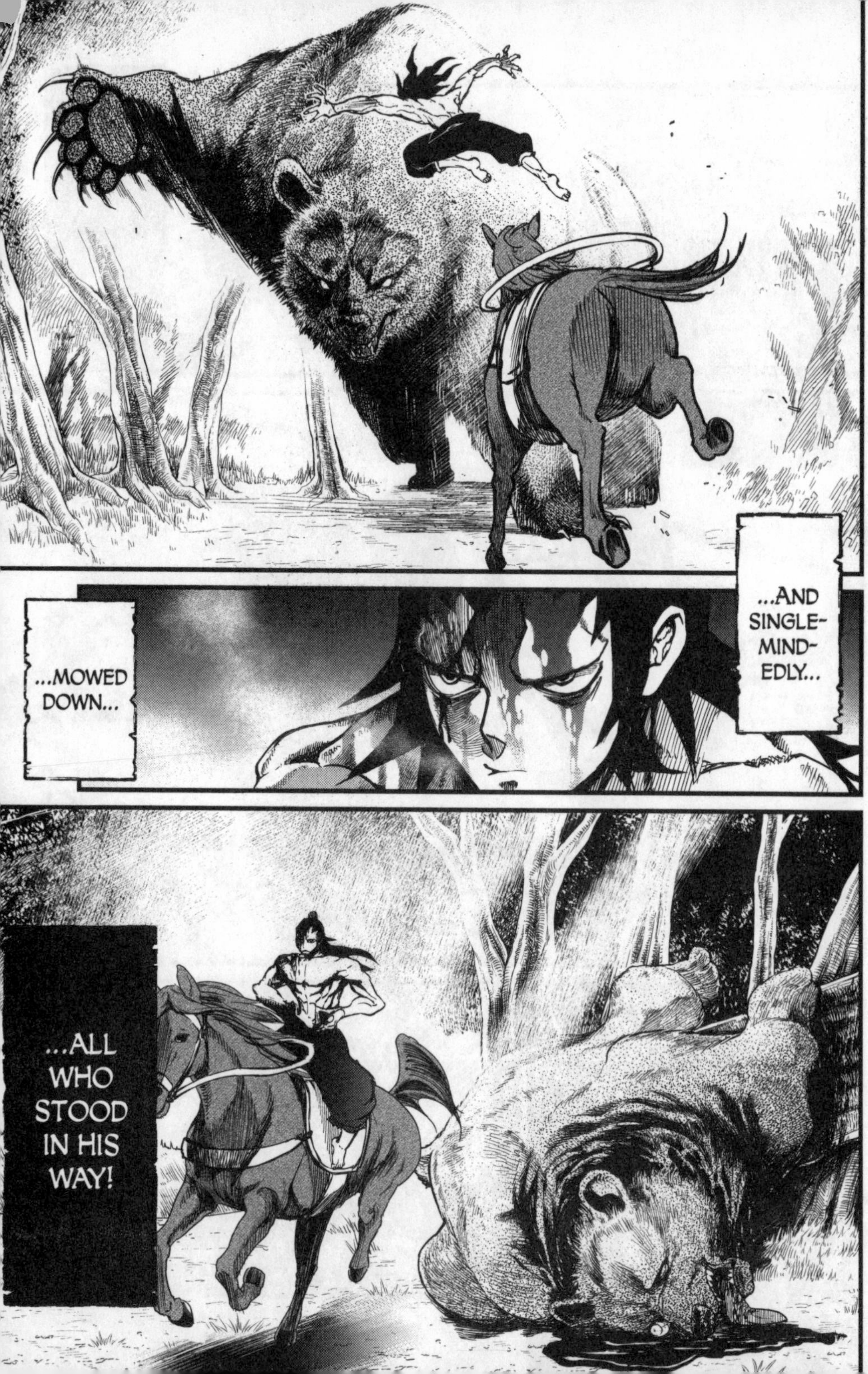
...AND SINGLE-MINDEDLY...
...MOWED DOWN...
...ALL WHO STOOD IN HIS WAY!

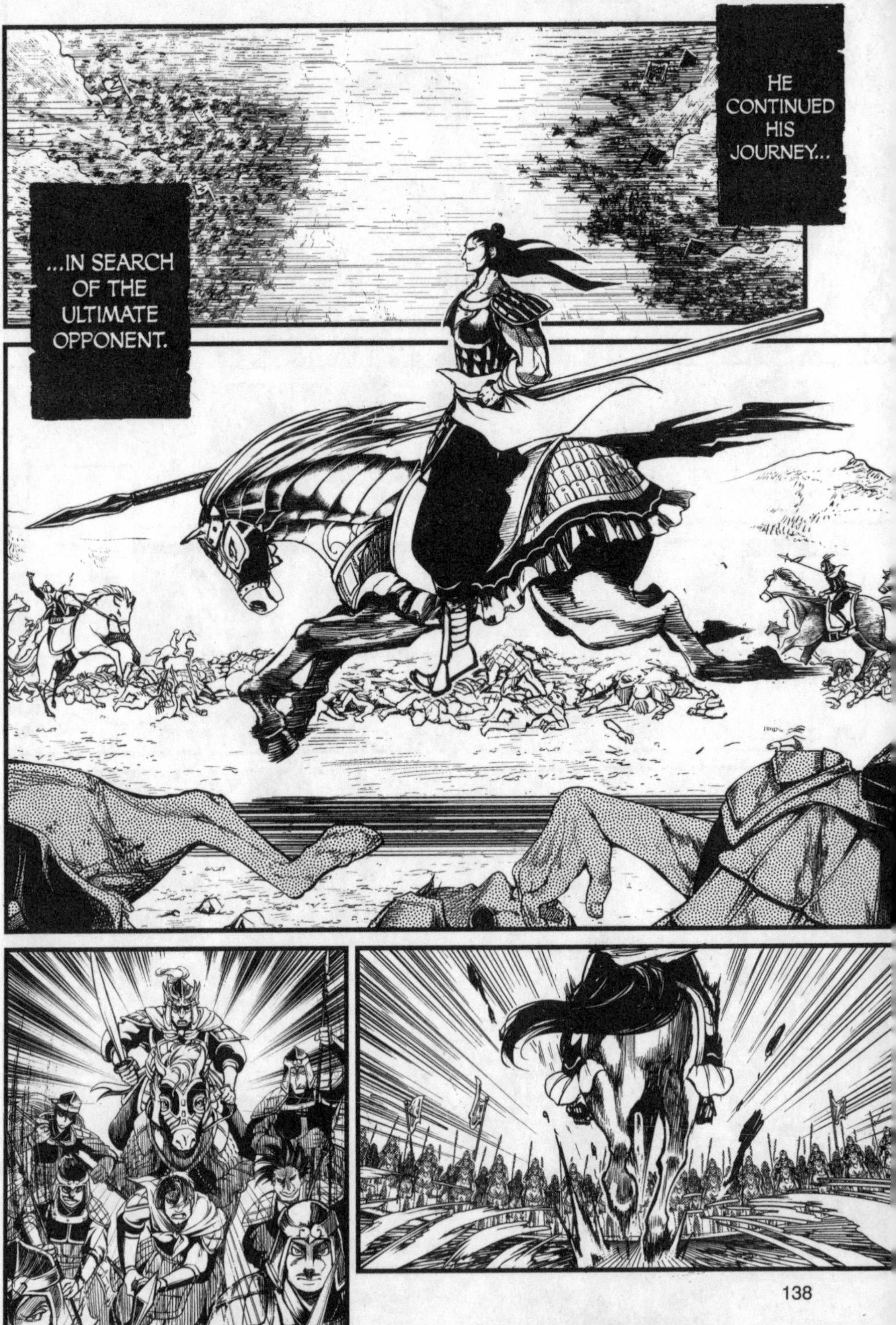
HE CONTINUED HIS JOURNEY...
...IN SEARCH OF THE ULTIMATE OPPONENT.

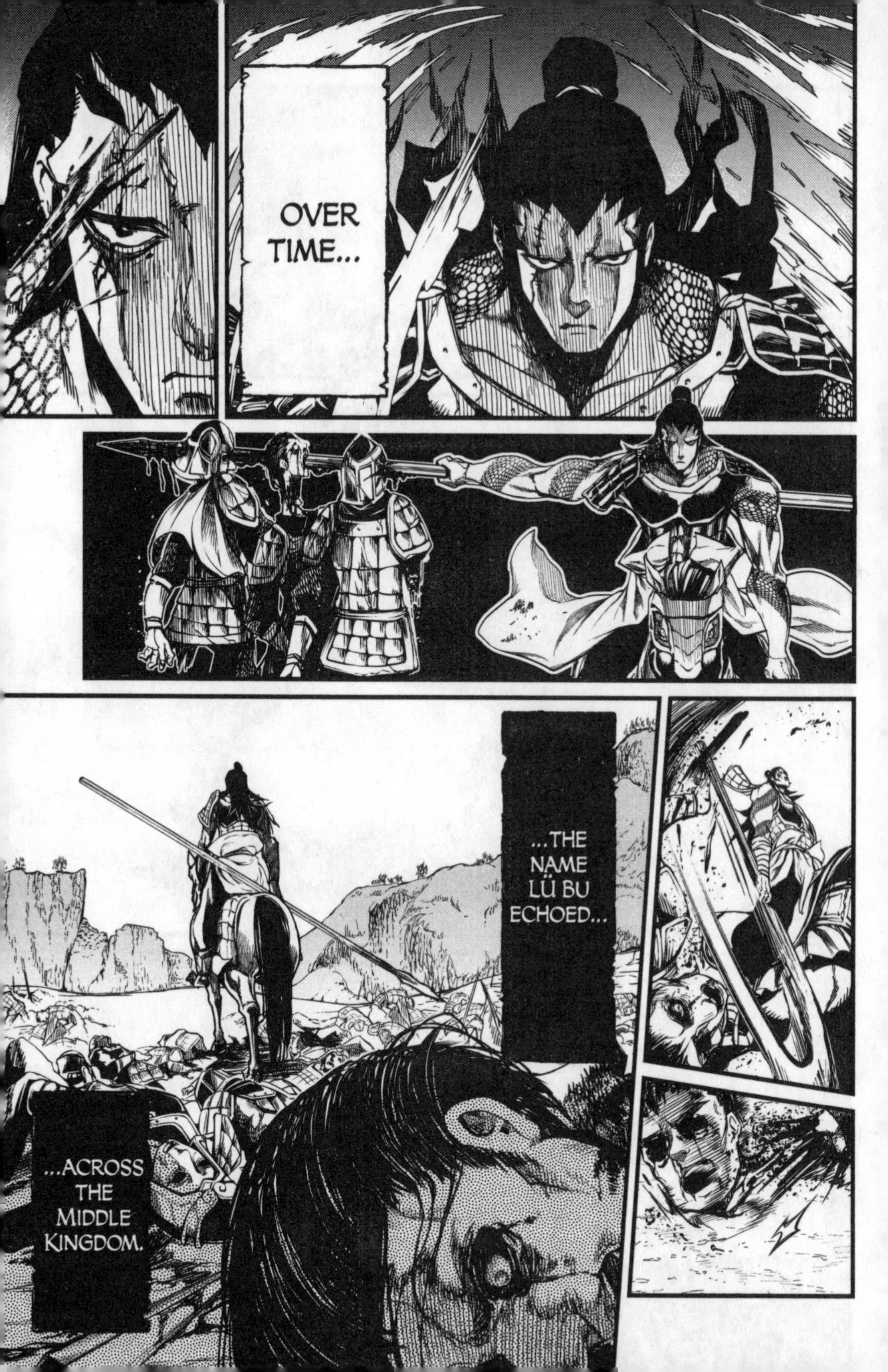
OVER TIME...
...THE NAME LÜ BU ECHOED...
...ACROSS THE MIDDLE KINGDOM.

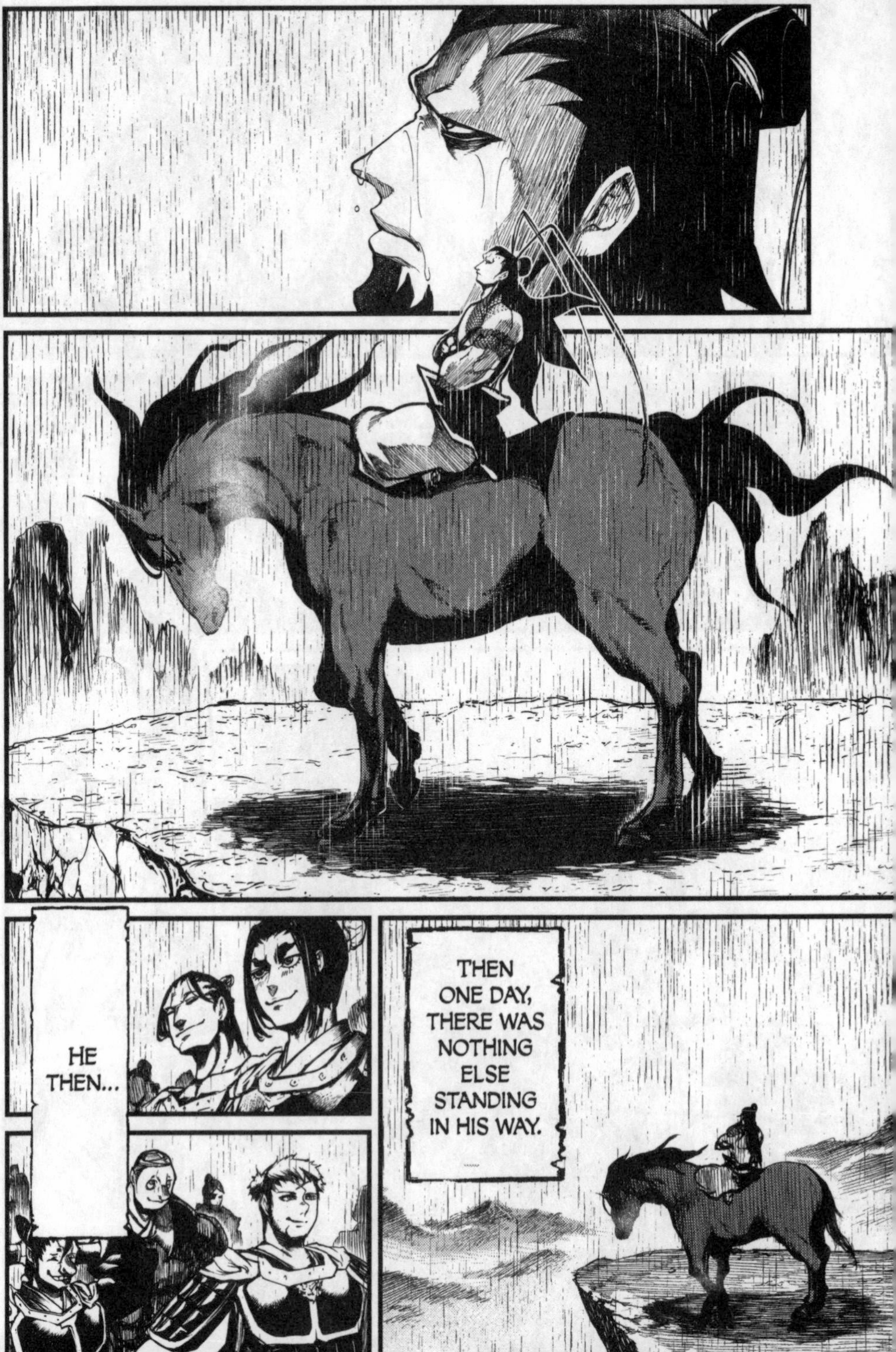
THEN ONE DAY, THERE WAS NOTHING ELSE STANDING IN HIS WAY.
HE THEN...

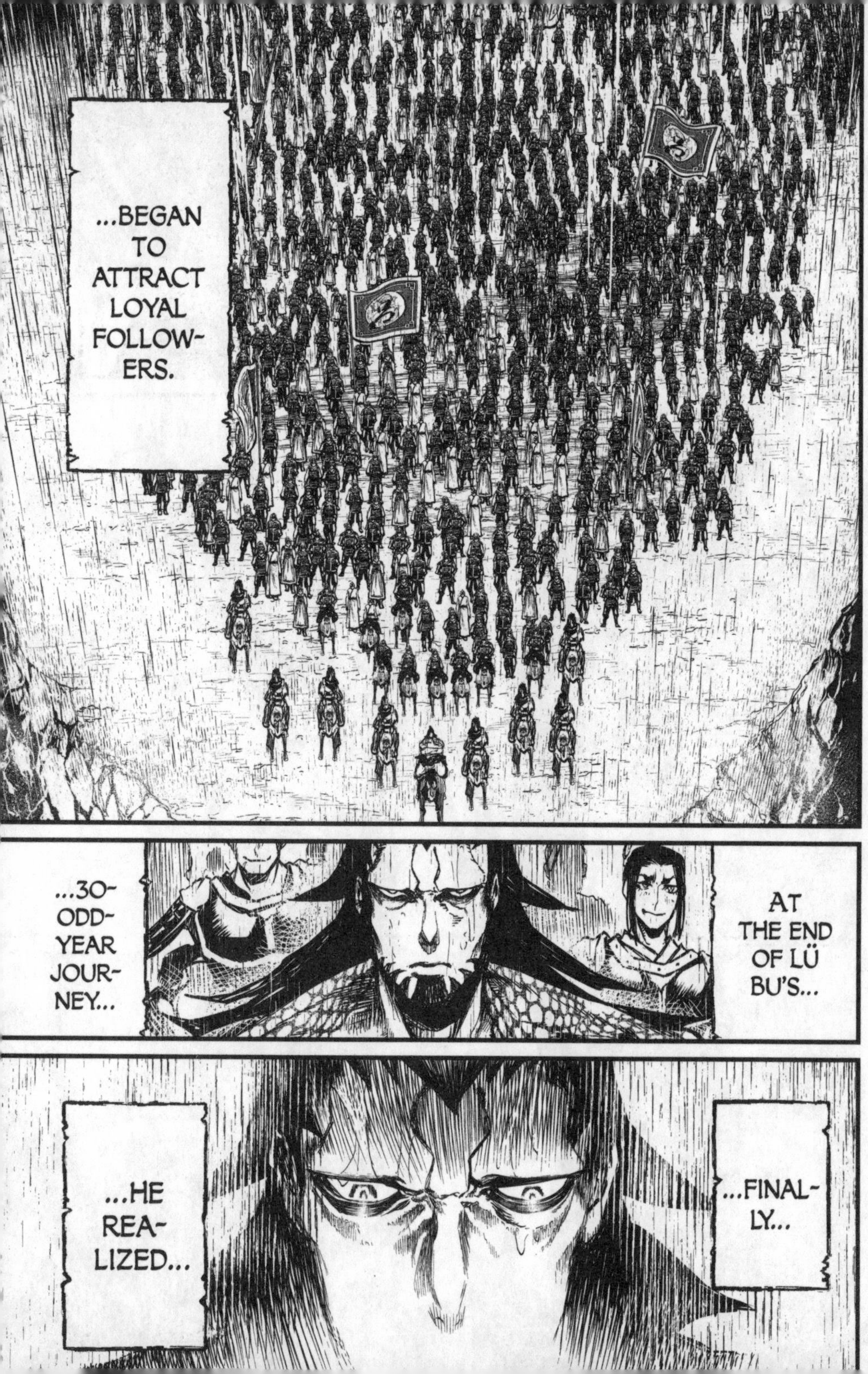
...BEGAN TO ATTRACT LOYAL FOLLOWERS.
AT THE END OF LÜ BU'S...
...30-ODD-YEAR JOURNEY...
...FINALLY...
...HE REALIZED...

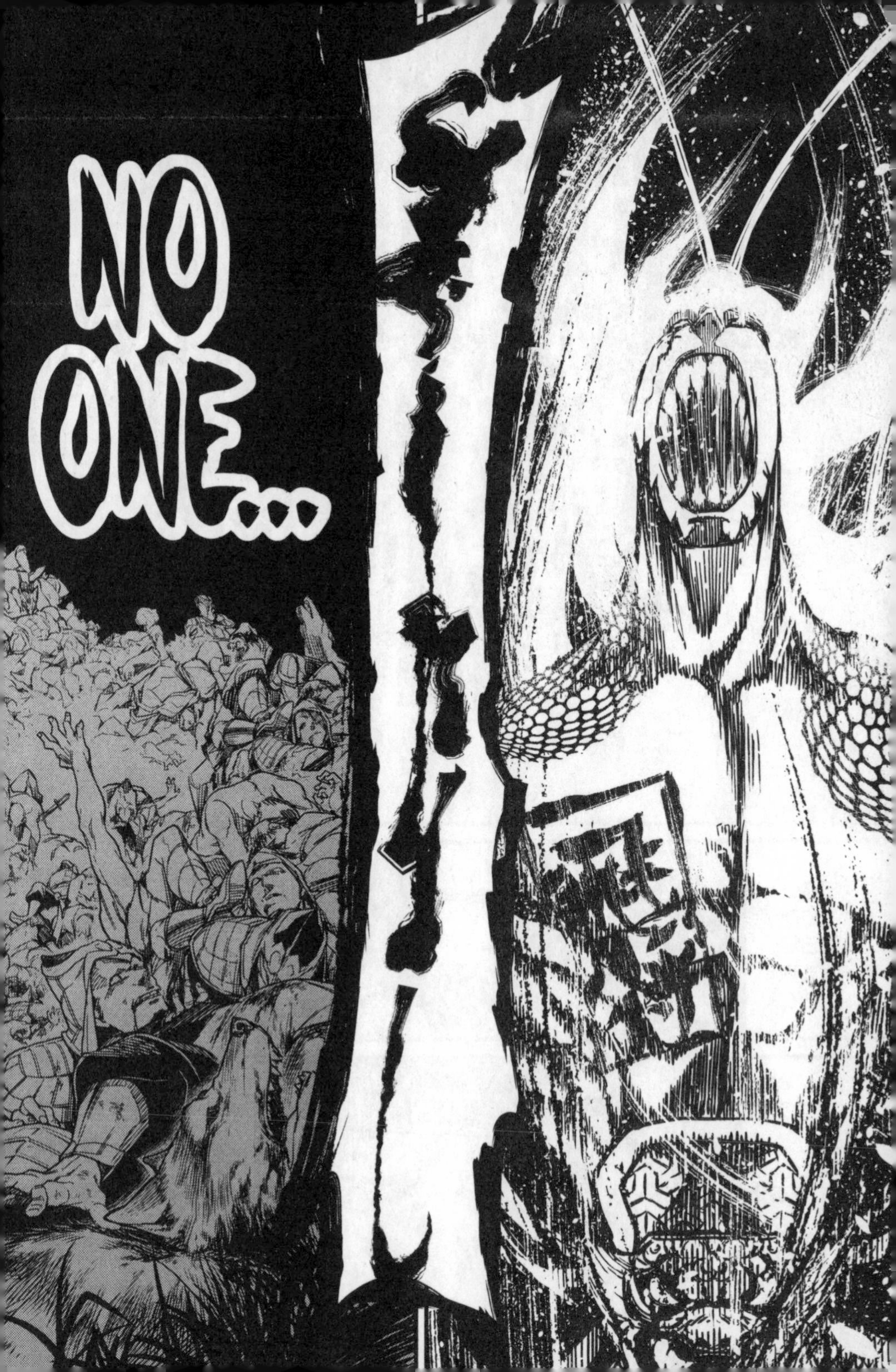
NO ONE...

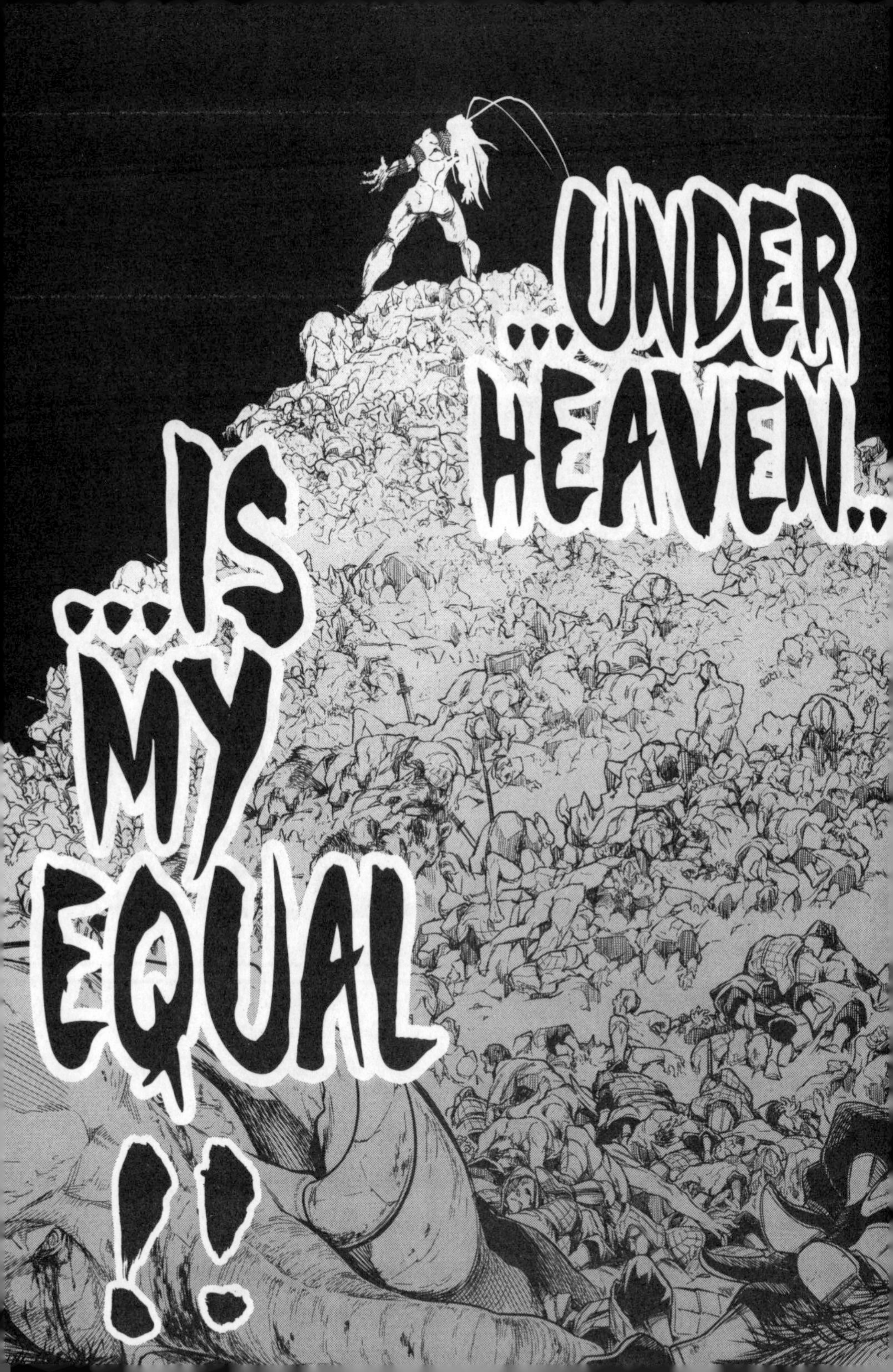
...UNDER HEAVEN...
...IS MY EQUAL!!

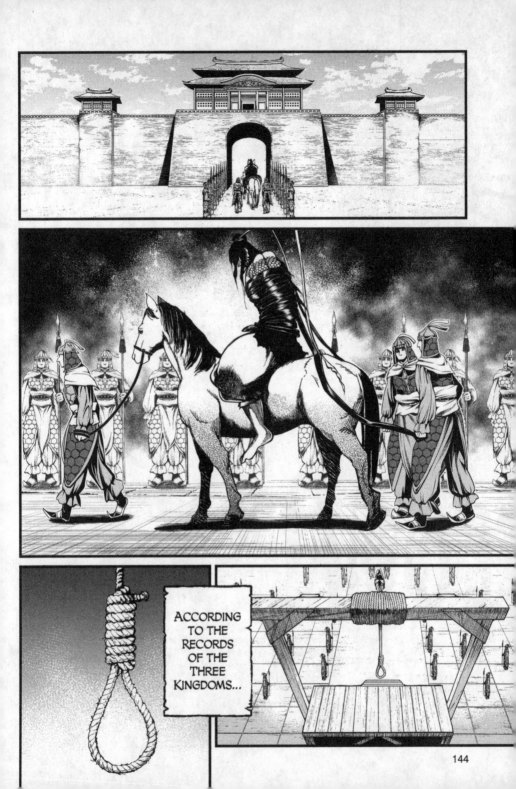

ACCORDING
TO THE
RECORDS
OF THE
THREE
KINGDOMS...

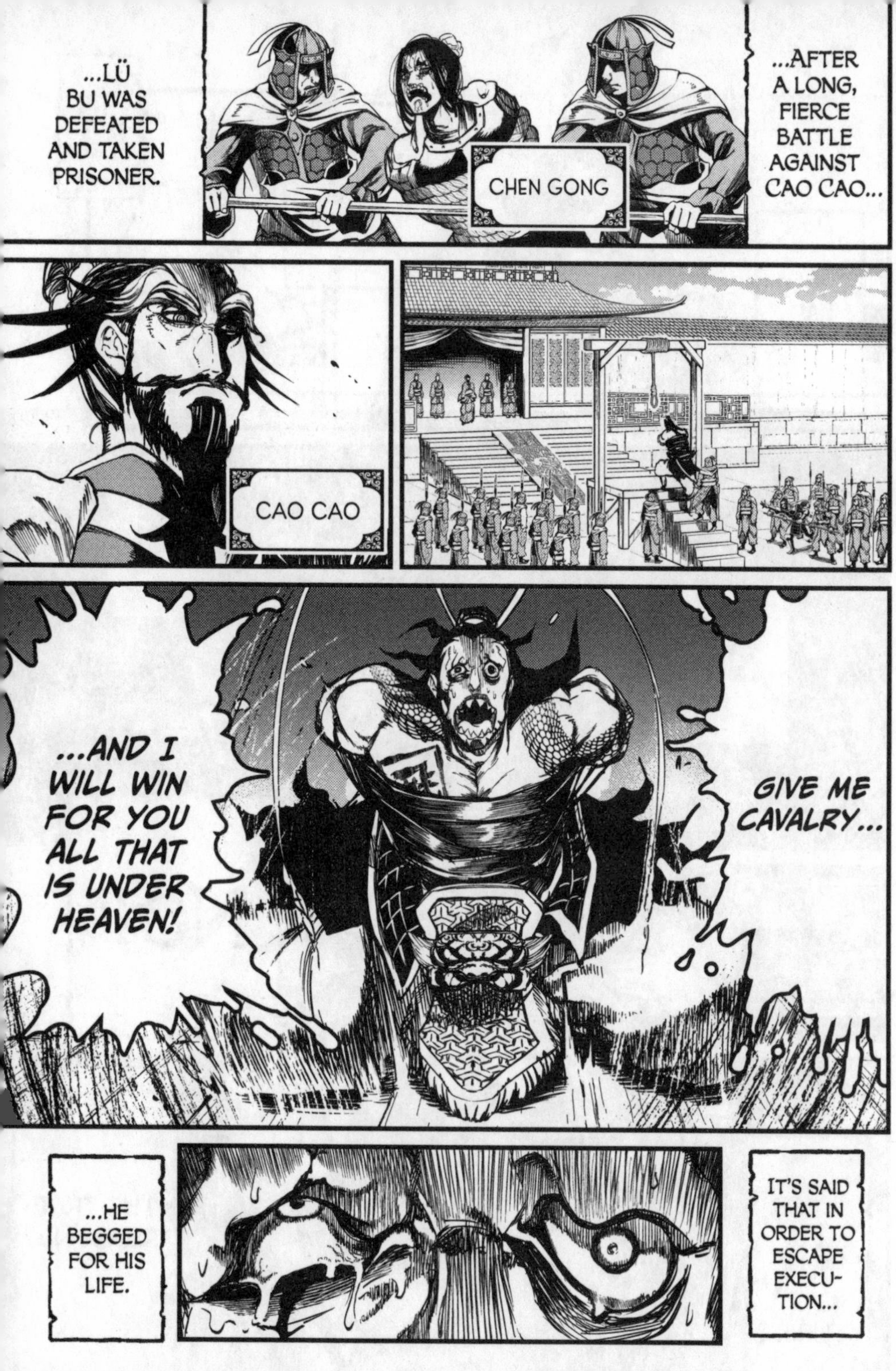
...AFTER A LONG, FIERCE BATTLE AGAINST CAO CAO...
CHEN GONG
...LÜ BU WAS DEFEATED AND TAKEN PRISONER.
CAO CAO
GIVE ME CAVALRY...
...AND I WILL WIN FOR YOU ALL THAT IS UNDER HEAVEN!
IT'S SAID THAT IN ORDER TO ESCAPE EXECU-TION...
...HE BEGGED FOR HIS LIFE.

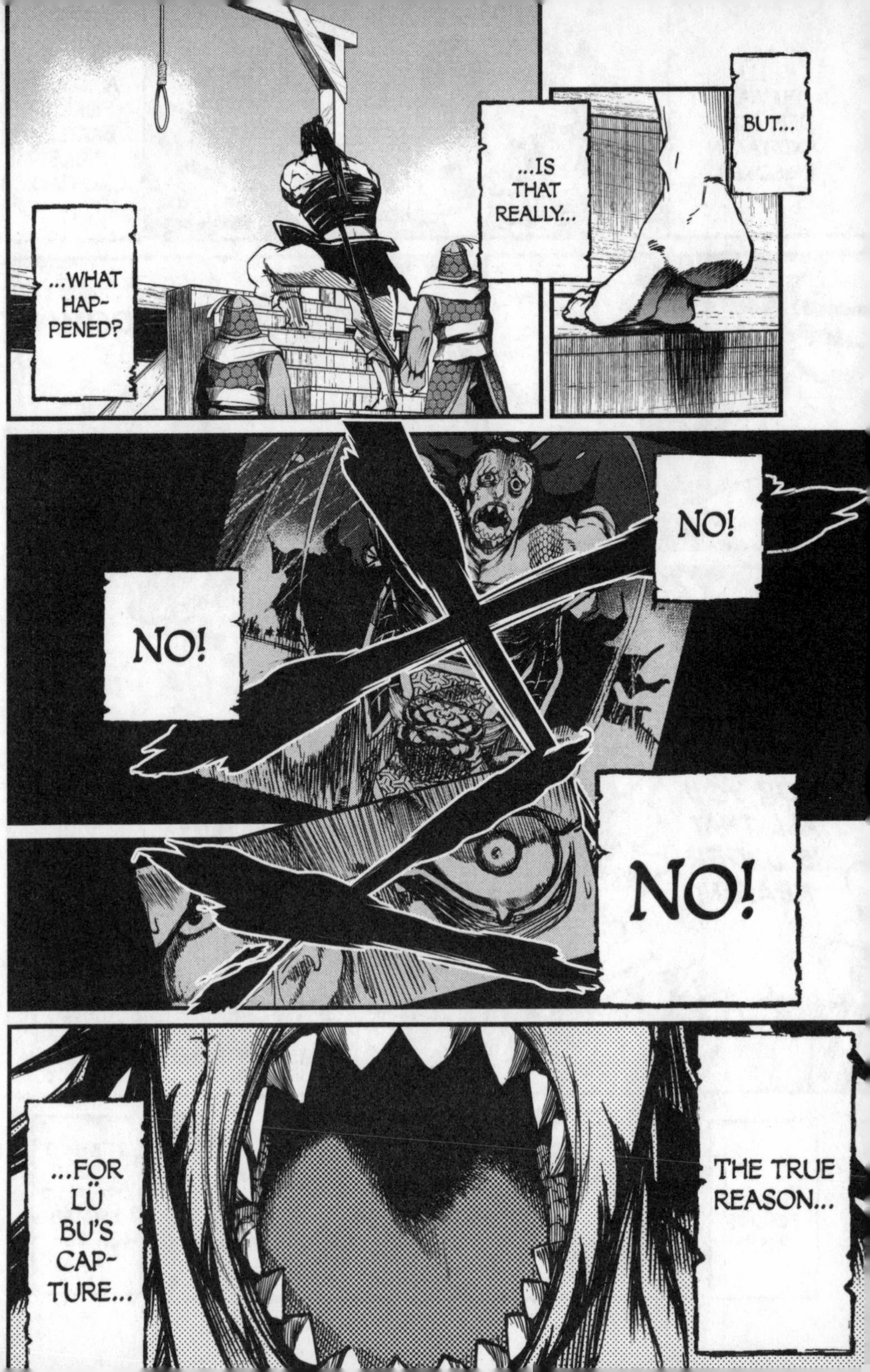
BUT...
...IS THAT REALLY...
...WHAT HAP-PENED?
NO!
NO!
NO!
THE TRUE REASON...
...FOR LÜ BU'S CAP-TURE...

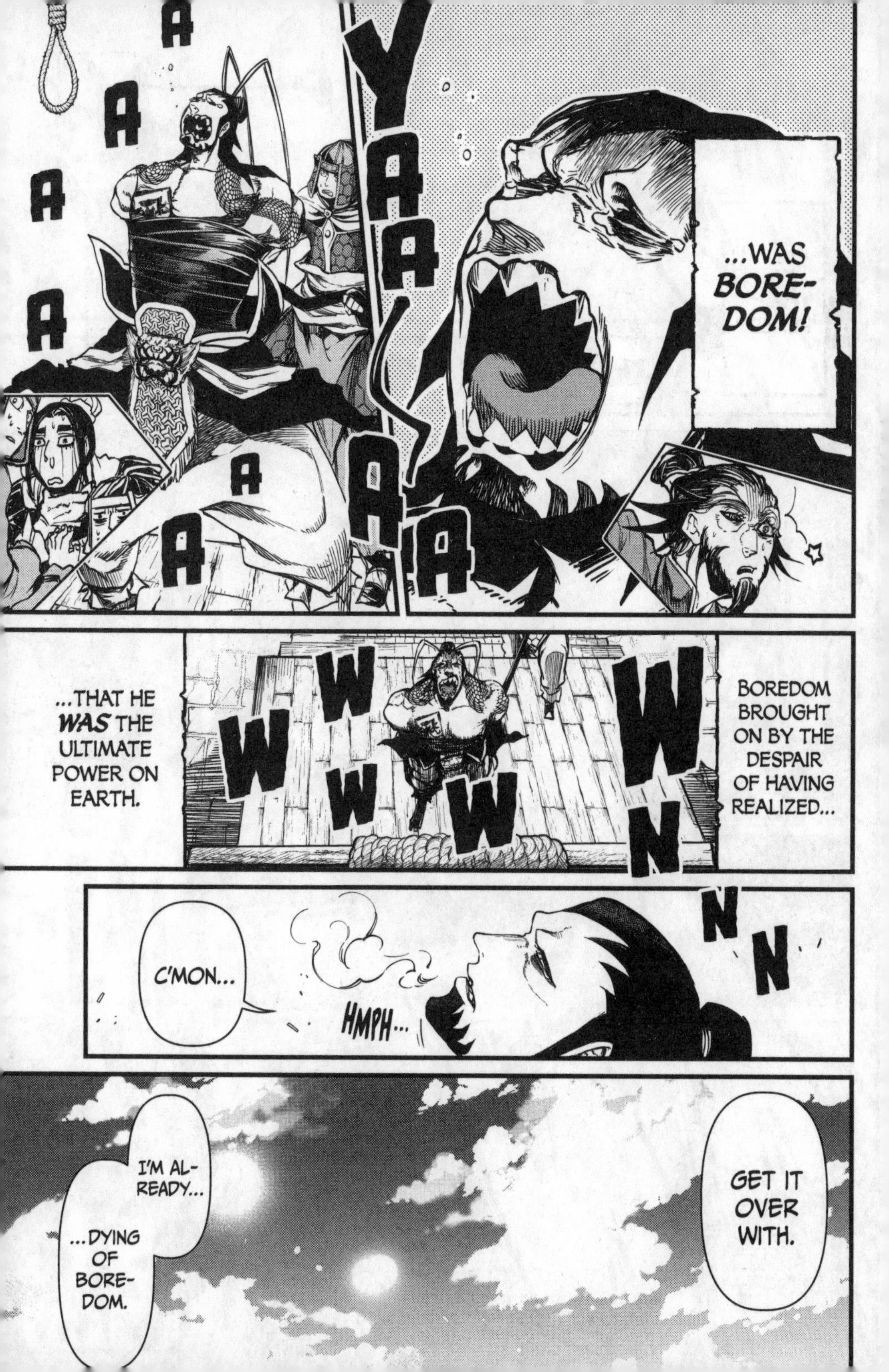
...WAS *BORE-DOM!*
YAAAAAAA
AAAAAAA
BOREDOM BROUGHT ON BY THE DESPAIR OF HAVING REALIZED...
WWWWWWNN
...THAT HE *WAS* THE ULTIMATE POWER ON EARTH.
NNN
HMPH...
C'MON...
GET IT OVER WITH.
I'M AL-READY...
...DYING OF BORE-DOM.

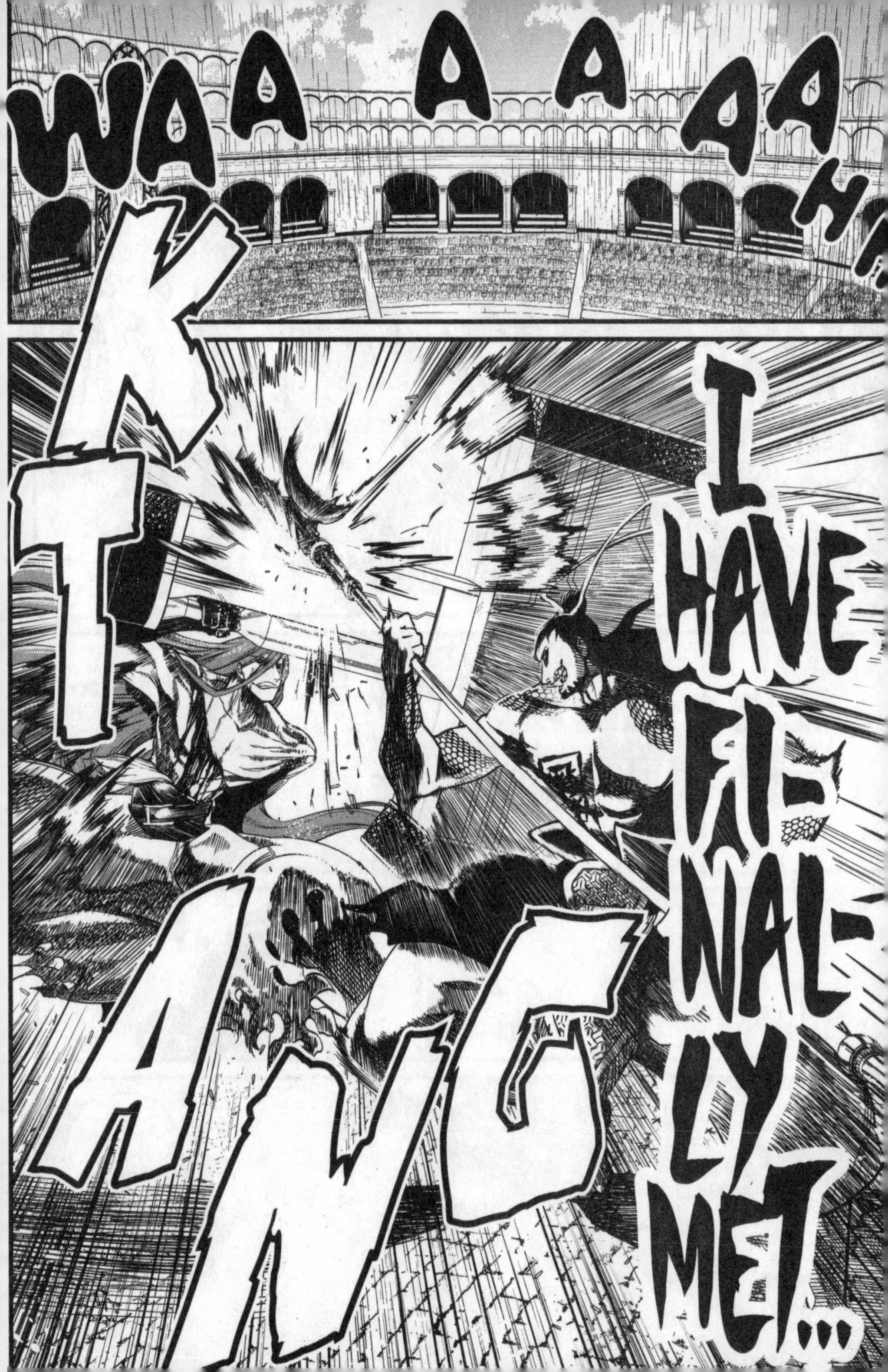
WAAAAAAAH!!
I HAVE FI-NAL-LY MET...
KTANG

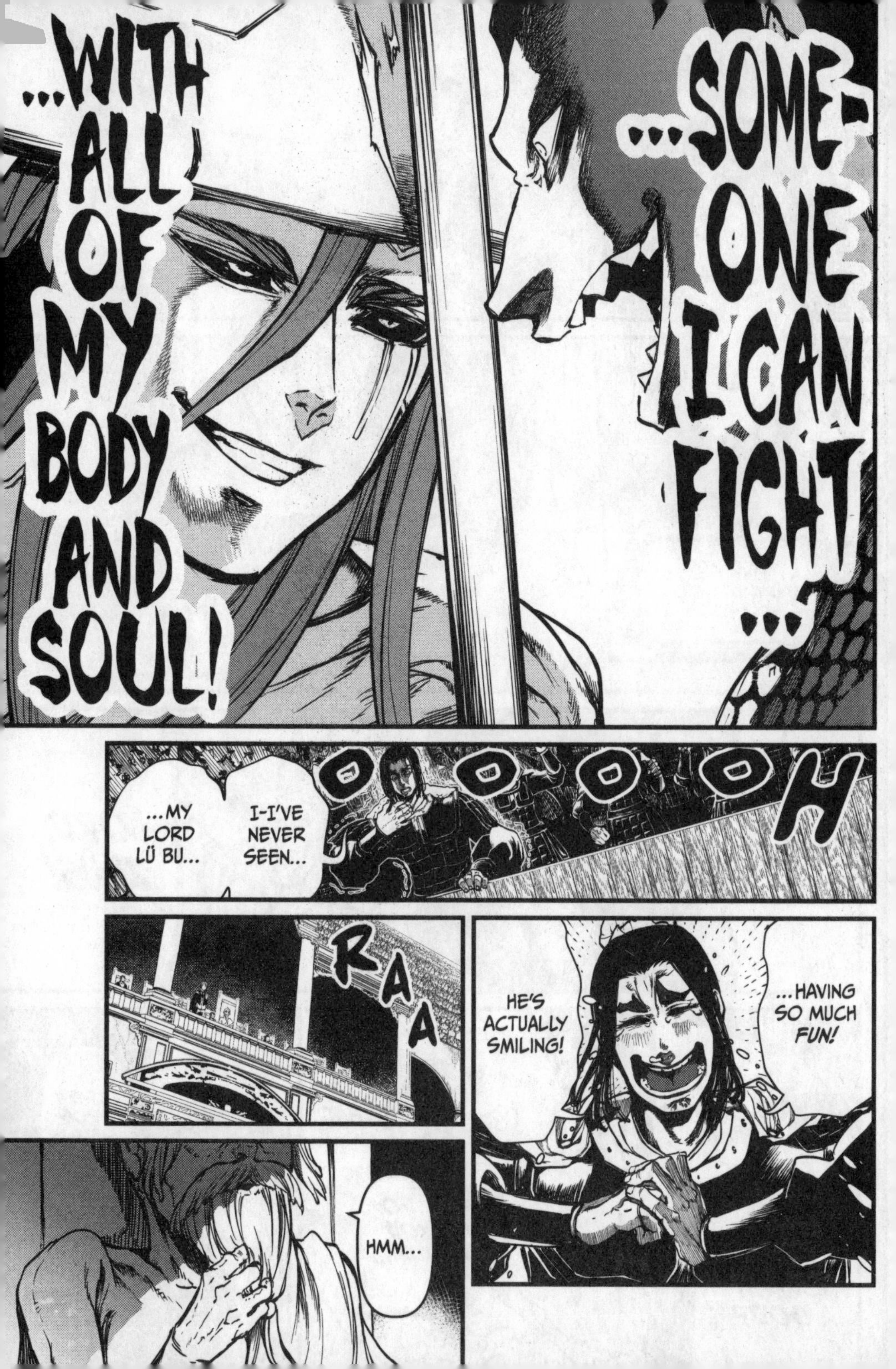
...SOME-ONE I CAN FIGHT...
...WITH ALL OF MY BODY AND SOUL!
OOOOOH
I-I'VE NEVER SEEN...
...MY LORD LÜ BU...
...HAVING SO MUCH FUN!
HE'S ACTUALLY SMILING!
RAA
HMM...

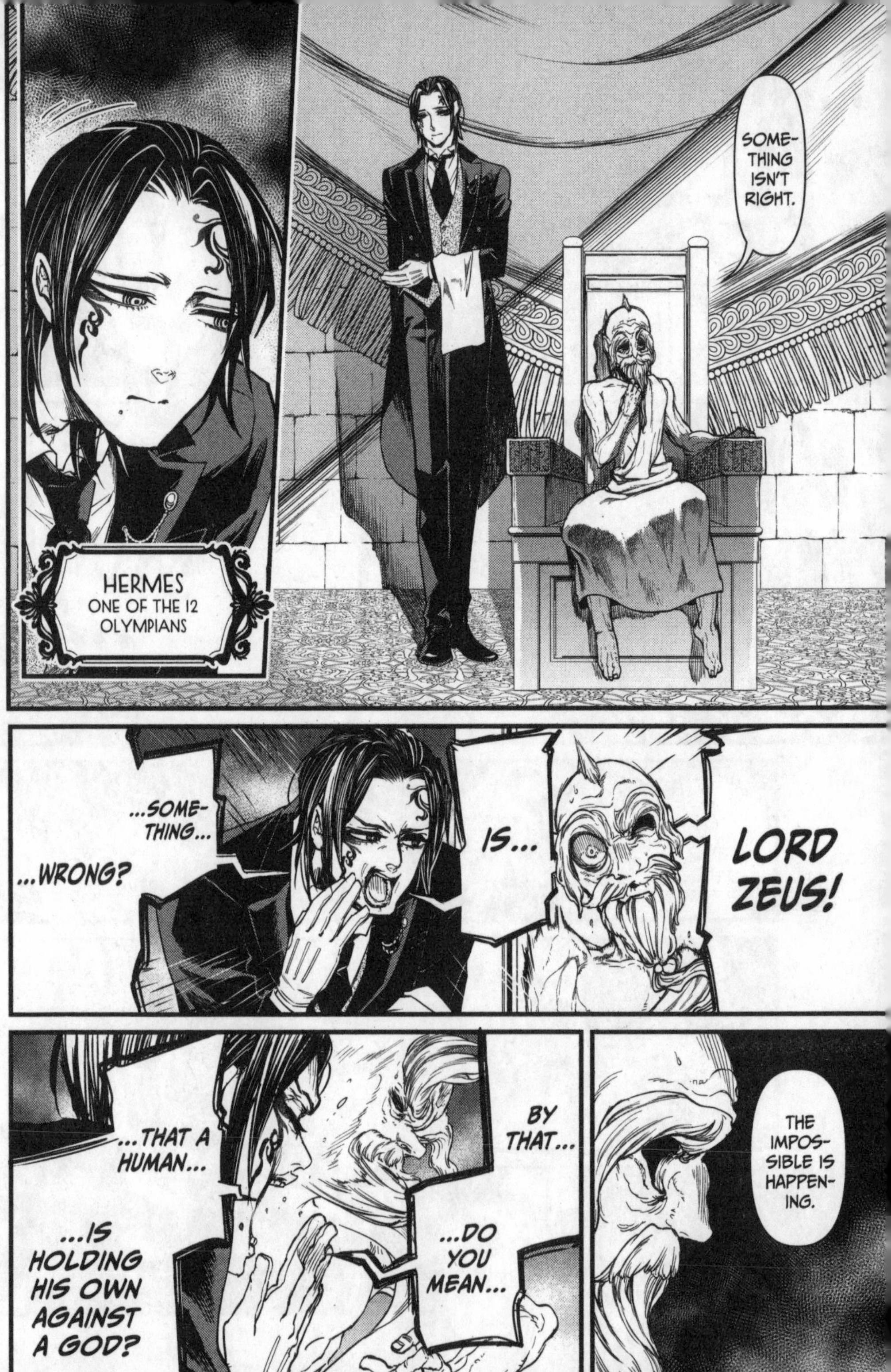
SOMETHING ISN'T RIGHT.
HERMES
ONE OF THE 12 OLYMPIANS
LORD ZEUS!
IS...
...SOMETHING...
...WRONG?
THE IMPOSSIBLE IS HAPPENING.
BY THAT...
...DO YOU MEAN...
...THAT A HUMAN...
...IS HOLDING HIS OWN AGAINST A GOD?

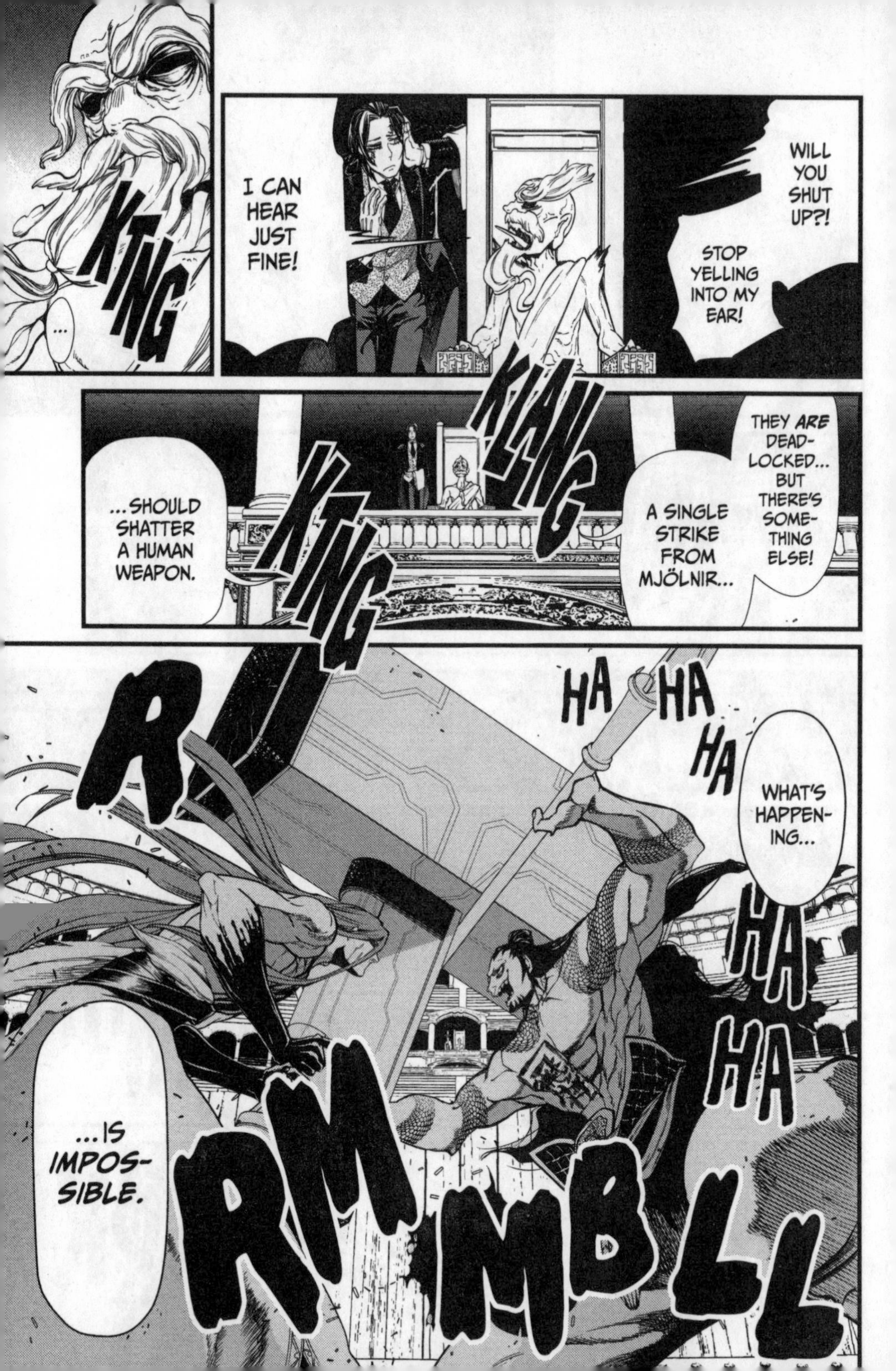
WILL YOU SHUT UP?!
STOP YELLING INTO MY EAR!
I CAN HEAR JUST FINE!
KTNG
...
KTANG
THEY *ARE* DEAD-LOCKED... BUT THERE'S SOME-THING ELSE!
A SINGLE STRIKE FROM MJÖLNIR...
...SHOULD SHATTER A HUMAN WEAPON.
KTNG
HA HA HA HA
WHAT'S HAPPEN-ING...
HA HA HA
RMMBLL
...IS IMPOS-SIBLE.

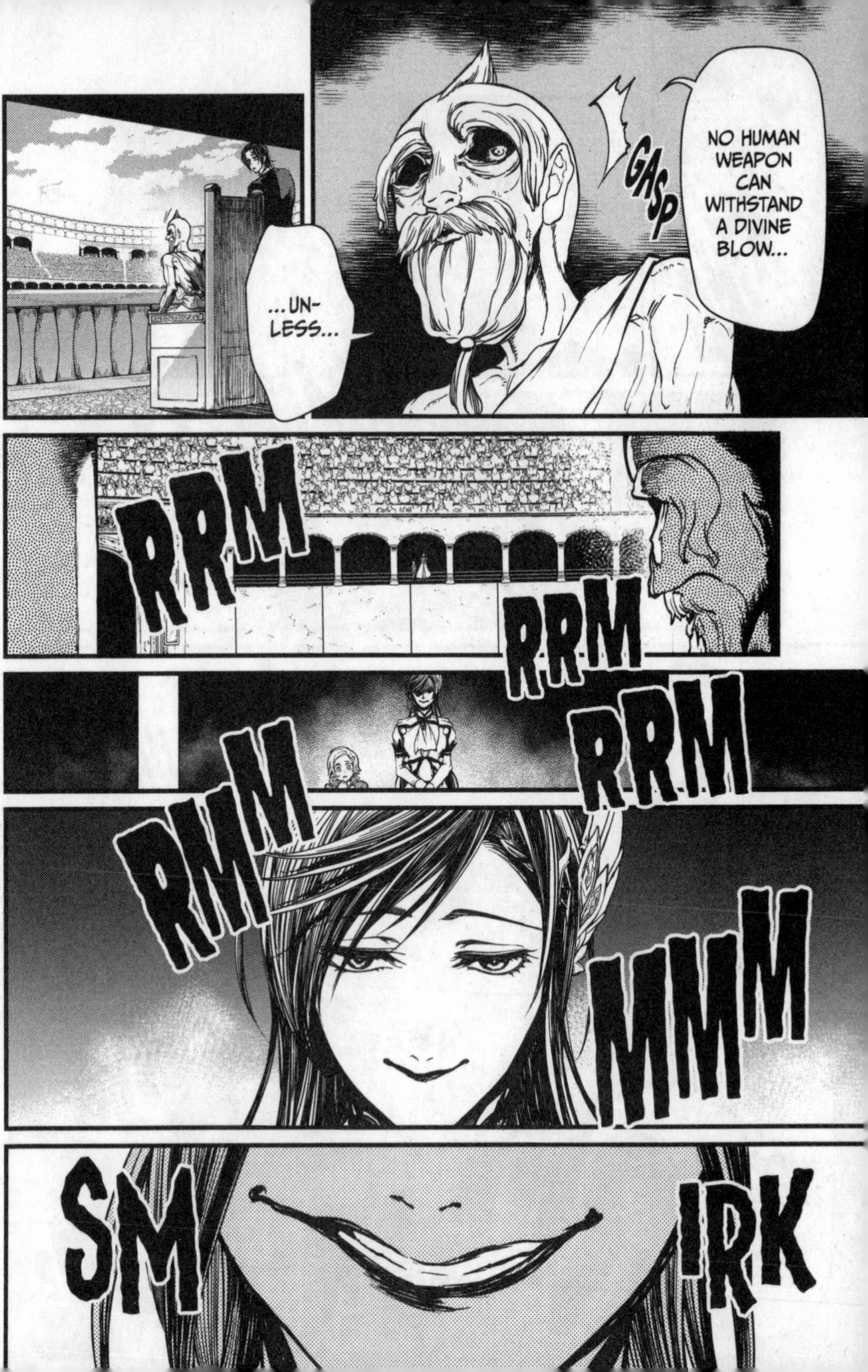
NO HUMAN WEAPON CAN WITHSTAND A DIVINE BLOW...
GASP
...UN-LESS...
RRM
RRM
RRM
RMM
MMM
SM
IRK

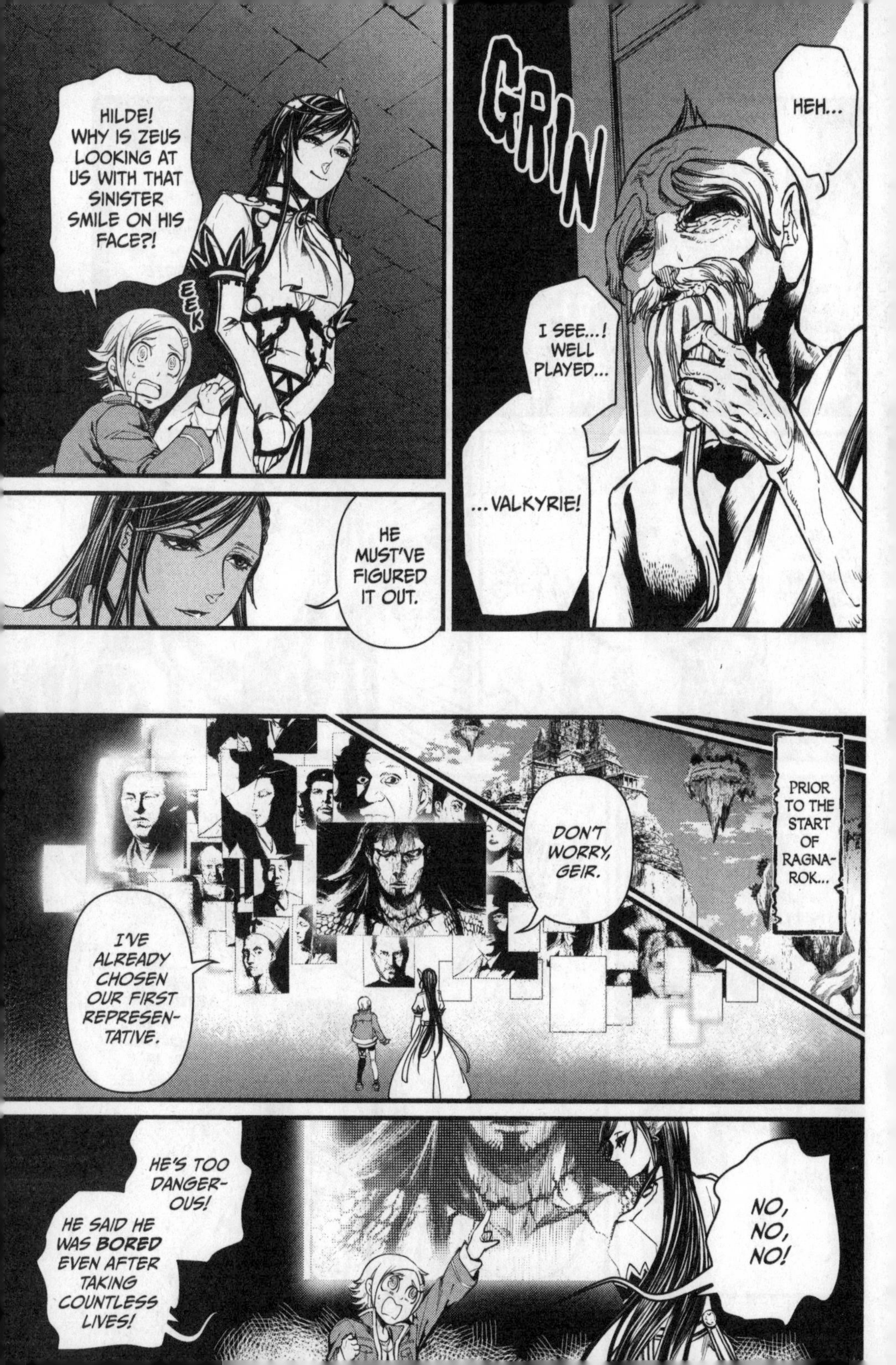

GRIN
HEH...
I SEE...! WELL PLAYED...
...VALKYRIE!
HILDE! WHY IS ZEUS LOOKING AT US WITH THAT SINISTER SMILE ON HIS FACE?!
EEK
HE MUST'VE FIGURED IT OUT.
PRIOR TO THE START OF RAGNA-ROK...
DON'T WORRY, GEIR.
I'VE ALREADY CHOSEN OUR FIRST REPRESEN-TATIVE.
NO, NO, NO!
HE'S TOO DANGER-OUS!
HE SAID HE WAS BORED EVEN AFTER TAKING COUNTLESS LIVES!

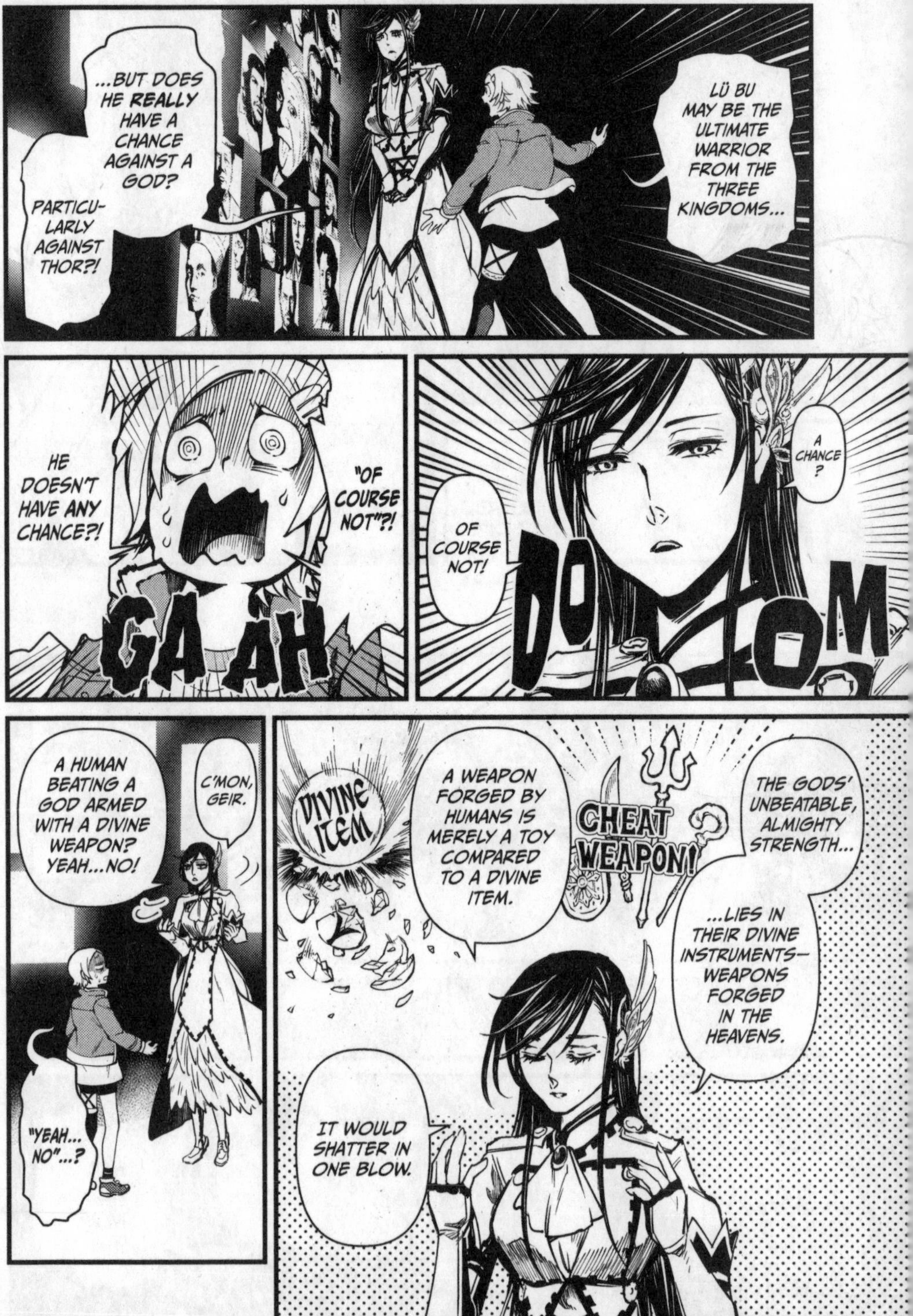
LÜ BU MAY BE THE ULTIMATE WARRIOR FROM THE THREE KINGDOMS...
...BUT DOES HE REALLY HAVE A CHANCE AGAINST A GOD?
PARTICU-LARLY AGAINST THOR?!
A CHANCE?
OF COURSE NOT!
DOOM
"OF COURSE NOT"?!
HE DOESN'T HAVE ANY CHANCE?!
GAAH
THE GODS' UNBEATABLE, ALMIGHTY STRENGTH...
...LIES IN THEIR DIVINE INSTRUMENTS—WEAPONS FORGED IN THE HEAVENS.
CHEAT WEAPON!
A WEAPON FORGED BY HUMANS IS MERELY A TOY COMPARED TO A DIVINE ITEM.
DIVINE ITEM
IT WOULD SHATTER IN ONE BLOW.
C'MON, GEIR.
A HUMAN BEATING A GOD ARMED WITH A DIVINE WEAPON? YEAH...NO!
"YEAH... NO"...?

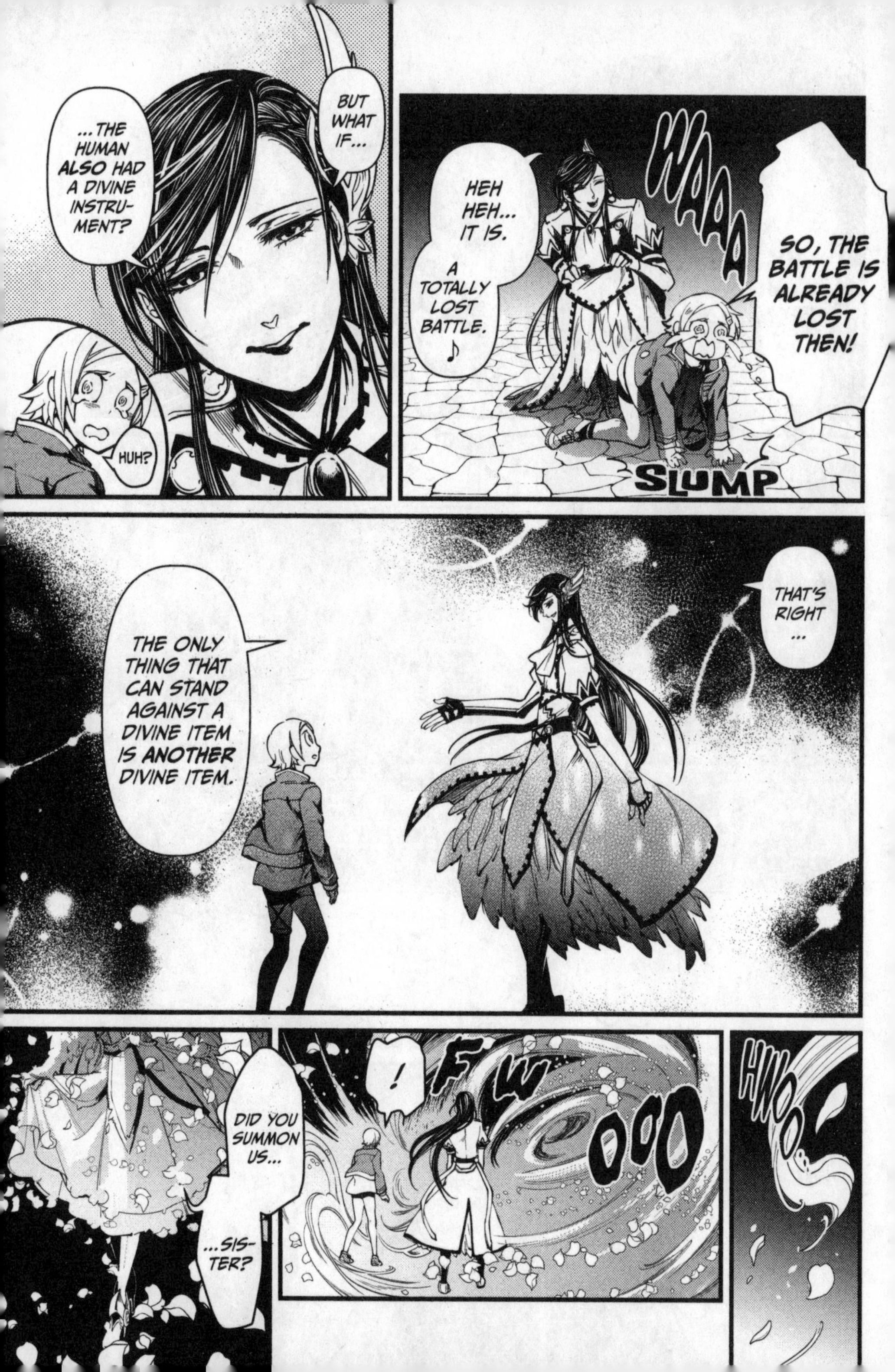
WAAAA
SO, THE BATTLE IS ALREADY LOST THEN!
HEH HEH... IT IS.
A TOTALLY LOST BATTLE. ♪
SLUMP
BUT WHAT IF...
...THE HUMAN ALSO HAD A DIVINE INSTRU-MENT?
HUH?
THAT'S RIGHT ...
THE ONLY THING THAT CAN STAND AGAINST A DIVINE ITEM IS ANOTHER DIVINE ITEM.
HWOO
!
FWOOO
DID YOU SUMMON US...
...SIS-TER?

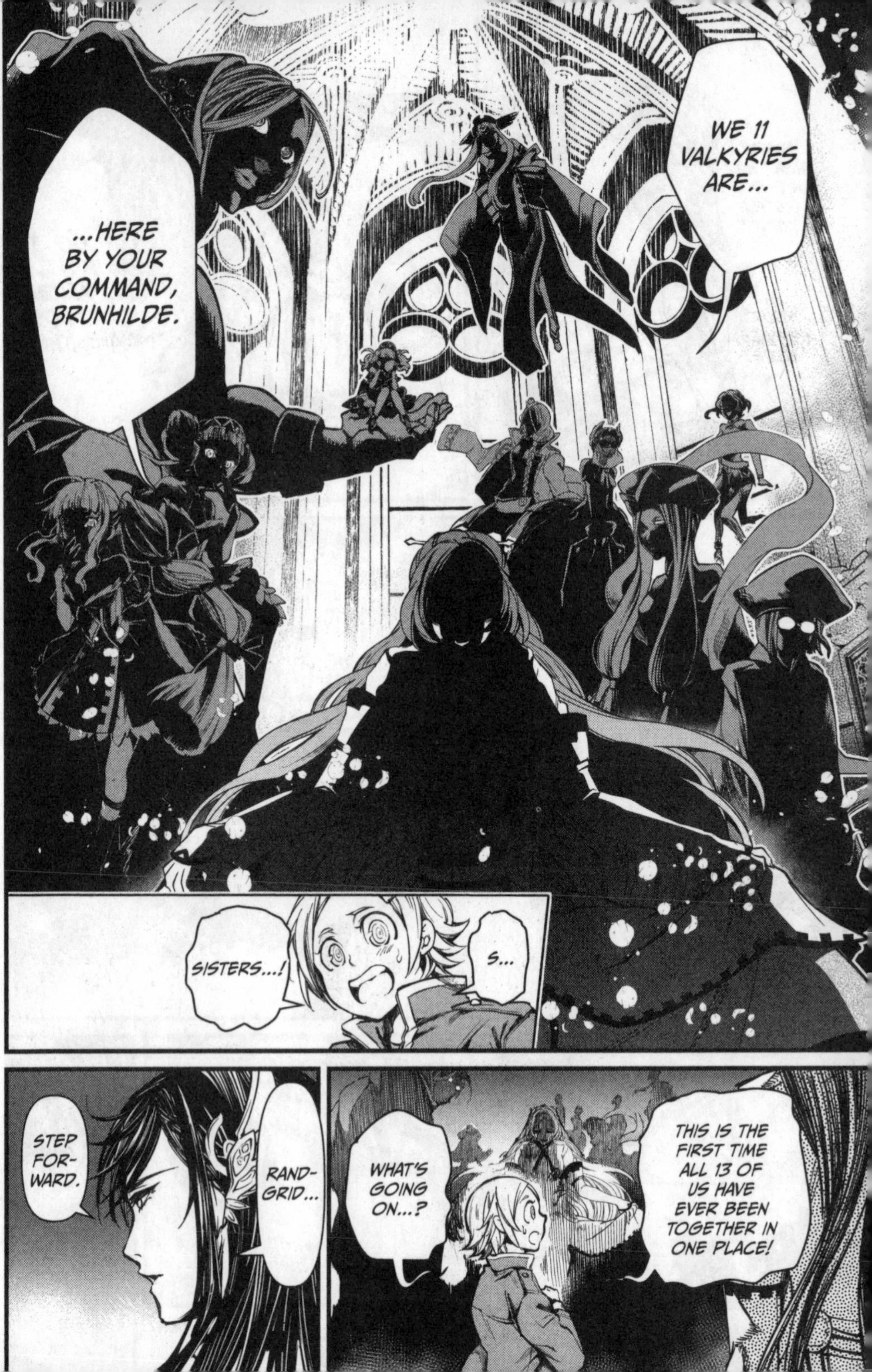
WE 11 VALKYRIES ARE...
...HERE BY YOUR COMMAND, BRUNHILDE.
S...
SISTERS...!
THIS IS THE FIRST TIME ALL 13 OF US HAVE EVER BEEN TOGETHER IN ONE PLACE!
WHAT'S GOING ON...?
RAND-GRID...
STEP FOR-WARD.

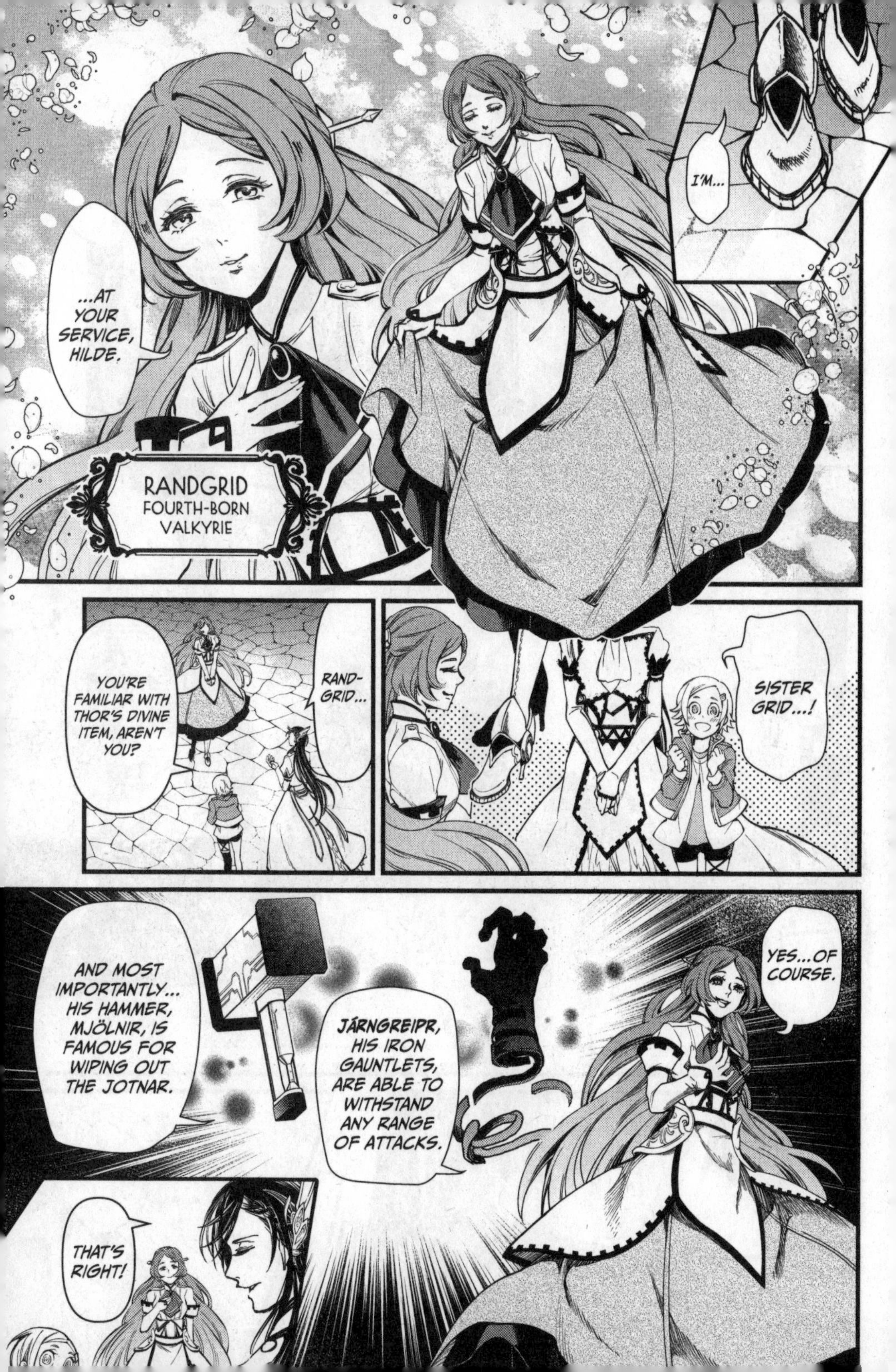
I'M...
...AT YOUR SERVICE, HILDE.
RANDGRID
FOURTH-BORN VALKYRIE
SISTER GRID...!
RAND-GRID...
YOU'RE FAMILIAR WITH THOR'S DIVINE ITEM, AREN'T YOU?
YES...OF COURSE.
JÁRNGREIPR, HIS IRON GAUNTLETS, ARE ABLE TO WITHSTAND ANY RANGE OF ATTACKS.
AND MOST IMPORTANTLY... HIS HAMMER, MJÖLNIR, IS FAMOUS FOR WIPING OUT THE JOTNAR.
THAT'S RIGHT!

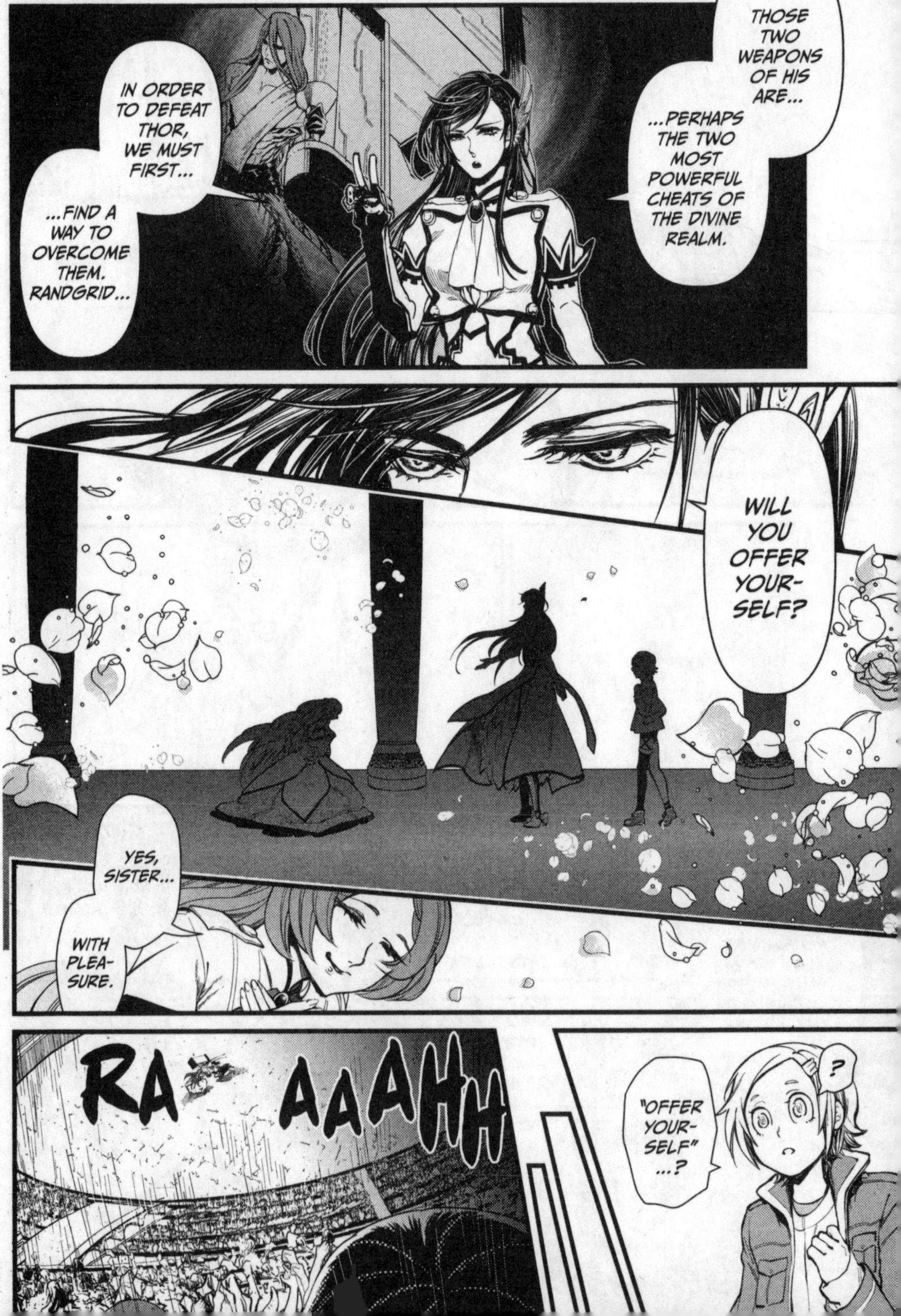
THOSE TWO WEAPONS OF HIS ARE...
...PERHAPS THE TWO MOST POWERFUL CHEATS OF THE DIVINE REALM.
IN ORDER TO DEFEAT THOR, WE MUST FIRST...
...FIND A WAY TO OVERCOME THEM. RANDGRID...
WILL YOU OFFER YOUR-SELF?
YES, SISTER...
WITH PLEA-SURE.
?
"OFFER YOUR-SELF" ...?
RA AAAHH

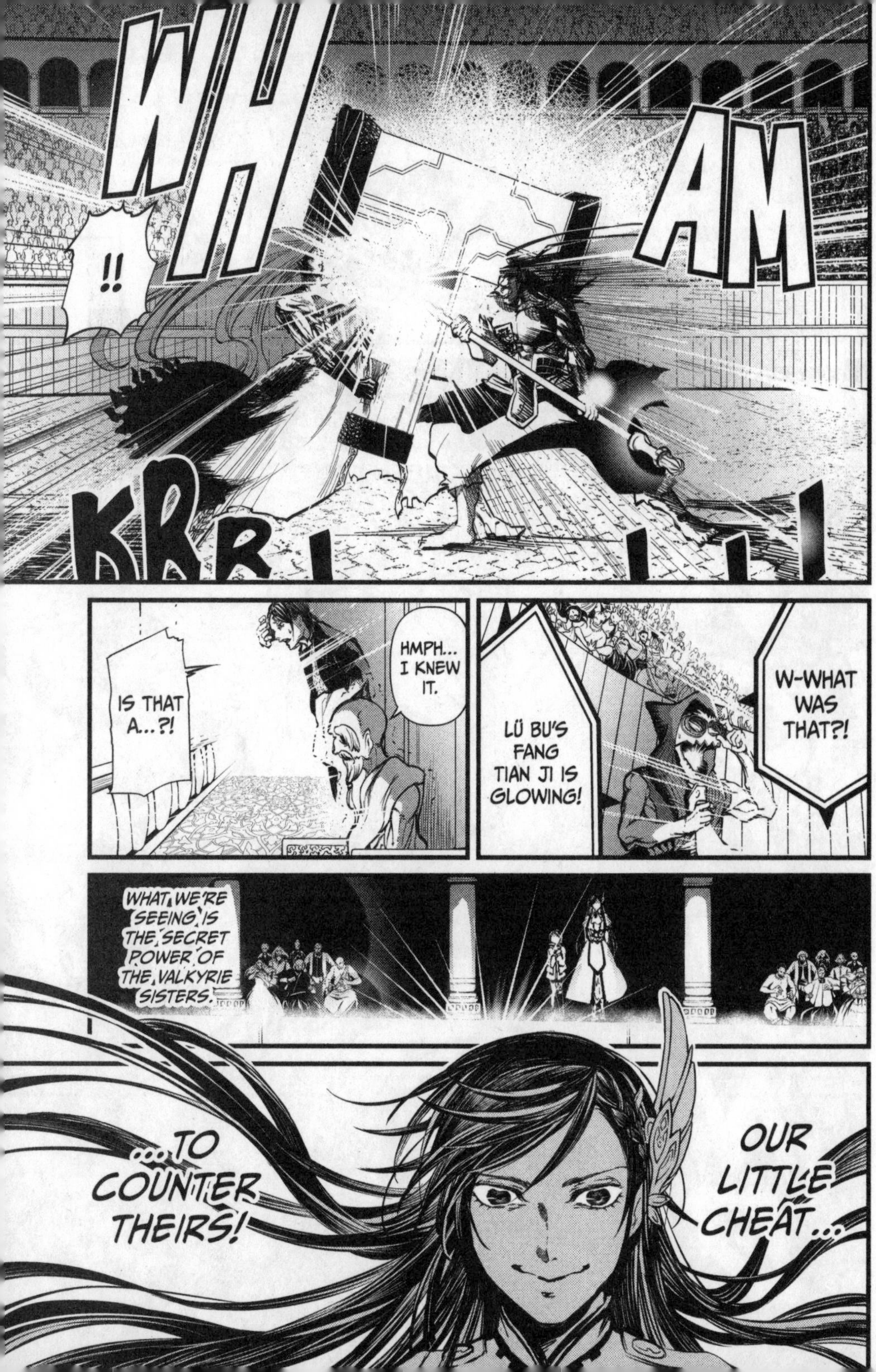
WHAM
!!
KRR
W-WHAT WAS THAT?!
LÜ BU'S FANG TIAN JI IS GLOWING!
HMPH... I KNEW IT.
IS THAT A...?!
WHAT WE'RE SEEING IS THE SECRET POWER OF THE VALKYRIE SISTERS.
OUR LITTLE CHEAT...
...TO COUNTER THEIRS!

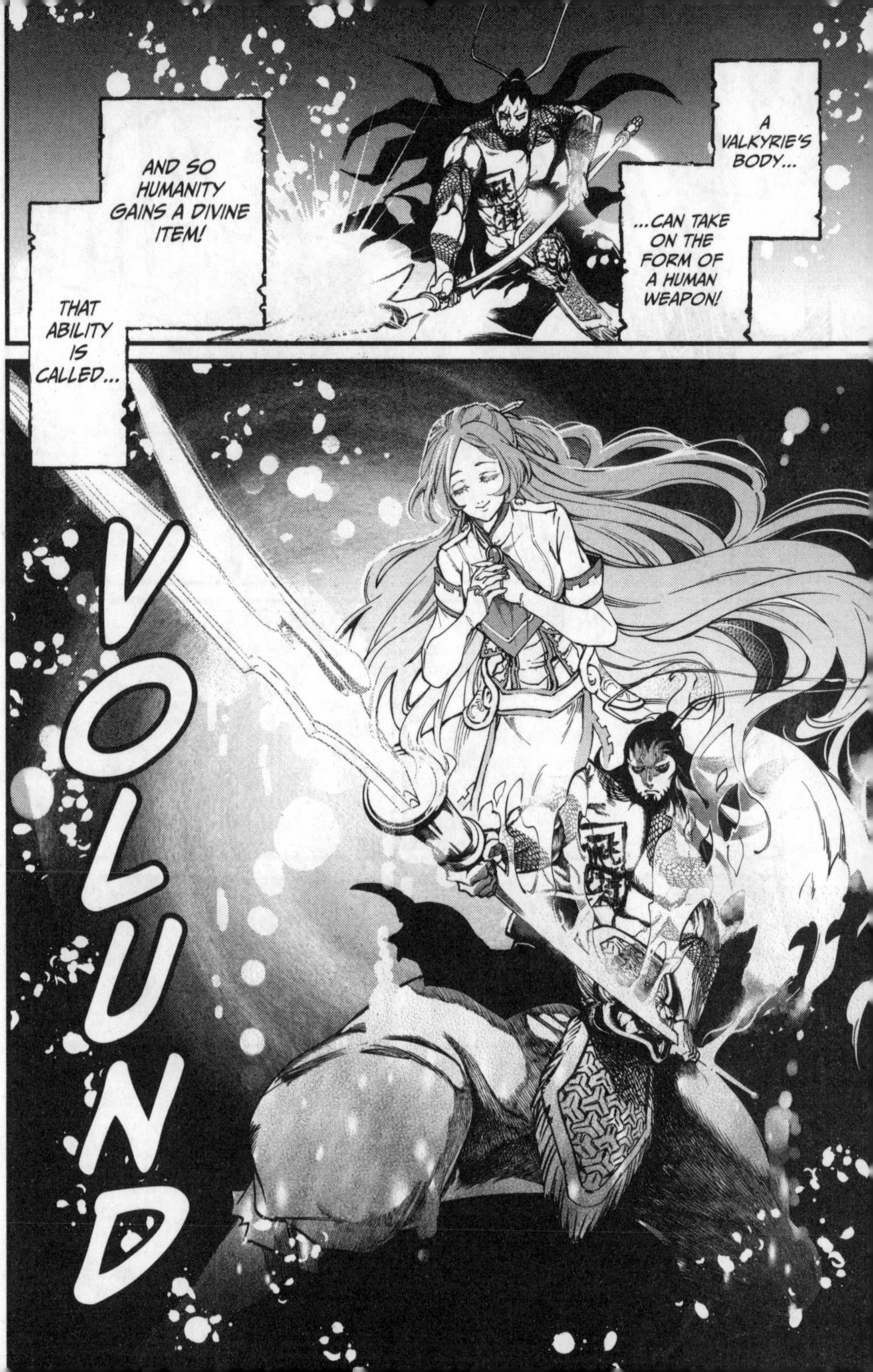
A VALKYRIE'S BODY...
...CAN TAKE ON THE FORM OF A HUMAN WEAPON!
AND SO HUMANITY GAINS A DIVINE ITEM!
THAT ABILITY IS CALLED...
VOLUND

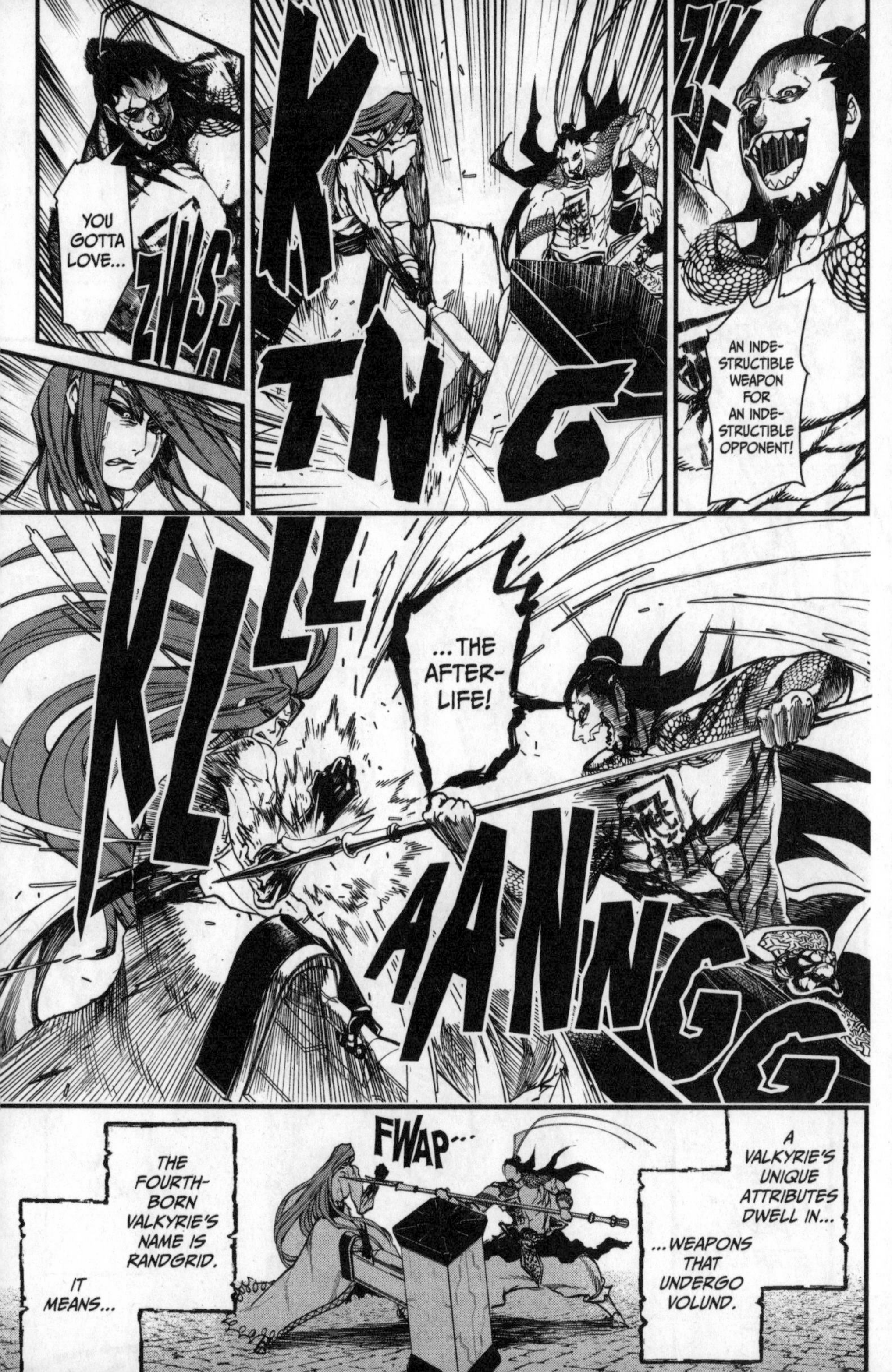
AN INDE-STRUCTIBLE WEAPON FOR AN INDE-STRUCTIBLE OPPONENT!
YOU GOTTA LOVE...
...THE AFTER-LIFE!
A VALKYRIE'S UNIQUE ATTRIBUTES DWELL IN...
...WEAPONS THAT UNDERGO VOLUND.
FWAP...
THE FOURTH-BORN VALKYRIE'S NAME IS RANDGRID.
IT MEANS...

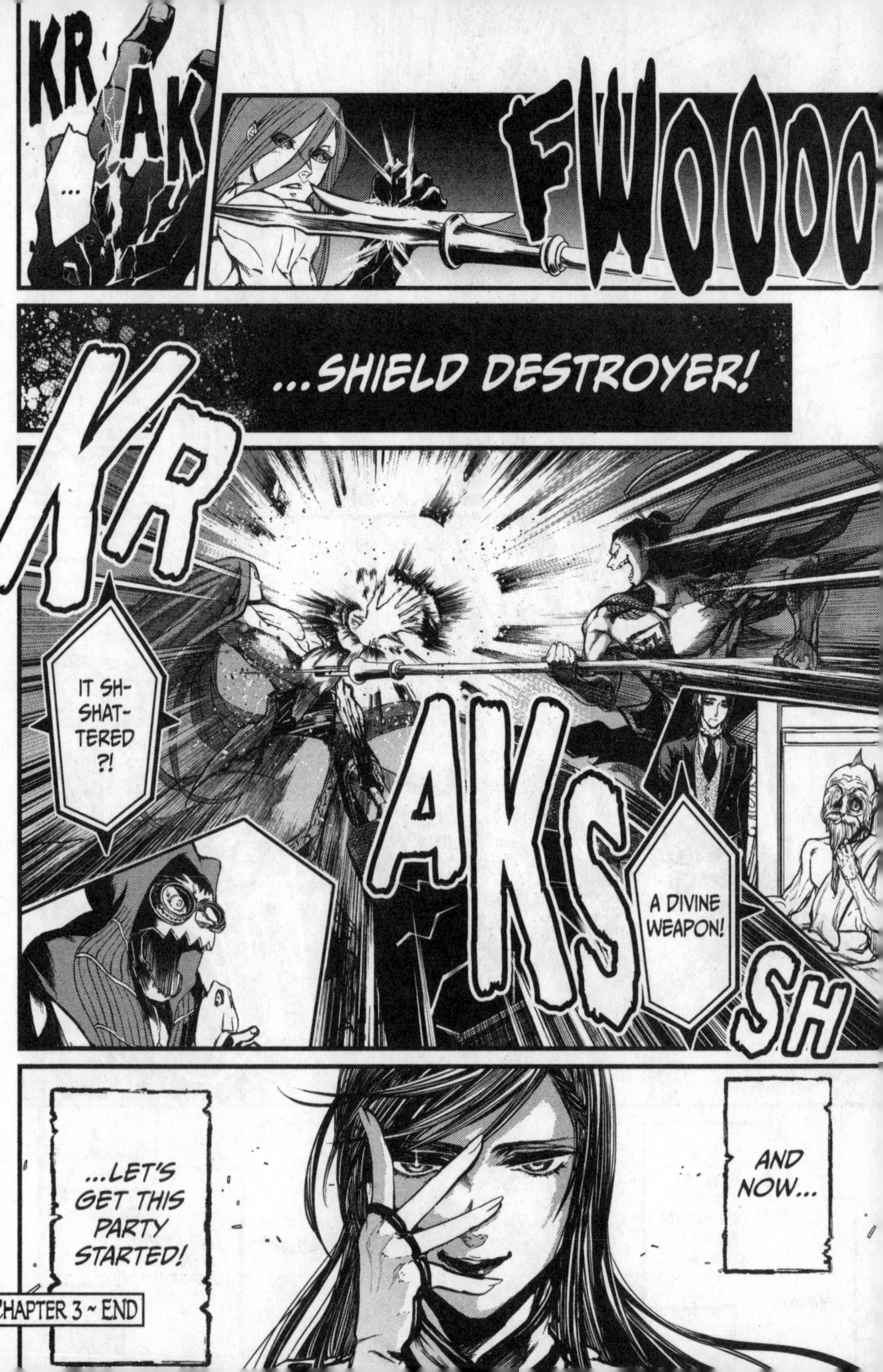
FWOOOO
KR AK
...
...SHIELD DESTROYER!
KR AKS SH
A DIVINE WEAPON!
IT SH-SHATTERED?!
AND NOW...
...LET'S GET THIS PARTY STARTED!
CHAPTER 3 ~ END

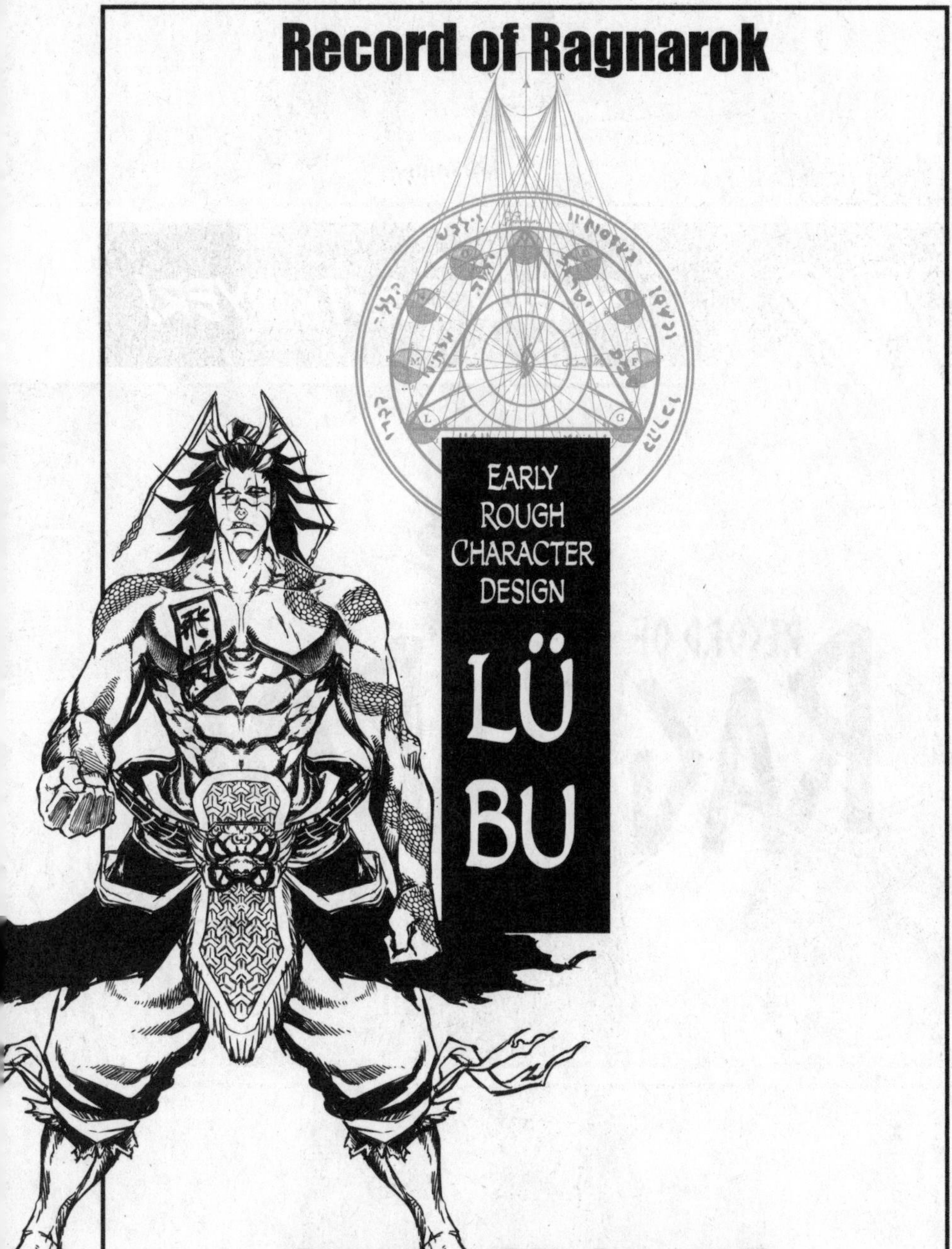
Record of Ragnarok
EARLY
ROUGH
CHARACTER
DESIGN
LÜ
BU

RECORD OF

RAGNAROK

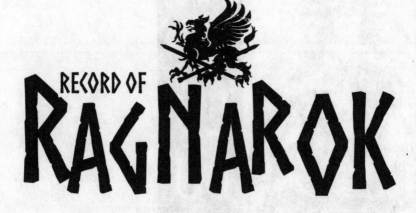

Chapter 4: Thirteen Gods and Thirteen Humans

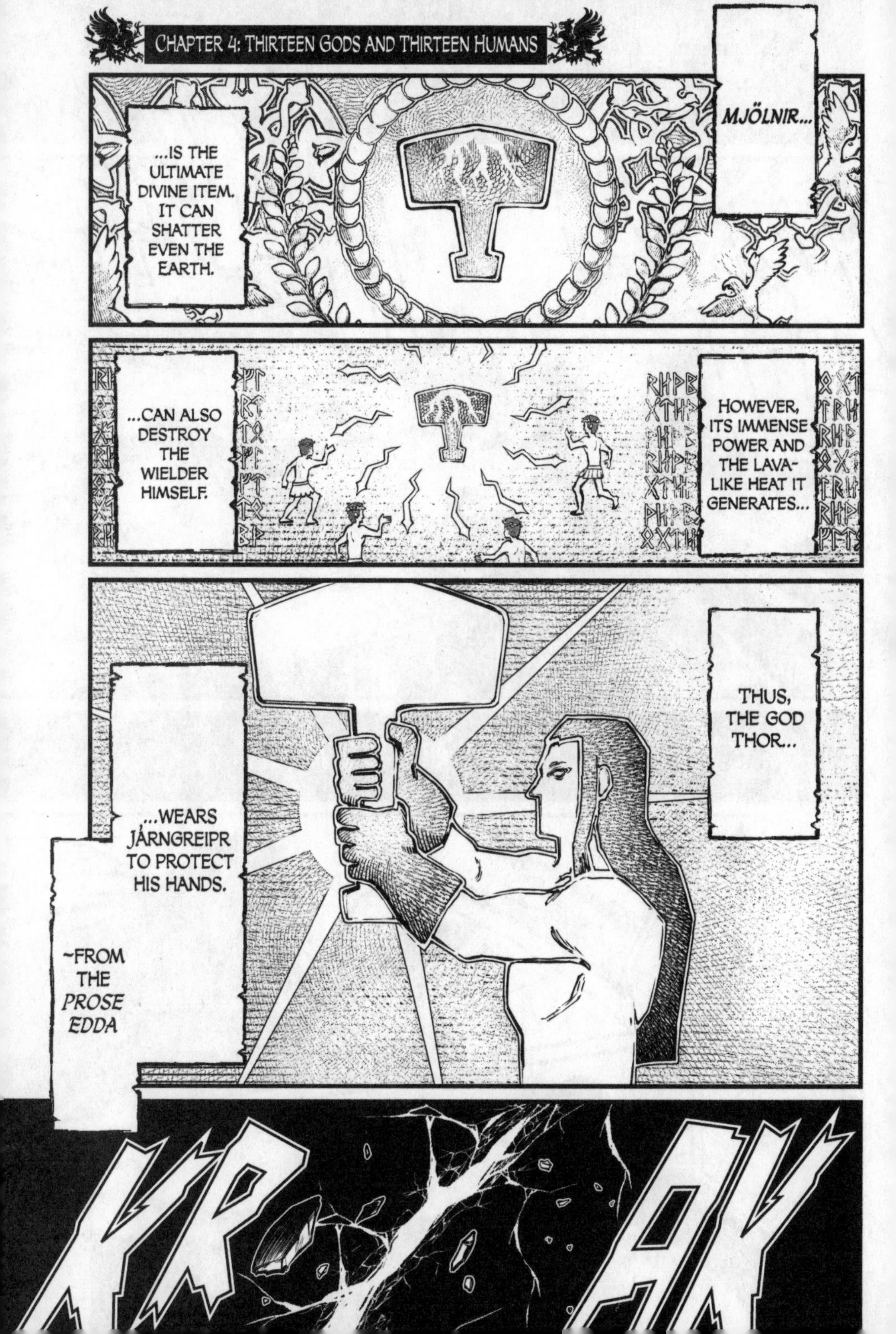
MJÖLNIR...
...IS THE ULTIMATE DIVINE ITEM. IT CAN SHATTER EVEN THE EARTH.
HOWEVER, ITS IMMENSE POWER AND THE LAVA-LIKE HEAT IT GENERATES...
...CAN ALSO DESTROY THE WIELDER HIMSELF.
THUS, THE GOD THOR...
...WEARS JÅRNGREIPR TO PROTECT HIS HANDS.
~FROM THE *PROSE EDDA*
KRAK

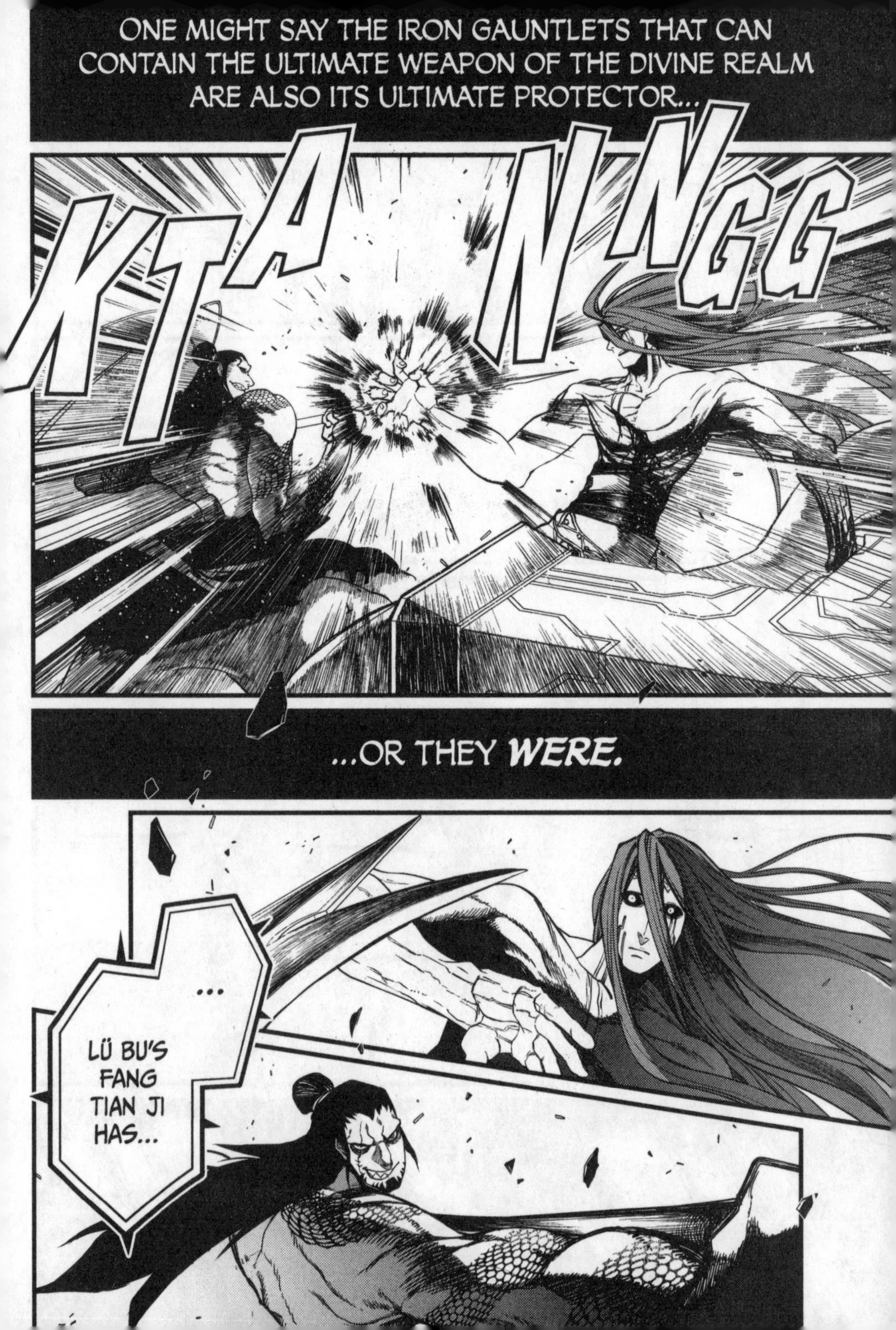
ONE MIGHT SAY THE IRON GAUNTLETS THAT CAN CONTAIN THE ULTIMATE WEAPON OF THE DIVINE REALM ARE ALSO ITS ULTIMATE PROTECTOR...
KTANNGG
...OR THEY **WERE.**
...
LÜ BU'S FANG TIAN JI HAS...

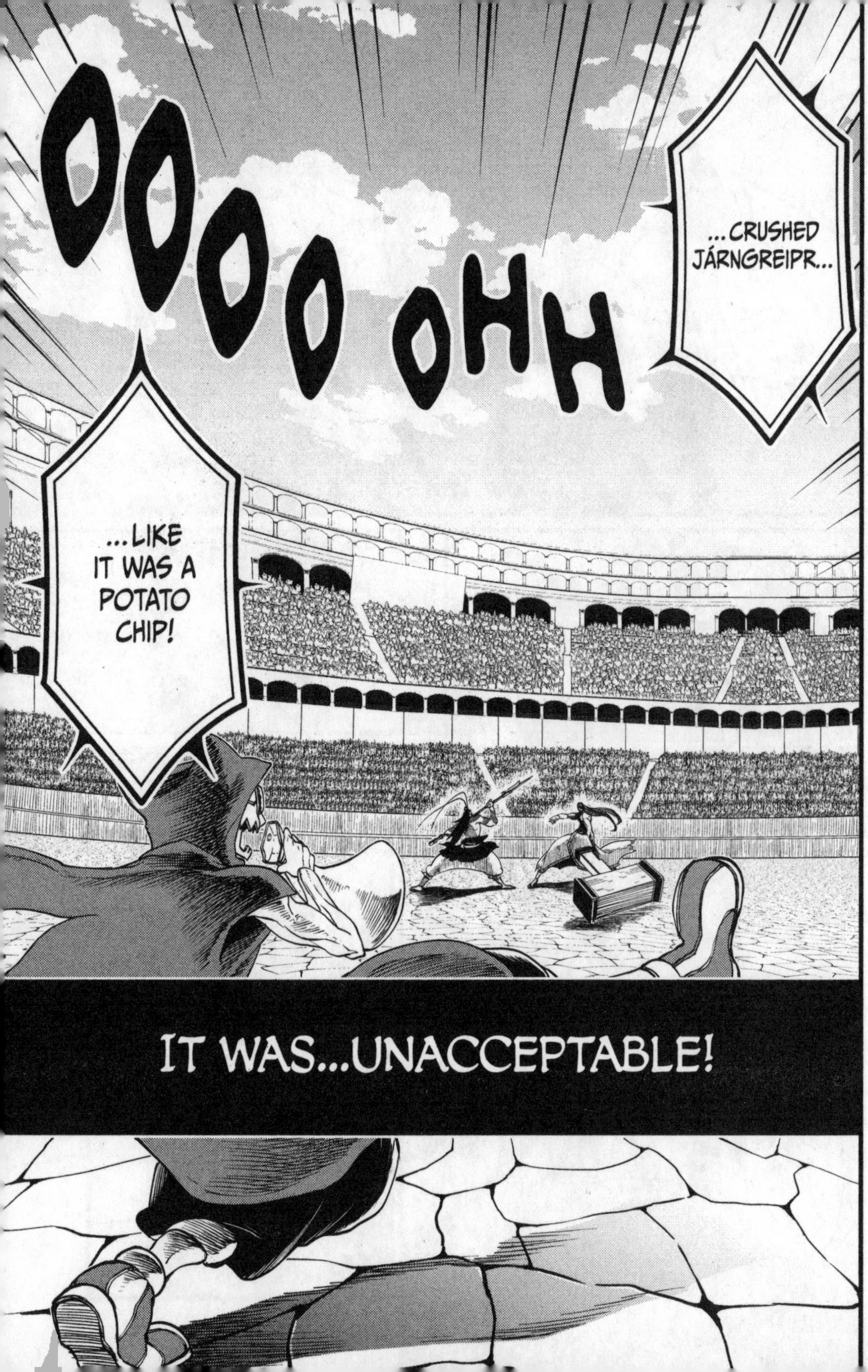
...CRUSHED JÁRNGREIPR...
OOOO OHH
...LIKE IT WAS A POTATO CHIP!
IT WAS...UNACCEPTABLE!

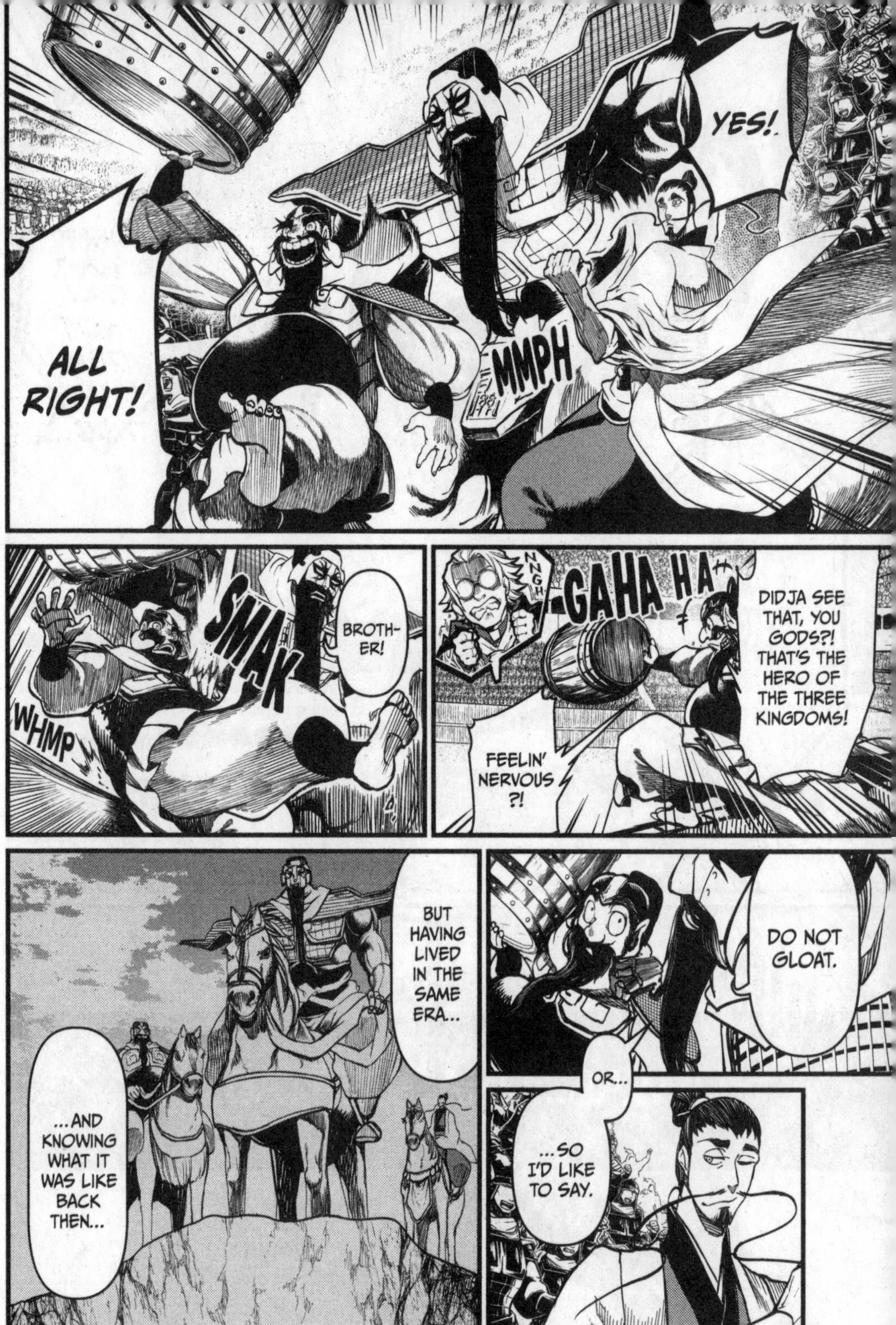
YES!
MMPH
ALL RIGHT!
GAHA HA
NNGH
DIDJA SEE THAT, YOU GODS?! THAT'S THE HERO OF THE THREE KINGDOMS!
FEELIN' NERVOUS?!
BROTHER!
SMAK
WHMP
DO NOT GLOAT.
OR...
...SO I'D LIKE TO SAY.
BUT HAVING LIVED IN THE SAME ERA...
...AND KNOWING WHAT IT WAS LIKE BACK THEN...

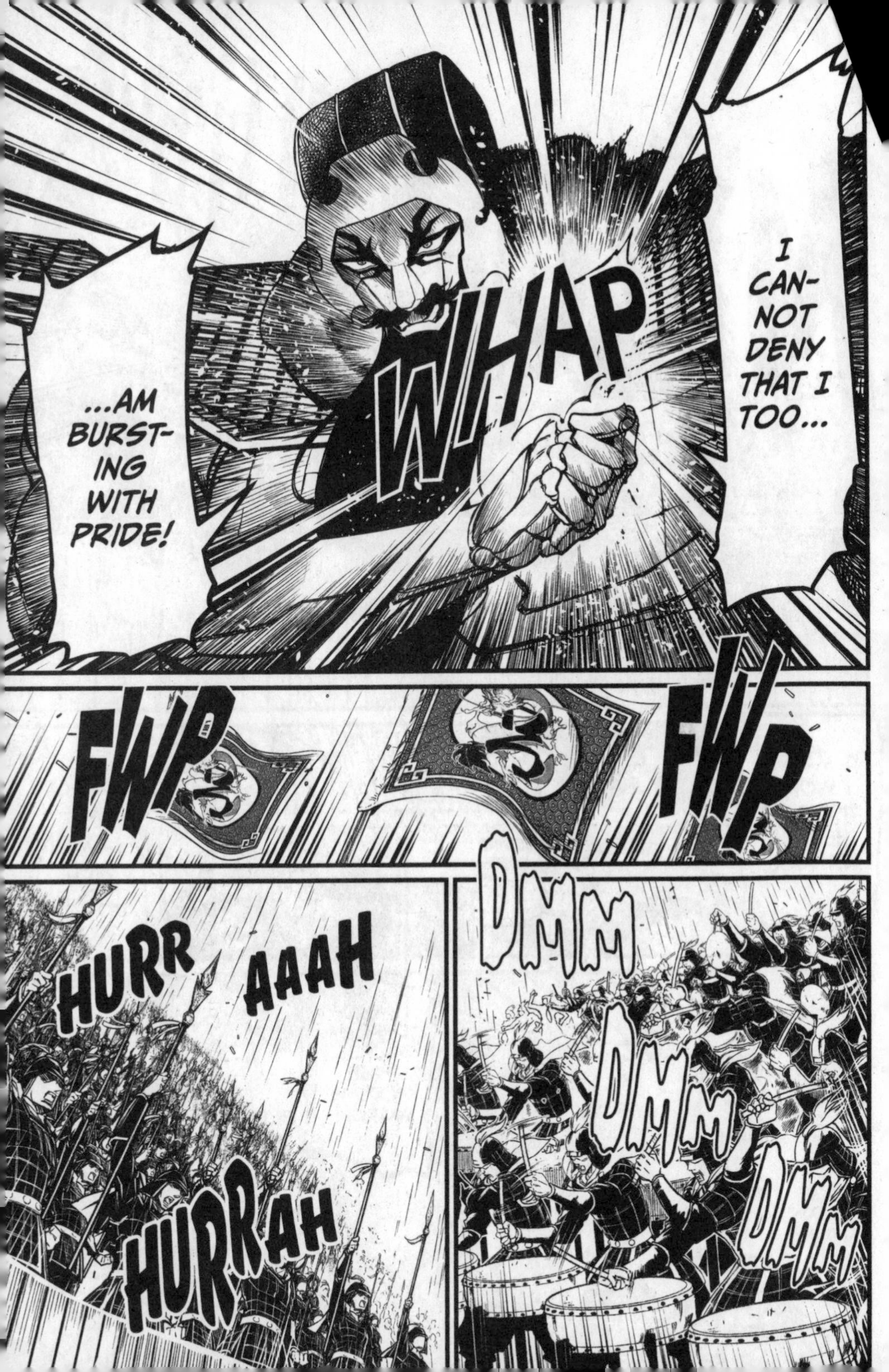
I CAN-NOT DENY THAT I TOO...
WHAP
...AM BURST-ING WITH PRIDE!
FWP
FWP
DMM
DMM
DMM
HURR
AAAH
HURRAH

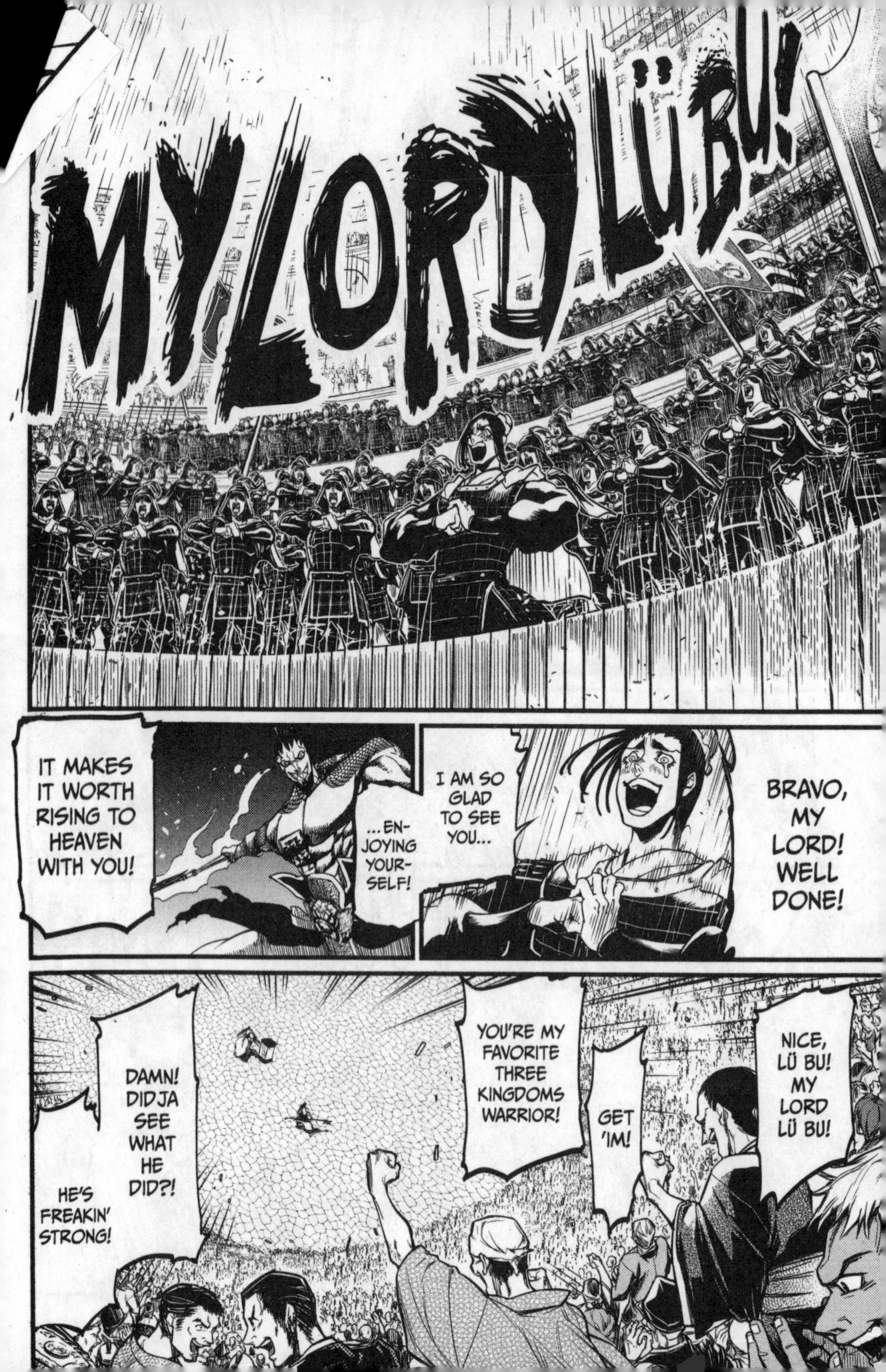
MY LORD LÜ BU!
BRAVO, MY LORD! WELL DONE!
I AM SO GLAD TO SEE YOU...
...ENJOYING YOURSELF!
IT MAKES IT WORTH RISING TO HEAVEN WITH YOU!
NICE, LÜ BU! MY LORD LÜ BU!
GET 'IM!
YOU'RE MY FAVORITE THREE KINGDOMS WARRIOR!
DAMN! DIDJA SEE WHAT HE DID?!
HE'S FREAKIN' STRONG!

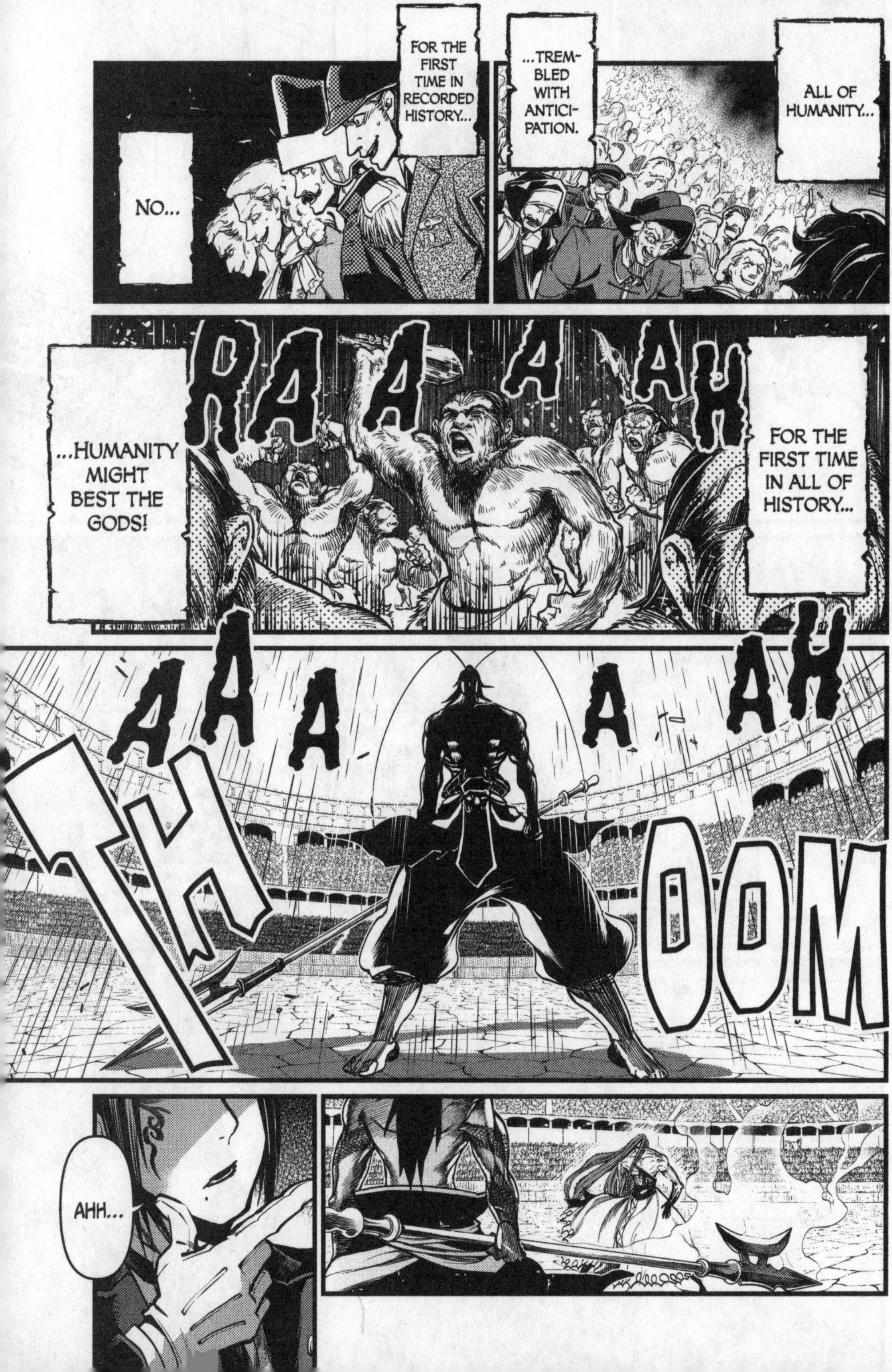
ALL OF HUMANITY...
...TREM-BLED WITH ANTICI-PATION.
FOR THE FIRST TIME IN RECORDED HISTORY...
NO...
FOR THE FIRST TIME IN ALL OF HISTORY...
RAAAAH
...HUMANITY MIGHT BEST THE GODS!
AAAAAH
THOOM
AHH...

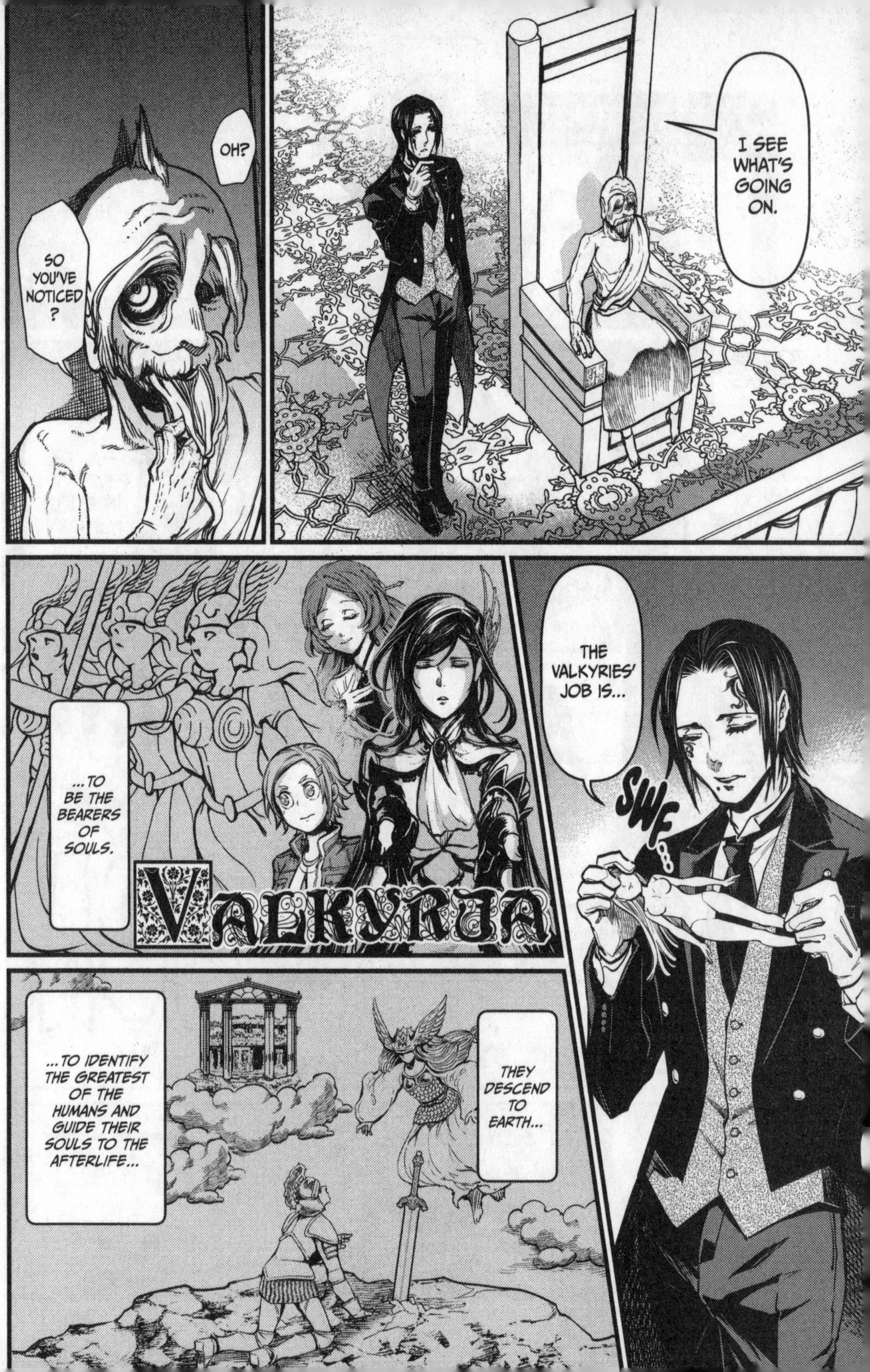
I SEE WHAT'S GOING ON.
OH?
SO YOU'VE NOTICED?
THE VALKYRIES' JOB IS...
SWF
...TO BE THE BEARERS OF SOULS.
VALKYRJA
THEY DESCEND TO EARTH...
...TO IDENTIFY THE GREATEST OF THE HUMANS AND GUIDE THEIR SOULS TO THE AFTERLIFE...

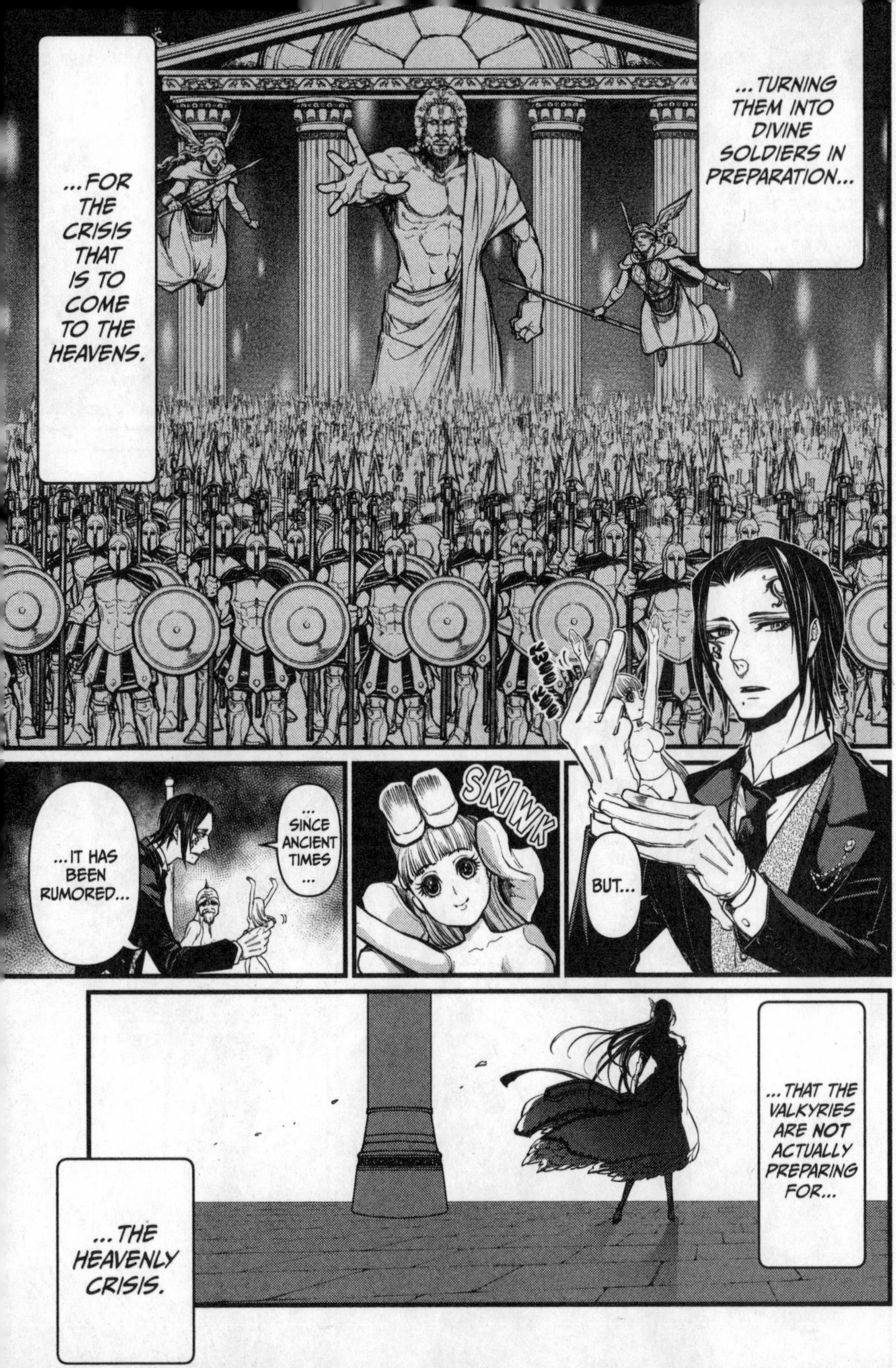
...TURNING THEM INTO DIVINE SOLDIERS IN PREPARATION...
...FOR THE CRISIS THAT IS TO COME TO THE HEAVENS.
BUT...
SKIWK
...SINCE ANCIENT TIMES...
...IT HAS BEEN RUMORED...
...THAT THE VALKYRIES ARE NOT ACTUALLY PREPARING FOR...
...THE HEAVENLY CRISIS.

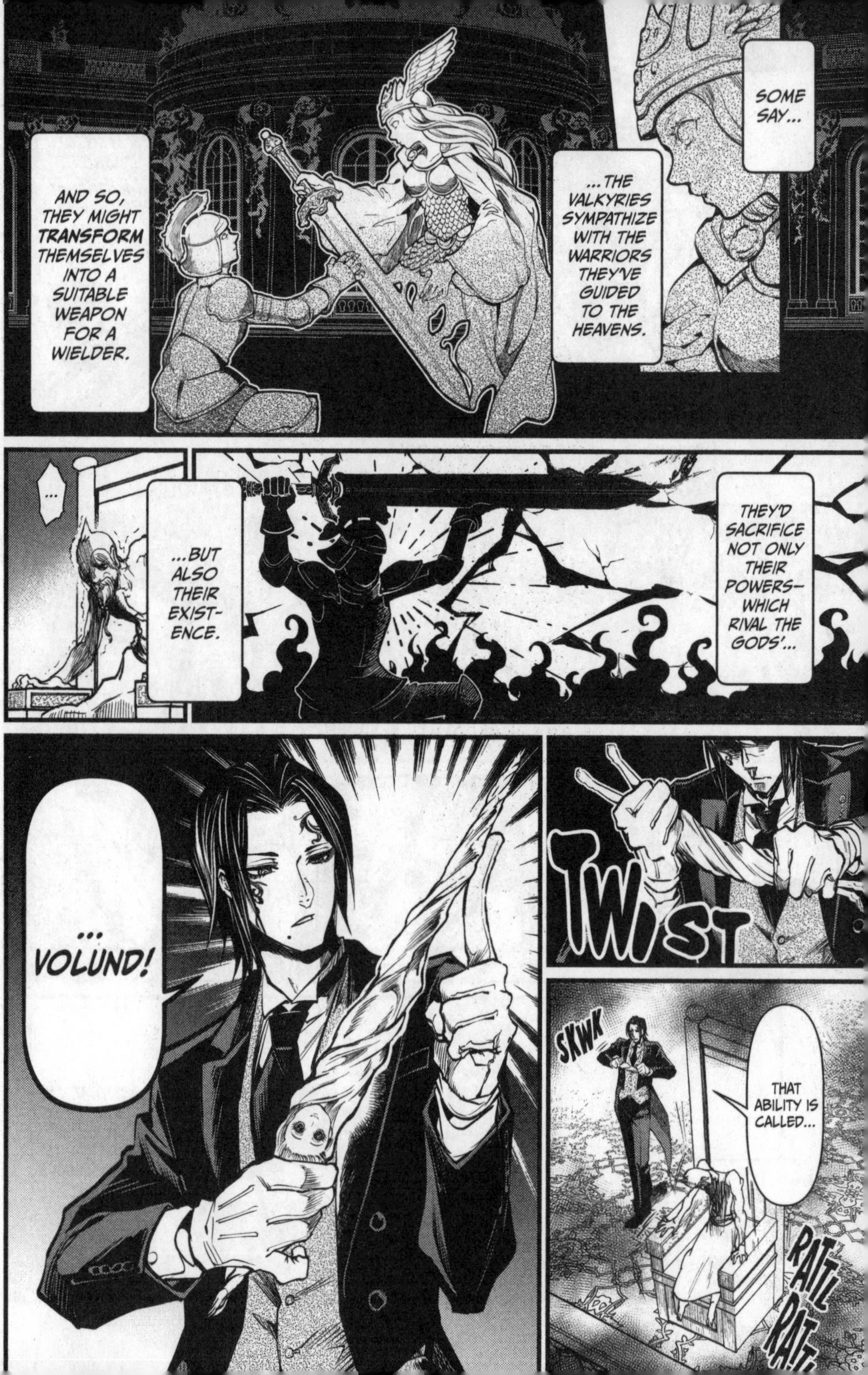
SOME SAY...
...THE VALKYRIES SYMPATHIZE WITH THE WARRIORS THEY'VE GUIDED TO THE HEAVENS.
AND SO, THEY MIGHT TRANSFORM THEMSELVES INTO A SUITABLE WEAPON FOR A WIELDER.
THEY'D SACRIFICE NOT ONLY THEIR POWERS—WHICH RIVAL THE GODS'...
...BUT ALSO THEIR EXISTENCE.
...
TWIST
THAT ABILITY IS CALLED...
SKWK
RATTL
RATTL
...VOLUND!

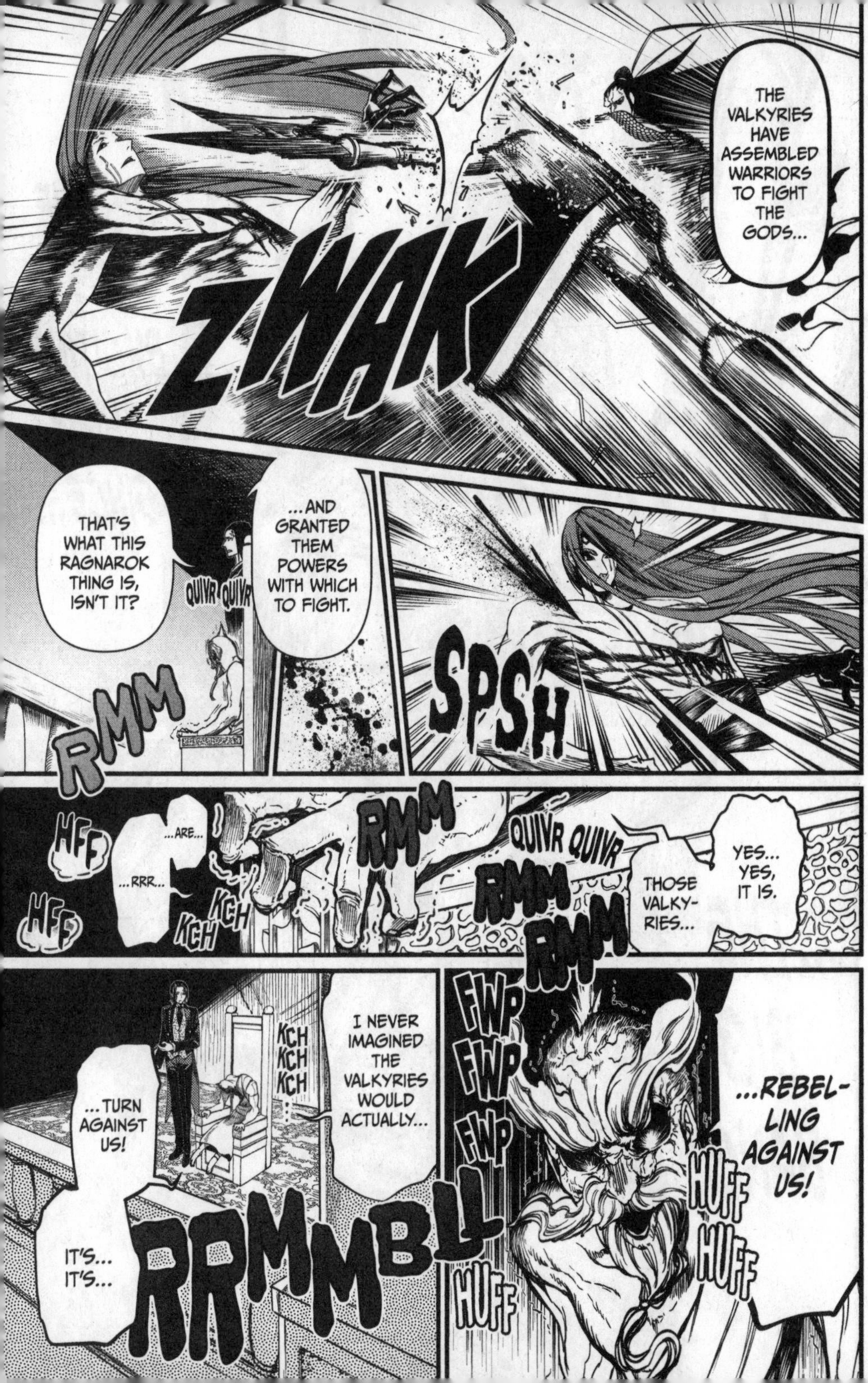
THE VALKYRIES HAVE ASSEMBLED WARRIORS TO FIGHT THE GODS...
ZWAK
SPSH
...AND GRANTED THEM POWERS WITH WHICH TO FIGHT.
THAT'S WHAT THIS RAGNAROK THING IS, ISN'T IT?
QUIVR QUIVR
RMM
YES... YES, IT IS.
THOSE VALKY-RIES...
RMM
RMM
QUIVR QUIVR
RMM
KCH KCH
...ARE...
...RRR...
HFF
HFF
...REBEL-LING AGAINST US!
RMM
FWP FWP FWP FWP
HUFF HUFF HUFF
I NEVER IMAGINED THE VALKYRIES WOULD ACTUALLY...
KCH KCH KCH
...TURN AGAINST US!
IT'S... IT'S...
RRMMBLL

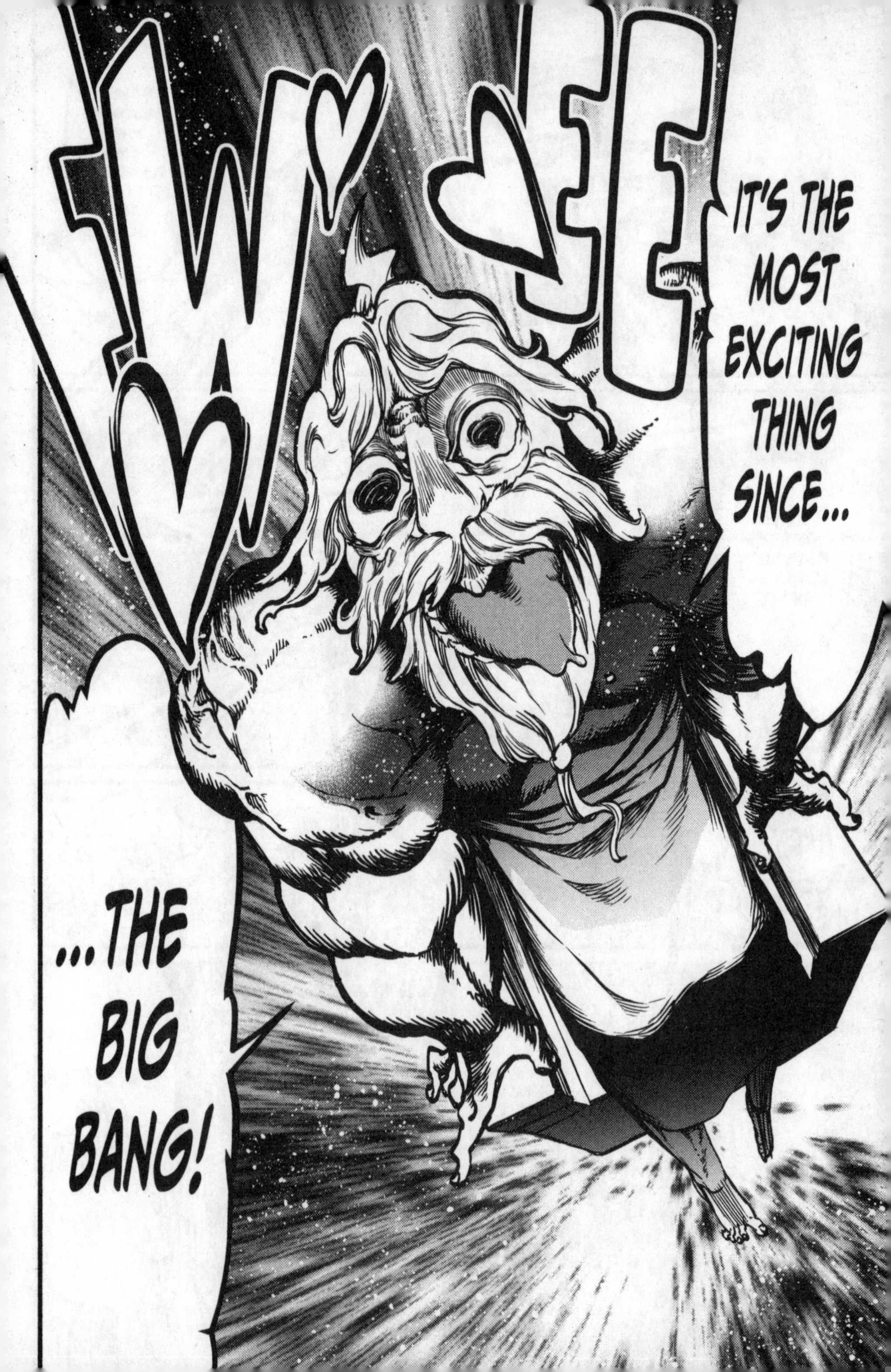
IT'S THE MOST EXCITING THING SINCE...
...THE BIG BANG!

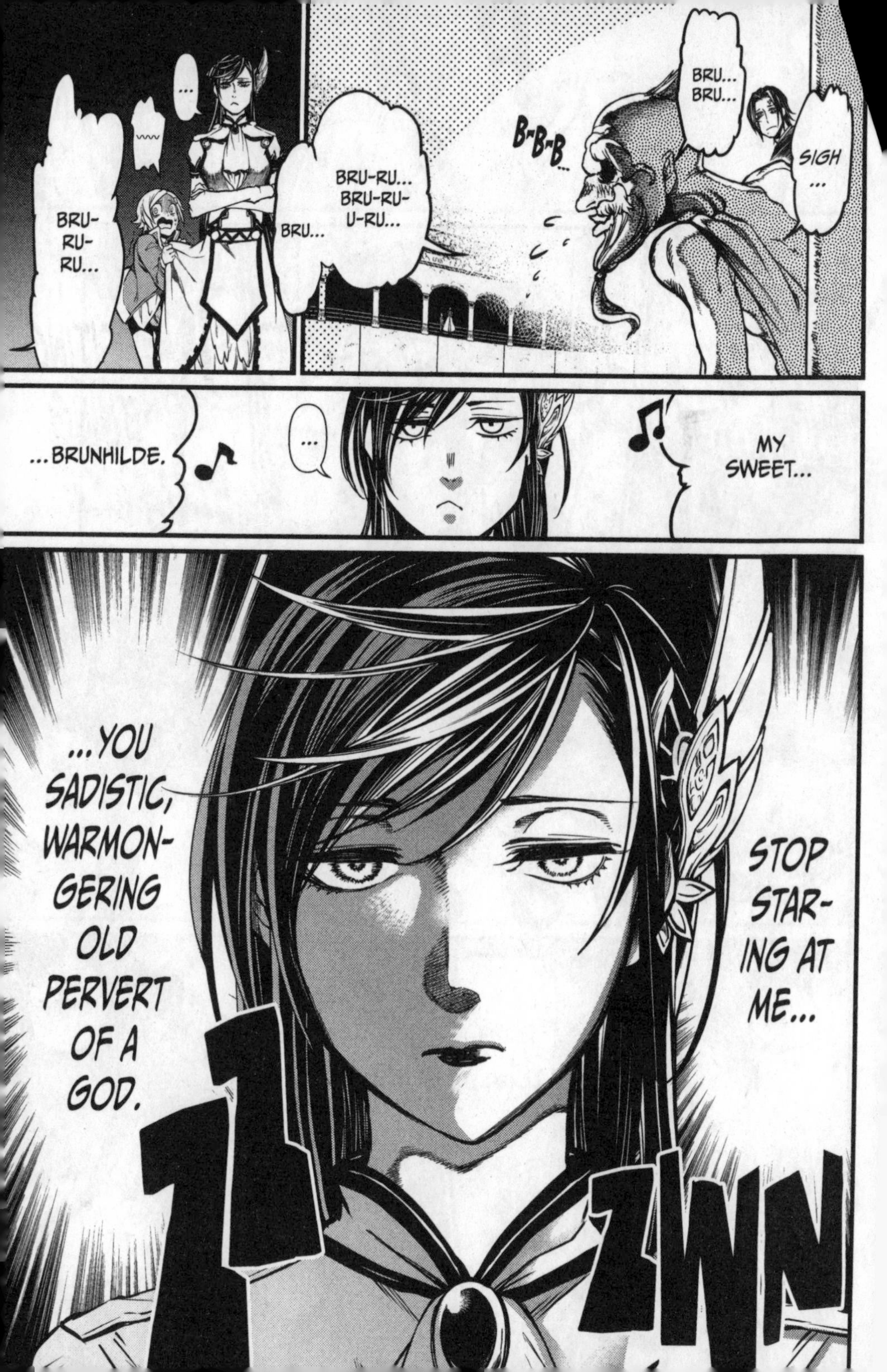
BRU... BRU...
SIGH ...
B-B-B...
BRU-RU... BRU-RU-U-RU...
BRU...
...
BRU-RU-RU...
MY SWEET...
...
...BRUNHILDE.
STOP STARING AT ME...
...YOU SADISTIC, WARMONGERING OLD PERVERT OF A GOD.

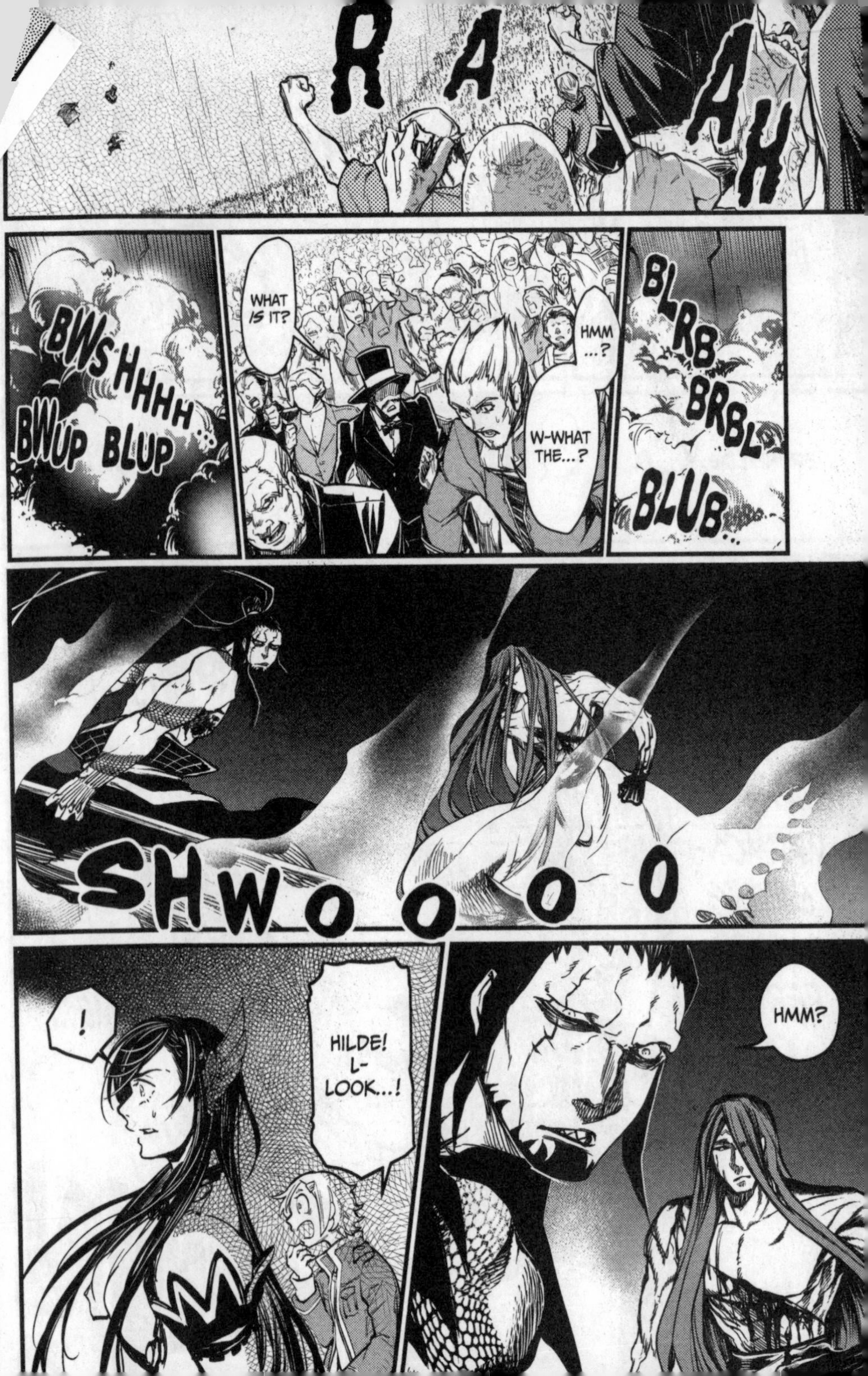
RAAH
BLRB BRBL BLUB...
HMM ...?
W-WHAT THE...?
WHAT IS IT?
BWSHHHH... BWUP BLUP
SHWOOOO
HMM?
HILDE! L-LOOK...!
!

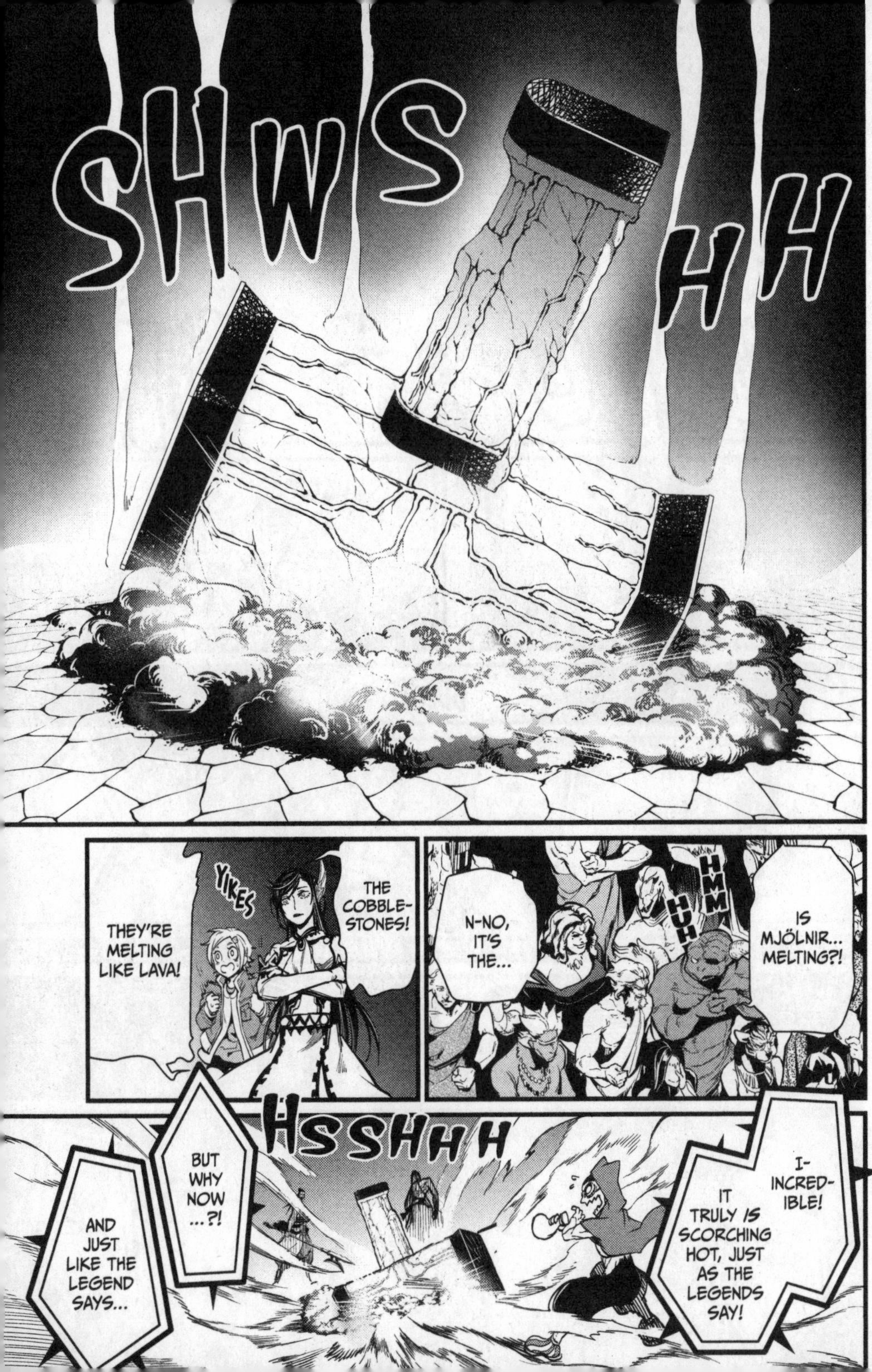
SHWSHH
IS MJÖLNIR... MELTING?!
HMM
HUH
N-NO, IT'S THE...
THE COBBLESTONES!
YIKES
THEY'RE MELTING LIKE LAVA!
HSSHHH
I-INCREDIBLE!
IT TRULY *IS* SCORCHING HOT, JUST AS THE LEGENDS SAY!
BUT WHY NOW...?!
AND JUST LIKE THE LEGEND SAYS...

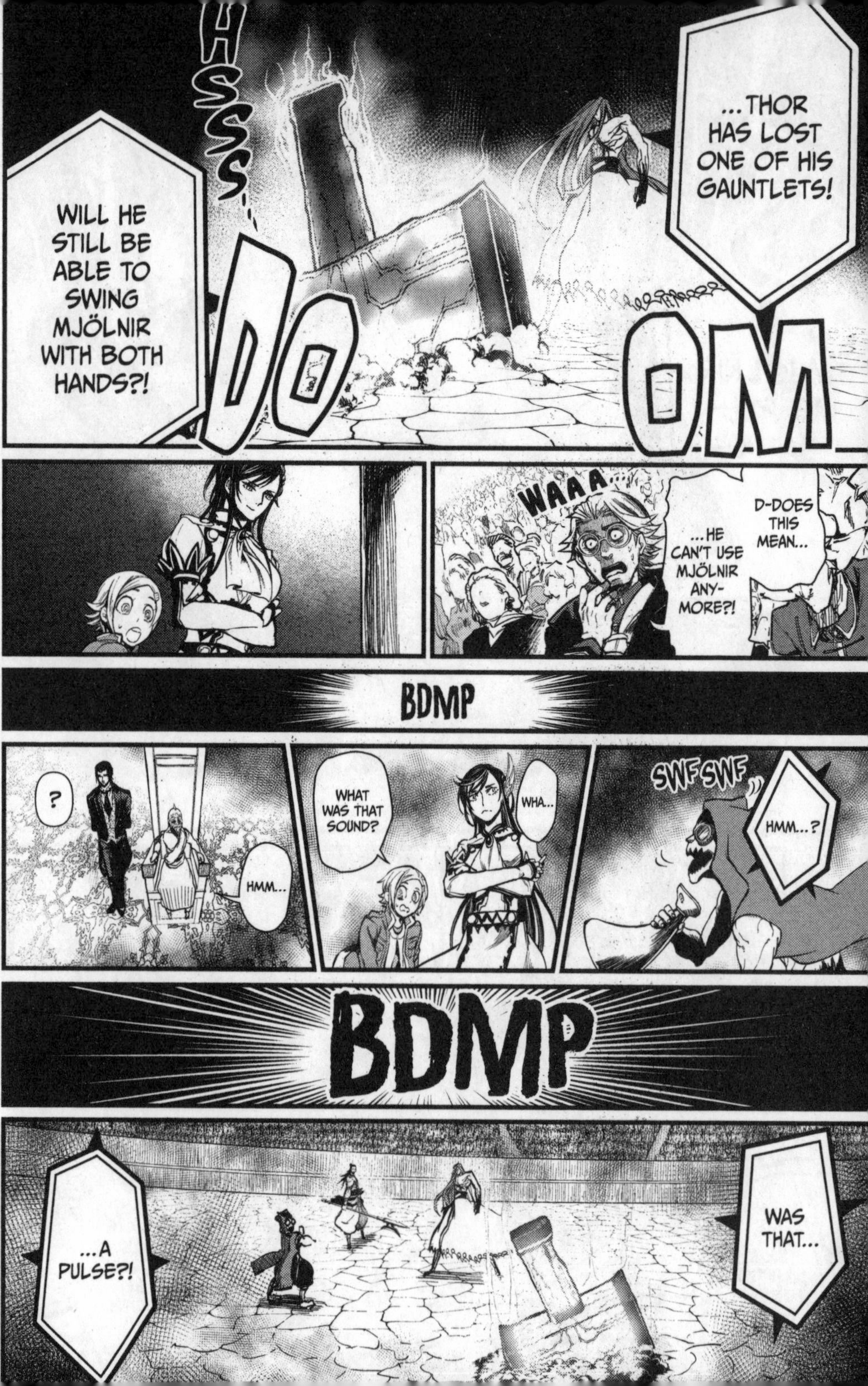
HSSS...
...THOR HAS LOST ONE OF HIS GAUNTLETS!
WILL HE STILL BE ABLE TO SWING MJÖLNIR WITH BOTH HANDS?!
DOOM
WAAA...
D-DOES THIS MEAN...
...HE CAN'T USE MJÖLNIR ANYMORE?!
BDMP
SWF SWF
HMM...?
WHA...
WHAT WAS THAT SOUND?
?
HMM...
BDMP
WAS THAT...
...A PULSE?!

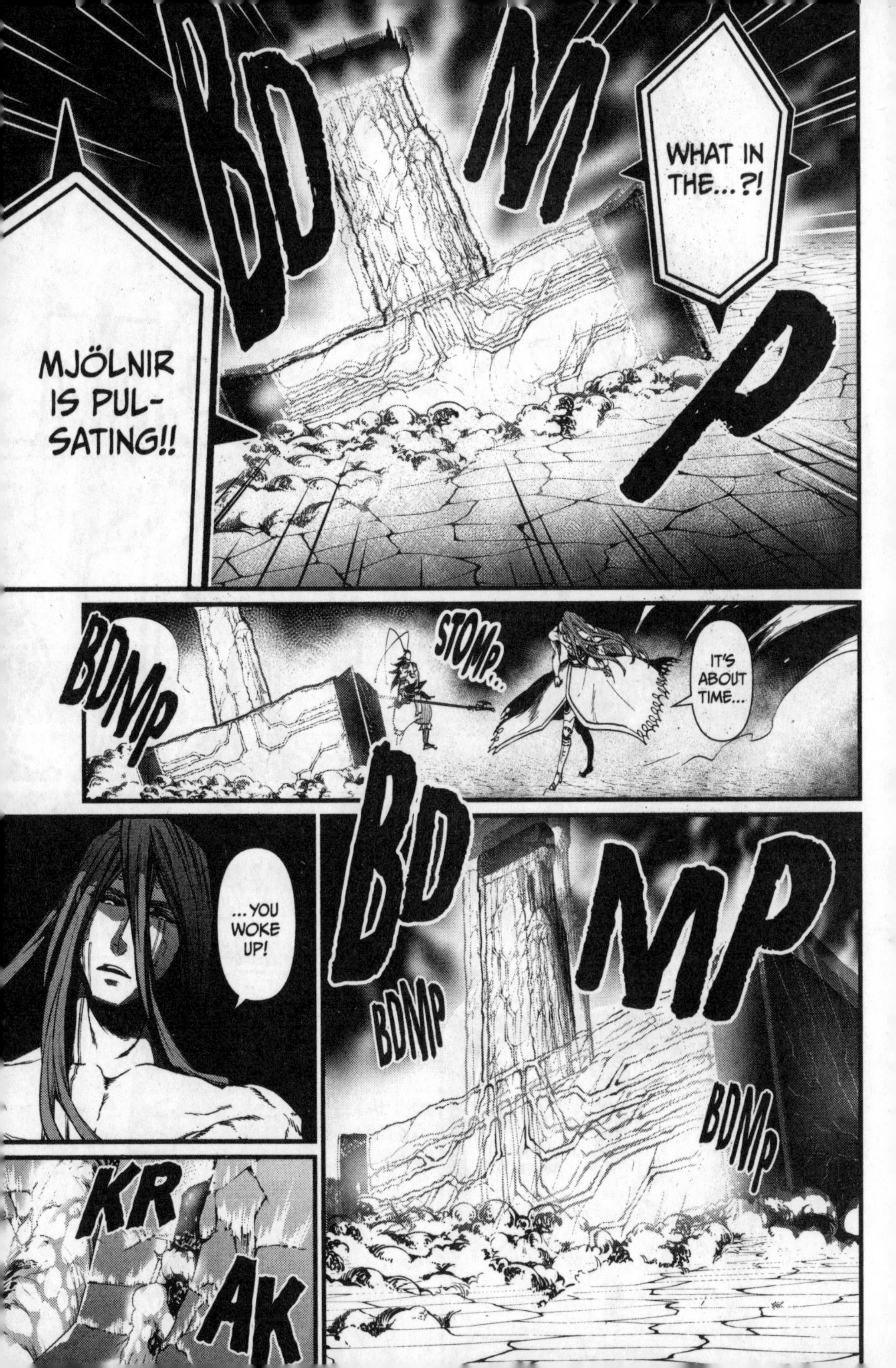
WHAT IN THE...?!
BDMP
MJÖLNIR IS PUL-SATING!!
IT'S ABOUT TIME...
STOMP...
BDMP
BDMP
BDMP
BDMP
...YOU WOKE UP!
KRAK

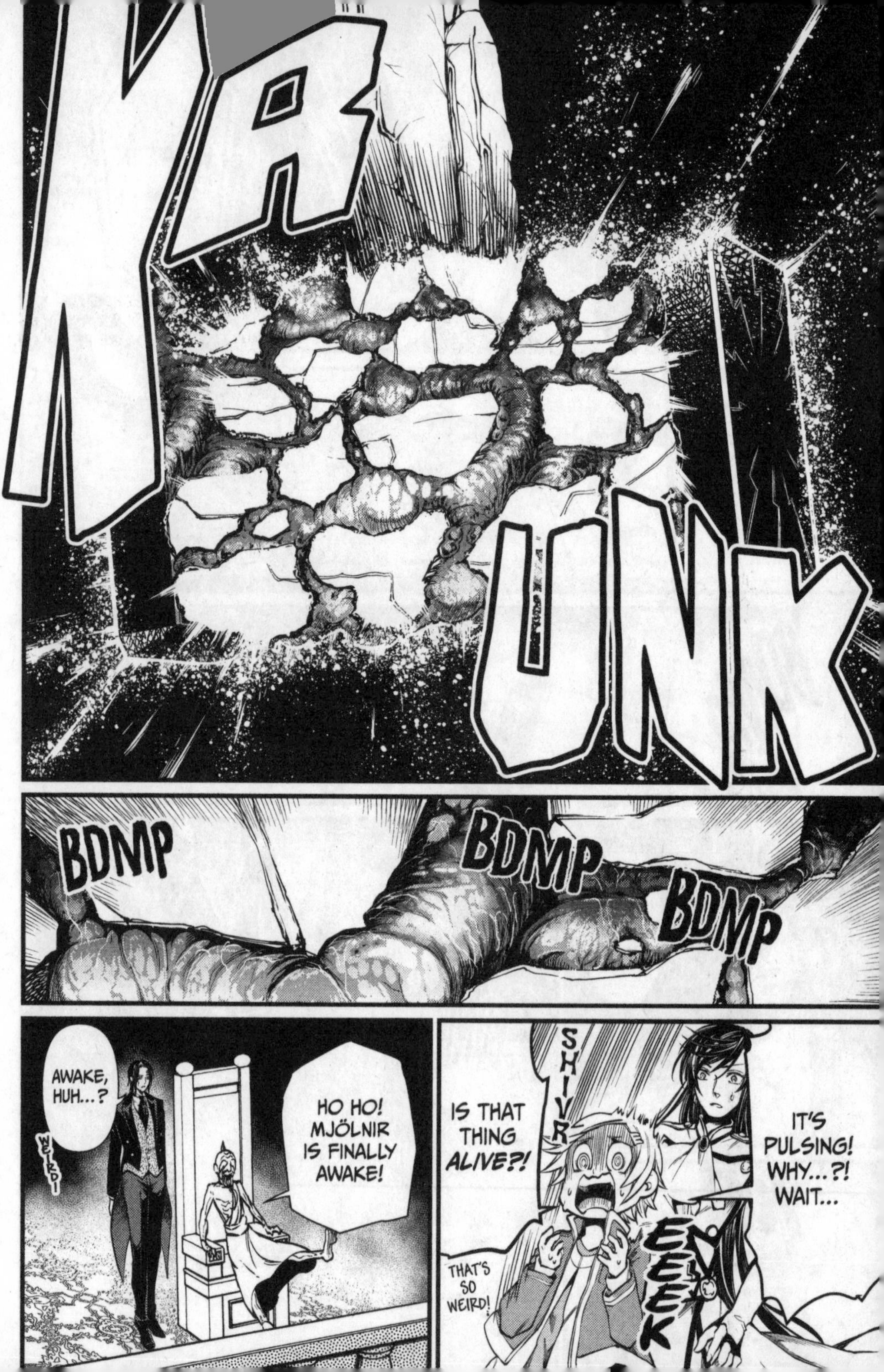
UNK
BDMP
BDMP
BDMP
SHIVR
IT'S PULSING! WHY...?! WAIT...
IS THAT THING ALIVE?!
EEEEK
THAT'S SO WEIRD!
HO HO! MJÖLNIR IS FINALLY AWAKE!
AWAKE, HUH...?
WEIRD!

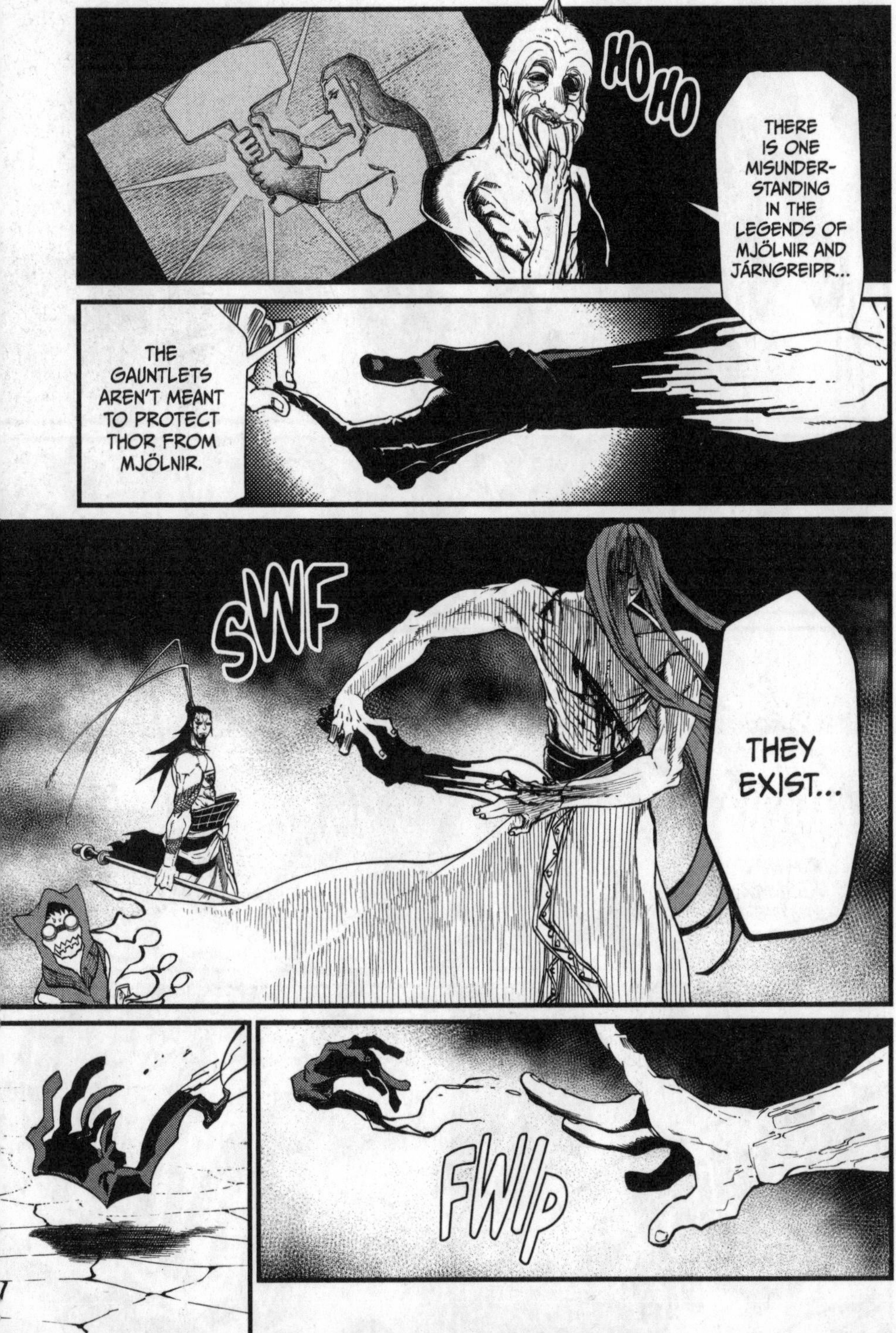
HOHO
THERE IS ONE MISUNDER-STANDING IN THE LEGENDS OF MJÖLNIR AND JÁRNGREIPR...
THE GAUNTLETS AREN'T MEANT TO PROTECT THOR FROM MJÖLNIR.
THEY EXIST...
SWF
FWIP

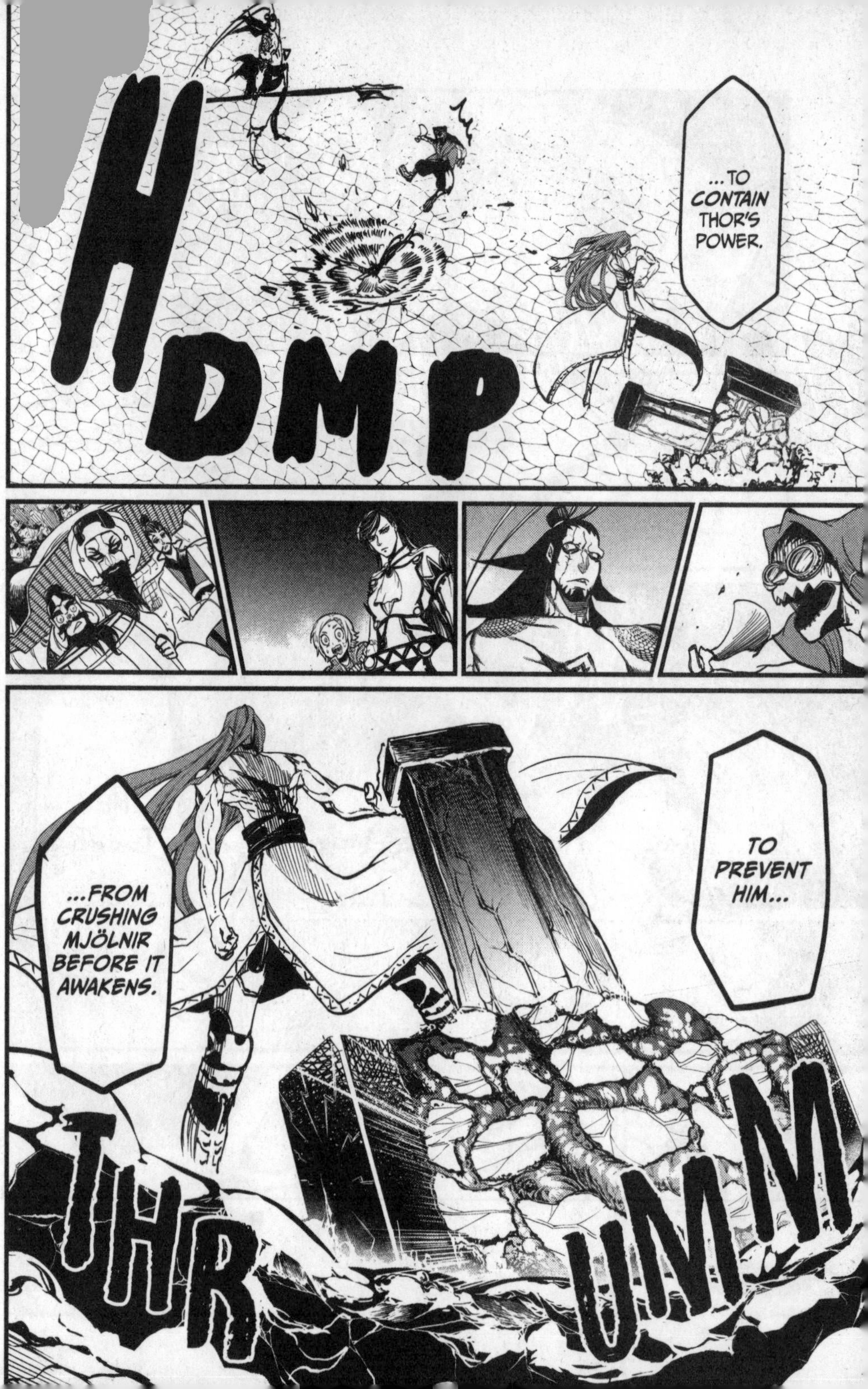
...TO CONTAIN THOR'S POWER.
HDMP
TO PREVENT HIM...
...FROM CRUSHING MJÖLNIR BEFORE IT AWAKENS.
THRUMM

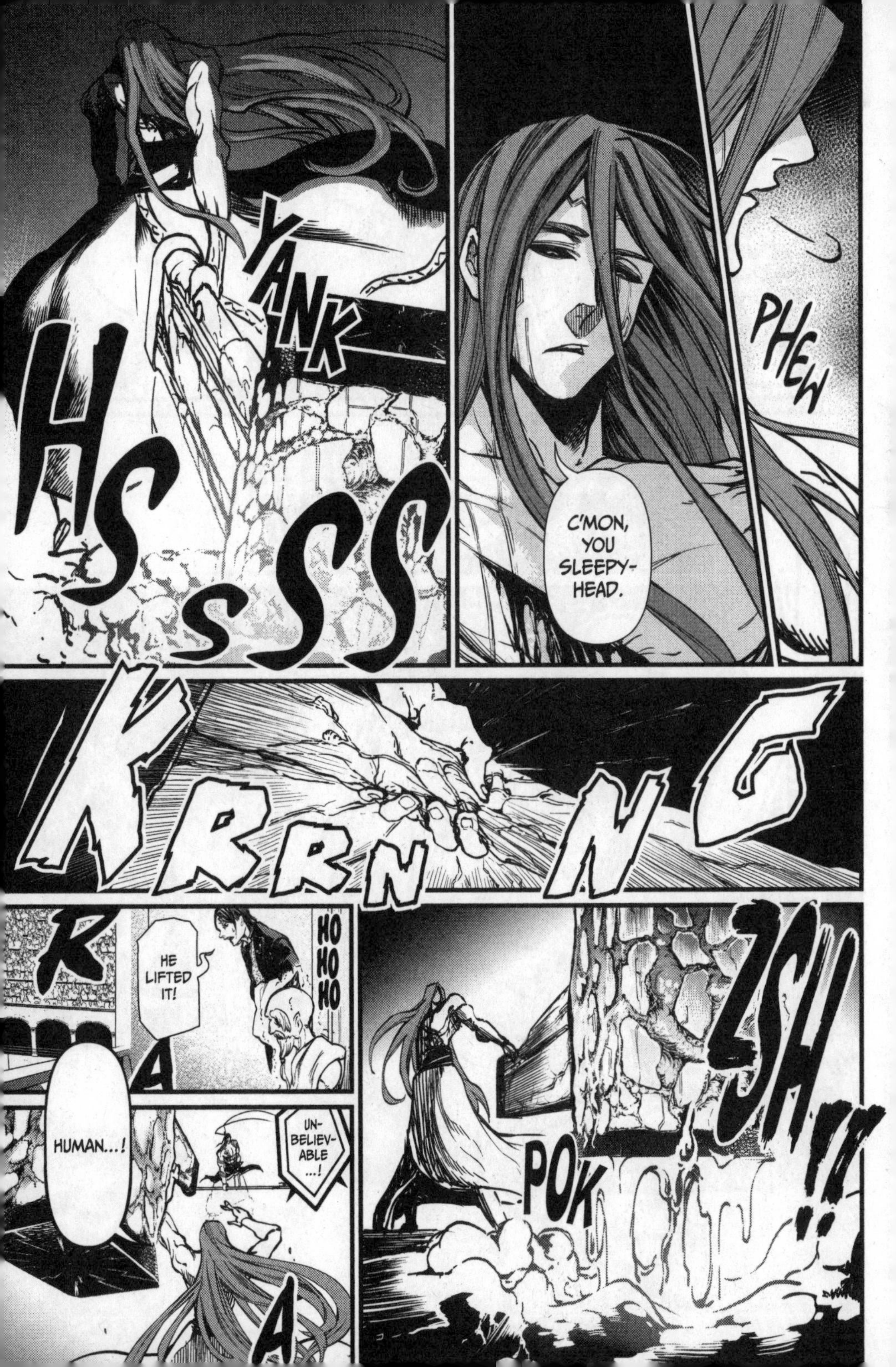
PHEW
C'MON, YOU SLEEPY-HEAD.
YANK
HSSSS
K'RRNNG
ZSH!!
POK
HOHOHO
HE LIFTED IT!
R
A
UN-BELIEVABLE...!
HUMAN...!
A

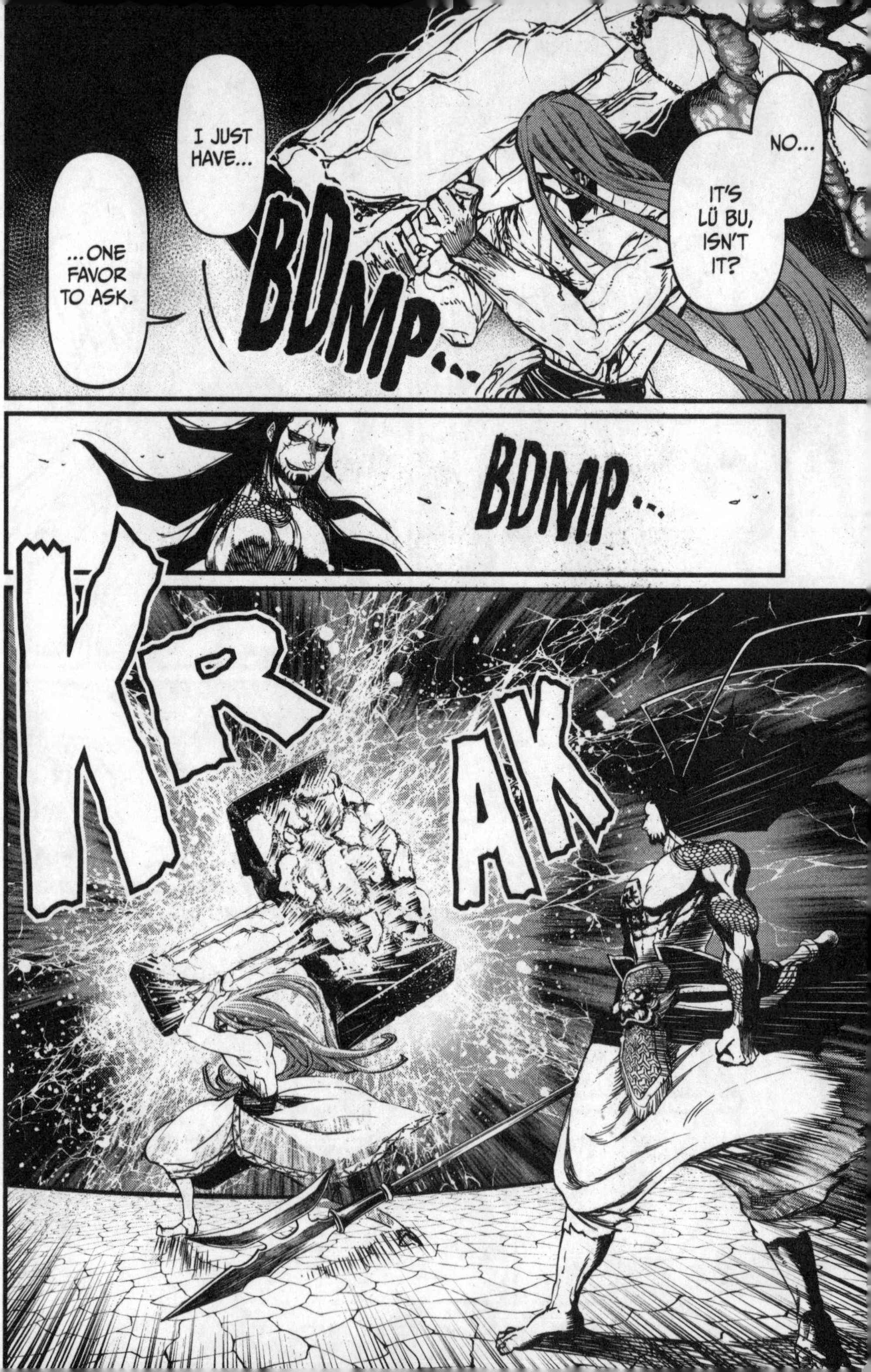
NO...
IT'S LÜ BU, ISN'T IT?
BDMP...
I JUST HAVE...
...ONE FAVOR TO ASK.
BDMP...
KRAK

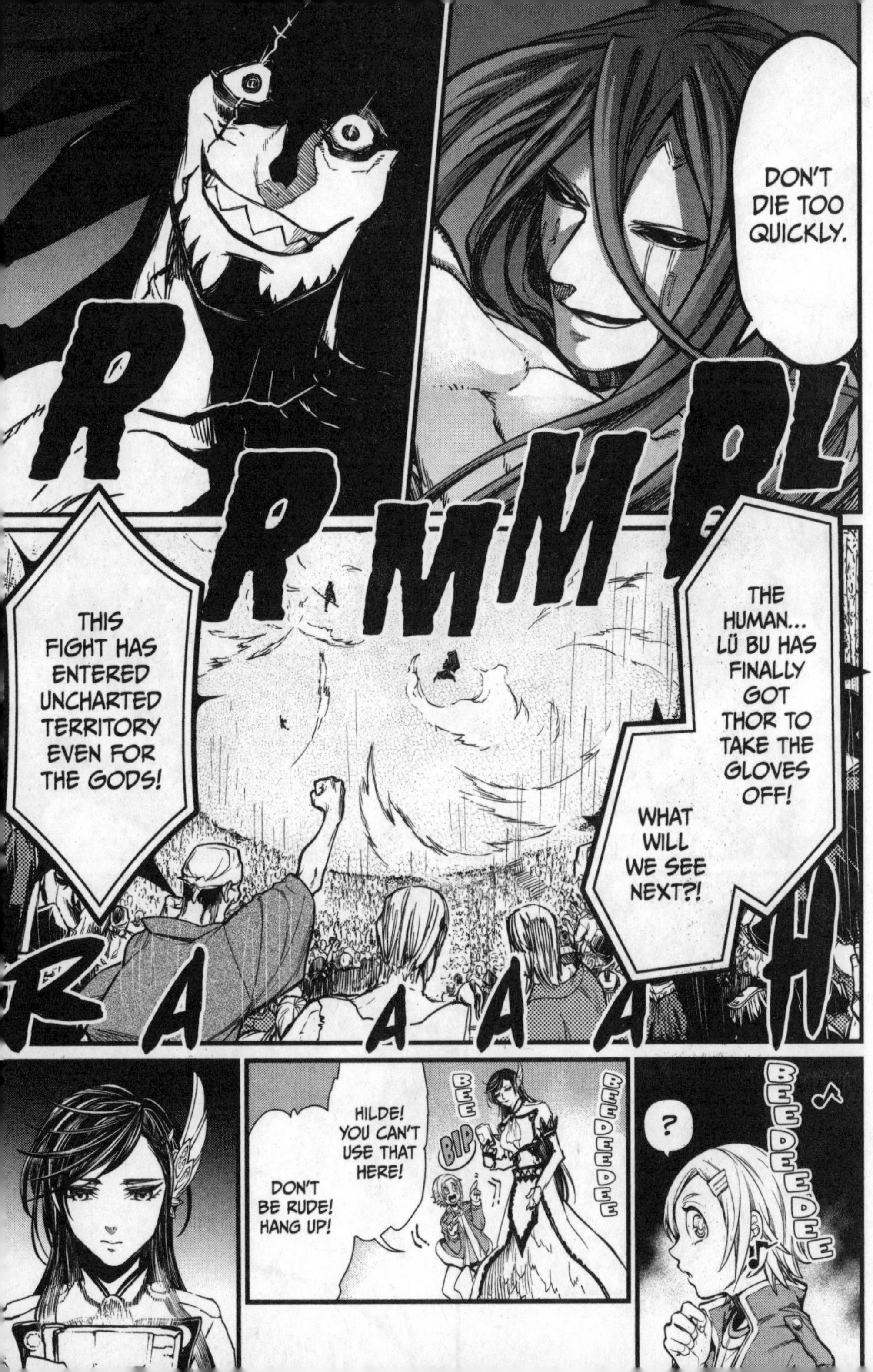
DON'T DIE TOO QUICKLY.
RRMMBL
THE HUMAN... LÜ BU HAS FINALLY GOT THOR TO TAKE THE GLOVES OFF!
WHAT WILL WE SEE NEXT?!
THIS FIGHT HAS ENTERED UNCHARTED TERRITORY EVEN FOR THE GODS!
RAAAAH
BEEDEEDEEDEE
?
BEEDEDEE
BEE
BIP
HILDE! YOU CAN'T USE THAT HERE!
DON'T BE RUDE! HANG UP!

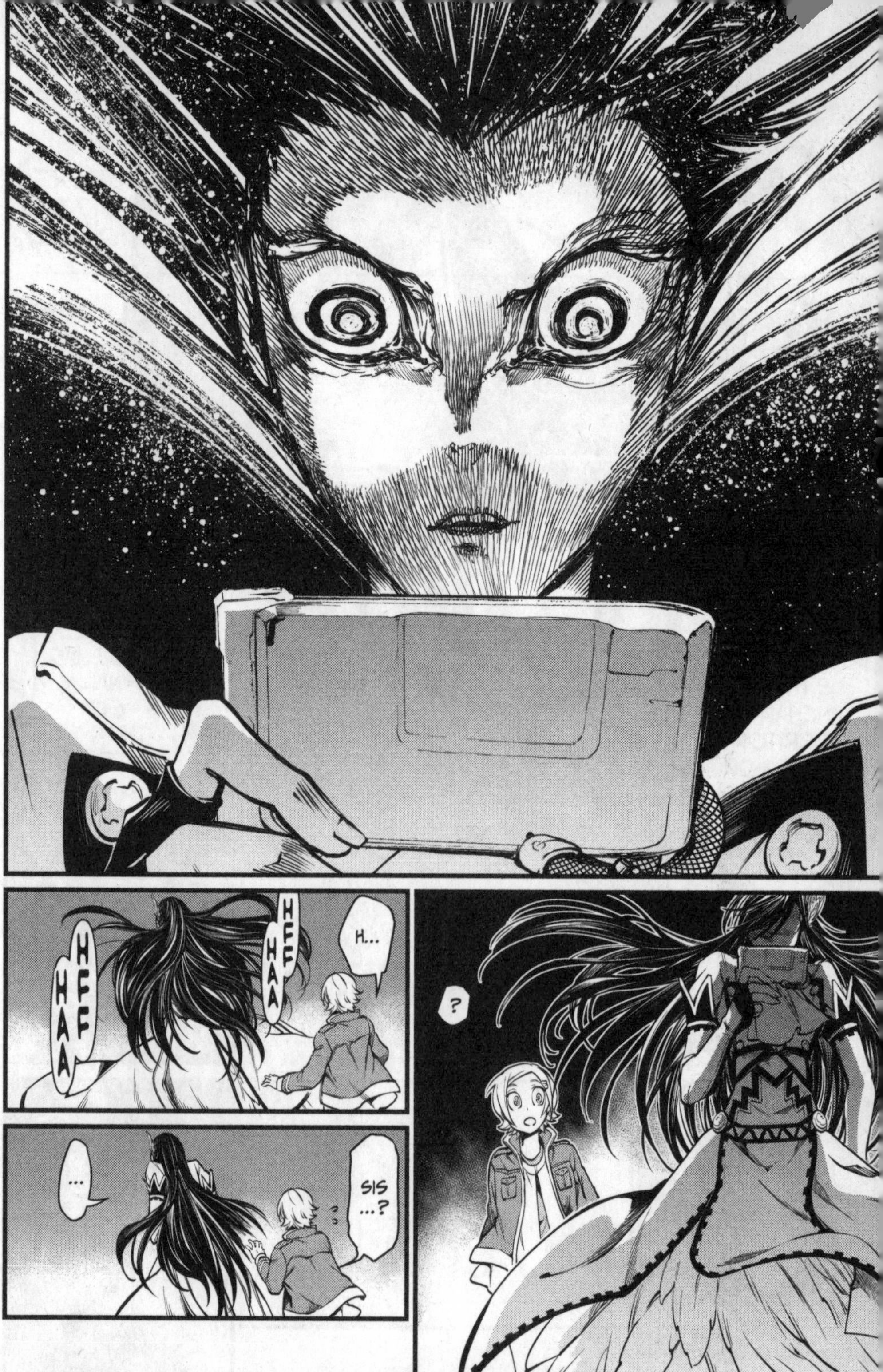
?
H...
HFF HAA
HFF HAA
SIS ...?
...

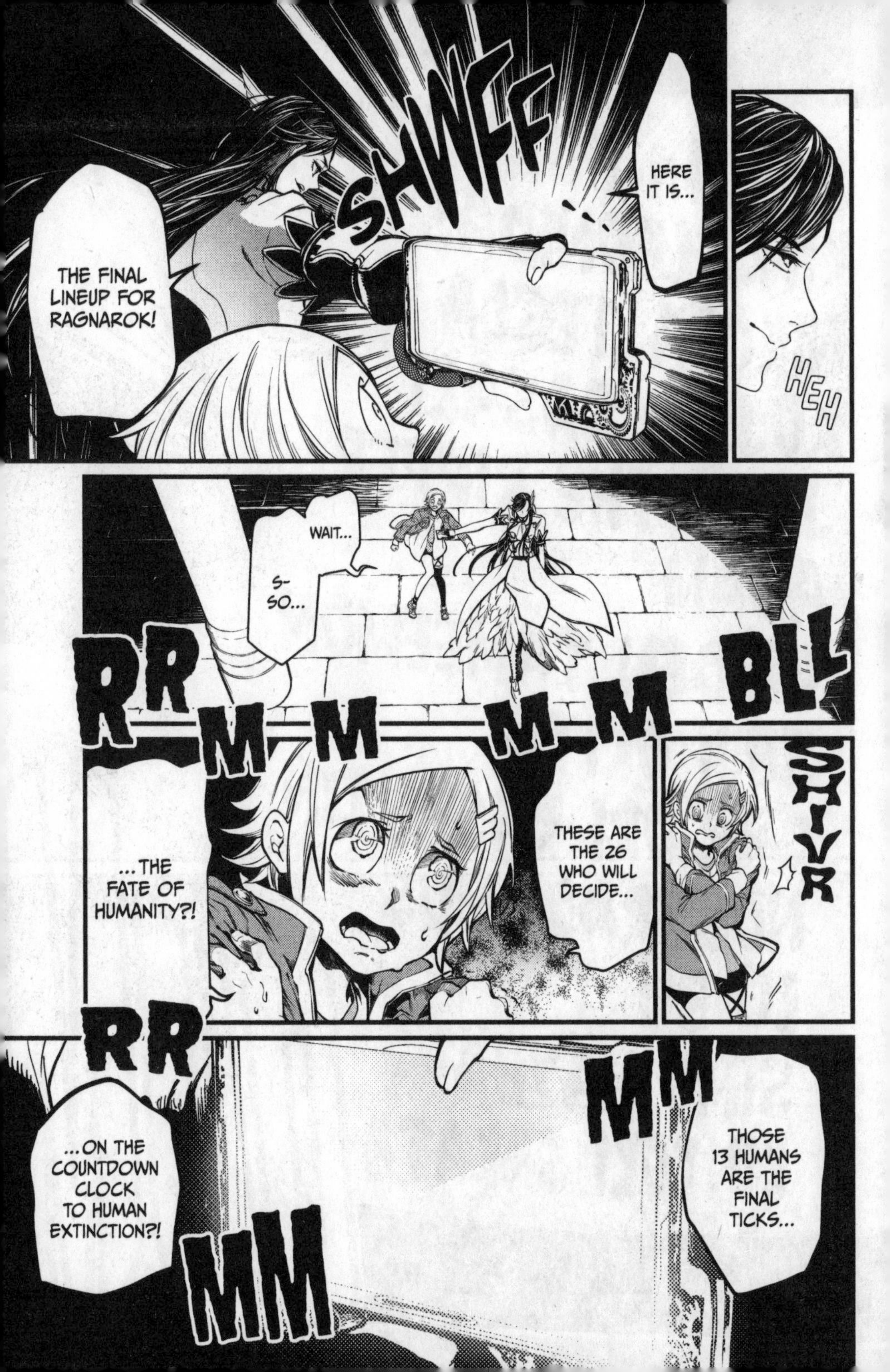
HERE IT IS...
HEH
SHWFF
THE FINAL LINEUP FOR RAGNAROK!
WAIT...
S-SO...
RRMMMMMMBLL
SHIVR
THESE ARE THE 26 WHO WILL DECIDE...
...THE FATE OF HUMANITY?!
RRMMMM
THOSE 13 HUMANS ARE THE FINAL TICKS...
...ON THE COUNTDOWN CLOCK TO HUMAN EXTINCTION?!

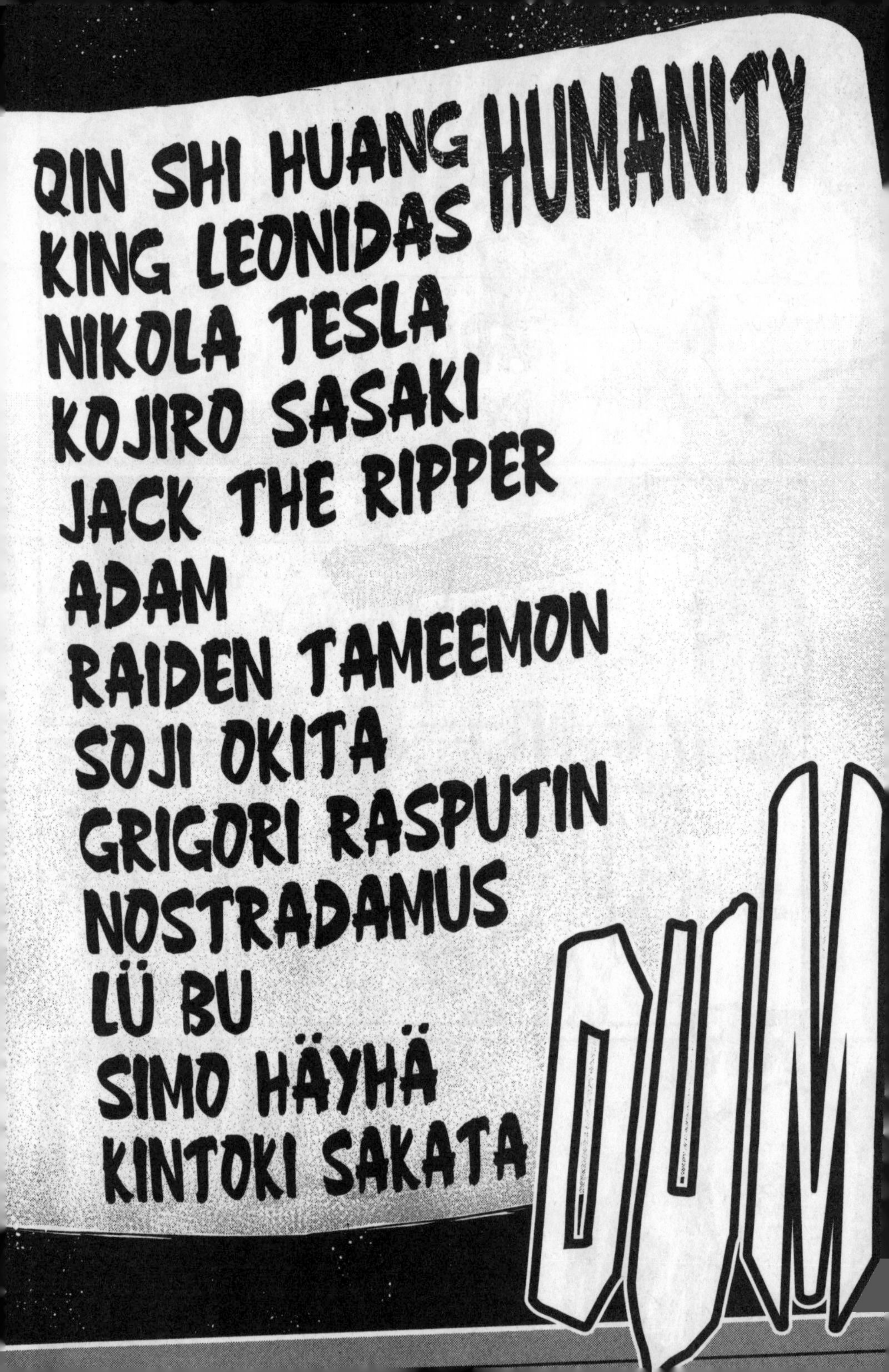
HUMANITY
QIN SHI HUANG
KING LEONIDAS
NIKOLA TESLA
KOJIRO SASAKI
JACK THE RIPPER
ADAM
RAIDEN TAMEEMON
SOJI OKITA
GRIGORI RASPUTIN
NOSTRADAMUS
LÜ BU
SIMO HÄYHÄ
KINTOKI SAKATA
DUN

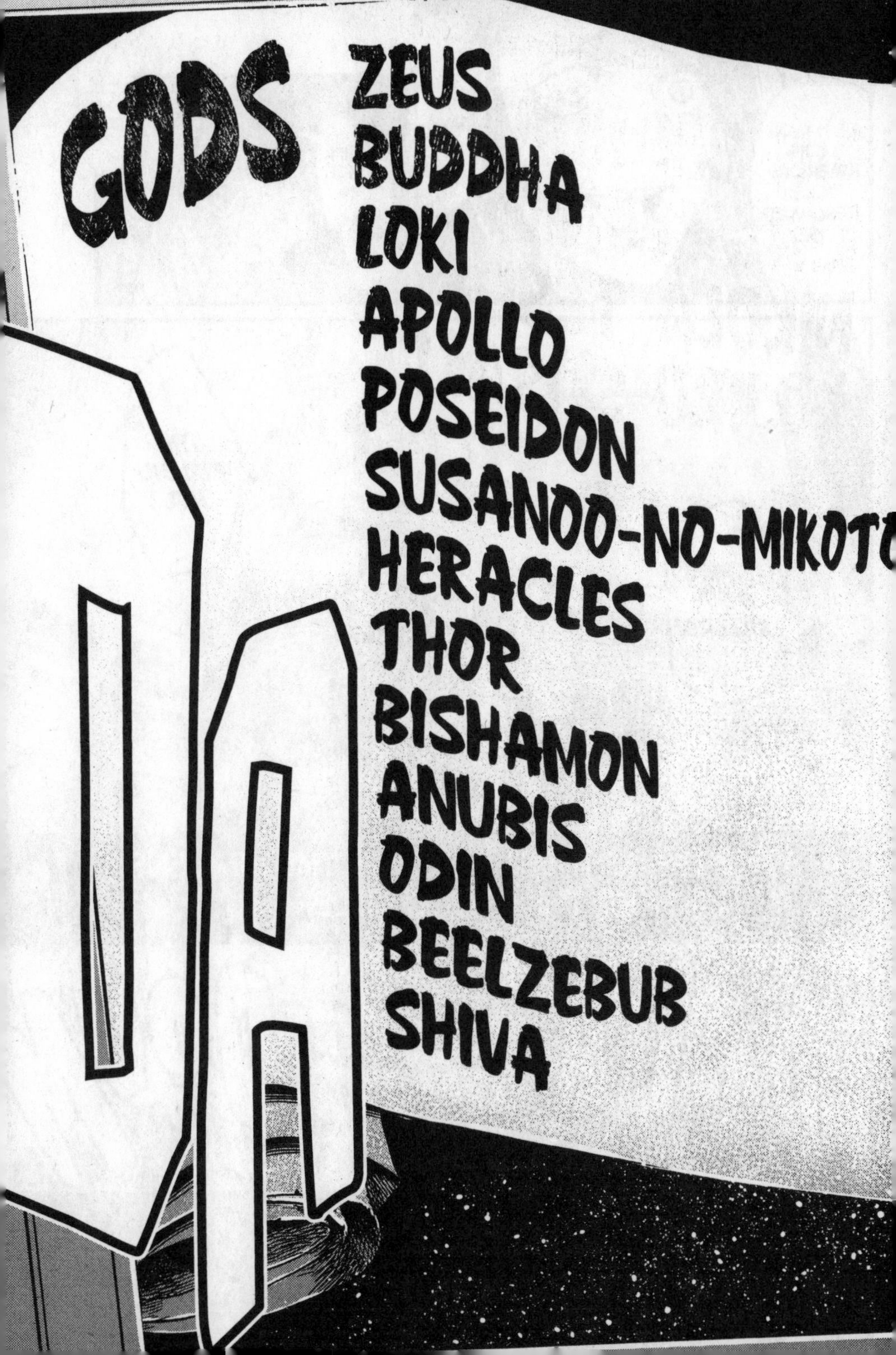
GODS
ZEUS
BUDDHA
LOKI
APOLLO
POSEIDON
SUSANOO-NO-MIKOTO
HERACLES
THOR
BISHAMON
ANUBIS
ODIN
BEELZEBUB
SHIVA

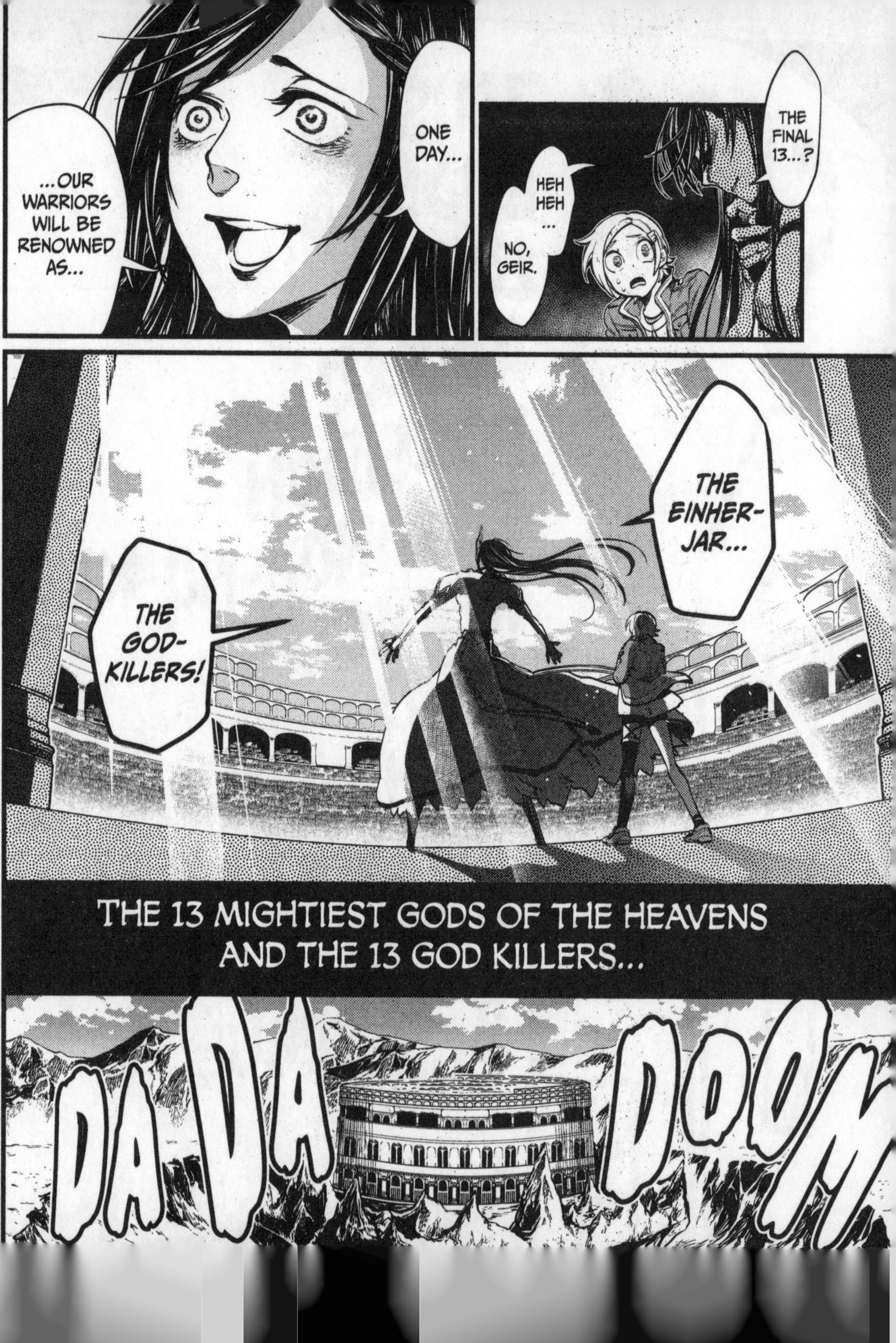
THE FINAL 13...?
HEH HEH ...
NO, GEIR.
ONE DAY...
...OUR WARRIORS WILL BE RENOWNED AS...
THE EINHER-JAR...
THE GOD-KILLERS!
THE 13 MIGHTIEST GODS OF THE HEAVENS AND THE 13 GOD KILLERS...
DA DA DOOM

RECORD OF RAGNAROK

VOLUME 1
VIZ Signature Edition

Art by **Azychika**

Story by **Shinya Umemura**

Script by **Takumi Fukui**

Translation / Joe Yamazaki
Touch-Up Art & Lettering / Mark McMurray
Design / Julian (JR) Robinson
Editor / Mike Montesa

Shumatsu no Walkure
©2017 by AZYCHIKA AND SHINYA UMEMURA AND TAKUMI FUKUI/COAMIX
Approved No. ZCW-123W
First Published in Japan in Monthly Comic ZENON by COAMIX, Inc.
English translation rights arranged with COAMIX Inc., Tokyo
through Tuttle-Mori Agency, Inc., Tokyo

The stories, characters, and incidents mentioned in this publication are entirely fictional.

No portion of this book may be reproduced or transmitted in any form or by any means without written
permission from the copyright holders.

Printed in Canada

Published by VIZ Media, LLC
P.O. Box 77010
San Francisco, CA 94107

10 9 8 7 6 5 4 3 2 1
First printing, January 2022

viz.com

PARENTAL ADVISORY
RECORD OF RAGNAROK is rated T+ for
Older Teen and is recommended for ages
16 and up. Contains graphic violence.

VIZ SIGNATURE

vizsignature.com